AF621660

SOCIAL RESPONSIBILITY, TECHNOLOGY AND AI

DEVELOPMENTS IN CORPORATE GOVERNANCE AND RESPONSIBILITY

Series Editor: David Crowther

Recent Volumes

Volume 1:	NGOs and Social Responsibility
Volume 2:	Governance in the Business Environment
Volume 3:	Business Strategy and Sustainability
Volume 4:	Education and Corporate Social Responsibility: International Perspectives
Volume 5:	The Governance of Risk
Volume 6:	Ethics, governance and Corporate Crime: Challenges and Consequences
Volume 7:	Corporate Social Responsibility in the Digital Age
Volume 8:	Sustainability After Rio
Volume 9:	Accountability and Social Responsibility: International Perspectives
Volume 10:	Corporate Responsibility and Stakeholding
Volume 11:	Corporate Responsibility and Corporate governance: Concepts, Perspectives and Emerging Trends in Ibero-America
Volume 12:	Modern Organisational Governance
Volume 13:	Redefining Corporate Social Responsibility
Volume 14:	Stakeholders, Governance and Responsibility
Volume 15:	Governance and Sustainability
Volume 16:	CSR in an Age of Isolationism
Volume 17:	The Equal Pillars of Sustainability
Volume 18:	Social Entrepreneurs: Mobilisers of Social Change
Volume 19:	Socially Responsible Plastic: Is This Possible?
Volume 20:	Achieving Net Zero: Challenges and Opportunities
Volume 21:	Corporate Resilience: Risk, Sustainability and Future Crises
Volume 22:	Innovation, Social Responsibility and Sustainability

DEVELOPMENTS IN CORPORATE GOVERNANCE AND RESPONSIBILITY VOLUME 23

SOCIAL RESPONSIBILITY, TECHNOLOGY AND AI

EDITED BY

DAVID CROWTHER
Social Responsibility Research Network, UK

AND

SHAHLA SEIFI
Social Responsibility Research Network, UK

emerald PUBLISHING

United Kingdom – North America – Japan
India – Malaysia – China

Emerald Publishing Limited
Emerald Publishing, Floor 5, Northspring, 21-23 Wellington Street, Leeds LS1 4DL

First edition 2025

Editorial matter and selection © 2025 David Crowther and Shahla Seifi.
Individual chapters © 2025 The authors.
Published under exclusive licence by Emerald Publishing Limited.

Reprints and permissions service
Contact: www.copyright.com

No part of this book may be reproduced, stored in a retrieval system, transmitted in any form or by any means electronic, mechanical, photocopying, recording or otherwise without either the prior written permission of the publisher or a licence permitting restricted copying issued in the UK by The Copyright Licensing Agency and in the USA by The Copyright Clearance Center. Any opinions expressed in the chapters are those of the authors. Whilst Emerald makes every effort to ensure the quality and accuracy of its content, Emerald makes no representation implied or otherwise, as to the chapters' suitability and application and disclaims any warranties, express or implied, to their use.

British Library Cataloguing in Publication Data
A catalogue record for this book is available from the British Library

ISBN: 978-1-83608-497-6 (Print)
ISBN: 978-1-83608-496-9 (Online)
ISBN: 978-1-83608-498-3 (Epub)

ISSN: 2043-0523 (Series)

Printed and bound by CPI Group (UK) Ltd, Croydon, CR0 4YY

INVESTOR IN PEOPLE

CONTENTS

PART 3
SOCIAL CHALLENGES FROM TECHNOLOGY

LIST OF CONTRIBUTORS

Aysha A-Zayani	The George Washington University, USA
Noor Al Mawlani	The George Washington University, USA
Muneer Al Mubarak	Ahlia University, Bahrain
Hiba AlSaidi	University of Bedfordshire, UK
Ahmed Ali Alkuwaiti	The George Washington University, USA
Zaleekha Aman	The George Washington University, USA
Nurudeen Babatunde Bamiro	Lagos State University, Nigeria
David Crowther	University of Bedfordshire, UK
Teodor Dumitru	Petroleum Gas University of Ploiesti, Romania
Sheereen Fauzel	University of Mauritius, Mauritius
Aleksandra Gaweł	Poznan University of Economics and Business, Poland
Iza Gigauri	St. Andrew the First-Called Georgian University, Georgia
Răzvan Ionescu	School of Advanced Studies of the Romanian Academy, Romania
Astha Jaiswal	Manipal University, India
Bibi Nabeeha Jaunoo	University of Mauritius, Mauritius
Nandikesh Juglal	University of Mauritius, Mauritius
Dinesh Kumar	Shree Rangniketan Foundation, India
Syamimi Ariff Lim	Universiti of Brunei Darussalam, Brunei
Mirela Panait	Petroleum-Gas University of Ploiesti, Romania
Marius Gabriel Petrescu	Petroleum Gas University of Ploiesti, Romania
Lukman Raimi	Universiti of Brunei Darussalam, Brunei
Maria Tănase	Petroleum Gas University of Ploiesti, Romania
Verena Tandrayen-Ragoobur	University of Mauritius, Mauritius
Ningyu Zhai	Macau University of Science and Technology, Macao
Scarlett Ruopiao Zhang	Macau University of Science and Technology, Macao

PART 1

TECHNOLOGY AND SUSTAINABILITY

SUSTAINABLE TECHNOLOGIES FOR ROAD MAINTENANCE AND REHABILITATION

Marius Gabriel Petrescu, Maria Tănase and Teodor Dumitru

Petroleum Gas University of Ploiesti, Romania

ABSTRACT

Human society is going through an interesting period in terms of the challenges it faces. The most interesting problems are environmental problems. In support of protection of the environment in which we live, we must find efficient and clean (ecological) solutions, at the same time, for the materials and technologies that are the basis of the goods production. In this context, the problem of means of transport, in general, and land road transport, in particular, will remain one whose solution will probably mark multiple stages in the attempt to abandon fossil fuels. Even if this problem will be solved, the travel routes – roadways – represent an additional challenge in terms of construction materials and technologies but also in terms of maintenance and rehabilitation technologies. In the context of Industry 4.0, the concerns in the field of road execution and repair are more and more obviously aimed at elements of the circular economy. Solutions are sought and experimented for: reuse of degraded asphalt material, incorporating reused/reusable materials into the asphalt mixtures and the implementation of ecological execution technologies. In this work, it is intended to carry out an analysis regarding the technical and technological solutions implemented or in the proposal/experiment stage that respond to the desired "Sustainable technologies for road maintenance and rehabilitation".

Keywords: Ecological solutions; environment; sustainable technologies; maintenance; transport infrastructure; sustainable construction

Social Responsibility, Technology and AI
Developments in Corporate Governance and Responsibility, Volume 23, 3–28
Copyright © 2025 Marius Gabriel Petrescu, Maria Tănase and Teodor Dumitru
Published under exclusive licence by Emerald Publishing Limited
ISSN: 2043-0523/doi:10.1108/S2043-052320240000023001

1. ASPECTS SPECIFIC TO ROAD CONSTRUCTION, MAINTENANCE AND REPAIR ACTIVITIES

Millions of kilometres of paved roads and highways exist worldwide, with several hundred 1000 of them in need of significant rehabilitation efforts. Governments and local authorities around the world allocate approximately $100 billion annually to maintain the functionality and safety of these road networks ("Martec - Recycler Comprises", n.d.). However, even with this substantial investment, there remains a considerable global shortfall in modern roads. This shortfall is primarily due to insufficient budgets allocated for transportation and the steep expenses associated with conventional road rehabilitation methods.

Technologies used in road construction have evolved throughout human history. From the mundane paths blazed by camels 8,000 years ago to the scientific paper published by Clifford Richardson in 1905 establishing the composition of asphalt as we know it today, technology has always adapted to the new types of vehicles used, from those with animal traction and up to motorised vehicles that appeared more than 100 years ago (Popescu, 2022).

If we are to refer to what, generically, we call the road, i.e. the asphalt or cement concrete surface on which vehicles move, we must say that this represents only the "visible part of the iceberg". The structure of the road, in the section, is much more complex, the successive layers fulfilling several roles (Fig. 1 ["What are the functions of layers in a flexible pavement?", n.d.]): a protective layer – having in its composition a varied range of materials, from gravel to sand, but various resulting materials can also be used following some demolished constructions – with the role of water drainage and frost protection; a base layer – composed of gravel and sand, and in some cases bitumen for compacting the materials or cement – with the role of evenly distributing the forces generated by road traffic to the foundation; a binder layer, with the role of absorbing the forces generated by road traffic and distributing them to the basic start of the

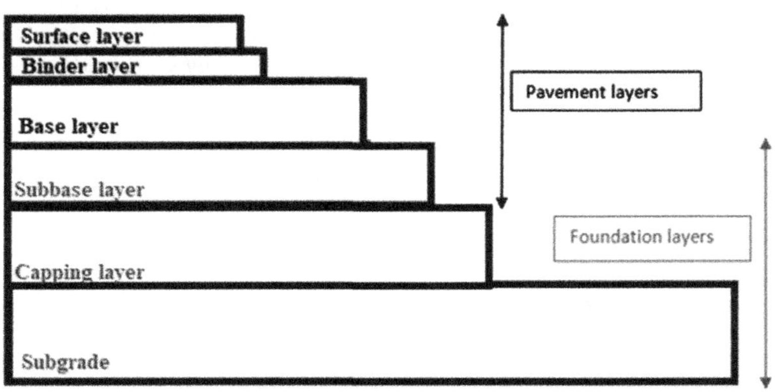

Fig. 1. The Conventional Structure of an Asphalt Road.

foundation; the surface (wear) layer, resistant to pressure forces generated by traffic and waterproof to avoid water seeping through the lower layers.

Usually, to create each of the four layers, mineral aggregates (ground rock, river gravel, sand) of various sizes are used; materials specific to the recipe, to give the mixture elasticity and strength; bitumen (artificially obtained by processing petroleum) to ensure the adhesion of the components and to obtain a compact mixture.

Specialists estimate that the manufacturing process of the foundation of a conventional two-lane road with a total width of 4 metres generates emissions of about 276 tons of carbon dioxide for each kilometre worked, without taking into account aspects such as pouring the wear asphalt layer – i.e. the actual running surface – or the long-term maintenance of the road (Popescu, 2022).

At present, there is a global emphasis on enhancing mechanisation within the realm of road infrastructure projects. This includes the integration of cutting-edge technologies aimed at boosting both technical and economic efficiency. The primary goal is to promote the judicious utilisation of resources and equipment in road construction and maintenance endeavours ("https://documents1.worldbank.org/curated/en/240821468196173343/pdf/Solu%C5%A3ii-tehnice-%C5%9Fi-tehnologii-eficiente-%C5%9Fi-inovatoare-pentru-investi%C5%A3iile-%C3%AEn-infrastructura-public%C4%83-din-Rom%C3%A2nia-raport-final.pdf", n.d.). The interest in identifying new solutions in the field of road construction is all the greater as the degree of damage and, consequently, the volume of repairs increases.

As can be seen in the graph in Fig. 2 ("Martec - Recycler Comprises", n.d.), the asphalt road surface undergoes an accelerated deterioration process a few years into its operation. However, implementing timely rehabilitation measures

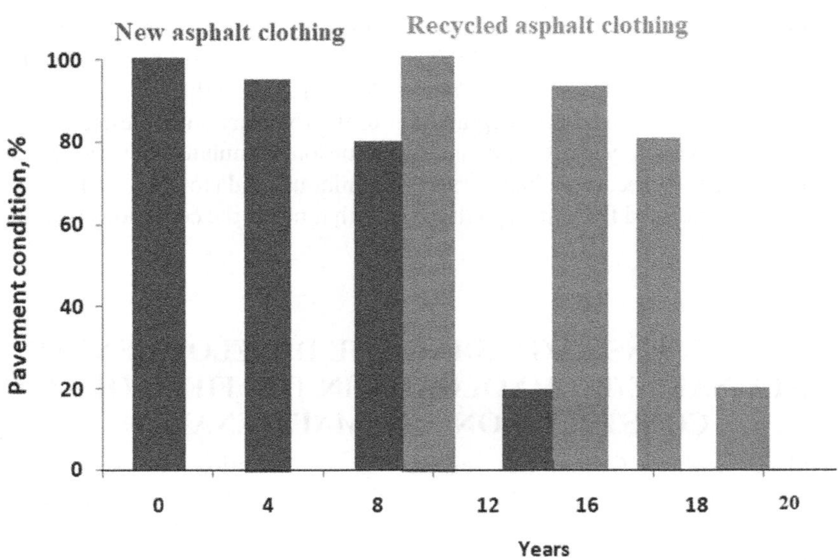

Fig. 2. The Process of Damage to the Asphalt Pavement.

such as reasphalting or recycling can effectively restore the quality of the road surface, ultimately prolonging the lifespan of the road.

Maintaining the road in optimal operating parameters requires monitoring the evolution over time of the state of degradation and carrying out maintenance by immediately remedying the defects. Road maintenance requires, on a case-by-case basis, the implementation of corrective actions – as part of current maintenance works, especially – or preventive – as part of periodic maintenance works – with the aim of partially compensating for wear and tear and maintaining the respective road structure in the technical conditions necessary for uninterrupted traffic in safety and comfort, as well as for maintaining it in a permanent state of cleanliness, order and appearance aesthetic, corresponding to the functional category of the road ("Normativul privind reciclarea la cald a îmbrăcăminţilor rutiere bituminoase, indicativ NE-026-2004 din 16.03.2004 - Lege5.ro", n.d.; "Referat Drumuri | PDF", n.d.; "Sr-599-Lucrari-De-Drumuri-Tratamente-Bituminoase-Conditii-De-Calitate 2022 | PDF", n.d.).

The current maintenance works aim at the maintenance of the asphalt coating, the degraded surfaces and their protection measures, sealing, combating cracks and fissures.

Periodic maintenance works refer to those activities that are performed periodically and planned for the purpose of partially compensating the wear produced on the road structure, works of art, road safety or in order to completely remove the effects of wear produced on the road structure, to return the technical characteristics to the initial technical condition by replacing, restoring or repairing sectors or parts that have suffered degradation. In this category are mainly included the periodic maintenance operations of the running surface through bituminous treatments. The treatments are thin layers made by spraying with bituminous binder, screening and fixing by rolling. The role of the treatments is protection (waterproofing) and roughening of the surface on which it is performed ("Referat Drumuri | PDF", n.d.; "Sr-599-Lucrari-De-Drumuri-Tratamente-Bituminoase-Conditii-De-Calitate 2022 | PDF", n.d.).

In the situation of excessive degradation of the roadway – manifested by local degradations with very great depth and/or expansion, cumulated, very large – it is recommended to execute asphalt carpets (bituminous road clothing made up of a single layer, executed from an asphalt mixture that meets the conditions of a wear layer).

2. CONCERNS REGARDING THE DEVELOPMENT OF SUSTAINABLE TECHNOLOGIES IN THE FIELD OF ROAD CONSTRUCTION AND MAINTENANCE

Road construction technologies require high consumption of non-renewable resources (Luo et al., 2013). The specialised literature (Montoya-Alcaraz et al., 2019) provides interesting information regarding the approach to the sustainability of road construction technologies. Along with policies in the field of road construction and maintenance, sustainability assessment programmes have been developed. Among them, we can mention (Montoya-Alcaraz et al., 2019): the

Greenroads programme ("Greenroads Manual v1.5", 2011), FHWA's Voluntary Infrastructure Sustainability Assessment Tool (INVEST), European Union Road Federation (ERF) Sustainability Programme (Mendoza Sanchez, 2014), Environmental quality in civil engineering (CEEQUAL) (Bryce et al., 2017). These programmes offer a comprehensive set of strategies and facilitate the integration of sustainability criteria across various stages of the road life cycle, encompassing aspects such as material selection and production, road design and construction as well as road operation and maintenance (Montoya-Alcaraz et al., 2019; Ozer et al., 2016).

The matter concerning the sustainability of road construction technologies extends beyond considerations solely focused on road design and construction. It encompasses various elements related to road construction and maintenance technologies, which have environmental and natural resource implications. These elements encompass:

- The sourcing, transportation and processing of road construction materials, including materials like rock, gravel, concrete and bitumen.
- The fuel consumption associated with construction and maintenance machinery, along with its environmental impacts.
- The production and application of paints used for road markings.
- The manufacturing and processing of semi-finished products derived from plastic materials, which are utilised in road safety equipment production.

These factors collectively contribute to the broader sustainability picture within the realm of road infrastructure.

In this context, a sustainable strategy in the field of road execution and maintenance must benefit from (see also Fig. 3):

- The choice of construction/maintenance materials in accordance with environmental protection policies.
- Planning the stages of road construction taking into account the efficient use of equipment and machinery, to reduce fuel consumption.
- Planning of road maintenance works based on a systematic road condition evaluation programme.
- Evaluation of maintenance costs by reference to the implementation of a new roadway.
- Assessment of the situation of roads with exceeded life span.

The paper (Montoya-Alcaraz et al., 2019) offers an overview of the key economic, social, and environmental principles related to the sustainability of roads and their construction technologies: in (Mao et al., 2018) is proposed a method to enhance pavement durability under reasonable traffic conditions. Corriere and Rizzo (2012) offer guidance on approaching sustainability in road design. The factors contributing to traffic safety were analysed by (Demasi et al., 2018; Farooq et al., 2019; Yang et al., 2018). Regarding the

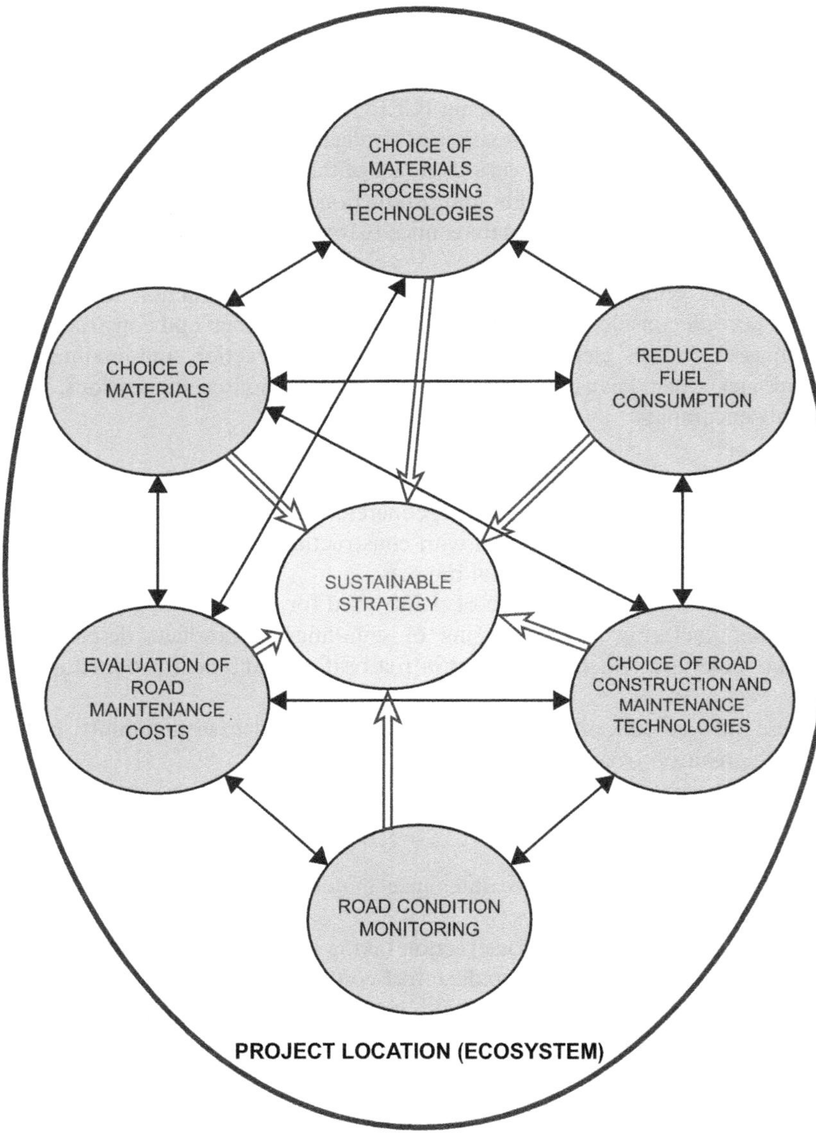

Fig. 3. The Issue of Strategies for Road Construction and Maintenance. Connections of Determining Factors (in the View of the Authors).

environmental sustainability, (Montgomery et al. (2015) present numerous ideas to incorporate environmental considerations across the road project life cycle; adapted structural failure models for Moroccan conditions were developed by Bannour et al. (Bannour et al., 2015); Jain et al. (Jain & Thube, 2007) present calibrated pavement damage models for general network conditions in

India; Rodhe et al. (Jooste, 1998) suggest a number of calibrations to improve the prediction of performance models in South Africa; Pantuso (Pantuso et al., 2019) used Rodhe's model to integrate pavement condition assessment studies into the implementation of Pavement Management Systems (PMS) in Kazakhstan.

It is observed that, in general, road sustainability strategies are highly dependent on the characteristics of location where the project is to be implemented (area, region, country, etc.), as seen in Fig. 3.

The development of projects in the field of road construction essentially depends on the local policy/policies in the fields: social, economic, environmental, etc.

2.1 Local Policies on Sustainable Road Development (Sustainable Roads). Example from ("Sustainable Construction, Maintenance and Operations", n.d.)

According to "Sustainable Construction, Maintenance and Operations" (n.d.), the sustainable construction involves the application of sustainable development principles within the construction industry, encompassing planning, construction, maintenance and infrastructure and building usage. Its goal is to foster environmentally friendly community development, long-term prosperity and improved resident quality of life. It also extends to areas like procurement, design and innovation, aligning with broader sustainable development objectives (Apostu et al., 2023).

Exploring Sustainable Construction from a Global Perspective.

The concept of sustainable construction has undergone scrutiny and adaptation in various countries worldwide, including New Zealand, Australia, Japan, South Africa, China, Hong Kong and the United States. The insights gathered through internet research, literature reviews and personal contacts reveal the unique circumstances of each nation. For instance, Japan, an island nation with limited landfill space, aspires to achieve zero-net waste. In contrast, South Africa, a developing nation facing social and economic pressures, focuses its legislation and strategies on addressing these challenges.

Section 2.1 from "Sustainable Construction, Maintenance and Operations" (n.d.) lays the foundation for sustainable construction within these countries, analysing overarching legislation that promotes sustainability in diverse sectors, including climate change, renewable energy, air quality/emissions, waste management and resource management. In the same document, section 2.2 explores how legislation shapes national-level strategies, influencing the actions of government departments. An example is New Zealand's Transport Strategy, reflecting the impact of such policies, while section 2.3 aims to showcase exemplary practices and case studies from each of the countries in focus.

As an illustration, consider Queensland's waste management policies, which lay out a comprehensive strategy for handling waste. These policies establish a prioritised hierarchy of waste management methods, ranging from the most desirable to the least preferred, namely:

- Waste avoidance.
- Waste reuse.
- Waste recycling.
- Energy recovery from waste.
- Waste disposal.

These fundamental principles and the hierarchical structure serve as the foundational framework for waste management initiatives. They are applied across various contexts, including prerequisites for environmentally significant industry activities, voluntary efforts to reduce waste and the development of waste management strategies at the state and local government levels.

Also, it is specified in "Sustainable Construction, Maintenance and Operations" (n.d.) that the Hong Kong Highways Department places a strong emphasis on executing public infrastructure projects with efficiency and a deep commitment to environmental responsibility. This commitment has been an integral part of the department's management approach since 2003. The environmental protection policies embraced by the department encompass the following key components:

- Systematic identification and management of environmental aspects across all operational activities, with a core objective of effectively controlling their impact and minimising pollution.
- Vigilant monitoring of contractors' performance to ensure the delivery of high-quality work while proactively mitigating potential environmental consequences associated with project execution.
- Strict adherence to all pertinent legal requirements and regulations pertaining to environmental preservation and sustainability.
- An unwavering dedication to resource efficiency and waste reduction throughout the course of projects.
- An ongoing commitment to identifying and pursuing opportunities for continuous enhancement and improvement within the realm of environmental responsibility and project management.

In Japan, the Construction Materials Recycling Law enacted in 2000 serves as a pivotal instrument aimed at the recycling and reuse of potential construction materials, thereby promoting the efficient utilisation of resources. Under this legislation, contractors are mandated to meticulously segregate and recycle any waste arising from building demolition activities. Moreover, they are obligated to use specified construction materials, including concrete (including precast panels), asphalt/concrete and wooden construction materials.

This policy framework encompasses specific numerical targets designed to ensure rigorous adherence to sustainable practices. For instance, it sets forth an ambitious goal of achieving a recycling rate of 95% for specified construction materials by 2010. Additionally, it establishes the objective of completely eliminating the final disposal of waste generated from specified construction materials

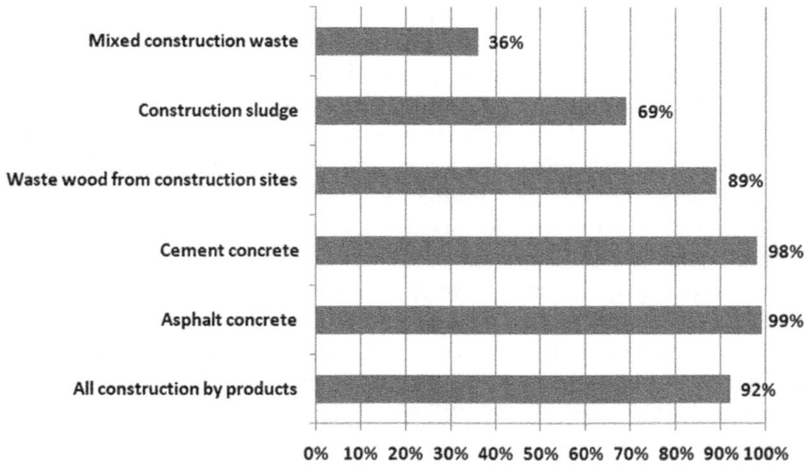

Fig. 4. The Recycling Rate for Construction By-Products in Japan in the Year 2002.

in government-ordered projects by 2005. As illustrated in Fig. 4, the construction industry in Japan had already achieved an impressively high recycling rate as early as 2002, indicative of the law's proactive impact on sustainable resource management.

The Law for Promoting Resource Efficient Utilization (2000) aims to establish a robust economic system of material cycles by:

- Strengthening recycling measures for goods and resources through the implementation of collecting and recycling used products by commercial entities.
- Reducing waste generation by promoting resource conservation and ensuring longer product lifespans.
- Implementing new measures for reusing parts recovered from collected used products.
- Introducing measures to address the reduction of industrial waste by accelerating the reduction of by-products and recycling.

In Japan, this law was considered innovative because it mandated the implementation of the 3Rs (Reduce, Reuse and Recycle) from the product design stage to the collection and recycling of used products.

2.2 Sustainable Technologies for Road Maintenance and Rehabilitation

On the world level, there is an unprecedented evolution of road transport both in terms of dynamic parameters – travel speed and distances covered – and in terms of transport capacity – the volume and mass of transport – goods or people. In order to deal with these situations, all those responsible in the field of transport –

producers of raw materials for roads, road builders, road administrators, traffic regulatory authorities – are involved in identifying solutions to deal with: high traffic speeds, increasing axle load, increased tyre pressure and increased traffic volume. These requirements lead to the need to use stronger and more durable roads, which ensure, at the same time, the reduction of traffic interruptions due to maintenance and rehabilitation works ("https://documents1.worldbank.org/curated/en/240821468196173343/pdf/Solu%C5%A3ii-tehnice-%C5%9Fi-tehnologii-eficiente-%C5%9Fi-inovatoare-pentru-investi%C5%A3iile-%C3%AEn-infrastructura-public%C4%83-din-Rom%C3%A2nia-raport-final.pdf", n.d.)

In the current stage of human development, in response to the above-mentioned aspects, the road infrastructure must benefit from projects – construction, maintenance and rehabilitation – reliable, ecological, safe and intelligent. In detail, it can be said that ("https://documents1.worldbank.org/curated/en/240821468196173343/pdf/Solu%C5%A3ii-tehnice-%C5%9Fi-tehnologii-eficiente-%C5%9Fi-inovatoare-pentru-investi%C5%A3iile-%C3%AEn-infrastructura-public%C4%83-din-Rom%C3%A2nia-raport-final.pdf", n.d.):

- A reliable infrastructure is in operation for a long time, without major interventions, and presents superior quality characteristics, which gives it increased durability. This concept is closely related to that of "lifetime engineering", which implies optimisations project, with special emphasis on maintenance, modernisation and renovation.
- An ecological infrastructure is based on technical solutions with low energy consumption and low impact on the environment. The concept of ecological infrastructure must be adopted and respected in all phases of the project: in the design stage, by specifying the inputs and outputs of the processes in accordance with social, economic and environmental policies; in the construction stage, by imposing ecological solutions for the equipment/machinery used and regarding the application of technologies; in the exploitation stage, especially by choosing efficient and environmentally friendly maintenance programmes.
- A safe infrastructure is an infrastructure that minimises the risk of accidents both during the commissioning phase and during the respective use and maintenance. A safe infrastructure benefits, from the design phase, of a risk analysis – applicable throughout the life of the project – whose conclusions ensure the reduction of the consequences of any accident situation.
- An intelligent infrastructure is able to ensure interconnection (communication) with users, operators and other infrastructures. In the current stage – of the transition to the era of Industry 5.0 – modern infrastructures must benefit from connections with real and virtual environments in the sense of gathering information, issuing solutions and transmitting them to road users and administrators.

Sustainable technologies applicable to road infrastructure are initiated in the design phase and finalised, respectively, developed and perfected in the operation and maintenance phases. Road maintenance and repair technologies must take into account the improvement of mechanisation and the rational use of available resources and equipment.

From the design phase of the road infrastructure, its integration into the environment must be taken into account, to ensure habitats have a chance to survive. This requirement is a challenge for designers and builders who must guarantee the creation of ecological zones, without obstacles – using, for example, ecological approaches and underpasses – for the conditions and requirements of the site.

A good example of an ecological technical solution for roads is represented by permeable drainage systems, which are frequently used in the vicinity of roads, starting from the idea that they will be much drier, even in very rainy areas ("https://documents1.worldbank.org/curated/en/240821468196173343/pdf/Solu%C5%A3ii-tehnice-%C5%9Fi-tehnologii-eficiente-%C5%9Fi-inovatoare-pentru-investi%C5%A3iile-%C3%AEn-infrastructura-public%C4%83-din-Rom%C3%A2nia-raport-final.pdf", n.d.). Such a solution is called "shallow ecological ditches". It was found that most of the critical water pollution in the road area, such as oil and gasoline, will be destroyed by bacteria in the soil. If the permeability of the soil is low, a solution with underground pipes is recommended.

The current trends, internationally, regarding the materials and technologies used for the construction, maintenance and rehabilitation of road infrastructure, refer to ("https://documents1.worldbank.org/curated/en/240821468196173343/pdf/Solu%C5%A3ii-tehnice-%C5%9Fi-tehnologii-eficiente-%C5%9Fi-inovatoare-pentru-investi%C5%A3iile-%C3%AEn-infrastructura-public%C4%83-din-Rom%C3%A2nia-raport-final.pdf", n.d.):

- The use on a wider scale of bitumens modified with polymers and the use of additives.
- Recycling asphalt mixtures and road cement concrete. The concept of recycling makes its presence felt more and more in the field of road construction and rehabilitation, contributing to the optimisation of the use of natural resources, to the introduction into the economic system of materials improperly called "waste", all of which ultimately contribute to the implementation of high-performance materials, with high durability.
- The use of prefabricated cement concrete linings, the use of continuously reinforced linings, as well as the use of road cement concrete in the rehabilitation of road structures with asphalt mixtures as a wear layer.
- The use of cold recycling for the construction and maintenance of roads, using various technologies such as foamed bitumen, bituminous emulsions or cement, with beneficial effects from the point of view of reducing burnt gas emissions and reducing energy consumption.
- The use of technologies that reduce the temperature of mixing and putting into operation asphalt mixtures – the concept of asphalt mixtures with reduced temperature ("warm mix" or "cold mix") (Fig. 5 ["https://marini.fayat.com/", n.d.]).

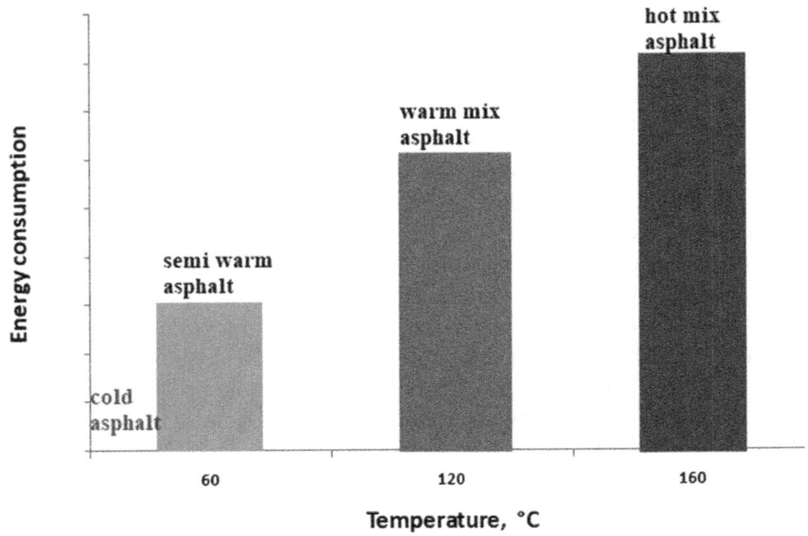

Fig. 5. Energy Consumption in Relation to the Temperature of the Asphalt.

- Using raceways to store and release energy from the sun. Currently, new technologies are being developed that can be applied to road infrastructure through the use of various systems – piezoelectric elements, networks of collector pipes – that absorb the heat from the summer, so that it can be returned in the winter to combat the phenomena of the production of snow and ice. Reducing the temperature of the layers bituminous during the summer has a beneficial effect on the appearance of ruts, which would lead to the prevention of road degradation.
- Use of photocatalytic pavers, especially in urban areas. They consist of materials that have the role of minimising air pollution. The laboratory results indicated an increased efficiency in reducing air pollution, being increasingly used in Belgium, Great Britain, Italy, Japan and France.

2.2.1 Recycling of Road Clothing

The use of the existing material in the road structure to be rehabilitated – very degraded road structure or exceeded in terms of bearing capacity – ensures the use of a material located in the work area while limiting, at the same time, the costs related to the extraction/production and transport of the materials from remote areas. The technologies for recycling the road surface material used in practice are: hot recycling in the asphalt mixture station, hot recycling in situ, cold recycling in situ and recycling of the entire road structure (Fig. 6 [https://documents1.worldbank.org/curated/en/240821468196173343/pdf/Solu%C5%A3ii-tehnice-%C5%9Fi-tehnologii-eficiente-%C5%9Fi-inovatoare-pentru-investi%C5%A3iile-%C3%AEn-infrastructura-public%C4%83-din-Rom%C3%A2nia-raport-final.pdf, n.d.]).

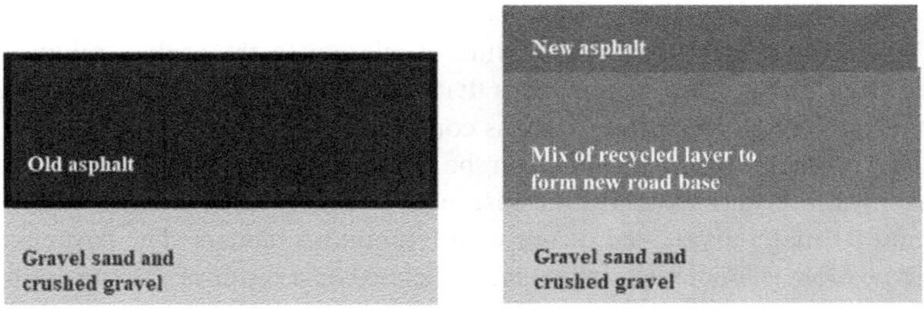

Fig. 6. Flexible Road Clothing Before and After Recycling.

The use of recycling helps to save energy, reduces the cost of transporting aggregates and the amount of waste left after the deconstruction process and does not lead to the depletion of non-renewable natural resources such as bitumen or new aggregates. The recycling of asphalt mixture creates an optimal cycle of use of natural resources and supports the asphalt manufacturing industry ("https://documents1.worldbank.org/curated/en/240821468196173343/pdf/Solu%C5%A3ii-tehnice-%C5%9Fi-tehnologii-eficiente-%C5%9Fi-inovatoare-pentru-investi%C5%A3iile-%C3%AEn-infrastructura-public%C4%83-din-Rom%C3%A2nia-raport-final.pdf", n.d.).

The hot recycling of old road layers can be done through a wide range of technologies, respectively, with an important variety of machines and devices. These technologies can be developed on site or in recycling factories of recovered asphalt mixtures (Belc, n.d.).

Hot recycling in situ is a method of rehabilitating clothing-degraded road asphalt. The operation is performed entirely on the spot by means of a set of machines (recycler train) and starts by applying heat to "soften" the rolling layer of the asphalt road surface. Asphalt material softened is removed by means of milling devices and later mixed with or without the addition of any recycling agent. The recycled asphalt mixture is then laid along the way and compacted to complete the recycling process. Although this recycling-based method is absolutely 100% effective, certain remixing options such as adding new hot mix asphalt or new mineral aggregates may be necessary for structural correction and improvement of the geometrical elements of the road (Popescu & Burlacu, 2017).

Recycling in fixed factories consists in the homogenisation in different types of mixers of the properly crushed asphalt mixture (sizes below 40 mm, respectively, 13…32 mm for use in connecting or wearing layers) with new natural aggregates (35…90 %) and binder (currently 1…3%), followed by its transport and commissioning. The binder used may or may not be characterised by regenerative properties, depending on the characteristics of the old bitumen, and the old asphalt mixture must be well disaggregated when introduced into the technological flow. Industrial-scale recycling of asphalt mixtures has been implemented in the United States in 1976, on the occasion of the first global oil crisis. In Europe (in France, for example), the development of these technologies accelerated in the first half of the 80s. After this period, entrepreneurs focused on the promotion of hot recycling technologies in fixed factories that allow the reuse of a small percentage of old asphalt mixture in relation to the asphalt mixture produced (10...25 %), while technologies that allow recycling a larger amount of old asphalt mixture were viewed with less confidence (Belc, n.d.).

Cold recycling (retreatment) can be applied to old bituminous coatings, including milling a thickness of the base layer or the upper foundation layer made of granular materials treated or not with bituminous binders. The particularities of the possible technologies are generally defined as a result of the type of binder used, namely: cement, bituminous emulsion, foamed bitumen or a composite binder made up of cement and a bituminous binder (bituminous emulsion or foamed bitumen [Belc, n.d.]). Cold recycling reuses old, polluting, existing road materials, without the need to transport natural aggregates to the factories for the preparation of the mixtures, nor the composite materials from the factories to the place of work.

Recycling of material waste through the use of asphalt pavement layers. A varied range of materials from various industries – civil construction, chemical industry, glass industry, textile industry, electrotechnical and electronic industry, telecommunications – find their use with difficulty after being taken out of use, becoming, in most cases, waste. A large part of this waste can, however, find a new use in the construction of road infrastructure.

The types of materials that lend themselves to recycling within the works of the roads are (Popescu & Burlacu, 2017):

- ***Slag:*** Slag generated as a by-product resulting from the steel and iron production process can be broadly classified as blast furnace slag and steel slag. Blast furnace slag is a by-product of iron production in the furnace and is mainly composed of silicates and limestone silicates of limestone or other basic substances. Depending on the cooling method used, it is classified either as "airborne" slag or granular slag, rapidly cooled by immersion in water (Popescu & Burlacu, 2017). The first experiences in using slag as an aggregate in asphalt mixes date back since 1969, when an experimental stretch of road was built in Toronto. Within this section, steel mill slag was used both as an aggregate in the layer base, but also in the wear layer (Emery, 1982). The studied asphalt mixes demonstrated very good properties in terms of bearing capacity, resistance to the action of external factors and durability (Emery, 1982; Popescu & Burlacu, 2017).
- ***Powder rubber:*** Bitumen with the addition of powder rubber is a mixture of hot bitumen and ground rubber from waste or scrap tyres. It is widely used in the transport industry both in Europe and in the United States. In terms of noise, the Rubber Pavements Association (RPA) has stated that using rubber in open asphalt mixes reduces noise by up to 50%,
- ***Glass:*** Currently, in the United States, up to 10% glass can be used instead of aggregates for base layers. Maximum bottle size must be 4.75 mm due to safety measures, but also due to the fact that a surface which is composed of large size glass will not have the roughness corresponding to. The best results were

obtained when the content of glass was no more than 10% of the total weight, and the size of the glass was less than 6 mm.

- ***Plastic:*** The idea of using waste plastics in road construction is relatively new. Laboratory tests have shown positive results when a small amount (5–10% by weight) of plastic is incorporated in bituminous mixes (asphalt), resulting in improved pavement stability, strength and durability (Sasidharan et al., 2019). This solution appeared in the early 2000s in India, when chemistry professor Rajagopalan Vasudevan managed to replace 10% of the traditionally used bitumen with recycled plastic. The new raw material was used in the construction process of some roads in India and was later implemented on a local scale in Great Britain or the Netherlands (Popescu, 2022). However, the solution is not really efficient in the context where the total amount of recycled plastic used in the process is very small compared to the total amount of materials required for a complete infrastructure project. Moreover, for this reason, the use of such a small amount of plastic in the bitumen composition has the effect of reducing carbon dioxide emissions by only 3 tons for every kilometre of road, emissions that would normally have been generated by burning plastic ("Asfalt din plastic și sticle reciclate: soluție ecologică inventată în Cluj-Napoca - Autocritica", n.d.). Studies carried out in Great Britain on asphalt mixtures containing recycled plastic materials, mainly low-density polyethylene (LDPE – low-density polyethylene), which replace approximately 30% of aggregates with dimensions of 2.36–5 mm, present a number of advantages such as growth Marshall stability and increased indirect tensile strength. The major advantage is that no change is required in the manufacturing process existing facilities for mixing recycled LDPE with the asphalt mixture (Chesner, 1998). Dennis Debie and Sebastian Tudose founded in Cluj-Napoca the start-up The Climate Change Company with the aim of putting into practice a recipe by which recycled plastic is not used in the composition of bitumen but is used as a raw material instead of gravel and sand together with recycled glass The final product made by the start-up is called Littar and can be used for the three classic layers of the foundation. The Climate Change Company uses plastic and glass waste that ends up in recycling facilities. Here, plastic and glass are processed to start-up stability standards and then transported to asphalt plants to be used with bitumen and other aggregates to make road foundation material. Also, in addition to plastic and glass, Littar can also include fibre optic cables, for which recycling solutions are currently limited ("Asfalt din plastic și sticle reciclate: soluție ecologică inventată în Cluj-Napoca – Autocritica", n.d.).
- ***Crushed concrete:*** The American Concrete Pavement Association estimates that approximately 322 kilometres of road cement concrete is recycled each year, and that approximately 1750 tons of crushed concrete can be recovered from 1.0 km of road cement concrete with an average thickness of 25 cm. This thing shows that 2.6 million tons of concrete are recycled annually in the United States. Concrete from roads, sidewalks, buildings and other sources can be crushed for reuse. It is recommended that before the concrete crushing operation, reinforcements or other embedded materials be removed. By

crushing concrete, granular aggregates are obtained, hard, composed of inert minerals such as sand, gravel or crushed stone. Due to the adhesion of cement mortar to aggregates embedded in concrete, aggregates resulting from concrete crushing, they have a hard texture, low bulk density and higher water absorption than the comparative natural aggregates in size (Popescu & Burlacu, 2017).

2.3 Transition to Non-polluting Means of Transport in the Context of Ensuring Sustainable Roads

In order to complete the picture of what it means to build and maintain sustainable roads, we must also remember the role of the means of transport and operation used in road service processes.

Humanity's intention to reduce pollutant emissions, harmful to people's health and the integrity of the environment, is known. The current trend is to widely use electricity as a source of movement, to the detriment of fossil fuels. Intentions at European and global level are to invest in electric and/or hydrogen-based means of transport, including those intended for heavy transport or agricultural or construction machinery ("The future of mobility 2020 | McKinsey", n.d.).

At the European level, significant companies from Germany and France, which are developing electrical trucks, invest in research to optimise steady accumulators and enhance their performances. In this race, undoubtedly, major producers, traditionally not targeting the car market, enter with extraordinary know-how in developing such products ("Epoca vehiculelor electrice bate la ușă, cum ne putem pregăti pentru ea?", n.d.).

The French Agency for Environmental and Energy Management (ADEME) recently published a report based on surveys, examining new technological solutions for transport. The report presents an analysis of the new trends in electrification, including vehicles already available on the market or under development. It appears that by 2030, electric vehicles have the potential to compete with diesel vehicles in many respects, with an exception represented by trucks with a greater Gross Total Weight (GTW) from 12 to 40 tons ("Adevăruri și mituri despre rentabilitatea camioanelor electrice | trans.info", n.d.)

Considering that the economic factor is crucial when analysing a new solution for transportation, ADEME evaluated various road transport technologies. Economic terms such as total cost of ownership (TCO) and the environmental impact were taken into account, utilising vehicle life cycle analysis (LCV). Consequently, the environmental impact of a vehicle during its contractual period of existence was estimated based on:

- Identification of raw materials and energy usage.
- Release of pollutants and generated waste.
- Assessment of potential effects they can cause.

The studied results indicate that electrification of vehicles will only be feasible if the profits from reduced usage costs become competitive compared to internal combustion engines (Tables 1 and 2). A comparison of the total cost of owning vehicles is made using the World Harmonised Light Vehicle Test Procedure (WLTP) cycle ("Adevăruri și mituri despre rentabilitatea camioanelor electrice | trans.info", n.d.).

Even and on a long term, such a scenario is not possible for the big trucks. Transport on long distances will be, through therefore, dominated by diesel engines with the possibility to develop technologies that allow the use of some alternative types of fuel, such as gases natural.

Although the fuel costs will increase, ADEME ("Adevăruri și mituri despre rentabilitatea camioanelor electrice | trans.info", n.d.) considers that until in 2030, the total cost of use trucks with diesel engines will decrease by up to 30%. Thus, it will be the result of technological improvements, including reduction the vehicles weight more than 15%, reducing the tyres friction by 20% and reducing aerodynamic resistance by 30%.

Because, moreover, reference was made to the wear of the tyres, of course, in the case of electric vehicles, a more pronounced wear is noted due to, including, the mass of the accumulators (the mass of the accumulators, in the case of heavy transport, is not negligible). At the same time, an increased friction between the tyres and the road surface also accentuates the phenomenon of degradation of the asphalt coating. This is a simple example which demonstrates the complexity of the problem related to the exploitation and maintenance of roads.

The idea of introducing the wide-scale transport with electric drive should also be taken up by road administrators when referring to light machinery. Regarding the trucks and dump trucks used to transport the raw material – mineral aggregates, asphalt mixtures, cement concrete – the aspects mentioned above are valid. In this case, the companies involved in road maintenance activities are developing, in their own bases, efficient charging systems with electrical energy. The problem is more difficult to solve in the case of specialised machinery such as:

Table 1. Comparison Regarding the Total Cost of Owning Vehicles From the WLTP Cycle (*World Harmonised Light Vehicle Test Procedure*) ("Adevăruri și mituri despre rentabilitatea camioanelor electrice | trans.info", n.d.).

Type of Operation	Total Cost of Ownership, in Eurocents/km, in 2015	Estimated Total Cost of Ownership, in Eurocents/km in 2030
Diesel	40.1	41.6
System hybrid light (MHEV 48V)	39.3	40.6
Plug – in hybrid electric vehicle (PHEV)	44.2	42.3
Vehicle (BEV)	40.2	36.4

Table 2. Comparison Regarding the Total Cost of Owning Trucks With a GTA of up to 12 tons ("Adevăruri și mituri despre rentabilitatea camioanelor electrice | trans.info", n.d.).

Type of Operation	Total Cost of Ownership, in Eurocents/km, in 2015	Estimated Total Cost of Ownership, in Eurocents/km in 2030
Diesel	76.8	79.1
Hybrid parallel	80.2	77.7
Serial hybrid	83.3	77.3
Vehicle (BEV)	110.2	80.3

milling machines, asphalt dressing machines, bulldozers and backhoe excavators. For these, the solution is either hybrid drive or the development of autonomous sources, each useful, with charging using solar energy. Beyond the reduction to zero of carbon emissions harmful to the environment, this way, the vehicle can operate with much reduced noise ("CASE 580 EV, primul buldozer/excavator electric - EVmagazine.ro", n.d.).

In conclusion, it can be affirmed that, like all the branches of the economy, also in the field of road construction and maintenance, ecological, sustainable solutions are constantly being sought and developed. These refer to the two components:

(1) Increasing the durability of the asphalt surfaces by reducing friction with the tyres,
(2) Use of clean energy sources to operate work equipment.

2.4 Research on the Development of Ecological Technologies for Repairing Roads

The authors developed an experimental programme with the aim of developing ecological, efficient solutions in road maintenance processes. The behaviour of the teeth of asphalt pavement milling machines (Fig. 7) which are subjected to the restoration operation was studied.

As part of the research programme, in the laboratory, experiments were carried out that allowed the comparison of the results corresponding to the operation of the asphalt cutters in the presence of different work environments (cutting fluids): air (therefore, without a cutting fluid), water and, respectively, a cutting fluid proposed by the authors of the study.

In the laboratory, the experimental tests were performed on a Baroid tribometer presented in Fig. 8. The test consists in applying a pressure force on the test specimen using a torque generated by the rotation of the lever arm under a predetermined load (Dumitru et al., 2023; Niă et al., 2023). Under these conditions, the sample (taken from the tooth of the asphalt cutter – Fig. 9) presses on the test roll (Fig. 10) in rotation (made of a mineral material similar to the aggregates in the asphalt mixtures), ensuring the displacement relative between

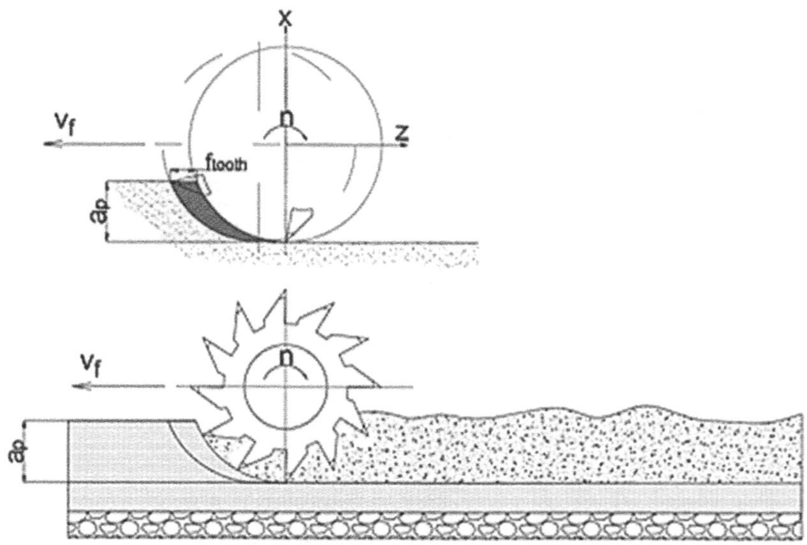

Fig. 7. Milling Schematisation: n – milling drum rotation speed, rpm; v_f – speed in the advance direction, m/min; a_p – milling depth, mm; f_{tooth} – tooth advance, mm/tooth (Dumitru et al., 2023).

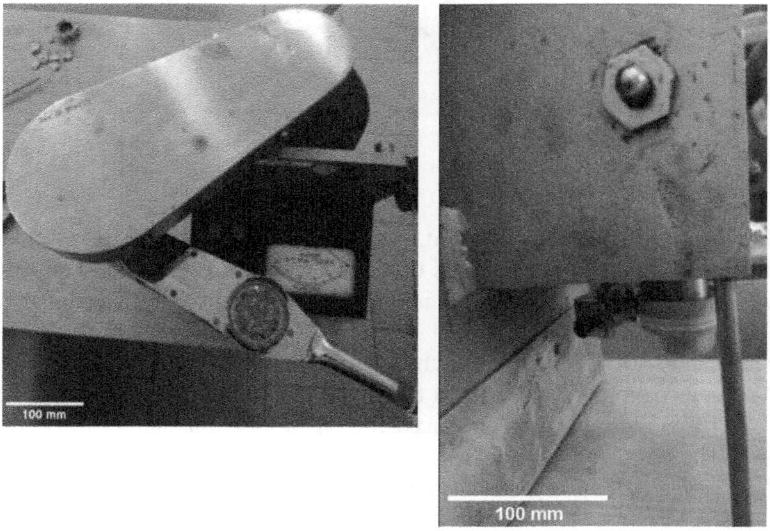

Fig. 8. Baroid Lubricity Tester Tribometer (Dumitru et al., 2023).

the two components of the coupling. The tester allows the simulation, under accelerated conditions, of the abrasion/erosion processes specific to the movement of mineral aggregates on the active surface of the milling tooth, and the results are expressed in gravimetric units.

(a) (b)

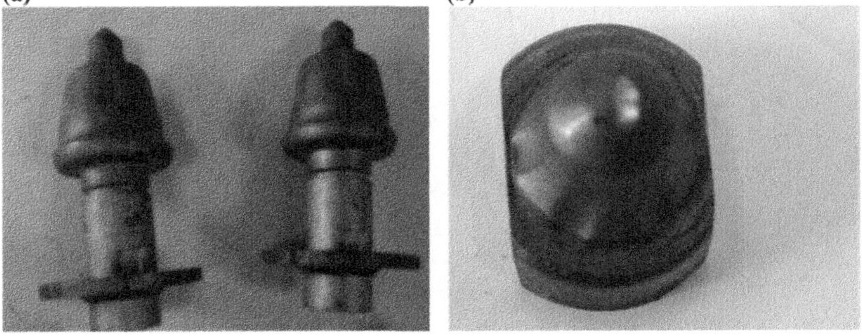

Tooth for milling Processed specimen

Fig. 9. Sample Used in the Experimental Investigation.

Fig. 10. Granite Rollers.

Starting from the hypothesis that, in the composition of the asphalt mixtures, the mineral aggregates are the ones that excessively load the cutter teeth causing their abrasive wear, the rollers used in the experimental programme were made of granite.

The results of the tests are presented in the graphs from Fig. 11.

As results from the experimental tests, it can be said that water, in addition to the role of cooling, has a pronounced role of lubrication, significantly contributing to the reduction of the wear rate. The use of water as a working fluid in asphalt pavement milling operations has several practical implications. First, water serves as an effective coolant during the milling process, reducing friction and heat generated at the cutting interface, helping to prevent excessive wear and damage to the milling teeth, thus extending their life and reducing the frequency of replacements. Second, water acts as a lubricant, facilitating smoother and more efficient asphalt cutting, minimising adhesion of asphalt particles to the milling teeth, preventing clogging and ensuring uninterrupted operation. This

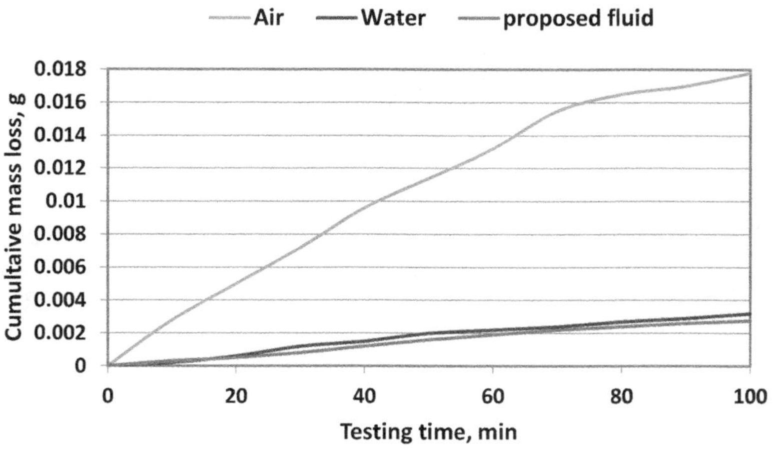

Fig. 11. The Results of the Second Set of Wear Tests.

leads to improved milling performance, increased productivity and reduced downtime for equipment maintenance.

In case of the cutting fluid proposed by the authors of the study to be used in practice, there is a decrease in the wear of the milling tooth (estimated by the gravimetric loss measured by the experiments carried out on the Baroid tribometer) by 14% compared to the situation where straight water is used in cutting fluid and by 84% compared to the case when milling is performed in a dry environment. At the same time, it is stated that the experienced chipping fluid is, by its composition, ecological (its composition mainly contains secondary products from the agricultural products processing industry). Moreover, by wetting, this fluid keeps compact the mass of dust resulting during milling for a long period of time (Fig. 12), preventing the dispersion of particles in the ambient environment (atmosphere). It was found that, mixed with water, the dust resulting from the milling of asphalt pavements is reconstituted after a maximum of 84 hours (under laboratory conditions), while in combination with the new chipping fluid, the reconstitution is practically absent after 168 hours.

3. CONCLUSIONS AND PERSPECTIVES FOR A SUSTAINABLE INFRASTRUCTURE

Vehicles, of any type or category, are not the only ones responsible for harmful emissions in the transport industry. Road construction has been found to have a major responsibility in terms of environmental pollution and waste generation. That is precisely why it is necessary to find solutions to reduce polluting emissions due to the construction and maintenance of road infrastructure. Such solutions have in mind:

(a)

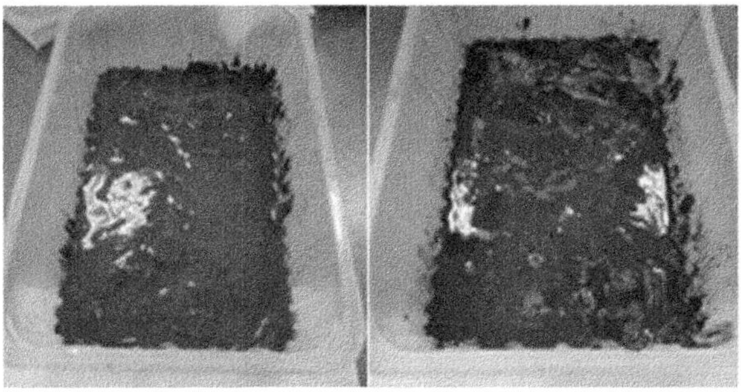

fresh mixtures

(b)

dust mixed with water after 48 hours of exposure

(c)

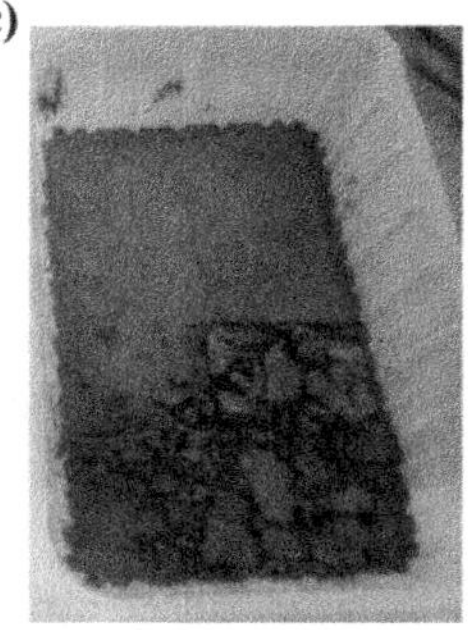

dust mixed with the fluid proposed by the authors, after 168 hours of exposure

Fig. 12. The Behaviour of Dust Mixed With Water, Respectively, the Fluid Proposed by the Authors.

- Reducing the quantities of raw materials and materials needed for road construction.
- Shortening the length of the routes on which construction materials are transported.
- Identification of constructive solutions friendly to the environment.
- Increasing safety in the use and maintenance of road infrastructure.

If the technologies that involve the partial or total reuse of the old material in the tread composition have a relatively long history – being applied with efficiency by most builders – at the present time, designers and builders are looking for new, unconventional solutions that ensure high efficiency of road construction technologies, guarantee increased service life and, more than ever, save natural resources. In this sense, the development of new technologies capable of incorporating residual materials from various sources is noted: manufacturing industries, domestic activities, waste from the decommissioning of various equipment/components/constructions.

The research performed by the authors, presented above, aimed to develop ecological and efficient solutions for road maintenance processes, with a particular focus on the behaviour of asphalt pavement milling machine teeth subjected to restoration operations. The study explored the influence of different work environments, specifically air, water and a cutting fluid proposed by the authors, on the wear and performance of these milling teeth. The results obtained from this comprehensive experimental programme offer several significant conclusions. Regarding the impact of water on milling teeth performance, the experiments revealed that water plays a crucial role in asphalt pavement milling. Beyond its cooling function, water serves as an effective lubricant, reducing friction and preventing excessive wear of the milling teeth. This dual role of water significantly extends the lifespan of milling teeth, decreases the frequency of replacements and contributes to an improved overall milling performance. Also, the use of water as a working fluid during asphalt pavement milling operations has practical implications for road maintenance. It not only reduces wear but also prevents the adhesion of asphalt particles to the milling teeth. This minimises clogging issues and ensures uninterrupted milling operations, leading to enhanced productivity and reduced equipment downtime for maintenance.

The research findings outlined in this study underscore several essential conclusions with respect to sustainability in road maintenance processes. The cutting fluid proposed by the authors of the study demonstrated impressive results, reducing milling tooth wear by 84% compared to the dry environment and 14% compared to using water as the cutting fluid. Furthermore, this cutting fluid's composition, primarily derived from secondary products of the agricultural processing industry, positions it as an eco-friendly alternative. The study also addressed the issue of dust management resulting from asphalt milling. When combined with the new cutting fluid, the dust reconstitution time was significantly longer compared to dust mixed with water. This not only contributes to cleaner working environments but also helps in preventing the dispersion of harmful particles into the atmosphere. Extending the lifespan of milling teeth and reducing the frequency of replacements through water lubrication minimise the need for raw materials in tooth production. This resource efficiency is a vital aspect of sustainability, as it conserves resources and decreases the environmental footprint associated with manufacturing. The lubrication not only enhances equipment life but also reduces downtime for maintenance. This means more efficient and productive road maintenance processes, resulting in less resource consumption and more sustainable road infrastructure.

In conclusion, this research programme has made valuable contributions to the field of road maintenance equipment and practices. The findings emphasise the importance of water as a cooling and lubricating agent in asphalt pavement milling operations, with practical implications for extending equipment life and enhancing productivity. Additionally, the introduction of an eco-friendly cutting fluid offers a promising alternative to further reduce wear and improve the working environment. The study's accelerated testing methods and use of granite rollers have proven effective in simulating real-world conditions, providing valuable insights into wear and performance. These findings have the potential to transform road maintenance processes, making them more efficient, eco-friendly and cost-effective.

No matter what the means of transport of the future will be, the road infrastructure will not end its existence anytime soon. The roads of the future will be able, beyond the basic function – providing support for the movement of road vehicles, to communicate with administrators and users. The road infrastructure of the future will benefit from self-maintenance solutions – cooling, defrosting, drying – ecological, which will use renewable energy sources. The roads of the future will amplify its mission to contribute to the elimination of waste by reusing it in its own constructive structure. All these will be the attributes of the road infrastructure of the future, following which designers, builders and road administrators will apply the principles of sustainable development in their activities.

REFERENCES

Adevăruri și mituri despre rentabilitatea camioanelor electrice | trans.info. (n.d.). https://trans.info/ro/adevaruri-si-mituri-despre-rentabilitatea-camioanelor-electrice-109495. Accessed 13 November, 2023.

Apostu, S.-A., Vasile, V., Panait, M., & Sava, V. (2023). Exploring the ecological efficiency as the path to resilience. *Economic Research-Ekonomska Istraživanja*, *36*(2), 2108476. https://doi.org/10.1080/1331677X.2022.2108476

Asfalt din plastic și sticle reciclate: Soluție ecologică inventată în Cluj-Napoca - Autocritica. (n.d.). https://www.autocritica.ro/feature/littar-asfalt-plastic-sticle-reciclate-cluj/. Accessed 6 October, 2023.

Bannour, A., Lakhal, E., Mohamed, E., Mohammed, A., Bouchra, L., & Pierre, J. (2015). Calibration study of HDM-4 Model of structural cracking models for flexible pavements in Moroccan Context. Unpublished. https://doi.org/10.13140/RG.2.1.2657.1600

Belc, F. (n.d.). *RECICLAREA STRATURILOR RUTIERE EXISTENTE.* https://www.ct.upt.ro/studenti/cursuri/belc/Reciclarea_straturilor_rutiere.pdf

Bryce, J., Brodie, S., Parry, T., & Lo Presti, D. (2017). A systematic assessment of road pavement sustainability through a review of rating tools. *Resources, Conservation and Recycling*, *120*, 108–118. https://doi.org/10.1016/j.resconrec.2016.11.002

CASE 580 EV, primul buldozer/excavator electric - EVmagazine.ro. (n.d.). https://evmagazine.ro/2020/03/12/case-580-ev-primul-buldozer-excavator-electric/. Accessed 13 November, 2023.

Chesner, W. H. (1998). *User guidelines for waste and by-product materials in pavement construction. U.S. Dept. of Transportation*, Federal Highway Administration, Research and Development, Turner-Fairbank Highway Research Center.

Corriere, F., & Rizzo, A. (2012). Sustainability in road design: A methodological proposal for the drafting of guideline. *Procedia - Social and Behavioral Sciences*, *53*, 39–48. https://doi.org/10.1016/j.sbspro.2012.09.858

Demasi, F., Loprencipe, G., & Moretti, L. (2018). Road safety analysis of Urban roads: Case study of an Italian municipality. *Safety Now*, *4*(4), 58. https://doi.org/10.3390/safety4040058

Dumitru, T., Petrescu, M. G., Tănase, M., & Laudacescu, E. (2023). The application of tribological tests to study the wear behavior of asphalt cutter teeth: An experimental investigation using baroid tribometer. *Coatings*, *13*(7), 1251. https://doi.org/10.3390/coatings13071251

Emery, J. J. (1982). *Slag utilization in pavement construction.//Extending aggregate resources.* American Society for Testing and Materials, pp. 95–119.

Epoca vehiculelor electrice bate la uşă, cum ne putem pregăti pentru ea?" (n.d.). https://airmotion.ro/blog/epoca-vehiculelor-electrice-bate-la-u-cum-ne-putem-pregti-pentru-ea. Accessed 13 November, 2023.

Farooq, D., Moslem, S., & Duleba, S. (2019). Evaluation of driver behavior criteria for evolution of sustainable traffic safety. *Sustainability*, *11*(11), 3142. https://doi.org/10.3390/su11113142

Greenroads Manual v1.5. (n.d.). https://www.transportcouncil.org/files/236.pdf. Accessed 22 July, 2024.

https://documents1.worldbank.org/curated/en/240821468196173343/pdf/Solu%C5%A3ii-tehnice-%C5%9Fi-tehnologii-eficiente-%C5%9Fi-inovatoare-pentru-investi%C5%A3iile-%C3%AEn-infrastructura-public%C4%83-din-Rom%C3%A2nia-raport-final.pdf. (n.d.).

https://marini.fayat.com/. (n.d.). Accessed 6 October, 2023.

Jain, S. S., & Thube, D. T. (2007). HDM-4 based optimal maintenance strategies for low-volume roads in India. *Road and Transport Research*, *16*(4).

Jooste, F. (1998). The calibration and use of HDM-IV performance models in a pavement management system. In *4th International Conference on Managing Pavements.*

Luo, G. Z., Fu, J. S., & Yan, P. (2013). Highway construction based on sustainable concept. *Advanced Materials Research*, *726–731*, 4086–4090. https://doi.org/10.4028/www.scientific.net/AMR.726-731.4086

Mao, X., Wang, J., Yuan, C., Yu, W., & Gan, J. (2018). A dynamic traffic assignment model for the sustainability of pavement performance. *Sustainability*, *11*(1), 170. https://doi.org/10.3390/su11010170

Martec - recycler Comprises. (n.d.). https://martec.ca/. Accessed 6 October, 2023.

Mendoza Sanchez, J. F. (2014). Criterios de sustentabilidad para carreteras en México. *Publicación Técnica*, (392).

Montgomery, R., Schirmer, H. J., & Hirsch, A. (2015). *Improving environmental sustainability in road projects.* World Bank.

Montoya-Alcaraz, M., Mungaray-Moctezuma, A., & García, L. (2019). Sustainable road maintenance planning in developing countries based on pavement management systems: Case study in Baja California, México. *Sustainability*, *12*(1), 36. https://doi.org/10.3390/su12010036

Niţă, A., Petrescu, M. G., Dumitru, T., Burlacu, A., Tănase, M., Laudacescu, E., & Ramadan, I. (2023). Experimental research on the wear behavior of materials used in the manufacture of components for cement concrete mixers. *Materials*, *16*(6), 2326. https://doi.org/10.3390/ma16062326

Normativul privind reciclarea la cald a îmbrăcăminţilor rutiere bituminoase, indicativ NE-026-2004 din 16.03.2004 - Lege5.ro". (n.d.). https://lege5.ro/Gratuit/gu3tcnju/normativ-din-2004-privind-reciclarea-la-cald-a-imbracamintilor-rutiere-bituminoase-indicativ-ne-026-2004. Accessed 6 October, 2023.

Ozer, H., Al-Qadi, I. L., Harvey, J., & United States. Federal highway administration. Office of Asset management, P., and construction. (2016), *Strategies for improving the sustainability of asphalt pavements: [Techbrief].* No. FHWA-HIF-16-012.

Pantuso, A., Loprencipe, G., Bonin, G., & Teltayev, B. B. (2019). Analysis of pavement condition survey data for effective implementation of a network level pavement management program for Kazakhstan. *Sustainability*, *11*(3), 901. https://doi.org/10.3390/su11030901

Popescu, D. (2022). Asfalt din plastic şi sticle reciclate: Soluţie ecologică inventată în Cluj-Napoca. *Autocritica*, 24 November. https://www.autocritica.ro/feature/littar-asfalt-plastic-sticle-reciclate-cluj/. Accessed 6 October, 2023.

Popescu, D., & Burlacu, A. (2017). Considerations on the benefits of using recyclable materials for road construction. *Romanian Journal of Transport Infrastructure*, *6*(1), 43–53. https://doi.org/10.1515/rjti-2017-0053

Referat Drumuri | PDF. (n.d.). https://www.scribd.com/document/677068309/referat-drumuri. Accessed 23 July, 2024.

Sasidharan, M., Torbaghan, D. M. E., & Burrow, D. M. (2019). *Using waste plastics in road construction.* Helpdesk Report.

Sustainable Construction, Maintenance and Operations. (n.d.). https://s3.eu-west-2.amazonaws.com/assets.highwaysengland.co.uk/specialist-information/knowledge-compendium/2009-11-knowledge-programme/Sustainable_Construction_Literature_Review.pdf

The future of mobility 2020 | McKinsey. (n.d.). https://www.mckinsey.com/industries/automotive-and-assembly/our-insights/the-future-of-mobility-is-at-our-doorstep. Accessed 22 July, 2024.

What are the functions of layers in a flexible pavement? (n.d.). https://www.tensar.co.uk/resources/articles/what-are-the-function-of-layers-in-a-flexible-pavement. Accessed 10 October, 2023.

Yang, Y., Easa, S. M., Lin, Z., & Zheng, X. (2018). Evaluating highway traffic safety: An integrated approach. *Journal of Advanced Transportation*, *2018*, 1–11. https://doi.org/10.1155/2018/4598985

B2B MARKETING RATIONAL DECISION USING BIG DATA AND AI TECHNOLOGY

Aysha A-Zayani[a] and Muneer Al Mubarak[b]

[a]*The George Washington University, USA*
[b]*Ahlia University, Bahrain*

ABSTRACT

This chapter explains the phenomenon of artificial intelligence (AI) powered by big data in technology and its contribution in knowledge-based marketing in B2B and its impact on rational decision-making in B2B marketing that affects business performance. This chapter is literature review prepared by compiling and reviewing previous literature, studies, articles, books and other sources related to the contribution of big data-enabled AI to B2B marketing. According to the information analysed, the findings show that big data supported by AI plays a significant role in creating user knowledge, external knowledge and customer knowledge, all of which are factors that significantly influence the ability of business-to-business marketers to make rational decisions that affect the performance of their companies. This chapter explains to them the phenomena of AI powered by big data and its effect on B2B marketing rational decision that will enhance company performance and its contribution on knowledge-based marketing in B2B. This chapter contributes to understanding main functions and interactions of AI system powered by big data and how such a system helps in B2B marketing by generating knowledge about customers, users and markets.

Keywords: B2B marketing; artificial intelligence; knowledge-based marketing; big data; knowledge management

Social Responsibility, Technology and AI
Developments in Corporate Governance and Responsibility, Volume 23, 29–47
Copyright © 2025 Aysha A-Zayani and Muneer Al Mubarak
Published under exclusive licence by Emerald Publishing Limited
ISSN: 2043-0523/doi:10.1108/S2043-05232024000023002

1. INTRODUCTION

Value creation in B2B in general has changed recently due to increasing digitisation, increased entry of information and communication technologies (ICTs) (Paschen et al., 2019) and how B2B companies handle their data and knowledge (Gupta et al., 2017). Large amounts of data have been developed by ICTs, such as the almost universal use of social media and the advent of the internet of things (IoT) (Paschen et al., 2019). These recent and still emerging data have limited individual significance compared to their rich collective significance (Pigni et al., 2016). Big data, which is huge in terms of volume, speed, variety, validity and value, is a useful source of market intelligence for B2B companies. According to Abbate et al. (2019) new information technologies can help organisations find, organise and share the knowledge contained in big data. On the other hand, one information technology that is gaining popularity among professionals is artificial intelligence (AI) (Paschen et al., 2020). For example, the professional services sector was one sector most likely to use AI, according to a 2018 survey of more than 1,400 B2B marketing experts (MIT Technology Review Insights, 2018). The theory is that AI may help B2B companies transform (big) data into the knowledge and skills required to develop effective marketing and sales plans and approaches.

B2B marketers have historically found it difficult to analyse customer behaviour and the market environment because they need to focus on getting to know their customers – those who make the purchase decision – and their users – those who will ultimately benefit from the service (Abrell et al., 2016). By using big data to power AI technology, marketing professionals may gain a competitive advantage that is reflected in marketing plans, influences consumer behaviour and produces better results (Jabbar et al., 2020). As a result, sales force's function is evolving, and success is becoming more dependent on technology and analytics (Sleep et al., 2020). Innovations in technology had a crucial impact on marketing. Even though it may be difficult to fully understand, big data has enabled AI to the extent that it has revolutionised marketing management and made the traditional "4P" method more out of date (Rust, 2020), and since more widely available big data sets will allow robots to think and act more logically, they will be more beneficial for AI applications. AI technology can also assist in the selection of successful marketing efforts and global marketing strategies (Katsikeas et al., 2019).

Big data could be helpful for extracting important information from inputs of structured and unstructured data, such as web surfing habits, demographic traits and purchasing patterns, and it can give beneficial consumer knowledge for rational decision-making. For developing new goods, innovating and simplifying processes, user information is essential. Understanding psychographic features can help B2B marketers come up with innovative solutions (Paschen et al., 2019). For competitive advantage, it is crucial to have knowledge of external markets. By analysing unstructured data, such as news and social media information, competitive intelligence may be generated using AI. This can be useful in making better decisions in B2B marketers, increasing their analytical and decision-making capacity and fostering their creativity (Paschen et al., 2019). Therefore, for firms to succeed in the age of technology, knowledge management and decision-making methods are important (Abubakar et al., 2019).

To make the best decisions, the rational decision-making approach needs reliable information. When making decisions, this methodological approach requires careful consideration of all accessible options. The performance of the organisation is also improved (Smolka et al., 2018). According to the literature (Abubakar et al., 2019), knowledge management procedures are positively correlated with organisational performance. Organisations can use knowledge management systems to improve decision-making processes and get rid of operational bottlenecks (Powell & Swart, 2010). Although AI-enabled knowledge presents opportunity for marketers, there is a gap in our understanding of how to implement AI for B2B marketing operations and decision-making (Martínez-López and Casillas, 2013; Singh et al., 2020; Syam & Sharma, 2018). In other words, B2B marketers frequently refer to and use various terms and concepts when talking about AI, which causes misunderstandings and uncertainty about what AI can and cannot achieve.

Understanding what AI is, what the many related phrases and concepts represent and how they all work together to give various value propositions to B2B marketing is a first crucial step in helping B2B managers and executives analyse AI appropriately (Paschen et al., 2019). There is a gap in our understanding on the implications of big data-powered AI with respect to market knowledge in a B2B and its impact on B2B marketing rational decision-making to influence firm performance.

In this chapter, we first provide an overview of the framework for AI systems by outlining the fundamental components of all AI systems and how they interact, after that we explain the phenomenon of big data-powered artificial intelligence (BDAI) in technology and the knowledge management theory (KMT), which can be used to deal with the diffusion and development of knowledge and to analyse the knowledge features of a relationship in order to handle it more efficiently. The study will next address the implications for BDAI in relation to various forms of market information in the setting of B2B marketing decision-making, as well as how knowledge production will affect the B2B marketing rational decision-making. The paper's value is in contributing to understanding the fundamental components and their interactions that make up any AI system and BDAI role in B2B marketing and the generation of information about customers, users and external markets to gain a better understanding of how this impacts the rational decision-making used in B2B marketing to influence business performance. The research claims that even if B2B firms employ digital marketing technologies, most of them don't fully utilise them. There aren't many scholarly articles in this area (Pandey et al., 2020).

2. LITERATURE REVIEW

2.1 AI Systems Framework

Human context defined the word intelligence as a person's capacity for learning, dealing with novel circumstances, comprehending and managing complex ideas and using knowledge to influence their environment (Sternberg, 2017). The word "intelligence" in the more general definition, we can say, is the ability to observe, process turn data into information and eventually knowledge and use that knowledge to engage in goal-directed action (Paschen et al., 2019). By exploring the above definitions, we can say AI is computational agents that act intelligently and perceive their environments to perform actions that maximise probability of success; this definition departs from previous views that AI is about machines displaying humanlike intelligence as computational agents. AI agents perceive and act upon their environment performing processes, such as perception, learning, memorising, reasoning and problem-solving towards goal-directed action (Poole & Mackworth, 2010).

Information systems, at any level of intelligence, consist of hardware, software, data, people and procedures, operate or maintain an information system interact with its environment in a basic input–process–output model in which the system itself will be as a separate entity from its environment. Accordingly, systems require input as raw data from human or physical sources to manipulate it in value-creating ways (processes) and feed information (outputs) back to the environment (Paschen et al., 2020). After defining AI and the role of its information system, the concept of AI systems are discussed. There are six building blocks that make up AI systems, as shown in Fig. 1 (Paschen et al., 2019).

The building blocks are essential for the design and assembly of AI systems. The basic functionality that each building block possesses is provided, and the blocks are often modified to create custom applications. The simplest AI use cases often consist of a single building block, and over time, they evolve to combine two or more blocks. The exhibition below organises the building blocks according to whether they relate primarily to data, processing or work (Baier & McIlraith, 2022).

Each building piece's responsibilities are briefly described in the sections that follow.

2.1.1 Inputs

Information from the environment will be sent into the input–process–output transformation of an AI information system. Either structured or unstructured data make up the data format.

2.1.1.1 Structure Data. Structured data is the core of intelligence and business analytics. It is data that can be organized and standardized using a well-defined schema or data model. Structured data can be either internal or external. Internal data includes inventory figures, sales data, and customer demographics while external data includes ratings of social media and transactions of stock exchange. AI can frequently perform computations on various sorts of structured data, in real time, due to rapidly advancing machine learning (ML) algorithms and increased computational efficacy (Paschen et al., 2020).

2.1.1.2 Unstructured Data. Data that comes from different sources and applications such as social media, IoT and mobile applications are challenging and

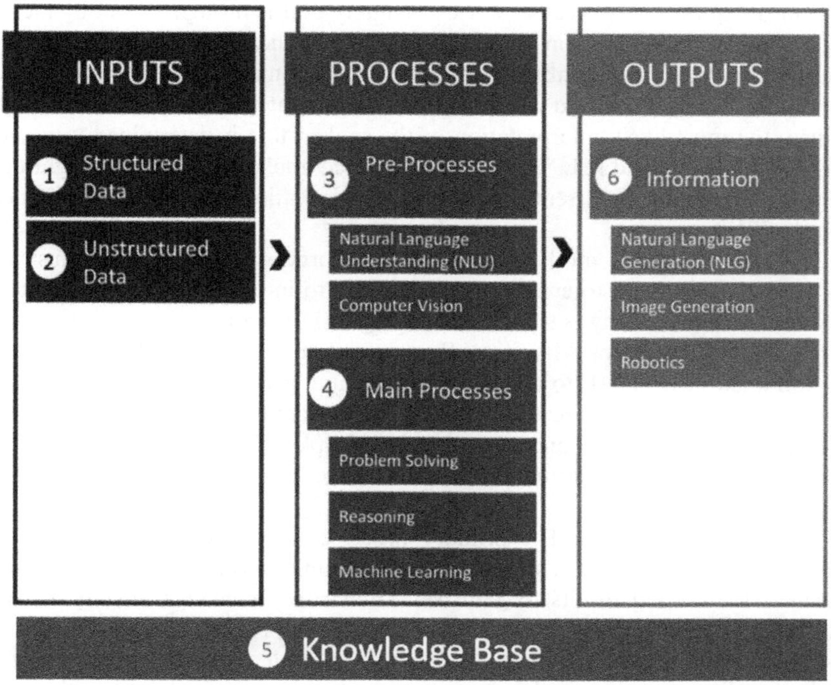

Fig. 1. Building Blocks of Artificial Intelligence Systems. *Source:* Paschen et al., 2019.

need to be well analyzed and organized. Therefore, AI has a unique ability to handle these data (Paschen et al., 2020; Zhuang et al., 2017).

2.1.2 Processes

At the pre-processing stage, the first action will involve AI systems formatting and standardising unstructured data to convert it into structured data, which the primary AI processes will eventually alter (O'Leary, 2013).

2.1.2.1 Pre-processes. To enable value-adding processing of the remaining data, pre-processing of unstructured data in its different forms involves data cleaning, normalisation, transformation, feature extraction and selection (Paschen et al., 2020).

By using natural language understanding (NLU), AI assigns meaning to the vast and complicated human language in spoken and written form. AI systems in the pre-processes understand spoken and written language from humans using NLU. NLU captures spoken language during real-time speech, transcribes it and outputs text. This enables the system to recognise spoken words but prevents it from giving those words meaning. The most difficult aspect of NLU is defining the meaning of words because of the ambiguity that is brought about by factors like context, dialect, jargon or discourse. Most applications for comprehending natural language use vocabulary and a set of grammatical rules to analyse the structure, connections and context of words or sentences in natural language. Then, the most likely interpretation of the spoken text is determined using statistical modelling and ML. The most widely used applications of NLU right now are text summarisation, sentiment analysis and relationship extraction (Zhuang et al., 2017).

Computer vision is another example of a pre-processed AI system. In this case, images are converted to enable representations to interface with the AI system. Because this processing is such a demanding task for computers to carry out, it creates a bottleneck for AI systems that are trying to utilise the data. Computer vision makes use of ML to recognise patterns and generate meaning from them. The success rates of face recognition software are comparable to those of human recognition (Forsyth & Ponce, 2011). One example of this would be using facial recognition software to scan surveillance footage for criminal suspects.

2.1.2.2 Main Processes. The primary processes comprise three categories of intelligent behaviour: ML, problem and reasoning solving. To more efficiently achieve the desired results to gain new knowledge or change already existing knowledge, ML employs the other two stages. A problem must be solved by selecting the best option to achieve the desired result. When there is no perfect solution, diverse problem-solving produces and assesses various options that may be equally advantageous. Contrarily, convergent issue resolution seeks to identify a single, best solution and benefits immensely from AI systems that make use of big data sets to produce results that are appropriate for the circumstance (Tecuci, 2012). AI systems store both divergent and convergent issue solutions, and knowledge is updated (Tecuci, 2012).

Problem-solving is to select the best option from a variety of options to solve a problem. AI systems have two essentially distinct ways of solving problems, just like people do. AI systems create and assess multiple solutions to a given problem in divergent problem-solving. It is crucial to remember that there is no one ideal answer in this situation; instead, a variety of options may be just as beneficial. Convergent problem-solving, on the other hand, focuses on reducing the number of possible solutions to identify the best – or even the only – solution to a given issue. The brute force that AI systems can use to process large amounts of data is especially useful for this (Paschen et al., 2020).

Reasoning refers to applying logic to generate conclusions from available data. Reasoning uses logic to reach conclusions from the available data. When it comes to thinking under ambiguous circumstances, AI systems exceed traditional capacities. Deductive reasoning, often known as top-down reasoning, tries to derive new conclusions from presupposed truths. The goal of inductive or bottom-up thinking is to derive generalisations from specific observations. AI systems use both types of reasoning to look for patterns and guidelines that can be used to solve both current and upcoming challenges (Pecora, 2014).

If the aim of AI is to create intelligent machines, then those machines must have the capacity to learn from their mistakes. The term ML refers to methods that let computers learn from experience, that is, gradually get better at what they do, without the need for a clear-cut set of predefined rules that are kept in memory. In traditional supervised ML, the systems learned by pre-programming particular behaviour and defining input features through human decision-making. Effective systems would require large amounts of data to be analyzed to gain insight, as well as experience and knowledge, without requiring explicit reprogramming each time. Advanced ML techniques are required to create algorithms and statistical techniques that can extract knowledge from data (Paschen et al., 2020).

As a result, AI researchers created algorithms that could extract new information from huge quantities of data, making sophisticated or "deep" ML the essential element of modern AI systems. Deep ML improves the system's capacity for problem-solving and boosts the precision of repeated task solutions. Today, one of the potent techniques utilised in ML is artificial neural networks. They are made up of a series of computational steps called network layers. Each network layer executes comparatively simple calculations before passing the results to the next, deeper layer. Even while each non-linear calculation may be mathematically simple, the cascading design creates a powerful system that can depict complex mappings (Sebag, 2014).

There are many different types of learning algorithms; however, three main categories exist: supervised (i.e. learning from data where the desired outcome is known), unsupervised and reinforcement learning. Computer vision applications, such as object or speech recognition, are examples of supervised learning techniques. In these applications, training data and appropriate labels are given to the computer so that it can identify patterns and create rules that it can use to solve the same problem in the future. The goal of unsupervised learning techniques, such as clustering and dimensionality reduction, is to find structure in high-dimensional data to make it easier to access reasoning processes. Consequently, ML improves an AI system's ability to tackle a larger variety of problems and raises the precision with which repetitive tasks are completed. This may also indicate increases in productivity in terms of memory usage or amount of time dedicated to a task.

2.1.2.3 Knowledge Base. Intelligent behaviour depends on the preservation of historical data, knowledge or information so that the experiences represented in that knowledge can shape future conduct. Prior information systems used relational or hierarchical databases with structured data to store and retrieve data from previous procedures. These representations in AI systems can be generated by the system itself for the AI operations mentioned in the previous section, as well as from unstructured data, structured data or data from preprocessing. Implicit knowledge is a result of deep learning, and it prevents the interpretation of stored data from a single network layer in isolation. Artificial neural network's function is an example of implicit knowledge (Huang et al., 2006).

2.1.3 Outputs

After completing the processes operation, the AI system is required to transmit the meaningful data that have been produced to its environment. This information might be used as the basis for a human decision call or as input into another information system. In addition, several for-profit applications leverage AI-generated data for tasks that do not require human interaction. Natural language production, on the other hand, results in the output of complete narratives of conversations, making it the opposite of natural language comprehension. When the AI system converts large data sets into business intelligence insights and reports, it will take the format of synthesised voice or, more complexly, written text. These can also be voices that have been artificially created.

The most current iteration of Google assistant has demonstrated its capacity for significant two-way exchanges that were allegedly comparable to human communication, and this technology is already extensively employed in marketing and customer support (Kietzmann & Pitt, 2020). Using this technology in marketing and customer service is already widespread. Picture creation, which is the reverse of picture identification, produces entire images even when the information is insufficient (for instance, if the backdrop is absent). "Drawing bots" can already generate visuals from text descriptions, even though this technology is still in its early phases (Lu & Zhang, 2002). Robotics gives robots the ability to engage physically with and their surroundings updates. AI-powered machines can navigate challenging physical settings, selecting things in warehouses, bending, moving with amazing coordination and balance and even running or jumping (Evans, 2003).

2.2 Big Data Powered AI Technology (BDAI)

With the reference of AI definition, we can refer the AI as the theory and the development of machine intelligence that replicates aspects of human intelligence such as visual perception, reasoning ability, problem-solving, learning from previous experience, communication, perception and acting (Petrescu et al., 2022). AI is enabling the creation of intelligent machines. Intelligence empowers an entity to function appropriately and anticipate the conditions of its environment. It is programmed to "self-learn" from data and make predictions and intelligent decisions based on automated ML, artificial neural networks, robotic process automation and text mining (Petrescu et al., 2022).

The use of AI methods is increasingly utilising a vast array of substitute data sources as well as data analytics that are constantly utilising huge amounts of substitute data sources and data analytics that are called big data. ML considers a category of AI, and it is where computers get the ability to learn from data using appropriate algorithms, making it possible for computers to identify the hidden patterns in data without having a user programming it actively in order to do so with the main goal of conducting a solid task. On the other hand, the term "big data analytics" (BDA) refers to enormous amounts of data that can be generated, processed and increasingly utilised by digital tools and information systems for predictive, descriptive and prescriptive analyses (Nallaperuma et al., 2019).The ability to process unstructured data, increase in data storage capacity and increased availability of structured data, all contribute to the development of this capability. In society today, there is increased availability of novel data sources that can be processed using complex and powerful algorithms that include AI systems. That leads to several benefits, but there are some challenges, too (Zhou et al., 2017).

As a result, marketing science has been included in the scope of AI research. Marketing professionals can better understand which variables can enhance marketing performance by analysing big data sets that are derived from numerous sources and demographics. Big data analysis identifies themes and patterns that AI can employ to increase the effectiveness of marketing efforts (Paschen et al., 2019). Regarding big data studies, De Camargo Fiorini et al. (2018) considered several organisational theories. They provide a research framework to link organisational theories to empirical study based on big data sets. De Camargo Fiorini et al. (2018) point out explicitly that KMT can be useful to investigate different facets of adopting big data. Knowledge management is a popular approach for boosting an organisation's competitive position (DeTienne & Jackson, 2001; Dwivedi et al., 2011). Organisational learning can support the development of new knowledge or offer perceptions that may change behaviour (McElroy, 2000).

The two types of knowledge are explicit and tacit. Tacit knowledge exists among personnel and is regarded as a significant knowledge resource in any organisation; explicit knowledge is the knowledge that is already been recorded such as files, databases, documents, etc.. An organisation can significantly improve performance by gaining access, share and implementing both explicit and tacit knowledge (DeTienne & Jackson, 2001). Knowledge has been demonstrated to be a crucial component of production in the 21st century. Any company that wishes to raise its profit margins must constantly learn and adjust to the ever-changing external environment. Consequently, a knowledge-based approach is a crucial foundation for any organisation (Tzortzaki & Mihiotis, 2014). According to Abubakar et al. (2019), KMT will largely concentrate on the institutional, cultural and technical enablers for managing knowledge and related activities. KMT may be used for innovative notions that offer a logical justification for managing knowledge and may support construct knowledge management ways to organise the completion of a process, even though it is more frequent in information systems research (Baskerville & Dulipovici, 2006).

Relationship marketing has been included in KMT's scope (Rowley, 2004). Communication is a part of both knowledge management and relationships, even though they may be separate concepts, as has been shown in the pertinent literature. Customer data are beneficial for relationship management, and knowledge management afterwards creates an appealing interface for more study (Rowley, 2004). Due to the importance of B2B marketing's transactions from an economic standpoint (Cortez & Johnston, 2017), theoretical advances have been made over the past 10 years, and future research should concentrate on innovation, customer interactions, data analytics and the industrial environment

(Cortez & Johnston, 2017). In this chapter, we will provide a theoretical model that was created based on the talks that came before (Fig. 2). In the context of the mining sector, the model considers big data, AI technologies and organisational performance elements. Knowledge management may be used to address the growth and dissemination of information as well as to examine the knowledge characteristics of a relationship to manage it more successfully (Powell & Swart, 2010). According to Abubakar et al. (2019), knowledge is a confluence of relevant facts, professional understanding and values that may inspire innovation. Organisational effectiveness and creativity may both be enhanced through knowledge management.

Enablers for knowledge management are motivational components that might enhance tasks linked to knowledge management. These significant factors include corporate structure, organisational culture and technology. It is interesting how information technology has made communication more straightforward. Information technology aims to promote communication, mutual learning and knowledge exchange (Abubakar et al., 2019). To enhance organisational performance, the knowledge management process includes activities including gathering, creating, managing and communicating knowledge. Inputs, outputs and brokers are all crucial components of the knowledge generation process. The method of decision-making can be influenced by knowledge management. Intuition or reason can be used in decision-making. The rational decision-making style, on the other hand, is a methodological procedure that necessitates extensive information. Individual or organisational performance can be the eventual result. Systems for managing knowledge can increase organisational effectiveness and reduce operational obstacles. They facilitate improved decision-making and raise revenue (Abubakar et al., 2019).

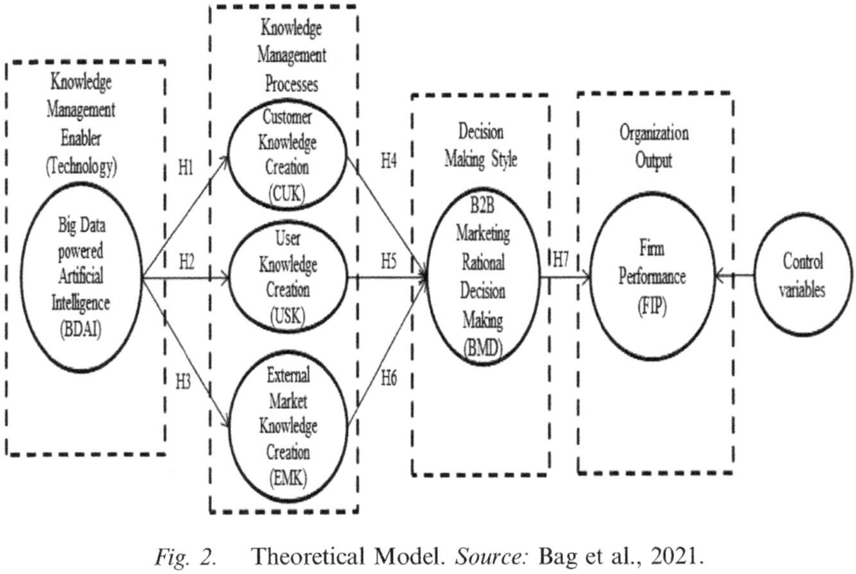

Fig. 2. Theoretical Model. *Source:* Bag et al., 2021.

Our theoretical model's primary pillars are organisational output, decision-making style, knowledge management methods and enablers of knowledge management (Paschen et al., 2019). The technology (BDAI) that facilitates the knowledge management process by generating user knowledge, customer knowledge and external market knowledge is the knowledge management enabler considered in our paper. Additionally, this knowledge generation promotes rational B2B decision-making, which improves business performance (Paschen et al., 2019). The administration of unstructured and structured data sets as well as their usage in automating some B2B marketing and sales procedures are the key focuses of the BDAI architecture that was taken into consideration. The customer knowledge creation concept relates to the application of AI to analyse customer attitude and behaviour by utilising structured and unstructured data of various types. USK in a B2B environment is therefore considered in this theoretical model. AI-enabled user knowledge may reveal how users customise items, and this knowledge might be useful for new product improvements (Paschen et al., 2019).

External market knowledge (EMK) creation is considered in the theoretical model since it provides B2B marketers with a competitive advantage. Because BDAI may be used to gather information regarding external market dynamics and stakeholders, it focuses on it (Paschen et al., 2019). As rational decision-making in B2B marketing is essential in this uncertain business climate, B2B marketing rational decision making is another key idea applied here. The use of BDAI technology enables the completion of difficult tasks and the ability to make better informed judgements (Duan et al., 2019). According to Wamba et al. (2017), the endogenous construct, or firm performance, measures the company's financial and marketing success, including its superior capacity to retain customers as compared to competitors and its rise in return on investment (ROI) and market share. The effects of control factors like firm size and age must be considered. The research suggests that size boosts a company's capacity to access and acquire resources. Like this, an organisation becomes more mature and more likely to accept cutting-edge technology as it becomes older. Both variables must be controlled for the study to yield accurate results (Bag et al., 2021).

2.3 Market Knowledge in B2B Marketing and the Implications of BDAI

The knowledge of customers, users and the external market, which are important elements of the knowledge management process, is what drives knowledge generation in B2B marketing the most (Abubakar et al., 2019). To better understand how AI driven by big data influences the creation of user, customer and external market information that impacts firm performance in B2B marketing, we analyse the impact of this technology on these three different knowledge-producing processes (Bag et al., 2021).

2.3.1 Customer Knowledge

Customers are those who purchase a B2B service, whether they utilise it or not. Customer knowledge includes steps for creating, codifying, distributing and utilising such knowledge as well as an inventory of the knowledge that already exists about customers. What, how, and why of a purchase, as well as its causes and effects, are a few examples of this information (Abrell et al., 2016). Since it pertains to the urgent performance needs of an item or service and may be a beneficial resource for refining an offering, customer knowledge is vital for B2B organisations (Syam & Sharma, 2018). Big data sets that are both structured and unstructured are available to organisations in the digital era for analysis (Gupta et al., 2020). However, using data from social media presents marketers with two significant difficulties. First, the data are unstructured; second, the large number of data sets renders the normal analysis technique impractical (Liu et al., 2016).

Balducci and Marinova (2018) contributed to the literature by conducting analysis on the marketing applications of unstructured data. Such data sets must be analysed using sophisticated analytical and computational approaches (Dubey et al., 2020). Data visualisation techniques aid B2B marketers in understanding complex data and gaining perceptions for making decisions (Duan et al., 2019). Recently, AI bots have become more popular since they can automate sales tasks and enhance the capabilities of the current sales staff (Leung et al., 2019; Panchen et al., 2019). BDA may extract crucial information from both structured and unstructured data, including how frequently a user visits the web, the kinds of industrial products they look for, their previous purchases and buyer characteristics that can be used to learn more about their demographic (Chintagunta et al., 2016). Additionally, B2B marketers can utilise ML and predictive analytics technologies to create a profile of current and potential clients and then construct an appropriate relationship strategy (Hofacker et al., 2020; Paschen et al., 2019).

With BDAI, every step of the B2B sales process may be improved. Without using a lot of human resources, B2B marketers can uncover high-quality business leads by using the predictive modelling approach. B2B marketers can utilise AI presentation bots to create outstanding presentations at the very end of the sales process. When negotiating commercial deals, emotion AI might be helpful in overcoming any client doubts that could surface. AI can also aid in lessening competition and improving an organisation's own value propositions. AI-based chat bots can be useful for automating order processing tasks and following up on orders with business clients (Paschen et al., 2019). The use of BDAI technology can therefore triple the effectiveness of B2B marketing (Jabbar et al., 2020; Liu, 2020). According to Davenport et al. (2019), advanced technologies like AI might change the course of marketing in the future. This becomes possible by utilising BDAI technology to generate customer knowledge and further develop effective B2B marketing strategies (Bonnin & Rodriguez, 2019).

2.3.2 User Knowledge

Users are those who use a B2B company's product or service and are often located farther down the value chain than customers, which in the context of a B2B company includes purchasers (Abrell et al., 2016). The firm's efforts to generate and codify these insights are included in user knowledge, as are insights related to the experience of using a product, such as users' attitudes, beliefs and future requirements and wants. Because it may assist a B2B firm in effectively adapting to long-term updates in market demands and because it can be used to enhance present goods and services, the literature that is now available recognises the value of user knowledge. Therefore, user knowledge is essential for developing new products, innovating and streamlining processes (Abrell et al., 2016; Pedeliento et al., 2018).

Big data appears to have lately increased the capability of AI, and the digital revolution has enhanced processing capacities (Duan et al., 2019). The growth of user knowledge for improved decision-making may be assisted by BDAI, according to the literature (Paschen et al., 2019). According to Dwivedi et al. (2015), digital marketing is becoming more popular. The content of social media platforms may be used for BDA and to find out more about user preferences and attitudes towards commercial goods. AI may infer the sentiments and feelings of potential clients from text-based data. Psychographic traits may be quite useful when developing new things. Additionally, BDAI-enabled user data can provide crucial information on how customers modify products and services, which (Paschen et al., 2019) may be useful for product development (Huang & Rust, 2017).

2.3.3 Market Knowledge

Finally, based on market orientation framework, B2B companies need to understand more about the external market factors such competitors, politics-legal, economic, technology, new companies as outside forces could affect customer or user preferences and behaviours (Kohli & Jaworski, 1990). BDAI has shown to be quite useful in this digital era. Duan et al. (2019 and Paschen et al. (2019) claim that AI models can be helpful for obtaining market intelligence data on rival activities, rival product releases, governmental changes and the entry of new businesses into the market. AI aids in the creation of market knowledge by applying BDA to decipher online web-based material. To assess the accuracy of market news and spot fake information, tools for natural language processing (NLP) and ML might be helpful. This greatly enhances B2B marketing campaigns. BDAI can outperform competitors by extracting vital information from documents created by them, such as news articles or social media postings (Paschen et al., 2019).

2.4 Knowledge Creation and B2B Marketing Rational Decision-Making

Customer knowledge creation is crucial as it brings a competitive edge over rivals. B2B marketers can make intelligent judgements using customer knowledge (Paschen et al., 2019). A methodological technique called rational decision-making entails evaluating options and choosing the best course of action. Knowledge generation has been demonstrated to be a dynamic, complicated process based on KMT (Abubakar et al., 2019). By transforming tacit information into explicit knowledge, customer knowledge is a resource that can aid in knowledge development. Customer information is pertinent, may be utilised as a basis for large data studies and can be considered when making crucial decisions. The standard of decision-making is substantially higher because rational decision-making is a conscious, deliberate and intuition-free process. B2B marketing can be made more effective by making logical judgements based on customer understanding (Paschen et al., 2019).

Utilising the BDAI technology enabling outlined in the preceding sections, user knowledge creation can be obtained. According to Paschen et al. (2019), user knowledge includes psychographic traits as well as user experiences, likes, dislikes, attitudes and behaviours about a company's product and service offerings. Making informed judgements on the creation of new products and service offerings for the B2B market can benefit from these insights. These comprehensive data sets can be collected, managed and processed by B2B marketers to generate knowledge that will help to further enhance B2B marketing and sales procedures. When making sensible decisions by considering alternative possibilities and likely outcomes, user knowledge development gives B2B marketers an added advantage (Abubakar et al., 2019). B2B marketers can stay current on market developments by using external market knowledge. It enables B2B marketers to be watchful of rivals' actions and vigilant about potential influences on their own brands. Competitors frequently spread false information to disparage other businesses, but these dangers can be effectively controlled by staying up to date with new developments and utilising BDAI technology (Paschen et al., 2019).

Making rational decisions includes a deliberate evaluation of the facts through a planned procedure that takes time and effort. For use in problem-solving and decision-making, external market knowledge production can be collected, saved, analysed and organised utilising BDAI technology. Duan et al. (2019) and Prior and Keränen (2020) noted that B2B marketing must be understood from an information requirement viewpoint, and that effort must be made to decoding information for improved solutions. They also provided prospective paths for future study. Rational decision-making requires B2B decision-makers to weigh many factors and the likelihood of each alternative before deciding. Rational decision-making criteria are developed to consider all choices. To make rational decisions, it is crucial to have access to trustworthy and pertinent information. Assumptions and biases are eliminated during the rational decision-making process, which results in better decisions and increased organisational performance (Smolka et al., 2018). The state of the organisation affects its performance. Performance can be evaluated by contrasting desired results with actual results. By encouraging rational decisions, knowledge management can improve organisational processes and remove other obstacles (Abubakar et al., 2019; Johnston & Chandler, 2012). Rational business-to-business decisions can increase profit margins and help retain clients. B2B marketers can swiftly enter new markets and introduce new products (Singh et al., 2020) and can dramatically increase market share (Yu et al., 2008; Wamba et al., 2017; Wilson & Bettis-Outland, 2019).

3. CONCLUSION

This chapter explains the phenomenon of AI powered by big data in technology and its contribution in knowledge-based marketing in B2B and its impact on rational decision-making in B2B marketing that affects business performance. As per the chapter results, we conclude that advanced technologies powered by BDAI play a crucial role in determining the success or failure of a company. During this time of massive upheavals caused by digitalisation, information technology and communication technology, the first argument that this chapter made was that current breakthroughs in AI will have important implications for businesses in general and for B2B marketing. The process by which massive amounts of data could be converted into information and, eventually, knowledge will be profoundly altered by the introduction of AI.

The problem is that, as is the case with many new technologies, B2B managers who are eager to employ them do not understand how they work or what potential effects they may have on knowledge management strategies and tactics. This is a problem because it is common for new technologies to have this problem. Considering this, the purpose of this chapter is to provide B2B companies with an explanation of the essential components of AI systems as well as their interrelationships. Therefore, this chapter focuses on the potential for BDAI to liberate value based on knowledge of customers, users and external markets. Additionally, describe how the KMT Model was adopted. This covers BDAI, customer knowledge development, user knowledge creation, external market information generation, B2B marketing rational decisions and business performance, according to research by Abubakar et al. (2019).

The article addresses the requirements for information management and decision-making about B2B marketing in the digital era and proposes a model for those activities. The model illustrates how the BDAI, a knowledge management enabler, affects the knowledge management process for B2B marketing choices. Additionally, our chapter includes a structured assessment of how BDAI systems may affect market analysis in B2B marketing. B2B marketers can benefit from the usage of BDAI systems to transform data into information, which can then be further processed to produce various sorts of knowledge, including user, customer and other external market knowledge. By empowering businesses to generate, organise and use knowledge about their clients, users and external market forces, it is expected to assist B2B companies in becoming more market oriented. We hope that by providing real-world advice for B2B managers, this chapter will encourage management and marketing researchers to explore the application of BDAI technologies in organisational settings in more depth.

3.1 Theoretical Implications

This chapter explores the theoretical model based on KMT. Knowledge is a collection of relevant data, skill and information acquired through experience and creating value that stimulates innovation (Abubakar et al., 2019). It may be applied to handle knowledge growth and dispersion as well as to examine the knowledge characteristics of an interaction to manage it more effectively (Powell

& Swart, 2010). The original theoretical framework of the study also generated several testable hypotheses and investigated KMT theory in B2B sales and marketing. The study provides two different explanations for it in a body of literature through this procedure. The power of digital technology (BDAI), which essentially acts as a knowledge management enabler, has been demonstrated by this effort in the first place. Second, this study has shown how crucial knowledge management procedures, such the generation of user and external market knowledge, are to B2B rational decision-making. Thus, by highlighting the importance of digital technology-based knowledge facilitator in knowledge development and improving B2B decision making for improving organisational performance, this study contributes to the body of knowledge.

3.2 Practical Implications

Advanced technologies powered by BDAI can help B2B marketers in the collection of market data, and it can also provide essential information on plant operations, which in turn can assist in the development of products and solutions that are suitable for the market. The marketing managers in the firm can utilise this technology to keep track of all salespeople's daily calls and meetings. On their own tablets or mobile devices, the sales staff can capture information concerning meetings by using certain applications. Through the analysis of large data sets, it is also possible to get beneficial information regarding the purchasing patterns, sentiments and perspectives of consumers about certain businesses. Additional applications of AI could be helpful for business-to-business marketing. As a result, B2B marketers can better optimise knowledge management procedures by employing AI driven by big data. It is essential to practise effective knowledge management to advance and improve corporate performance.

Our paper led us to draw several findings useful to marketing practices. First and foremost, senior leaders have an obligation to pay close attention to big data sets, since these can be leveraged to make AI more valuable. To make educated decisions regarding B2B marketing, it is very necessary to place a strong emphasis on knowledge management processes that include the development of knowledge regarding clients, users and external markets. In conclusion, the decisions that are made about B2B marketing need to be of a high quality because they have a significant effect on the organisation's performance. In addition to this, they may call attention to the possibility of the need for action from management. When problems are solved in a significantly shorter amount of time, efficiency is increased.

3.3 Study Limitations and Future Research

Since AI applications are still in their infancy, future studies can study the effects of the different types of collaborative relationships on AI and business performance such as supplier collaboration, human and machine collaboration, project teams' collaboration. Currently, there is a pressing need for additional research on the institutional structures that are the driving forces behind big data and AI. Particularly in the context of business-to-business marketing, big data and AI create severe privacy problems. Fears on the part of customers regarding the disclosure of personal information could be a barrier to the implementation of BDAI, preventing big data from reaching its full potential. It is essential to carry out a study on the formulation of BDAI policies to protect from the inappropriate use of data by B2B marketers. In conclusion, the next generation of researchers ought to place a higher emphasis on B2B research as well as triple bottom line research.

REFERENCES

Abbate, T., Codini, A. P., & Aquilani, B. (2019). Knowledge co-creation in open innovation digital platforms: Processes, tools and services. *Journal of Business and Industrial Marketing*, *34*(7), 1434–1447.

Abrell, T., Pihlajamaa, M., Kanto, L., vom Brocke, J., & Uebernickel, F. (2016). The role of users and customers in digital innovation: Insights from B2B manufacturing firms. *Information and Management*, *53*(3), 324–335.

Abubakar, A. M., Elrehail, H., Alatailat, M. A., & Elçi, A. (2019). Knowledge management, decision-making style, and organisational performance. *Journal of Innovation & Knowledge*, *4*(2), 104–114.

Bag, S., Gupta, S., Kumar, A., & Sivarajah, U. (2021). An integrated artificial intelligence framework for knowledge creation and B2B marketing rational decision making for improving firm performance. *Industrial Marketing Management*, *92*, 178–189.

Baier, J. A., & McIlraith, S. A. (2022, February). Knowledge-based programs as building blocks for planning. *Artificial Intelligence*, *303*, 103634.

Balducci, B., & Marinova, D. (2018). Unstructured data in marketing, *Journal of the Academy of Marketing Science*, *46*(4), 557–590.

Baskerville, R., & Dulipovici, A. (2006). The theoretical foundations of knowledge management. *Knowledge Management Research and Practice*, *4*(2), 83–105.

Bonnin, G., & Rodriguez, M. A. (2019). The narrative strategies of B2B technology brands. *Journal of Business and Industrial Marketing*, *34*(7), 1448–1458.

Chintagunta, P., Hanssens, D. M., & Hauser, J. R. (2016). Marketing science and big data. *Marketing Science*, *35*, 341–342.

Cortez, R. M., & Johnston, W. J. (2017). The future of B2B marketing theory: A historical and prospective analysis. *Industrial Marketing Management*, *66*, 90–102.

Davenport, T., Guha, A., Grewal, D., & Bressgott, T. (2019). How artificial intelligence will change the future of marketing. *Journal of the Academy of Marketing Science*, *48*(1), 24–42.

De Camargo Fiorini, P., Seles, B. M. R. P., Jabbour, C. J. C., Mariano, E. B., & de Sousa Jabbour, A. B. L. (2018). Management theory and big data literature: From a review to a research agenda. *International Journal of Information Management*, *43*, 112–129.

DeTienne, K. B., & Jackson, L. A. (2001). Knowledge management: Understanding theory and developing strategy. *Competitiveness Review: An International Business Journal. 11*(1), 1–11.

Duan, Y., Edwards, J. S., & Dwivedi, Y. K. (2019). Artificial intelligence for decision making in the era of Big Data–evolution, challenges, and research agenda. *International Journal of Information Management*, *48*, 63–71.

Dubey, R., Gunasekaran, A., Childe, S. J., Bryde, D. J., Giannakis, M., Foropon, C., Roubaud, D., & Hazen, B. T. (2020). Big data analytics and artificial intelligence pathway to operational performance under the effects of entrepreneurial orientation and environmental dynamism: A study of manufacturing organisations . *International Journal of Production Economics*, *226*, 107–599.

Dwivedi, Y. K., Ismagilova, E., Hughes, D. L., Carlson, J., Filieri, R., Jacobson, J., Jain, V., Karjaluoto, H., Kefi, H., Krishen, A. S., Kumar, V., Rahman, M. M., Raman, R., Rauschnabel, P. A., Rowley, J., Salo, J., Tran, G. A., & Wang, Y. (2021). Setting the future of digital and social media marketing research: Perspectives and research propositions. *International Journal of Information Management*, *59*, 102168.

Dwivedi, Y. K., Kapoor, K. K., & Chen, H. (2015). Social media marketing and advertising. *The Marketing Review*, *15*(3), 289–309.

Dwivedi, Y. K., Venkitachalam, K., Sharif, A. M., Al-Karaghouli, W., & Weerakkody, V. (2011). Research trends in knowledge management: Analyzing the past and predicting the future. *Information Systems Management*, *28*(1), 43–56.

Evans, J. M. (2003). AI and robotics. Industrial Robot. *International Journal*, *30*(2).

Forsyth, D., & Ponce, J. (2011). *Computer vision: A modern approach*. Prentice Hall.

Gupta, S., Drave, V. A., Dwivedi, Y. K., Baabdullah, A. M., & Ismagilova, E. (2020, October). Achieving superior organizational performance via big data predictive analytics: A dynamic capability view. *Industrial Marketing Management*, *90*, 581–592.

Gupta, S., Keen, M., Shah, A., Verdier, G. & Walutowy, M. F. (2017), *Digital revolutions in public finance*. International Monetary Fund, Washington, DC.

Hofacker, C., Golgeci, I., Pillai, K. G., & Gligor, D. M. (2020). Digital marketing and business-to-business relationships: A close look at the interface and a roadmap for the future. *European Journal of Marketing*, *54*(6), 1161–1179.

Huang, M. J., Tsou, Y. L., & Lee, S. C. (2006). Integrating fuzzy data mining and fuzzy artificial neural networks for discovering implicit knowledge. *Knowledge-Based Systems*, *19*(6), 396–403.

Huang, M. H., & Rust, R. T. (2017). Technology-driven service strategy. *Journal of the Academy of Marketing Science*, *45*(6), 906–924.

Jabbar, A., Akhtar, P., & Dani, S. (2020). Real-time big data processing for instantaneous marketing decisions: A problematization approach. *Industrial Marketing Management*, *90*, 558–569.

Johnston, W. J., & Chandler, J. D. (2012). The organizational buying center: Innovation, knowledge management and brand. In *Handbook of business-to-business marketing*. Edward Elgar Publishing eBooks. https://doi.org/10.4337/9781781002445.00031

Katsikeas, C., Leonidou, L., & Zeriti, A. (2019). Revisiting international marketing strategy in a digital era. *International Marketing Review*, *37*(3), 405–424.

Kietzmann, J., & Pitt, L. F. (2020, March). Artificial intelligence and machine learning: What managers need to know. *Business Horizons*, *63*(2), 131–133.

Kohli, A. K., & Jaworski, B. J. (1990), Market orientation: The construct, research propositions, and managerial implications, *Journal of Marketing*, *54*(2), 1–18.

Leung, K. H., Luk, C. C., Choy, K. L., Lam, H. Y., & Lee, C. K. (2019). A B2B flexible pricing decision support system for managing the request for quotation process under e-commerce business environment. *International Journal of Production Research*, *57*(20), 6528–6551.

Liu, X. (2020). Analyzing the impact of user-generated content on B2B Firms' stock performance: Big data analysis with machine learning methods. *Industrial Marketing Management*, *86*, 30–39.

Liu, X., Singh, P. V., & Srinivasan, K. (2016). A structured analysis of unstructured big data by leveraging cloud computing. *Marketing Science*, *35*(3), 363–388.

Lu, R., & Zhang, S. (2002). *Automatic generation of computeranimation: Using AI for movie animation*. Springer.

Martínez-López, F. J., & Casillas, J. (2013). Artificial intelligence-based systems applied in industrial marketing: An historical overview, current and future insights. *Industrial Marketing Management*, *42*(4), 489–495.

McElroy, M. W. (2000). Integrating complexity theory, knowledge management and organisational learning. *Journal of Knowledge Management*, *4*(3), 195–203.

Nallaperuma, D., Nawaratne, R., Bandaragoda, T., Adikari, A., Nguyen, S., Kempitiya, T., De Silva, D., Alahakoon, D., & Pothuhera, D. (2019, December). Online incremental machine learning platform for big data-driven smart traffic management. *IEEE Transactions on Intelligent Transportation Systems*, *20*(12), 4679–4690.

O'Leary, D. E. (2013). Artificial intelligence and big data. *IEEE Intelligent Systems*, *28*(2), 96–99.

Pandey, N., Nayal, P., & Rathore, A. S. (2020). Digital marketing for B2B organizations: Structured literature review and future research directions. *Journal of Business and Industrial Marketing*, *35*(7), 1191–1204.

Paschen, J., Kietzmann, J., & Kietzmann, T. C. (2019). Artificial intelligence (AI) and its implications for market knowledge in B2B marketing. *Journal of Business and Industrial Marketing*, *34*(7), 1410–1419.

Paschen, J., Wilson, M., & Ferreira, J. J. (2020). Collaborative intelligence: How human and artificial intelligence create value along the B2B sales funnel. *Business Horizons*, *63*(3), 403–414.

Pecora, F. (2014). Is model-based robot programming a mirage? A brief survey of AI reasoning in robotics. *KI-Künstliche Intelligenz*, *28*(4), 255–261.

Pedeliento, G., Andreini, D., Bergamaschi, M., & Salo, J. (2018). End users' purchasing task involvement, power and influence strategies in organizational buying. *Journal of Business and Industrial Marketing*, *34*(1), 150–165.

Petrescu, M., Krishen, A. S., Kachen, S., & Gironda, J. T. (2022, May). AI-Based innovation in B2B marketing: An interdisciplinary framework incorporating academic and practitioner perspectives. *Industrial Marketing Management*, *103*, 61–72.

Pigni, F., Piccoli, G., & Watson, R. (2016). Digital data streams: Creating value from the real- time flow of big data. *California Management Review*, *58*(3), 5–25.

Poole, D. L., & Mackworth, A. K. (2010). *Artificial intelligence: Foundations of computational agents.* Cambridge University Press.

Powell, J. H., & Swart, J. (2010). Mapping the values in B2B relationships: A systemic, knowledge-based perspective. *Industrial Marketing Management*, *39*(3), 437–449.

Prior, D. D., & Keränen, J. (2020). Revisiting contemporary issues in B2B marketing: It's not just about artificial intelligence. *Australasian Marketing Journal*, *28*(2), 83–89.

Rowley, J. (2004). Partnering paradigms? Knowledge management and relationship marketing. *Industrial Management and Data Systems*. *104*(2), 149–157.

Rust, R. Y. (2020). The future of marketing, *International Journal of Research in Marketing*, *37*(1), 15–26.

Sebag, M. (2014). A tour of machine learning: An AI perspective. *AI Communications*, *27*(1), 11–23.

Singh, S. K., Marinova, D., & Singh, J. (2020). Business-to-business E-negotiations and influence tactics. *Journal of Marketing*, *84*(2), 47–68.

Sleep, S., Dixon, A. L., DeCarlo, T., & Lam, S. K. (2020). The business-to-business inside sales force: Oles, configurations and research agenda. *European Journal of Marketing*, *54*(5), 1025–1060.

Smolka, K. M., Verheul, I., Burmeister–Lamp, K., & Heugens, P. P. (2018). Get it together! Synergistic effects of causal and effectual decision–making logics on venture performance. *Entrepreneurship Theory and Practice*, *42*(4), 571–604.

Sternberg, R. J. (2017). Human intelligence. *Encyclopedia Britannica*. Available at: www.britannica.com/science/human-intelligence-psychology

Syam, N., & Sharma, A. (2018). Waiting for a sales renaissance in the fourth industrial revolution: Machine learning and artificial intelligence in sales research and practice. *Industrial Marketing Management*, *69*, 135–146.

Tecuci, G. (2012). Artificial intelligence. *WIREs: Computational Statistics*, *4*(2), 168–180.

Tzortzaki, A. M., & Mihiotis, A. (2014). A review of knowledge management theory and future directions. *Knowledge and Process Management*, *21*(1), 29–41.

Wamba, S. F., Gunasekaran, A., Akter, S., Ren, S. J. F., Dubey, R., & Childe, S. J. (2017). Big data analytics and firm performance: Effects of dynamic capabilities. *Journal of Business Research*, *70*, 356–365.

Wilson, D., & Bettis-Outland, H. (2019). Can artificial neural network models be used to improve the analysis of B2B marketing research data? *Journal of Business & Industrial Marketing*, *35*(3), 495–507. https://doi.org/10.1108/jbim-01-2019-0060.

Yu, Y. W., Yu, H. C., Itoga, H., & Lin, T. R. (2008). Decision-making factors for effective industrial e-procurement. *Technology in Society*, *30*(2), 163–169.

Zhou, L., Pan, S., Wang, J., & Vasilakos, A. V. (2017, May). Machine learning on big data: Opportunities and challenges. *Neurocomputing*, *237*, 350–361.

Zhuang, Y. T., Wu, F., Chen, C., & Pan, Y. H. (2017). Challenges and opportunities: From big data to knowledge in AI 2.0. *Frontiers of Information Technology and Electronic Engineering*, *18*(1), 3–14.

STRATEGIC FORESIGHT AND BUSINESS ANALYTICS: A SYSTEMATIC EXPLORATION OF MEDIATED IMPACTS ON ORGANISATIONAL RESILIENCE

Hiba AlSaidi and David Crowther

University of Bedfordshire, UK

ABSTRACT

This study delves into the interrelationships between business analytics (BA), strategic foresight (SF) and organisational resilience (OR) based on the systems theory. The research model was evaluated using Smart PLS 2.0. We found that both BA and SF have positive impacts on OR, explaining 32% of the change in OR. Additionally, BA was shown to have a positive effect on SF. We also discovered that BA partially mediates the relationship between SF and OR. However, no significant mediating effect was found in the relation of BA on OR through SF. These findings reveal the important role BA and SF play in enhancing OR, highlighting the mediating role of BA in the relationship between SF and OR. This research marks a significant advancement in the literature, being the first to establish this unique mediation effect and opens the way for future longitudinal research to validate and expand these findings.

Keywords: Business analytics (BA); Strategic foresight (SF); Organisational resilience (OR); research model evaluation; longitudinal research

1. INTRODUCTION

In an era defined by rapid technological progress, unpredictable market shifts and heightened global interconnectedness, businesses operate in an environment characterised by volatility, uncertainty, complexity and ambiguity; organisations

Social Responsibility, Technology and AI
Developments in Corporate Governance and Responsibility, Volume 23, 49–68
Copyright © 2025 Hiba AlSaidi and David Crowther
Published under exclusive licence by Emerald Publishing Limited
ISSN: 2043-0523/doi:10.1108/S2043-052320240000023003

must create shields to protect themselves from their surroundings (Taskan et al., 2022). The most seems to be the perfect response to these challenging conditions creating an organisational resilience (OR) environment, which has emerged as a crucial attribute for enterprises navigating this volatile landscape. OR refers to an organisation's capacity to absorb shocks, recover from disruptions and adapt. Resilience goes beyond merely surviving adversities to transforming challenges into opportunities for growth and improvement, therefore conferring a competitive advantage (Kantur & İşeri-Say, 2012).

> Organisations are complex systems made up of numerous interconnected subsystems, as articulated in the systems theory (Katina, 2015); each subsystem contributes to the overall system's functioning, adaptability and resilience. In the context of this study, two subsystems of particular interest are business analytics (BA) and strategic foresight (SF). The use of BA is powered by advanced technologies such as artificial intelligence (AI) and machine learning (ML), which allow organisations to process complex data, facilitating data-driven decision-making, risk identification and robust strategy formulation (Davenport, 2018), all of which can enhance an organisation's ability to adapt and recover, thereby augmenting resilience. On the other hand, SF provides a systematic way to envision potential futures, enabling organisations to prepare for various scenarios. By enhancing the readiness to adapt and evolve (Buehring & Bishop, 2020), SF is proposed to enhance the organisation's resilience.

While both subsystems – BA and SF – have been studied individually, comprehensive empirical research exploring their combined impact on OR in general and particularly from a systems perspective was not found. This research is thought to be the first in literature that seeks to fill this gap by examining how these subsystems collectively contribute to and interact to strengthen an organisation's resilience.

The following sections will detail the research questions and hypothesis that guide this study, followed by a thorough explanation of the methodology, analysis, findings and implications of the research.

2. LITERATURE REVIEW AND THEORETICAL CONSIDERATION

2.1 Organisational Resilience

The resilience concept was initially presented by Thomas Young and was influential across several fields including material sciences, psychology, ecological and engineering sciences (Holling, 1973; Mayar et al., 2022). In addition, its importance was notable in organisational studies as a concept for their survival, sustainability and continuity (Ince et al., 2017).

OR is a critical capability that allows businesses to navigate changing environments. This concept has evolved from merely recovering from adversities to transforming disruptions into opportunities for learning and growth. Resilience is a concept of sustainability, as it provides a comprehensive approach to managing risks (Sudmeier-Rieux, 2014), considering that resilient organisations demonstrate the ability to 'bounce forward' by not only recovering from disruptions but also adapting in ways that enhance their readiness and competitive advantage for future disruptions (Smith et al., 2008), in addition to a firm's capacity to withstand disorder resulted from unanticipated events (Antunes, 2011).

Although there is no universal definition for OR, OR offers an all-encompassing perspective by assessing how an organisation's structure, procedures and interactions respond to unpredictable situations, whether they stem from internal or external factors (Witmer, 2019). In this research, OR is defined as the organisational ability to adapt and recover from uncertainties (Antunes, 2011; Helm, 2015; Kim et al., 2016).

2.2 Business Analytics

The concept of "business analytics" is a relatively recent term, although it has been known for a long time ago because of all the changes and redefinitions of its application due to the technological advances, from simple business intelligence reports with drill-down options to dealing with massive amount of structured and unstructured data used to support knowledge creation, drive insights and solve problems (Holsapple et al., 2014). BA appeared in different fields as a helpful resource in all kinds of complicated situations (Gómez-Caicedo et al., 2022).

BA refers to technologies, applications and practices that transform raw business data into actionable insights (Davenport, 2006); by leveraging advanced technologies like AI and ML, they enable organisations to make informed decisions, identify potential risks, devise robust strategies, derive solutions from business data, thereby enhancing its capacity to describe, predict and optimise performance metrics (Delen & Ram, 2018). BA is classified into three dominant types: descriptive, predictive and perspective analytics (Holsapple et al., 2014):

Descriptive analytics is the initial stage that utilises data to understand past events. This type of analytics processes and scrutinises historical data to find patterns to create reports and performs procedures such as "data modelling, visualisation and regression analysis".

Predictive analytics is the more advanced of analytics compared to descriptive analytics; it projects future probabilities, identifies trends and uncovers correlations in data that might not be immediately noticeable with conventional analysis. This domain utilises techniques like data mining and predictive modelling.

Prescriptive analytics, on the other hand, is the most mature among the three domains, as it uses data to suggest the most beneficial method to enhance the likelihood of attaining the most favourable results. It explores and establishes innovative ways to conduct operations, aligns business goals and manages all restrictions. Optimisation and simulation techniques are largely used within this domain (Robinson et al., 2011).

Thus, this research defines BA as an asset of technologies, applications and practices that transform raw business data into actionable insights (Davenport, 2006).

2.3 Strategic Foresight

Environmental uncertainty led to the refinement of focused strategies to improve decision-making (Vecchiato, 2015) as traditional planning methods were no longer effective in deriving insights. SF merged as the ability to understand the future and gather related insights to be incorporated in decision-making (Rohrbeck et al., 2015) with a set of techniques that allows organisations to incorporate uncertainty into decision-making processes by allowing organisations to anticipate the future and adapt their strategies accordingly (Schwartz, 1997; Rhisiart et al., 2015). These SF techniques focused on the need for environmental scanning, scenario planning and knowledge creation capabilities (Vecchiato & Roveda, 2010).

Environmental scanning is one of the techniques that are essential in strategic management and organisational functions to understand the surroundings; they are associated with innovation activities and scenario planning needed to adapt to changes (Robinson et al., 2021). In addition, scenario planning creates potential events and finds suitable solutions (Wilkinson & Kupers, 2013). It is considered as a strategic planning component that manages uncertainties using available technological resources and tools (Vidal, 2007). Furthermore, environmental scanning techniques collect and use present information about what's happening and provide managers with needed information for knowledge-creation activities to form action plans responsible for stabilising the organisation's future (Haarhaus & Liening, 2020).

Therefore, this research considers these three elements for creating SF and defines SF as an organisation's ability to plan and scan the surrounding environments to create the needed knowledge that will help organisations deal with changes (Haarhaus & Liening, 2020), thereby contributing to its resilience.

2.4 Systems Theory on OR

Systems theory, as developed by *Bertalanffy, L. v.* (1968), provides a conceptual framework for understanding the complex interactions within entities. Later on, it was proposed (Ackoff, 1971) that a system is a composite entity and characteristics that result from the interactions between its components. According to (Nevo & Wade, 2010), the world comprises various entities, each with properties that have specific values, collectively determining the entity's state. These properties are derived from the interaction of the whole system and components, which determines the value of a system. By viewing this research through the lens of systems theory, an organisation is a holistic entity containing interrelated and interdependent subsystems, changes in one subsystem can spread across the entire system, influencing the whole organisation. This theory is often applied in organisational studies to analyse the interaction between various organisational subsystems and their impacts on organisational outcomes (Daft, 2015).

Drawing from the systems theory, which suggests that a system's properties may have an effect on their components' properties or present new "emergent properties" (Nevo & Wade, 2010), this is proposed to understand the interplay between BA, SF and OR. Within the systems theory framework, BA and SF can be considered critical components of the broader organisational system. Their use and implementation affect the system's overall functioning, dynamics and emergent properties which is OR. By applying the systems theory, we recognise that these components (BA and SF) do not function in isolation; instead, they interact with each other and other elements within a system, impacting the system's/organisation's overall resilience. Moreover, the systems theory also takes into account the complex, dynamic nature of organisational environments. It suggests that changes in one component of the system can reflect changes in other components and, therefore, the system's overall resilience. Hence, applying systems theory in our study is expected to provide a holistic understanding of how BA and SF impact OR. Finally, systems theory provides a valuable way to identify and understand the emergence of new properties within a system – in this case, OR. The 'emergence' concept offers a way to explore how the combination of BA and SF within an organisation can create a new property – resilience – that is more than the sum of its parts. Therefore, the application of systems theory in this research is justifiable as it can offer deeper insights into the relationships between BA, SF and OR.

3. RESEARCH MODEL AND HYPOTHESIS BUILDING

Leveraging the principles of systems theory, along with existing literature on BA, SF and OR, this study presents a research model, illustrated in Fig. 1. The following sections will provide an in-depth understanding of the literature review and hypothesis development to further explain this model.

3.1 Research Model

OR can be seen from many perspectives, yet a universal definition remains unavailable. For the context of this study, we define OR as "the ability of an organisation to adapt and recover from uncertainties". Central to this research is the exploration of how organisations can utilise BA and SF to enhance resilience, particularly focusing on the capacity to adapt to and recover from disruptions.

BA in the current digitised and data-driven era provides a pathway for organisations to gain in-depth insights from a huge amount of data, by detecting hidden patterns and unknown correlations. These insights can offer a competitive edge and lead to enhanced OR. For instance, Davenport (2006) has suggested

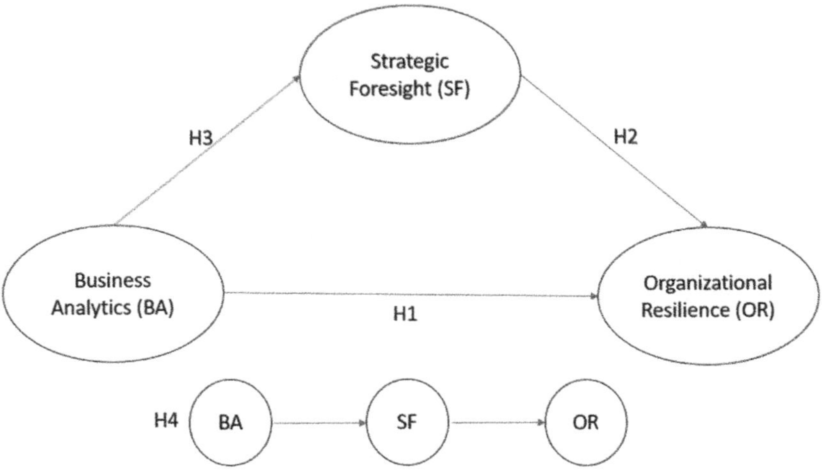

Fig. 1. Research Model.

that analytically driven organisations derive insights to innovate and secure competitive advantage. However, this assertion indicates a need for robust empirical investigation into the actual contribution of the use of BA in OR.

SF, on the other hand, is a systematic approach to intelligence that is related to building a medium- and long-term vision to inform on-time decisions and actions (Vecchiato, 2015). It is suggested to complement BA by adding a future-oriented perspective, enabling organisations to better anticipate and prepare for potential disruptions. BA is seen in this research as a powering tool to be used by decision-makers through SF to enhance OR.

Within the framework of systems theory, the interplay between BA, SF and OR becomes clearer. This research proposes that BA and SF, as key components of a system, can enhance the emergent property of this system which is OR. According to Nevo and Wade (2010), the value of these emergent properties is shaped by the complex interactions of the components within the system.

Thus, the research model for this study suggests that BA and SF influence the individual processes within an organisation, which collectively results in OR.

The forthcoming section details a series of hypothesis to be examined with empirical data in this research.

3.2 Hypothesis Building

Based on the research model supported by the underlying system theory and a review of literature, the following hypotheses are proposed. These hypotheses are intended to investigate the dynamic relationships among BA, SF and OR.

3.2.1 Business Analytics and Organizational Resilience

The use of BA is noted to enhance decision-making capabilities in organisations by revealing useful patterns and deriving insights from complex datasets (Lavalle et al., 2010). These insights, theoretically, facilitate a better comprehension of the operating environment, empowering organisations to handle disruptions more efficiently (Davenport, 2014), hence leading to an increase of resilience. This forms the basis of our first hypothesis:

> *H1*. The usage of business analytics (BA) has a positive influence on organizational resilience (OR).

3.2.2 Strategic Foresight and Organizational Resilience

SF enables organisations to anticipate and prepare for future possibilities (Schwartz, 1997), in addition to its aid in crafting efficient strategies to mitigate future risks (Rohrbeck & Kum, 2018) that can lead to creating needed knowledge to face the unexpected, hence proposes its contribution to OR. This forms the second hypothesis:

> *H2*. The employment of strategic foresight (SF) has a positive influence on organizational resilience (OR).

3.2.3 Business Analytics and Strategic Foresight

The interplay between BA and SF is critical, with each complementing the other as proposed in the system theory. BA-driven insights can serve as a robust foundation for SF activities, leading to efficient scenario planning and risk assessments (Chen et al., 2012; Lavalle et al., 2010; Sharma et al., 2014); in addition, BA can be used to improve environmental scanning (Duan et al., 2020) and knowledge creation process (Hair, 2007) that leads enhancing decision-making process, thus will be reflecting the leverage of BA usage in SF. This forms the third hypothesis:

> *H3*. The use of business analytics (BA) is positively related to the effectiveness of strategic foresight (SF).

3.2.4 Business Analytics, Strategic Foresight and Organizational Resilience

Drawing upon the systems theory, which posits that the value of an emergent property of a system is influenced by the values and interactions of its constituent elements (von Bertalanffy, 1950), this research proposes that OR – considered an emergent property – is shaped by the interplay of BA and SF.

Applying principles from mediating studies, this research proposes a possible interaction between the independent variable, BA, and SF as a mediator, which collectively influences the dependent variable (OR) (Preacher et al., 2007). Specifically, we propose that the use of BA influences OR not only directly but also indirectly through its mediating effect on SF. This proposition suggests a scenario where data-driven insights from BA use, when mediated by the capabilities of SF, can effectively enhance OR. As proposed by Rohrbeck et al. (2015), companies need to take advantage of available resources to prepare for changes and to meet their desired futures. Thus, the fourth hypothesis is proposed:

H4. The use of business analytics (BA) and its impact on organizational resilience (OR) is mediated by strategic foresight (SF).

Each of these hypotheses will be empirically tested to understand how BA and SF contribute to the enhancement of OR. It should be noted that these hypotheses are tentative and might be revised based on the data collected and the results of the study.

4. RESEARCH METHOD

Fig. 2 illustrates the proposed methodology's phases used to structure this research.

The research model and its corresponding hypothesis are evaluated through a survey method. Data are gathered via an online survey and drop-and-pick technique, targeting businesses based in Jordan.

4.1 Model Constructs and Measurements

Measurement of Constructs: All constructs were gauged using a five-point Likert scale (1 = strongly disagree, 5 = strongly agree).

Business Analytics (BA): This was measured with items adapted from Delen and Demirkan (2013) and Lavalle et al. (2010) and tested by Duan et al. (2020). That takes into consideration the types of analytics used within organisations: descriptive, predictive and perspective analytics.

Strategic Foresight (SF): This was assessed using items developed by Haarhaus and Liening (2020), which measure environmental scanning, scenario planning and knowledge creation as essentials for (Vecchiato & Roveda, 2010).

Organizational Resilience (OR): This was evaluated based on main two measurements (adaptation and recovery) as suggested by the OR definition by Antunes (2011), Helm (2015), Kim et al. (2016) and tested by Burnard and Bhamra (2011) and Sincorá et al. (2018) in resilient response framework.

4.2 Data Collection and Analysis Techniques

This section aims to provide greater transparency and context for the study by detailing the sample characteristics. As highlighted earlier, the primary focus is on Jordanian enterprises, but concerted efforts have been made to include a diverse range of industries and geographical locations within the country to improve the robustness and generalisability of the findings.

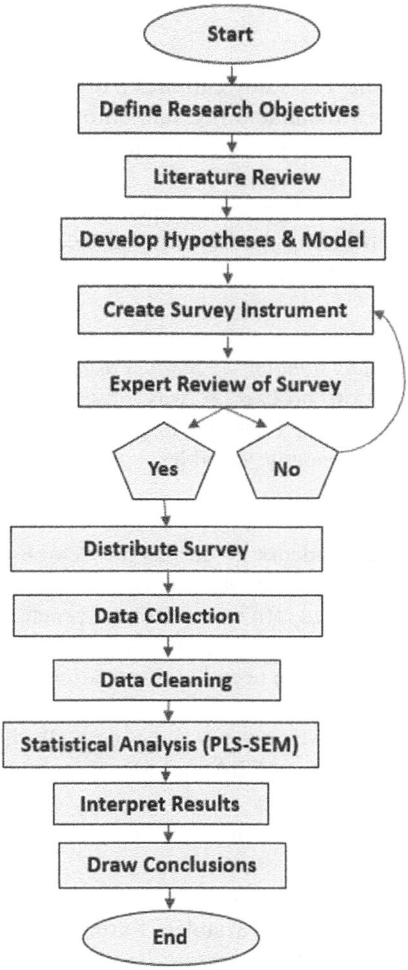

Fig. 2. Research Structure.

4.2.1 Definition of Medium and Large Enterprises

As defined in line with the EU standards, medium-sized enterprises in this study are organisations with a workforce ranging from 50 to 249 employees (Commission, 2003). Large enterprises consist of organisations with 250 or more employees. These categories were chosen specifically because organisations of these sizes are expected to have the resources and complexity to implement BA strategies effectively.

4.2.2 Data Collection Instrument

The survey instrument utilised a five-point Likert scale (ranging from 1 – strongly disagree to 5 – strongly agree). The survey was divided into four sections focusing on: Organizational information (enterprise size and industry type), BA usage, SF and OR.

4.2.3 Sample Characteristics

- Industry Representation: The study captures a diverse range of industries such as healthcare, finance, manufacturing and information technology, among others. This multi-sectoral approach aims to ensure that the results are not skewed by industry-specific factors.
- Geographical Distribution: The sample includes organisations from various cities across Jordan, including, but not limited to, Amman, Zarqa and Irbid. This serves to broaden the external validity of our findings.

4.2.4 Industry-specific Understanding of Study Variables

During the data collection process, it was observed that respondents from different industries as shown in Table 1.1 displayed varying levels of familiarity and understanding with the study variables – namely, BA usage, SF and OR. Notably:

- Financial Services: Respondents in this sector demonstrated a high level of understanding of all study variables. Their familiarity suggests that these constructs are well-integrated into organisational practices within this industry.
- Healthcare: This sector also showed a robust understanding of the study variables, although there was some need for clarification on specific aspects of BA usage.
- Technology: Companies in this sector were generally familiar with the variables, particularly in the areas of BA and SF.

Equally, the following observations were made about the other sectors:

- Others: This category, which makes up 24.5% of the sample, demonstrated the least familiarity with the study variables. Future research may benefit from more targeted information dissemination or training for respondents in this category to ensure accurate and informed responses.
- Additional Sectors: Respondents from other industries like manufacturing, services, retail/wholesale and education had varied levels of understanding, with some requiring more detailed explanations than others.

To maintain the content's validity, the survey was created on a Google survey instrument based on the literature review and the definitions discussed earlier and then scrutinised by subject experts. After a few revisions, the survey was reviewed by three senior academics in different areas (BA, business strategy and statistics) to ensure the clarity of the questions. The final version of the survey was distributed using the drop-and-pick technique, where the first author personally handed out the survey to managers in various enterprises and collected them at a later time and some answered surveys were sent back to email and WhatsApp numbers provided in the introduction section of the survey. In addition, the survey was distributed via emails to human resources departments of companies and directed to business directors and managers. These emails contained Google links, and responses were directed to a Google Sheet.

A total of 220 surveys were distributed, out of which 171 completed responses were received in the one-and-a-half-month collection period, giving a response rate of approximately 77.72 %. Fifty-eight surveys, manually completed by the participants, were entered into the Google Sheet by the first author. The hypotheses of this research were evaluated using the Partial Least Squares Structural Equation Modelling (PLS-SEM) technique on the collected survey data. PLS-SEM is considered suitable in similar cases, where the theory is not fully mature and the model includes newly defined constructs (Chen & Siau, 2020; Sarstedt et al., 2021).

Data cleaning was performed on Excel, and only 8 records showed incomplete respondents; these were removed from the dataset. The final dataset had 163 complete records as shown in the respondents' profile in Tables 1.1 and 1.2.

Table 1.1. Distribution of Participants by Industries.

Industry	# Of Subjects	%
Manufacturing	5	3.1
Services	22	13.5
Technology	12	7.4
Retail/Wholesale	19	11.7
Education	32	19.6
Healthcare	17	10.4
Financial services	16	9.8
Others[a]	40	24.5
Total	**163**	**100**

[a]Industry breakdown of others has been provided in Table 1.2.

Table 1.2. Industry Breakdown of (*Others*) Category.

Industries	# Of Subjects	%
Construction	7	17.5
Energy	4	10
Transportation	5	12.5
Media	6	15
Real estate	4	10
Legal services	8	20
Consulting	6	15
Total	**40**	**100**

Following the instructions used in the Chen and Siau's (2020) research and according to Hair et al. (2013), the minimum sample size for PLS-SEM should be 10 times the maximum number of paths directed to a particular construct in the structural model. In our research model, the largest number of such paths is three, indicating a minimum necessary sample size of 30.

Before beginning the analysis, this research performed an advanced power analysis following (Faul et al., 2007) guidelines, which takes into account a medium effect size of 0.30, an alpha of 0.05 and a power of 0.95. The calculated sample size for two-tailed *t*-tests is 134. With a survey sample size of 163, our sample is adequate for the PLS-SEM analysis. This analysis was processed using the SmartPLS 2.0 software.

4.3 Measurement Analysis Results

4.3.1 Common Method Bias

Common method bias is a usual problem in survey research analysis, so this research used the correlation method to investigate potential bias in the data. Table 2 displays the correlations among the main constructs of the study. According to Bagozzi et al. (1991), correlations score must not exceed 0.9, or it may be a sign of potential common method bias. As seen in Table 2, no bias is indicated.

4.3.2 Multicollinearity Test

Multicollinearity is another issue that can be captured in surveys, which is usually determined by the variance inflated factor (VIF) value as if the VIF value of 1 indicates the independent variables are not interrelated. If the VIF lies between 1 and 5, it indicates a moderate correlation among the variables. VIF values ranging from 5 to 10 are signals of a strong correlation with potential multicollinearity issues in the regression model (Barton & Peat, 2014; Shrestha, 2020). The VIF of this research construct was tested with results as the VIF of BA is 1.55 and VIF of SF is 2.245 and the VIF of OR is 2.425 which is lower than 5.

Table 2. Correlations Among Constructs.

	Construct Correlation					
	BA –Use	ES – SF	SP – SF	KC– SF	Adaptive – OR	Recovery – OR
BA – Use	1					
ES – SF	0.24	1				
SP – SF	0.27	0.34	1			
KC – SF	0.28	0.42	0.35	1		
Adaptive – OR	0.26	0.32	0.29	0.45	1	
Recovery – OR	0.28	0.35	0.36	0.32	0.49	1

4.3.3 Reliability and Validity Test

To check the reliability and validity of the survey questions, this research used the results of composite reliability, convergent validity and discriminant validity. At the start of any research, it's important to know if the questions being asked are reliable. Composite reliability checks this by seeing if questions consistently get similar answers. Next, convergent validity looks to make sure questions about a topic, all measure that topic correctly. And discriminant validity ensures that different topics don't get mixed up. All these steps make sure the research results can be trusted.

Composite reliability was calculated using the squared sum of the standardised loadings divided by the sum of the variances and error variances of the indicators. A composite reliability score of 0.7 or above is typically considered acceptable, and it is an indication of good internal consistency (Nunnally & Bernstein, 1994). The composite reliability score in Table 3 was above the recommended 0.7 score which means all scales are reliable. In addition, the criteria for convergent validity were fulfilled, as the average variance extracted (AVE) for each construct was not less than the recommended cut-off value of 0.50.

Convergent validity was confirmed by the AVE values for each construct, with all surpassing the recommended 0.5 threshold (Hair et al., 2013) as shown in Table 3. In addition, discriminant validity was tested following the criterion proposed by Fornell and Larcker (1981). Discriminant validity was established by ensuring the square root of the AVE of each construct was greater than its correlation with other constructs.

Thus, the above results confirmed confidence in the measurement scales used. It ensures that the questions consistently measure what they're meant to do and accurately reflect their intended topics without confusion or overlap, which leads to clear and trustworthy research results.

4.4 Evaluation of Structural Model and Hypothesis Testing

This research model was evaluated using Smart PLS 2.0, and the interaction effect was tested following the lead of Chen and Siau (2020) who followed the

Table 3. Constructs Average Variance Extracted (AVE), SQRT of AVE, Composite Reliability and Max Correlation With Other Constructs.

Construct	AVE	SQRT of AVE	Composite Reliability	Max Correlation with Other Constructs
BA – Use	0.58	0.76	0.89	0.5
ES – SF	0.69	0.83	0.87	0.6
SP – SF	0.66	0.81	0.88	0.57
KC – SF	0.67	0.82	0.86	0.58
Adaptive – OR	0.59	0.77	0.9	0.53
Recovery – OR	0.66	0.81	0.85	0.56

suggestions of Henseler and Chin (2010) using the two-stage approach by testing the path coefficient, then the significance of direct and indirect effect "using the bootstrapping method with 5,000 samples and 95% confidence interval as suggested by" (Vance et al., 2015). And "bias-corrected bootstrap that have the least biased confidence intervals, greatest power to detect non-zero effects and contrasts, and the most accurate overall Type I error" (Henseler & Chin, 2010).

To analyse control variables such as firm size and industry type influence on OR, these elements were tested using dummy variables. The findings demonstrated no significant impact on OR, with path coefficients of 0.07NS and 0.06NS, sequentially at the 5% significance level. It is noteworthy that despite varying levels of industry understanding of the study variables, as observed during data collection, these differences did not translate into statistically significant variations in OR outcomes. This strengthens the reliability of the study's core findings and suggests that the relationships between BA, SF and OR may be universally applicable across different industrial contexts.

To test the interaction effect of the model, we used the results of path coefficients where accepted scores are usually between −1 and +1, with coefficients closer to −1 representing strong negative relationships and those closer to +1 indicating strong positive relationships (Hair et al., 2021). In addition to the significant impact of probability value, if $p \leq 0.05$, the statement is true and far from the null hypothesis, and if ≥0.05, the statement is rejected and the null hypothesis is true. Thus, the results of hypothesis testing are shown in Table 4, where *H1*, 2 and 3 were supported, and *H4* was not supported.

This research is based on the lens of system theory, that suggests a system's properties may echo their components' properties or present new "emergent properties" (Nevo & Wade, 2010). We consider the OR to be this "emergent property, and BA, SF are the components" properties that work together to create a whole broader system in organisations. BA involves a range of techniques, including descriptive, predictive and prescriptive, that utilise various data sources. The use of these techniques enables organisations to make informed decisions that generate business value, ultimately aiding their survival in the highly competitive global market (Delen & Ram, 2018; Hindle & Vidgen, 2018). Therefore, this research suggests that the use of BA provides decision-makers with knowledge to understand the internal

Table 4. Summary Results of Hypothesis Testing.

Hypothesis	Independent Variable	Mediator	Dependent Variable	Path Coefficient	Empirical Evidence
H1	BA	N/A	OR	0.195*	Supported
H2	SF	N/A	OR	0.312**	Supported
H3	BA	N/A	SF	0.298**	Supported
H4	BA	SF	OR	0.006(a) NS	Not supported

N/A: Not applicable, NS: Not significant, a: total indirect path coefficient, **Significant at $p < 0.01$, * Significant at $p < 0.05$.

and external environment and provide insights to deal with changes. Thus, this research suggests that BA is a contributing component that affects the emergent property OR. The analysis showed the path coefficient for BA direct impact on OR is 0.195 and the significance level $p < 0.05$, thus; *H1* is supported. So, BA is proven to have a positive effect on OR.

SF is an organisation's ability to plan and scan the surrounding environments to create the needed knowledge that will help organisations deal with changes, whereas resilience is the ability to respond and recover (Helm, 2015), this research suggests that for organisations to be able to respond and recover, strategies must fit the new reality caused by uncertainties. Therefore, this research sees SF based on the systems theory as a contributing component that affects the emergent property OR, by creating new strategies and crafting current strategies to align with new needs and requirements to respond to changes, which will affect organisations' resiliency. The result of the analysis showed the path coefficient for SF's direct impact on OR is 0.312 and the significance level $p < 0.01$; thus, *H2* is supported. So, SF is proven to have a positive effect on OR. From the results of *H1* and *H2* and the variance results of OR, BA and SF explain 32% of the change in OR, which indicates that other factors play a major role in forming OR, which could be organisational culture, management, leadership styles, IT infrastructure, governance, ext.

IT systems can make complicated strategic planning methods easier to manage. They can help with different kinds of strategic planning methods and related tasks (Durst et al., 2015). This research proposes that BA has the needed capabilities to aid SF by gathering and scrutinising data, as well as automating tasks related to information research and analysis, so the use of BA by managers and decision-makers is proposed to help in developing needed changes and enhancements of current strategies and make better decisions. The results of the analysis showed the path coefficient for BA's direct impact on SF is 0.298 and the vsignificance level $p < 0.01$; in addition, the results showed that only 14% of the variance in SF is explained by BA, yet the effect of BA on SF is significant; thus, *H3* is supported. So, the use of BA has proved to have a positive effect on SF. The low variance score of BA on SF is reasonable as SF is affected by several other factors "related to the "participants" and factors related to the foresight "method and process"" (Iden et al., 2017). The findings show that BA is not just a factor affecting OR but also SF.

Mediating analysis results.

The results indicate a potential mediating effect on BA and SF relation; to test this, the mediating effect was tested using the boost strapping method following Chen and Siau (2020), to test the indirect effect of BA on OR through SF and the SF on OR through BA. Then variance accounted for (VAF) was calculated. If the VAF value > 0.8, there is a full mediating effect, if ≤ 0.8 and ≥ 0.2, then it's partial mediating and if <0.2, there is no mediating effect.

As shown in Table 5, the results show no significant indirect effect of BA on OR through SF with an indirect path coefficient of 0.006, *p*-value = 0.062 and VAF score = 0.12. This aligns with hypothesis test results in Table 3, where *H4* was not supported with a path coefficient of 0.006NS; therefore, *H4* is rejected,

Table 5. The Mediating Effects Results.

Effects	Path	Path Coefficient	Mediator	p Value	VAF	Mediating Effect
Indirect	BA SF OR	0.006 NS	SF	0.062	0.12	N/A
Indirect	SF BA OR	0.129[a]	BA	<0.01	0.52	Partial

[a]Significant at p <0.01.

and there are no significant effects of BA on OR through SF, so the relation of BA on OR is not mediated by SF. To extend the understanding of mediating relation, another test was conducted to test the relation of SF on OR through BA, and the results showed the significant indirect effect of SF on OR through BA with an indirect path coefficient of 0.129, $p < 0.01$ and VAF score of 0.52 which propose partial mediating effect. So, BA partially mediates the effect of SF on OR.

The finding that BA partially mediates the effect of SF on OR implies that BA is one of the channels through which SF influences OR but not the only one. This might be because BA and SF work together to improve OR or because BA helps put the insights from SF into action. BA might also have varying effects on different aspects of OR in different situations. Further research would be needed to confirm this.

5. CONCLUSION

This research has utilised the systems theory to examine the relationship between BA, SF and OR. This research relied on the system theory and proposed that BA and SF are components of the larger system, directly contributing to the emergent property, OR. Analysis results revealed that both BA and SF have a direct positive effect on OR, with path coefficients of 0.195 and 0.312, respectively, and their combined variance explains 32% of the change in OR. The positive effect of BA on SF was also substantiated with a path coefficient of 0.298, suggesting that the use of BA in strategic planning is significant, even though it only accounts for 14% of the variance in SF. However, this research failed to confirm a significant mediating effect of SF on the relationship between BA and OR. Instead, BA was found to partially mediate the impact of SF on OR, suggesting that the use of BA could enhance an organisation's SF capability and subsequently contribute to OR.

It is crucial to note that despite initial variations in industry understanding of these variables, statistical tests confirmed that such differences had no substantial influence on OR. This lends added robustness to the findings and suggests a potentially universal applicability of the identified relationships across diverse industry sectors that needs to be confirmed in future studies.

6. RESEARCH CONTRIBUTIONS

This research makes several notable contributions to the existing body of literature. It integrates systems theory with SF and OR, offering a fresh perspective on their interconnected relationship. Beyond theoretical connections, the research also empirically verifies the positive impacts of BA and SF on OR, enhancing the literature's understanding of the factors that drive OR. As far as researchers' knowledge, this is the first study to confirm this unique mediation effect of BA in the relationship between SF and OR.

7. LIMITATIONS

Despite its significant contributions, this study has several limitations that warrant consideration. First, the model used accounts for only 32% of the variance in OR, suggesting that other important factors like organisational culture, leadership styles or IT infrastructure were not included, thereby not covering the full spectrum of elements influencing OR. Second, the research sees that all organisations have the same capacity to adopt and implement BA and SF. This overlooks varying capabilities related to resources, skills and management commitment.

8. DIRECTIONS FOR FUTURE RESEARCH

This study opens up several avenues for future exploration. One promising direction would be to expand the current model to include additional variables that could influence OR, such as organisational culture, leadership styles and the role of IT infrastructure. Additionally, the partial influence of BA on the relationship between SF and OR warrants further investigation to ascertain under what conditions this influence becomes stronger or weaker. Lastly, while the cross-sectional design of this research has been instrumental in identifying key relationships, it provides only a snapshot in time, limiting the understanding of how these relationships might evolve. Future studies employing a longitudinal approach could offer a more comprehensive view of these dynamics, thereby enriching the findings and implications of this research. Although the varied familiarity with study variables across sectors did not influence the results, a confirmation of the thought to be a universally applicability of the identified relationships across diverse industry sectors and a sector-specific influences could be a valuable avenue for future research, providing deeper insights into the mechanisms through which BA and SF contribute to OR within different industrial contexts.

REFERENCES

Ackoff, R. L. (1971). Towards a system of systems concepts. *Management Science*, *17*(11), 661–671. https://doi.org/10.1287/mnsc.17.11.661

Antunes, P. (2011). BPM and exception handling: Focus on organizational resilience. *Systems, Man, and Cybernetics, Part C: Applications and Reviews, IEEE Transactions on*, *41*, 383–392. https://doi.org/10.1109/TSMCC.2010.2062504

Bagozzi, R. P., Yi, Y., & Phillips, L. W. (1991). Assessing construct validity in organizational research. *Administrative Science Quarterly*, *36*(3), 421–458. https://doi.org/10.2307/2393203

Barton, B., & Peat, J. (2014). *Medical statistics*. http://digilib.unkhair.ac.id/578/. Accessed on August 24, 2023.

Buehring, J., & Bishop, P. C. (2020). Foresight and design: New support for strategic decision making. *She Ji: The Journal of Design, Economics, and Innovation*, *6*(3), 408–432. https://doi.org/10.1016/j.sheji.2020.07.002

Burnard, K., & Bhamra, R. (2011). Organisational resilience: Development of a conceptual framework for organisational responses. *International Journal of Production Research*, *49*(18), 5581–5599. https://doi.org/10.1080/00207543.2011.563827

Chen, H., Chiang, L., & Storey, V. C. (2012) Business intelligence and analytics: From big data to big impact on JSTOR. https://www.jstor.org/stable/41703503. Accessed on June 22, 2023.

Chen, X., & Siau, K. (2020). Business analytics/business intelligence and IT infrastructure: Impact on organizational agility. *Journal of Organizational and End User Computing*, *32*(4), 138–161. https://doi.org/10.4018/JOEUC.2020100107

Commission, E. (2003) SME definition, European commission. https://single-market-economy.ec.europa.eu/smes/sme-definition_en. Accessed on October 18, 2023.

Daft, R. L. (2015). *Organization theory and design*. Cengage Learning.

Davenport, T. (2006). Competing on analytics. *Harvard Business Review*, *84*, 98–107, 134.

Davenport, T. (2014). Big data at work: Dispelling the myths, uncovering the opportunities. https://hbr.org/2014/03/big-data-at-work-dispelling-the-myths-uncovering-the-opportunities. Accessed on July 30, 2023.

Davenport, T. H. (2018). From analytics to artificial intelligence. *Journal of Business Analytics*, *1*(2), 73–80. https://doi.org/10.1080/2573234X.2018.1543535

Delen, D., & Demirkan, H. (2013). Data, information and analytics as services. *Decision Support Systems*, *55*(1), 359–363. https://doi.org/10.1016/j.dss.2012.05.044

Delen, D., & Ram, S. (2018). Research challenges and opportunities in business analytics. *Journal of Business Analytics*, *1*, 2–12. https://doi.org/10.1080/2573234X.2018.1507324

Duan, Y., Cao, G., & Edwards, J. S. (2020). Understanding the impact of business analytics on innovation. *European Journal of Operational Research*, *281*(3), 673–686. https://doi.org/10.1016/j.ejor.2018.06.021

Durst, C., Durst, M., Kolonko, T., Neef, A., & Greif, F. (2015). A holistic approach to strategic foresight: A foresight support system for the German Federal Armed Forces. *Technological Forecasting and Social Change*, *97*, 91–104. https://doi.org/10.1016/j.techfore.2014.01.005

Faul, F., Erdfelder, E., Lang, A.-G., & Buchner, A. (2007). G*Power 3: A flexible statistical power analysis program for the social, behavioral, and biomedical sciences. *Behavior Research Methods*, *39*(2), 175–191. https://doi.org/10.3758/BF03193146

Fornell, C., & Larcker, D. (1981). Evaluating structural equation models with unobservable variables and measurement error. *Journal of Marketing Research*, *18*(1), 39–50. https://doi.org/10.2307/3151312

Gómez-Caicedo, M. I., Gaitán-Angulo, M., Bacca-Acosta, J., Briñez Torres, C. Y., & Cubillos Díaz, J. (2022). Business analytics approach to artificial intelligence. *Frontiers in Artificial Intelligence*, *5*. https://www.frontiersin.org/articles/10.3389/frai.2022.974180. Accessed on June 15, 2023.

Haarhaus, T., & Liening, A. (2020). Building dynamic capabilities to cope with environmental uncertainty: The role of strategic foresight. *Technological Forecasting and Social Change*, *155*, 120033. https://doi.org/10.1016/j.techfore.2020.120033

Hair, J. F. (2007). Knowledge creation in marketing: The role of predictive analytics. *European Business Review*, *19*(4), 303–315. https://doi.org/10.1108/09555340710760134

Hair, J. F., Hult, G. T. M., Ringle, C. M., Sarstedt, M., Danks, N. P., & Ray, S. (2021). Evaluation of the structural model. In J. F. Hair Jr., G. T. M. Hult, C. M. Ringle, M. Sarstedt, N. P. Danks, & S. Ray (Eds.), *Partial least squares structural equation modeling (PLS-SEM) using R: A workbook* (pp. 115–138). Springer International Publishing. https://doi.org/10.1007/978-3-030-80519-7_6

Hair, J. F., Ringle, C. M., & Sarstedt, M. (2013). Partial least squares structural equation modeling: Rigorous applications, better results and higher acceptance. *Long Range Planning*, *46*(1), 1–12. https://doi.org/10.1016/j.lrp.2013.01.001

Helm, P. (2015). Risk and resilience: Strategies for security. *Civil Engineering and Environmental Systems*, *32*(1–2), 100–118. https://doi.org/10.1080/10286608.2015.1023793

Henseler, J., & Chin, W. (2010). A comparison of approaches for the analysis of interaction effects between latent variables using partial least squares path modeling. *Structural Equation Modeling*, *17*, 82–109. https://doi.org/10.1080/10705510903439003

Hindle, G. A., & Vidgen, R. (2018). Developing a business analytics methodology: A case study in the foodbank sector. *European Journal of Operational Research*, *268*(3), 836–851. https://doi.org/10.1016/j.ejor.2017.06.031

Holling, C. S. (1973). Resilience and stability of ecological systems. *Annual Review of Ecology and Systematics*, *4*(1), 1–23. https://doi.org/10.1146/annurev.es.04.110173.000245

Holsapple, C., Lee-Post, A., & Pakath, R. (2014). A unified foundation for business analytics. *Decision Support Systems*, *64*, 130–141. https://doi.org/10.1016/j.dss.2014.05.013

Iden, J., Methlie, L. B., & Christensen, G. E. (2017). The nature of strategic foresight research: A systematic literature review. *Technological Forecasting and Social Change*, *116*, 87–97. https://doi.org/10.1016/j.techfore.2016.11.002

Ince, H., Imamoglu, S. Z., Karakose, M. A., & Turkcan, H. (2017). *The search for understanding organizational resilience. In M. Özşahin (Ed.), Strategic management of corporate sustainability, social responsibility and innovativeness*. European Proceedings of Social and Behavioural Sciences (Vol 34, pp. 1–442). Future Academy. https://doi.org/10.15405/epsbs.2017.12.02.20

Kantur, D., & İşeri-Say, A. (2012). Organizational resilience: A conceptual integrative framework | *Journal of Management & Organization* | *Cambridge Core*. *18*(6), 762–773. https://doi.org/10.5172/jmo.2012.18.6.762

Katina, P. F. (2015). Emerging systems theory–based pathologies for governance of complex systems. *International Journal of System of Systems Engineering*, *6*(1–2), 144–159. https://doi.org/10.1504/IJSSE.2015.068806

Kim, K., Jung, K., & Chilton, K. (2016). Strategies of social media use in disaster management: Lessons in resilience from Seoul, South Korea. *International Journal of Emergency Services*, *5*(2), 110–125. https://doi.org/10.1108/IJES-02-2016-0005

Lavalle, S., Lesser, E., Shockley, R., Hopkins, M. S., & Kruschwitz, N. (2010). *Analytics: The new path to value*. MIT Sloan Management Review.

Mayar, K., Shen, X., & Carmichael, D. (2022). Stability and resilience—A systematic approach. *Buildings*, *12*, 1242. https://doi.org/10.3390/buildings12081242

Nevo, S., & Wade, M. R. (2010). The Formation and value of IT-enabled resources: Antecedents and consequences of synergistic relationships. *MIS Quarterly*, *34*(1), 163–183. https://doi.org/10.2307/20721419

Nunnally, J. C., & Bernstein, I. H. (1994) *Psychometric theory*. 3rd ed. McGraw-Hill (McGraw-Hill series in psychology). http://catdir.loc.gov/catdir/toc/mh022/93022756.html. Accessed on July 31, 2023.

Preacher, K. J., Rucker, D. D., & Hayes, A. F. (2007). Addressing moderated mediation hypotheses: Theory, methods, and prescriptions. *Multivariate Behavioral Research*, *42*(1), 185–227. https://doi.org/10.1080/00273170701341316

Rhisiart, M., Miller, R., & Brooks, S. (2015). Learning to use the future: Developing foresight capabilities through scenario processes. *Technological Forecasting and Social Change*, *101*, 124–133. https://doi.org/10.1016/j.techfore.2014.10.015

Robinson, C. V., Ahmad, F., & Simmons, J. E. L. (2021). Consolidation and fragmentation in environmental scanning: A review and research agenda. *Long Range Planning*, *54*(3), 101997. https://doi.org/10.1016/j.lrp.2020.101997

Robinson, A., Levis, J., & Bennett, G. (2011) *INFORMS to officially join analytics movement*, INFORMS. https://pubsonline.informs.org/do/10.1287/orms.2010.05.17in/full/. Accessed on August 3, 2023.

Rohrbeck, R., Battistella, C., & Huizingh, E. (2015). Corporate foresight: An emerging field with a rich tradition. *Technological Forecasting and Social Change*, *101*, 1–9. https://doi.org/10.1016/j.techfore.2015.11.002

Rohrbeck, R., & Kum, M. E. (2018). Corporate foresight and its impact on firm performance: A longitudinal analysis. *Technological Forecasting and Social Change*, *129*, 105–116. https://doi.org/10.1016/j.techfore.2017.12.013

Sarstedt, M., Ringle, C., & Hair, J. (2021). Partial least squares structural equation modeling. In *Handbook of market research* (pp. 1–47). Springer. https://doi.org/10.1007/978-3-319-05542-8_15-2

Schwartz, P. (1997) *Art of the long view: Planning for the future in an uncertain world.* Wiley. https://www.wiley.com/en-gb/Art+of+the+Long+View:+Planning+for+the+Future+in+an+Uncertain+World-p-9780471977858. Accessed on July 30, 2023.

Sharma, R., Mithas, S., & Kankanhalli, A. (2014). Transforming decision-making processes: A research agenda for understanding the impact of business analytics on organisations. *European Journal of Information Systems*, *23*, 433–441. https://doi.org/10.1057/ejis.2014.17

Shrestha, N. (2020). Detecting multicollinearity in regression analysis. *American Journal of Applied Mathematics and Statistics*, *8*, 39–42. https://doi.org/10.12691/ajams-8-2-1

Sincorá, L. A., de Oliveira, M. P. V., Zanquetto-Filho, H., & Ladeira, M. B. (2018). Business analytics leveraging resilience in organizational processes. *RAUSP Management Journal*, *53*, 385–403. https://doi.org/10.1108/RAUSP-04-2018-002

Smith, B. W., Dalen, J., Wiggins, K., Tooley, E., Christopher, P., & Bernard, J. (2008). The brief resilience scale: Assessing the ability to bounce back. *International Journal of Behavioral Medicine*, *15*(3), 194–200. https://doi.org/10.1080/10705500802222972

Sudmeier-Rieux, K. (2014). Resilience - An emerging paradigm of danger or of hope? *Disaster Prevention and Management: An International Journal*, *23*. https://doi.org/10.1108/DPM-12-2012-0143

Taskan, B., Junça-Silva, A., & Caetano, A. (2022). Clarifying the conceptual map of VUCA: A systematic review | Emerald insight. *International Journal of Organizational Analysis*, *30*(7), 196–217. https://doi.org/10.1108/IJOA-02-2022-3136

Vance, A., Lowry, P. B., & Eggett, D. (2015). Increasing accountability through user-interface design artifacts: A new approach to addressing the problem of access-policy violations. *39*. https://misq.umn.edu/increasing-accountability-through-user-interface-design-artifacts-a-new-approach-to-addressing-the-problem-of-access-policy-violations.html. Accessed on August 2, 2023.

Vecchiato, R. (2015). Strategic planning and organizational flexibility in turbulent environments. *Foresight*, *17*(3), 257–273. https://doi.org/10.1108/FS-05-2014-0032

Vecchiato, R., & Roveda, C. (2010). Strategic foresight in corporate organizations: Handling the effect and response uncertainty of technology and social drivers of change. *Technological Forecasting and Social Change*, *77*(9), 1527–1539. https://doi.org/10.1016/j.techfore.2009.12.003

Vidal, R. (2007). G. Ringland, Scenario planning – managing for the future, 2nd ed., John Wiley, 2006. ISBN 0-470-01881-X, p. xxii + 478, Euro 47.90. *European Journal of Operational Research*, 182, 1492–1493. https://doi.org/10.1016/j.ejor.2006.11.001

von Bertalanffy, L. (1950). An outline of general system theory. *The British Journal for the Philosophy of Science*, *1*(2), 134–165.

von Bertalanffy, L. (1968). *General system theory*. https://monoskop.org/images/7/77/Von_Bertalanffy_Ludwig_General_System_Theory_1968.pdf. Accessed on July 30, 2023.

Wilkinson, A., & Kupers, R. (2013). Living in the futures. *Harvard Business Review*, *91*.

Witmer, H. (2019). Degendering organizational resilience – The Oak and Willow against the wind. *Gender in Management: International Journal*, *34*(6), 510–528. https://doi.org/10.1108/GM-10-2018-0127

CONSTRUCTION 4.0 TECHNOLOGIES: USES AND CHALLENGES

Noor Al Mawlani[a] and Muneer Al Mubarak[b]

[a]*The George Washington University, USA*
[b]*Ahlia University, Bahrain*

ABSTRACT

The Architecture, Engineering and Construction (AEC) industry has been transformed by the increasing adoption of existing and emerging technologies of Industry 4.0, leading to the concept of Construction 4.0. However, the AEC industry is falling behind in comparison to other industries. The purpose of this chapter is to provide a comprehensive overview of digital transformation within the Construction 4.0 framework and explore the uses and challenges associated with adopting the most prominent digital technologies. This study is a literature-based exploration of published works to evaluate knowledge gaps and comprehend the Construction 4.0 concept in the context of the AEC industry. The results present a set of possible uses of 10 promising technologies in Construction 4.0 along with challenges that hinder its adoption. These are categorised as technical, legal, financial, organisational, industry and data security barriers. This research is limited to several promising technologies. Future studies should focus on rapidly developing technologies and finding better solutions for implementation. Besides increasing the awareness of practitioners, policymakers and clients towards Construction 4.0 technologies, it might assist them in making decisions on selecting and implementing key technologies. This chapter contributes to the literature by providing an updated and inclusive review that focuses on the uses and challenges of 10 trending technologies in the specific context of Construction 4.0. Therefore, the findings of this study provide a basis for different actors in the AEC industry to accelerate digital transformation and pave the way for future research.

Social Responsibility, Technology and AI
Developments in Corporate Governance and Responsibility, Volume 23, 69–90
Copyright © 2025 Noor Al Mawlani and Muneer Al Mubarak
Published under exclusive licence by Emerald Publishing Limited
ISSN: 2043-0523/doi:10.1108/S2043-052320240000023004

Keywords: Digital technologies; digital transformation; AEC industry; Construction 4.0; internet of things; Building Information Modelling; artificial intelligence

1. INTRODUCTION

In terms of economic growth and competitiveness, the Architecture, Engineering and Construction (AEC) industry is one of the biggest global sectors (Taher, 2021). Currently, the construction sector represents 6% of the global gross domestic product (GDP) growth and is expected to grow at about 14.7% by 2030 (Craveiro et al., 2019). However, the industry is characterised by low productivity in comparison to other industries such as manufacturing (Abioye et al., 2021). There is a consensus in the literature on the industry's being among the least digitalised sectors in the world (Perera et al., 2023; Tung et al., 2021). Several challenges are hindering the industry's growth such as project delays, the fragmentation of the industry, the difficulty of management, health and safety concerns (Chowdhury et al., 2019). In addition, cost inefficiencies, poor performance, uninformed decision-making and labour shortages are common issues (Abioye et al., 2021). Previous studies have concluded that these challenges are linked to the inadequate adoption and lagging implementation of digital technologies (Abioye et al., 2021). Therefore, digital technologies must be embraced to transform the industry, resulting in improved efficiency (Chowdhury et al., 2019).

The digital transformation of the AEC industry is achieved by pursuing Industry 4.0, characterised by the movement towards digitalisation and automation (Taher, 2021). The integration of advanced information and communication technologies across the project life cycle (Bosch-Sijtsema et al., 2021) has resulted in a significant shift in the processes and practices of the AEC industry (Forcael et al., 2020). Such advancements have revolutionised the sector (Manzoor et al., 2021), creating a new concept called Construction 4.0, the correspondent model of Industry 4.0 (Wang et al., 2022). Just like the definition of Industry 4.0, Construction 4.0 aims at the convergence of both digital and physical technologies (Taher, 2021). It is a transformative paradigm that explores digital technologies within the sector into three categories: industrial technologies, cyber-physical systems (CPS) and digital tools and technologies (Sawhney et al., 2020). Many digital technologies within this framework have witnessed a rising implementation to achieve higher efficiency and profitability (Mahajan, 2022). Some examples of these technologies are 3D printing, prefabrication, drones, sensors, internet of things (IoT), robots, Building Information Modelling (BIM), artificial intelligence (AI), Cloud computing, virtual reality (VR), 3D laser scanning and augmented reality (AR) (Sawhney et al., 2020).

The adoption of digital technologies has created many opportunities for enhancing the overall efficiency of the AEC industry (Chowdhury et al., 2019) and the quality of construction processes (Forcael et al., 2020). For instance, prefabrication enables faster construction, robotics improves safety and drones help to develop better design solutions (Mahajan, 2022). Supporting data-driven decision-making, improving productivity, reducing costs and providing digital access to information are several uses of digital technologies (Bosch-Sijtsema et al., 2021). For example, BIM has enabled better collaboration and data sharing between the projects' stakeholders (Manzoor et al., 2021). Moreover, it has shown that some technologies can be useful for improving the sustainability of building environments as well as decision orientation by making use of sensors and the IoT (Wang et al., 2022). In addition to that, digital technologies have an important role in expanding the dynamic capabilities of construction companies resulting in better utilisation of resources and response to the changing environment (Redwood et al., 2017).

In response to the increasing focus on digital technology trends towards digitalisation in the AEC industry (Bosch-Sijtsema et al., 2021), many studies have contributed to the knowledge in this field (Manzoor et al., 2021). However, several studies were limited to specific areas in which digital technologies are applied (Chowdhury et al., 2019). Procurement in the built environment (Yevu et al., 2021), off-site construction (Wang et al., 2020), prefabrication (Beulah et al., 2022), construction project management (Tung et al., 2021) and construction safety (Getuli et al., 2020) were among many discussed topics in literature. Some studies were confined to the uses and challenges of a particular digital technology such as AI (Abioye et al., 2021), digital twin (Opoku et al., 2023), IoT (Chen et al., 2020), cloud computing (Bello et al., 2020), BIM and immersive technologies (Khan et al., 2021). Furthermore, some studies were limited to the barriers to adopting digital technologies in developing economies (Oke et al., 2023). Manzoor et al. (2021) have provided a comprehensive framework of digital technologies in the AEC industry, whereas Bosch-Sijtsema et al. (2021) have identified the most promising technologies based on the hype curve. These studies have been based on the general context of the AEC sector, rather than a specific aspect of Construction 4.0. Besides the limitations of previous studies, digital technologies are rapidly evolving in Construction 4.0 which requires a continuous update of the literature (Forcael et al., 2020).

Thus, this chapter extends recent literature reviews on digital technologies by providing an updated overview of the uses and challenges of the most promising technologies by building upon the transformative framework of Construction 4.0 developed by Sawhney et al. (2020). To achieve the identified gap, the following objectives arise: (1) To identify the current situation and issues facing the AEC industry, (2) to define digital transformation in the context of the AEC industry, (3) to define Construction 4.0 and its transformative framework, (4) to explore the uses of the most promising technologies in Construction 4.0 and (5) to investigate the challenges and barriers to adopting the digital technologies of Construction 4.0.

By answering these questions, a detailed roadmap of Construction 4.0 and its prime technologies will emerge. Besides contributing to the knowledge body in the research domain, the findings will be beneficial to direct policymakers and industry stakeholders towards making better decisions to speed up the pace of digital transformation. Moreover, the results could be helpful for architecture, engineering and construction firms in assessing their status of digitalisation, improving processes and adopting more digitalised practices. As a result, these companies will gain and sustain their competitive advantage in the industry. This chapter paves the way for future studies on the rapidly evolving technologies as well as other neglected technologies in the context of the AEC industry. It is critical to proceed with future studies on finding better solutions to fully utilise the potential of digital technologies and overcome the barriers to their adoption with consideration of human–machine interaction.

2. LITERATURE REVIEW

2.1 The AEC Industry's Current State

Digital technologies have played a critical role in revolutionising the AEC industry from conventional labour-based practices to automation (Manzoor et al., 2021). According to recent literature aggregations, the global adoption of digital technologies within the industry has been on an increasing scale (Olanipekun & Sutrisna, 2021; Opoku et al., 2023). Several changes in design and construction approaches have been witnessed with the increasing use of digital technologies (Khan et al., 2021). It has yielded significant improvements in many critical aspects of construction projects such as quality, cost, efficiency and safety (Criado-Perez et al., 2022). For example, AI technology has been implemented in procurement management by monitoring safety, predicting risk and estimating cost (Abioye et al., 2021). Another application of digital technologies is the adoption of the IoT which is useful in tracking project progress, predicting maintenance and promoting efficiency (Oke et al., 2023).

Despite various applications of digital technologies, a consensus is reached that the AEC industry is slow and lags in adopting these technologies (Criado-Perez et al., 2022; Opoku et al., 2023). Due to inadequate digital adoption and expertise, the construction industry struggles to overcome many issues (Abioye et al., 2021). There are several workforce issues including a shortage of young talent and skilled labour (Sawhney et al., 2020), recruiting and retention problems (Taher, 2021), lack of competence and inadequate training (Bosch-Sijtsema et al., 2021). In addition, health and safety concerns are arising since workers may fail to report any safety concerns on the site due to busy schedules and workload which results in a higher rate of accidents (Tung et al., 2021). Besides the growing population, the high demand for sustainability and urbanisation adds more pressure on the AEC industry (Perera et al., 2023). Additionally, the sector's poor productivity image (Tung et al., 2021) is partially attributed to its fragmented nature, in which different parties operate in different silos (Bosch-Sijtsema et al., 2021).

The difficulty of transferring from one project to another is another issue that is justified by the instability and unpredictability of projects and the frequent change of the project stakeholders. Consequently, it is difficult for construction companies to transfer skills and work approaches across projects (Tung et al., 2021). The growth of this sector is hampered by low levels of collaboration, a lack of effective synergies in working relationships (Sawhney et al., 2020), the conservative character of the industry and the failure to accept a culture of change (Oke et al., 2023).

In addition, governments around the world are considering initiatives to address sustainability issues such as environmental pollution, high carbon emissions, health concerns and economic sustainability issues (Ammar et al., 2022). Moreover, the interdependency of tasks and lack of control over the construction process, waste of resources, poor management and fragmentation of the supply chain have led to low performance, cost inefficiencies and time overruns (Gholami, 2023). To address these issues, a digital transformation of the industry is needed (Sawhney et al., 2020).

2.2 Definition of Digital Transformation

It is important to understand first what digital technologies mean to comprehend the definition of digital transformation. Digital technologies have evolved across four phases from Industry 1.0 to Industry 4.0. In general, digital technology is an advanced information and communication technology that facilitates the capture, processing, storage, display, communication, integration and collaboration of information (Chowdhury et al., 2019). Several authors have later defined digital technologies in the AEC industry concerning the specific scope of their study. Advanced information and communication technologies that enhance productivity over the construction project's life cycle can be described as digital technologies (Bosch-Sijtsema et al., 2021). Digital technologies are also defined as a set of innovative tools and software used during all phases of construction projects (Oke et al., 2023). Moreover, it is addressed as innovations that assist the activities of construction projects such as management, procurement and delivery (Chowdhury et al., 2019).

Digital technologies are tools used to significantly improve the sector's performance (Oke et al., 2023). This definition underlines that the adoption of innovative technologies is accompanied by improvements, effects and changes leading to the concept of digital transformation. Digital transformation could be defined as the use of digital technology to change any aspect of human life (Taher, 2021). It is also defined as the utilisation of technology to develop the company's performance and reach (Schallmo et al., 2019). Furthermore, the transformational impact of digital technology implementation is described by Olanipekun and Sutrisna (2021) as digital transformation. The definition of digital transformation needs to be adapted to the context of the AEC sector since the previous definitions are general (Taher, 2021). The digital transformation of the AEC industry refers to a disruption in existing business models resulting from the application of digital technologies across all aspects of construction, including processes, undertakings and supply chains (Olanipekun & Sutrisna, 2021).

Those changes are usually an addition of value to the existing business. One example of such transformation is providing access to project information through BIM with 3D interaction (Olanipekun & Sutrisna, 2021). Taher (2021) adds to the previous definition that digital transformation yields four positive outcomes: retaining competitive advantage, increasing the efficiency of business processes, increasing customer satisfaction and facilitating better strategic decision-making. Furthermore, digital transformation is a process that seeks useful applications of internet technology in design, marketing, production, procurement and data-driven management models (Taher, 2021). Industry 4.0 provides a general framework for digital transformation known as Construction 4.0 to achieve optimum utilization of digital technologies in the AEC sector (Sawhney et al., 2020).

2.3 Construction 4.0 Definition and Technologies

Construction 4.0 is a concept that is still evolving, and there is no fixed definition of its meaning other than it is the counterpart of Industry 4.0 (Taher, 2021). Construction 4.0 explores the advanced digital technologies in the AEC industry (Wang et al., 2022). Its main goal is to overcome the industry's fragmentation through the digital transformation of organisations, project frameworks and the construction process across the entire project life cycle (Taher, 2021). It is based on a junction between digital and physical trends and technologies that dramatically transform the way built environments are designed and built (Sawhney et al., 2020). Such a transformative model in which CPS, digital technologies and industrial production and construction transitions occur is known as the Construction 4.0 framework (Taher, 2021). Based on the previous definition, Construction 4.0 framework divides technologies into three transformational categories (Sawhney et al., 2020).

2.3.1 Industrial Production and Construction Technologies

These refer to construction automated processes in which the physical production is linked to digital production enabling direct feed of instructions and production information between the two (Sawhney et al., 2020). The automation of activities reduces cost, increases efficiency, creates safer work environments and enables the use of new construction techniques and materials (Sawhney et al., 2020). This category includes digital prefabrication, 3D printing, assembly and offsite construction technologies.

2.3.2 Cyber-Physical Systems (CPS)

CPS are highly smart systems that are integrated and real-time interconnected primarily for data acquisition. A CPS system is usually composed of two parts. The cyber part is the data, software and network that controls or helps humans to take controlling actions of the physical part which is the device or building (Sawhney et al., 2020). This category includes robots, actuators, drones, sensors and IoT technology.

2.3.3 Digital Tools and Technologies

These technologies work on shared digital platforms and complementary digital tools creating a digital ecosystem. The ecosystem connects the physical layers with the digital layers allowing organisations that are part of the system to create innovative solutions for design, construction and delivery issues through real-time information processing and monitoring (Sawhney et al., 2020). BIM, AI, cloud computing, VR, AR and laser scanners are under this category.

2.4 The Uses of Construction 4.0 Technologies

Corresponding to the transformative model of Construction 4.0, a total of 10 trending technologies have been selected, and their current uses in the AEC industry are illustrated in (Table 1). These technologies represent the top prime digital technologies in the AEC industry (Mahajan, 2022).

Below is an overview of each technology in terms of definition, use and benefits including:

2.4.1 3D Printing

3D printing or additive manufacturing technology creates a physical structure or elements by adding material layers according to three-dimensional digital models (Mahajan, 2022). Although this technology has gained huge attention in Construction 4.0, the final product quality depends on the material, the speed of the printing process and the printing quality (Taher, 2021). It is used to improve the efficiency of production and construction processes by speedy printing of building components and automated production (Taher, 2021).

For example, 3D printing is more time and cost-efficient for on site or what is known as in-situ construction than off-site prefabrication which minimises the supply chain (Sawhney et al., 2020). In addition, 3D printing is used to improve work safety as it reduces labour requirements and enables access or repair to areas of limited human access (Chowdhury et al., 2019). As a result, it reduces labour costs (Chowdhury et al., 2019). Moreover, it contributes to achieving sustainability since it enables minimum waste of material (Wang et al., 2022). Moreover, it allows the development of new areas in the industry. For instance, it enables construction using new materials such as plastic and ultra-reinforced concrete (Forcael et al., 2020). Bridges in concrete, clay and metal have been printed by different technologists (Mahajan, 2022). Furthermore, it enables more flexibility and customisation in terms of building production (Forcael et al., 2020). Although this technology has faced several technical limitations such as shape optimisation and printing errors, it is continually developing (Forcael et al., 2020).

2.4.2 Prefabrication

Prefabrication or off-site construction is a comprehensive term that describes the off-site fabrication of building components, preassembly, modular construction and industrialised building systems and structures (Beulah et al., 2022). Prefabrication increases the efficiency of construction and supply chain through precise automated production of robots, machines and BIM (Sawhney et al., 2020). In addition, prefabrication improves productivity while reducing the time by up to 50% in comparison to conventional construction since the site can be prepared while modular building elements can be manufactured at the same time (Wang et al., 2020).

Table 1. The Uses of Construction 4.0 Technologies.

The Transformative Framework of Construction 4.0 (Sawhney et al., 2020).										
	Industrial Technologies		Cyber-Physical Systems			Digital Tools and Technologies				
Possible Use	1	2	3	4	5	6	7	8	9	10
Improving productivity	•	•	•			•	•			
Better management of the supply chain	•	•	•	•	•	•	•	•		
Improving efficiency in terms of time and cost	•	•	•	•	•	•	•	•	•	•
Improving work safety	•	•	•	•	•			•	•	•
Sustainability and reducing material waste	•	•			•	•	•	•		
Optimising resources	•	•	•			•	•	•		
Development of new potential	•							•	•	
Increasing the quality of processes		•	•		•					
Social viability		•	•				•		•	•
Enhancing digital visualisation of design						•			•	
Collecting, transferring and sharing data				•	•	•				•
Analysing volumes of data						•	•	•		
Tracking and monitoring assessment				•	•		•	•	•	•
Real-time communication and collaboration				•	•	•	•		•	
Providing a basis for better decision-making				•	•	•	•	•	•	•

Note: 1. 3D printing, 2. Prefabrication, 3. Robots and automation, 4. Drones, 5. Sensors and the internet of things (IoT), 6. Building Information Modelling (BIM), 7. Cloud computing, 8. Artificial intelligence (AI), 9. Virtual reality (VR) and augmented reality (AR), 10. 3D laser scanning.

Besides, prefabrication improves the quality of buildings as the production of building components is enhanced with quality control, productivity analysis and process optimisation (Sawhney et al., 2020). Moreover, this technology creates more energy-efficient buildings with better environmental performance reducing carbon emissions, water consumption and materials waste (Rocha et al., 2023). Prefabrication in combination with other digital technologies of Construction 4.0 can achieve a higher rate of safety (Wang et al., 2020). Furthermore, it has the benefit of social viability by reducing the working hours of construction workers while achieving a higher productivity level (Beulah et al., 2022). It also reduces the overall cost of construction across the project lifecycle with conditions of proper investment in prefabrication facilities, production optimisation and economies of scale (Rocha et al., 2023).

2.4.3 Robots and Automation

Automated devices that perform physical activities in real life and interact with the environment using sensors and actuators are known as robots (Abioye et al., 2021). Robots increase productivity with great accuracy and speed for a variety of tasks by combining automation with cognitive skills (Forcael et al., 2020). In addition, robots and automation enable the performing of repetitive or construction tasks with high efficiency (Chowdhury et al., 2019) and avoid human errors (Sawhney et al., 2020). This technology is very beneficial in the assembly of high-rise buildings and in conducting different operations such as painting, brick overlaying and earthwork. Besides performing tasks, robots provide better solutions to many site issues such as the transportation of materials (Forcael et al., 2020) resulting in the optimisation of logistics (Bosch-Sijtsema et al., 2021). In addition, robots increase safety by performing dangerous tasks and heavy lifting (Bosch-Sijtsema et al., 2021). Moreover, robots reduce labour costs (Mahajan, 2022) and leverage 3D printing technology (Chowdhury et al., 2019).

2.4.4 Drones

Drones known as unmanned aerial vehicles or robotics are one of the most used devices in Construction 4.0 (Sawhney et al., 2020). It is used for data collection as it enables remote observation and multiple tracking purposes during land surveys, construction and operations (Taher, 2021). Besides, it enables real-time coordination and monitoring of construction sites (Forcael et al., 2020). For example, drones perform inspections of systems on site, and the collected data are sent to the engineers through a wireless network where they can check if the system is properly installed and functional through a VR system (Forcael et al., 2020). It is also used for safety management and improving the work environment by assessing risks on site and enabling access to areas that are difficult to reach (Bosch-Sijtsema et al., 2021). Safety issues that are captured by drones in the format of photos are analysed, documented and recorded (Sawhney et al., 2020). Moreover, drones increase production efficiency (Chowdhury et al., 2019) and are very useful in terms of the traceability of materials on site and logistics (Bosch-Sijtsema et al., 2021).

2.4.5 IoT and Sensors

The IoT and sensors are rapidly transforming construction sites into smart working environments (Abioye et al., 2021). Automated sensors are devices that collect data from the physical world and are often connected to IoT (Bosch-Sijtsema et al., 2021). These two technologies combined enable effective data collection, generation, processing, sharing and fast storage (Taher, 2021) which is known as construction site analytics (Abioye et al., 2021). The installation of sensors on work uniforms, equipment and vehicles facilitates the monitoring of construction progress, captures real-time data and improves communication between stakeholders (Sawhney et al., 2020). In addition, sensors and IoT provide a basis for better decision-making and improve efficiency (Taher, 2021). Furthermore, sensors support the traceability of materials on site (Bosch-Sijtsema et al., 2021) with accurate estimations of the arrival time of different components which results in improving the logistics system and supply chain (Sawhney et al., 2020). In addition to reducing occupational safety risks, IoT is effective in controlling product quality through real-time risk monitoring systems (Abioye et al., 2021). The collected information by sensors helps improve sustainability and build operations tasks such as tracking equipment status, collecting data, safety and accessibility control (Sawhney et al., 2020).

2.4.6 Building Information Modelling (BIM)

BIM is the most central and important digital technology in the AEC industry (Manzoor et al., 2021). It is not just software but a collaborative data-based model to deliver projects more efficiently in which Revit is considered a tool (Redwood et al., 2017). It is a technology for visualising the building's design (Chowdhury et al., 2019) as it creates a digital illustration of the physical building and its functional aspects (Bosch-Sijtsema et al., 2021). A BIM system enables stakeholders to share, exchange and communicate information effectively (Wang et al., 2022). For instance, all the data related to the building such as size, dimensions, function and placement are projected into the digital model to provide a clear overview of the project (Redwood et al., 2017). With digital access to BIM, efficient data handling improves decision-making processes and reduces design errors (Chowdhury et al., 2019).

As a result, it reduces the project cost, time and errors substantially across the life span of the construction project including the design, procurement, manufacturing, operations and other construction activities (Taher, 2021). Besides improving productivity, BIM supports sustainability as well as the traceability of materials-related information on the digital model leading to effective management of resources (Bosch-Sijtsema et al., 2021). BIM is also used in safety management (Manzoor et al., 2021). Furthermore, BIM is usually integrated with other technologies to optimise its functionality such as AR, VR, IoT and laser scanning (Manzoor et al., 2021). For example, prefabrication has been integrated with BIM to enable the speedy construction of hospitals during the COVID-19 pandemic (Wang et al., 2022).

2.4.7 Cloud Computing

Cloud computing is a data processing technology that improves the capability of analysing a large volume of data at a high transmission speed (Chowdhury et al., 2019). It is often integrated with BIM and IoT creating a single point of data source (Mahajan, 2022) that enhances productivity and project management efficiency due to the timely sharing of information between the stakeholders (Sawhney et al., 2020). As a result, joint decision-making is generated across the construction supply chain resulting in value maximisation and avoiding time overruns (Sawhney et al., 2020). Moreover, it reduces the operational cost of project delivery by enabling direct access to the web-based cloud service without the need for IT personnel (Bello et al., 2020). In addition, the elasticity attribute of cloud computing allows users to request computing resources depending on the demand which increases the agility of construction companies and their competitive advantage (Bello et al., 2020). Cloud computing provides a low cost and direct access to project information by subscribing to software (Chowdhury et al., 2019). It is also used to trace materials by real-time tracking that provides automatically updated data reports on purchases and usage (Oke et al., 2023). In addition, cloud computing contributes to environmental and economic sustainability through effective material management, effective facilities management, optimising labour hours and minimising construction and overhead costs (Chowdhury et al., 2019).

2.4.8 Artificial Intelligence (AI)

AI represents how machines are capable of imitating human thinking to solve problems intelligently using algorithms (Wang et al., 2022). It creates intelligent behaviour through a system that can analyse the environment and act accordingly (Bosch-Sijtsema et al., 2021). In Construction 4.0, several adaptive vision systems have been used to identify certain elements on site with voice recognition abilities to keep track of construction labour progress (Taher, 2021). AI facilitates occupational safety and risk management, as well as effective monitoring of facility management data (Bosch-Sijtsema et al., 2021). AI provides solutions to address the existing labour shortage problem in the AEC industry and creates more opportunities for innovation (Forcael et al., 2020). In addition, implementing AI technology aids automation and helps construction organisations get a competitive advantage (Abioye et al., 2021).

Seven subfields of AI are used in the AEC industry (Abioye et al., 2021). Machine learning (ML) is one of them, and it refers to methods that enable computer systems to learn from existing data using algorithms to predict future behaviours without being deliberately programmed (Wang et al., 2022). Furthermore, AI is usually integrated with other technologies to expand its capabilities. For example, AI can be integrated with IoT to create sustainable and energy-efficient buildings (Abioye et al., 2021). Furthermore, AI improves production efficiency (Bosch-Sijtsema et al., 2021), automated decision-making processes, optimisation and logistics (Wang et al., 2022). The ongoing research on the capability of AI to predict new design and construction phenomena shows good indicators of developing intelligent manufacturing ability (Forcael et al., 2020).

2.4.9 Virtual Reality (VR) and Augmented Reality (AR)

VR and AR are types of computer-based visualisation tools for the future built environment (Bosch-Sijtsema et al., 2021). However, VR is one step ahead of AR as it provides a 360-degree vision of the visualised built environment using handsets (Taher, 2021). Alternately, AR combines real images and virtual worlds using screens, video visualisation and GPS to track information (Forcael et al., 2020).

Using a 3D platform, these technologies create interactive real-time experiences that are used in the planning and design stages (Chowdhury et al., 2019). Great results have been shown in enhanced spatial perception, design analysis and supporting better decision-making (Manzoor et al., 2021). VR and AR reduce design errors and detect any deviations in the execution of the project resulting in a reduction of costs (Chowdhury et al., 2019).

In addition, these technologies are useful for monitoring site activities, making rapid corrections, reducing unnecessary site visits, and controlling time and cost (Chowdhury et al., 2019). In addition, AR–VR technologies provide solutions to collaboration and communication problems between project parties (Manzoor et al., 2021). To leverage the use of robots in complex construction tasks, engineers or workers can use VR and AR tools to understand the design by visualisation (Sawhney et al., 2020). That intuitive and efficient visualisation enables getting more supporting information to carry out several tasks such as dimensions, processes and instructions (Sawhney et al., 2020). Furthermore, AR is useful for in situ assembly, identification of areas that need repair and facility management. In addition, VR increases work safety by incorporating it into construction health and safety training where it can reduce possible hazards and optimise procedures (Taher, 2021). For instance, VR can be used for fire evacuation training and exploring the effect of fire on building conditions (Sawhney et al., 2020).

2.4.10 3D Laser Scanning

Laser scanners are devices that can measure three-dimensional shapes of structures or objects and store their 3D coordinates, providing information about existing buildings and assisting in making better decisions (Bosch-Sijtsema et al., 2021). There are three modes of conducting laser scanning in construction: airborne scanning, mobile scanning and terrestrial scanning (Sawhney et al., 2020). Laser scanning (TLS) is most popular for measuring distances to targets and accreting 3D points at high speed and accuracy (Wang et al., 2022). For example, TLS has been successfully used to scan large amounts of 3D data of building facades in high-density urban areas to perform proper reconstruction (Manzoor et al., 2021). 3D laser scanning enables collecting data and tracking deviations in execution in comparison to the design by utilising photogrammetry (Chowdhury et al., 2019). In Construction 4.0, 3D laser scanners can be used for progress tracking, efficient cost management, quality control, assessment of existing structures and structural health monitoring of the site by capturing data and sending it to cloud-based platforms or data centres (Sawhney et al., 2020).

2.5 The Challenges to the Adoption of Construction 4.0 Technologies

Despite great improvements in design and construction deliverables due to the implementation of digital technologies, several challenges still exist for the adoption of digital technologies (Perera et al., 2023). A total of 34 barriers to the adoption of digital technologies in the AEC sector have been collected from previous papers. To simplify and clarify the understanding of the identified barriers in the literature, a classification of the barriers is suggested as shown in Table 2. This research follows a similar categorisation method as used by Opoku et al. (2023). These barriers are classified into six categories, namely (1) technical and technological barriers, (2) legal and regulatory barriers, (3) economic and financial barriers, (4) organisational resources and processes barriers, (5) market and industry barriers and (6) security and data management barriers. The six categories of barriers are further discussed and presented in the subsequent headings.

2.5.1 Technical and Technological Barriers

Technical and technological obstacles, such as the absence of system integration, are discussed in the first category. It refers to the incompatibility of digital technologies across various layers of hardware and software. As a result, interoperability occurs which limits the integration of new technology to one specific use that is not integrated with other systems. For example, the enterprise management system is used to record the wages of construction workers. However, it might not be linked to the system that keeps track of their productivity (Olanipekun & Sutrisna, 2021).

In addition, interconnectivity issues and network limitations prevent construction organisations from fully utilising the benefits of digital technologies. In cases of remote locations or incapable networks, it would not be possible to access and share information on digital platforms (Oke et al., 2023). Another barrier is the insufficient support for implementation to address the users' concerns and provide them with immediate assistance (Taher, 2021). Besides the non-conformity of some foreign software to the local standards or policies, the possibility of system failure and the complexity of using digital technologies hinder its effective adoption (Oke et al., 2023). Furthermore, the processing, analysis and transfer of a large amount of data during the design, construction and management of a project is a complex and lengthy process. This issue is very frequent in the use of BIM technology, especially when it involves the collaboration between different disciplines (Olanipekun & Sutrisna, 2021).

Table 2. The Barriers to Adopting Digital Technologies in the AEC Industry.

Category	Barrier	Reference
Technical and technological barriers	Interconnectivity issues and network limitations	(Oke et al., 2023; Opoku et al., 2023)
	System integration problems	(Olanipekun & Sutrisna, 2021; Opoku et al., 2023)
	Scalability and interoperability issues	(Opoku et al., 2023; Perera et al., 2023)
	Complexities of technological applications	(Oke et al., 2023),
	Complex data processing	(Bosch-Sijtsema et al., 2021; Criado-Perez et al., 2022; Olanipekun & Sutrisna, 2021)
	Design and system difficulties and failure	(Oke et al., 2023; Opoku et al., 2023)
	Non-compliance of foreign software to domestic standards	(Oke et al., 2023)
	Insufficient support for implementation	(Taher, 2021),
Legal and regulatory barriers	Legal and contractual uncertainty	(Sawhney et al., 2020; Perera et al., 2023; Oke et al., 2023),
	Lack or low industry standards	(Manzoor et al., 2021; Sawhney et al., 2020; Olanipekun & Sutrisna, 2021; Opoku et al., 2023)
	Inadequate government laws, and regulatory compliance	(Manzoor et al., 2021; Oke et al., 2023),
Economic and financial barriers	High implementation cost	(Manzoor et al., 2021; Perera et al., 2023; Sawhney et al., 2020; Taher, 2021)
	Lack of budgeting arrangements and incentives for innovation	(Oke et al., 2023),
	High computational and operating requirements	(Oke et al., 2023; Perera et al., 2023; Taher, 2021)
	Low investments in research and development	(Sawhney et al., 2020)
	ROI uncertainty	(Criado-Perez et al., 2022; Olanipekun & Sutrisna, 2021)
	Unclear value proposition and benefits	(Sawhney et al., 2020; Opoku et al., 2023)
Organisational resources and process barriers	Lack of knowledge and expertise	(Manzoor et al., 2021; Perera et al., 2023; Sawhney et al., 2020; Taher, 2021)
	Lack of digital strategies and supporting leadership or management	(Bosch-Sijtsema et al., 2021; Oke et al., 2023; Perera et al., 2023)

	Unsuitable framework to adopt digital technologies	(Oke et al., 2023),
	Poor long-term strategic planning	(Bosch-Sijtsema et al., 2021; Criado-Perez et al., 2022; Taher, 2021)
	Lack of competence and training	(Bosch-Sijtsema et al., 2021; Opoku et al., 2023)
	Professional disconnection and difficulties in setting realistic expectations	(Criado-Perez et al., 2022; Opoku et al., 2023)
	Lack of owner-buy-in	(Olanipekun and Sutrisna, 2021)
Market and industry barriers	The fragmentation of the industry	(Bosch-Sijtsema et al., 2021; Sawhney et al., 2020)
	The existing business models	(Bosch-Sijtsema et al., 2021; Olanipekun & Sutrisna, 2021)
	Nature of the industry and low-profit margins	(Criado-Perez et al., 2022; Perera et al., 2023)
	Insufficient demand from clients	(Criado-Perez et al., 2022; Manzoor et al., 2021)
	Project and design process complexity	(Opoku et al., 2023; Perera et al., 2023)
	Digital divide and inequality	(Olanipekun and Sutrisna, 2021)
	Resistance to change and low technology acceptance	(Manzoor et al., 2021; Sawhney et al., 2020; Taher, 2021)
Data security and management barriers	The lack of knowledge of management	(Oke et al., 2023),
	Data access and ownership	(Olanipekun & Sutrisna, 2021; Opoku et al., 2023)
	Data security risks and attacks and protection	(Manzoor et al., 2021; Olanipekun & Sutrisna, 2021; Opoku et al., 2023; Sawhney et al., 2020)
	Sharing information and collaboration issues	(Oke et al., 2023; Perera et al., 2023),
	Ethical issues	(Bosch-Sijtsema et al., 2021; Opoku et al., 2023)

2.5.2 Legal and Regulatory Barriers

The second category focuses on legal and regulatory barriers including lack of industry standards, inadequate government laws, regulatory compliance and legal uncertainty. Regulatory compliance is one of the reasons why most construction organisations have doubts about adopting digital technologies in their processes (Oke et al., 2023). This is supported by Criado-Perez et al. (2022) who point out that the AEC industry operates within a legal-bureaucratic frame that does not encourage advancement and innovation. Hence, most of the sector adheres to the existing norms, procedures and codes. Although notable progress has been made in setting global standards for digital transformation processes, more effort is needed to apply those standards in the AEC sector (Sawhney et al., 2020). Moreover, legal issues and uncertainties regarding data usage, tracking user behaviour and many other issues arise due to the lack of government laws and guidelines (Bosch-Sijtsema et al., 2021).

2.5.3 Economical and Financial Barriers

The third category focuses on economic and financial barriers such as the high implementation cost of digital technologies and high computational requirements (Taher, 2021). That includes the total cost of software licencing or purchase, digital tools, hardware, integration, technical support and IT personnel (Perera et al., 2023). The added cost of digital technologies might deviate companies from investing since most construction companies are struggling with materials and labour costs (Oke et al., 2023). In addition, the return-on-investment uncertainty increases hesitation, especially in small organisations that have fewer funds and resources (Olanipekun & Sutrisna, 2021). The unclear value proposition of digital technologies benefits for the stakeholders adds more hesitation as well (Sawhney et al., 2020). The AEC industry also performs and invests very poorly in research and development – R & D (Sawhney et al., 2020).

2.5.4 Organisational Resources and Process Barriers

The fourth category focuses on organisational barriers including lack of knowledge, expertise, competence and training (Taher, 2021). Since the implementation of digital technologies within construction operations requires a significant learning process, a skilled workforce is needed (Sawhney et al., 2020). Considering the shortage of labour, the necessity of training increases resulting in additional costs (Taher, 2021). Without a suitable framework and budgeting arrangements, the adoption of digital technologies would be difficult, especially with the lack of digital culture (Oke et al., 2023).

Another barrier is the lack of digital strategies and poor leadership support for digital innovations (Bosch-Sijtsema et al., 2021). Many researchers have confirmed that what drives a successful digital transformation is the integration of digital strategy with the business strategy rather than the technology itself (Criado-Perez et al., 2022). Furthermore, the lack of long-term strategic planning combined with the focus on the delivery of construction projects is a major barrier to investing, monitoring and experimenting with new technologies (Bosch-Sijtsema et al., 2021). Moreover, if the implementation of digital technologies does not fulfil the owner's expectations and requirements, a lack of owner-buy-in would result. It refers to the partial implementation of digital technologies and the inability to adapt to the resulting changes (Olanipekun & Sutrisna, 2021).

2.5.5 Market and Industry Barriers

The fifth category includes market and industry barriers such as the fragmentation of the industry due to the intensive use of traditional methods with different stakeholders at each stage of the construction project. As a result, gaps in communication and coordination occur resulting in cost and time overruns. This fragmented approach has hindered digitalisation greatly (Oke et al., 2023). Replacing the existing business models with new innovative ones is another obstacle to coping with technological innovation disruption (Olanipekun & Sutrisna, 2021).

For example, the use of IoT has transferred construction from just a physical process to selling buildings as a service (Olanipekun & Sutrisna, 2021). In addition, the AEC industry is characterised by declining revenues and low profit margins in comparison to large investments which results in an anti-innovation environment (Criado-Perez et al., 2022). Also, the industry is conservative with high resistance to change (Sawhney et al., 2020). Taher (2021) has underlined confusion and low acceptance of technology as barriers that affect employees' ability to respond to emerging technologies. Furthermore, the complexity of projects (Perera et al., 2023) and digital inequality between small and large organisations (Olanipekun & Sutrisna, 2021) are other barriers. Although clients exert some pressure on AEC organisations to speed up the adoption of digital technologies, the demand is insufficient. Some companies adopt a reactive strategy rather than a proactive strategy to retain clients (Criado-Perez et al., 2022).

2.5.6 Data Security and Management Barriers

The last category includes several barriers such as the lack of effective knowledge management which is one of the main reasons that blocks digitalisation (Oke et al., 2023). Achieving open data has become a challenge in the AEC industry due to data ownership, data access and privacy protection restrictions (Olanipekun & Sutrisna, 2021). That often leads to legal problems and limited data sharing as construction stakeholders treat data separately for every project phase (Olanipekun & Sutrisna, 2021). Due to data fragmentation, a lack of collaboration is observed which prevents the optimal use of smart technologies (Oke et al., 2023). Cyber security and data protection are critical barriers to implementing Construction 4.0 technologies since they require top cyber and physical security (Sawhney et al., 2020). In addition, ethical and integrity issues regarding data usage are another barrier, especially without proper regulatory laws and policies (Bosch-Sijtsema et al., 2021).

3. CONCLUSION

Through research presented in this review, a comprehensive understanding of transformational trends across the AEC sector has been attained. Surprisingly, the AEC industry is conspicuously under-represented in literature, despite being one of the most powerful industries in the world, contributing significantly to economic growth on a global level (Redwood et al., 2017). A myriad of complex challenges is limiting the industry's growth, including time and cost inefficiencies, workplace safety, labour shortages, low productivity, resistance to change and poor-quality performance (Abioye et al., 2021). Previous studies have indicated that these issues are caused by insufficient adoption of digital technologies (Abioye et al., 2021). Accordingly, many researchers are now looking at new trends in digitalisation as solutions and opportunities to address the most critical challenges of the AEC sector (Bosch-Sijtsema et al., 2021).

Digital transformation has taken place since Industry 4.0 and digital technologies have been integrated to enhance the industry's poor image (Tung et al., 2021). It encompasses transformational effects on the existing business models evident in the construction processes, organisations and supply chain (Olanipekun & Sutrisna, 2021). As a result of such advancements, a new concept has emerged which is known as Construction 4.0.

As former researchers have indicated, the concept of Construction 4.0 is still evolving, and it is perceived as the equivalent of Industry 4.0 (Taher, 2021). As the name suggests, Construction 4.0 focuses on exploring advanced digital technologies in the AEC sector (Wang et al., 2022). It is described as a transformative paradigm in which three digital trends occur: industrial technologies, CPS and digital tools and technologies (Sawhney et al., 2020).

Based on an extensive review of previous publications, this chapter identifies a total of 10 prime technologies under the classification of digital trends of the Construction 4.0 transformative framework. For instance, 3D printing and prefabrication are two promising industrial technologies whereas drones, robots, sensors and the IoT are CPS. Cloud computing, BIM, AI, VR, AR and 3D laser scanning are revolutionary digital tools and technologies. The adoption of such technologies has yielded several benefits that have revolutionised the industry towards automation (Manzoor et al., 2021). This chapter concludes that there are 15 possible uses of the previously identified digital technologies in the AEC industry such as increasing productivity across the project lifecycle, improving the quality of construction and enhancing the efficiency of design and construction processes (Taher, 2021). In addition, providing a data-driven basis for better decision-making and improving site safety are other uses (Taher, 2021).

Besides reducing building waste, contributing to sustainability and enabling better management of the supply chain (Manzoor et al., 2021), digital technologies are used to improve data generation and sharing between the project's stakeholders enabling real-time collaboration. Other examples of the usage of technologies are better data handling (Chowdhury et al., 2019), visualisation of the built environment (Bosch-Sijtsema et al., 2021), development of new potentials in terms of flexibility, customisation and building materials (Forcael et al., 2020). Moreover, optimising resources (Rocha et al., 2023), tracking project progress, monitoring site activities (Manzoor et al., 2021) and aiding social viability by reducing the working hours of labour (Beulah et al., 2022) are other possible uses.

Despite the various uses of digital technologies and their increasing implementation (Olanipekun & Sutrisna, 2021), the AEC sector is still digitally lagging in contrast to other industries (Bosch-Sijtsema et al., 2021). This is justified by the numerous challenges that hinder the productive adoption of digital technologies (Manzoor et al., 2021). The findings of this chapter identify a total of 34 barriers that have been collected from previous papers.

These barriers are classified into six categories, including technical and technological barriers, legal and regulatory barriers, economic and financial barriers, organisational resources and processes barriers, market and industry barriers and security and data management barriers. These challenges must be addressed by all actors in the industry to facilitate a smooth implementation and to fully utilise the benefits of digital technologies associated with Construction 4.0 (Taher, 2021). In addition, the industry risks losing its edge in digital transformation unless there is an adjustment of these barriers (Oke et al., 2023).

3.1 Theoretical Implications

From a theoretical standpoint, this chapter responds to the shortage of theoretical knowledge in the research domain. Thus, this chapter extends recent literature reviews on digital technologies in the AEC industry. It provides a groundwork for a better understanding of trending technologies in the era of Construction 4.0 and their role in changing the industry's landscape. It provides an updated overview of the uses and challenges of the most promising technologies by building upon the transformative framework of Construction 4.0 developed by Sawhney et al. (2020). The findings of this chapter amplify the transformative model where a total of 10 prime technologies have been identified with respect to the framework's categorisation of digital trends. This finding will contribute to the knowledge base by extending previous research efforts, as it is just one of several attempts at defining the uses and challenges of digital technologies in the AEC sector.

3.2 Practical Implications

The findings of this study may entail several practical implications: First, it will encourage policymakers and industry stakeholders to make more informed decisions on which digital technologies to prioritise and implement to accelerate digital transformation. Second, the results could make it easier for architects, engineers and construction firms to assess their state of digitalisation, improve processes and adopt more digital practices. Third, it might assist stakeholders in the construction sector in developing a strategic development plan towards achieving their vision of Construction 4.0 and retaining their competitive advantage. To achieve this objective, defining the potential uses of digital technologies and ways of overcoming the barriers to effective implementation are essential. However, the involved companies should consider that digital transformation requires using their innovative capabilities, new business models, approaches and organisational improvements in terms of human resources, production methods, governance practices, technical style and physical infrastructure (Taher, 2021).

3.3 Limitations and Future Studies

Despite the contribution of this study to the body of knowledge, it has several shortcomings because only 10 promising technologies are covered. Since digitalisation is inevitable, future studies on rapidly evolving technologies and other neglected technologies in the context of the AEC sector should be continued. In addition, the study is confined to the current uses and challenges of Construction 4.0 technologies without clarifying the future trajectory of these technologies. Therefore, it is deemed necessary to proceed with further studies on the future directions of digital technologies and find better strategies to overcome the numerous barriers. In addition, the need to conduct future research on the effects of emerging technologies on the sociocultural dimension and human–machine interaction is critical.

ABBREVIATIONS

AEC—Architecture, Engineering and Construction
BIM—Building Information Modelling
AI—Artificial intelligence
VR—Virtual reality
AR—Augmented reality
IoT—Internet of things
ML—Machine learning
R&D—Research and development
CPS—Cyber-physical systems

REFERENCES

Abioye, S. O., Oyedele, L. O., Akanbi, L., Ajayi, A., Davila Delgado, J. M., Bilal, M., Akinade, O. O., & Ahmed, A. (2021). Artificial Intelligence in the construction industry: A review of present status, opportunities, and future challenges. *Journal of Building Engineering*, *44*(1), 103299.

Ammar, A., Bou Hatoum, M., Nassereddine, H., & Dadi, G. (2022). Synergies between construction 4. 0 technologies and sustainable construction: A bibliometric analysis. In *CCC 2022: Creative Construction e-Conference*. 9–11 July.

Bello, S. A., Oyedele, L. O., Akinade, O. O., Bilal, M., Davila Delgado, J. M., Akanbi, L. A., Ajayi, A. O., & Owolabi, H. A. (2020). Cloud computing in construction industry: Use cases, benefits and challenges. *Automation in Construction*, *122*, 103441.

Beulah, F., Sudhakar, R., & Arivalagan, S. (2022). Challenges faced in prefabrication or modular construction. *International Journal for Research in Applied Science and Engineering Technology*, *10*(1), 168–178.

Bosch-Sijtsema, P., Claeson-Jonsson, C., Johansson, M., & Roupe, M. (2021). The hype factor of digital technologies in AEC. *Construction Innovation*, *21*(4), 899–916.

Chen, F., Jiao, H., Han, L., Shen, L., Du, W., Ye, Q., & Yu, G. (2020). Real-time monitoring of construction quality for gravel piles based on Internet of things. *Automation in Construction*, *116*, 103228.

Chowdhury, T., Adafin, J., & Wilkinson, S. (2019). Review of digital technologies to improve productivity of New Zealand construction industry. *Journal of Information Technology in Construction*, *24*, 569–587.

Craveiro, F., Duarte, J. P., Bartolo, H., & Bartolo, P. J. (2019). Additive manufacturing as an enabling technology for digital construction: A perspective on construction 4.0. *Automation in Construction*, *103*, 251–267.

Criado-Perez, C., Shinkle, G., Höllerer, M., Sharma, A., Collins, C., Gardner, N., Hank Haeusler, M., & Pan, S. (2022). Digital transformation in the Australian AEC industry: Prevailing issues and prospective leadership thinking. *Journal of Construction Engineering and Management*, *148*(1), 1–28.

Forcael, E., Ferrari, I., Opazo-Vega, A. & Pulido-Arcas, J. A.. (2020), Construction 4.0: A literature review, *Sustainability*, *22*(12), 9755.

Getuli, V., Capone, P., Bruttini, A., & Isaac, S. (2020). BIM-based immersive virtual reality for construction workspace planning: A safety-oriented approach. *Automation in Construction*, *114*, 103160.

Gholami, Y. (2023). *Investigating adoption of digital technologies in construction projects*. PhD thesis. Linköping University, Norrköping.

Khan, A., Sepasgozar, S., Liu, T., & Yu, R. (2021). Integration of BIM and immersive technologies for AEC: A Scientometric-SWOT analysis and Critical Content Review. *Buildings*, *11*(3), 126.

Mahajan, A. G. (2022). Swift rising pattern of New Emerging Construction Technology Trends in the construction industry. *International Journal of Innovative Technology and Exploring Engineering*, *11*(11), 55–64.

Manzoor, B., Othman, I., & Pomares, J. C. (2021). Digital technologies in the Architecture, Engineering and Construction (AEC) industry—A bibliometric—Qualitative literature review of research activities. *International Journal of Environmental Research and Public Health*, *18*(11), 6135.

Oke, A. E., Aliu, J., & Onajite, S. A. (2023). Barriers to the adoption of digital technologies for Sustainable Construction in a developing economy. *Architectural Engineering and Design Management*, 1–17.

Olanipekun, A. O., & Sutrisna, M. (2021). Facilitating digital transformation in construction—A systematic review of the current state of the art. *Frontiers in Built Environment*, *7*, 1–21.

Opoku, D.-G. J., Perera, S., Osei-Kyei, R., Rashidi, M., Bamdad, K., & Famakinwa, T. (2023). Barriers to the adoption of digital twin in the construction industry: A literature review. *Informatics*, *10*(1), 14.

Perera, S., Jin, X., Samaratunga, M., & Gunasekara, K. (2023). Drivers and barriers to digitalisation: A cross-analysis of the views of designers and builders in the construction industry. *Journal of Information Technology in Construction*, *28*(5), 87–106.

Redwood, J., Thelning, S., Elmualim, A., & Pullen, S. (2017). The proliferation of ICT and digital technology systems and their influence on the dynamic capabilities of construction firms. *Procedia Engineering*, *180*, 804–811.

Rocha, P. F., Ferreira, N. O., Pimenta, F., & Pereira, N. B. (2023). Impacts of prefabrication in the building construction industry. *Encyclopedia*, *3*(1), 28–45.

Sawhney, A., Riley, M., & Irizarry, J. (2020). *Construction 4.0: An innovation platform for the built environment*. Routledge.

Schallmo, D., Williams, C. A., & Boardman, L. (2019). Digital Transformation of business models—Best practice, enablers, and roadmap. *Digital Disruptive Innovation*, *36*, 119–138.

Taher, G. (2021). Industrial revolution 4.0 in the construction industry: Challenges and opportunities. *Management Studies and Economic Systems*, *6*(4–3), 109–127.

Tung, Y. H., Chia, F. C., & Yong, F. Y. Y. (2021). Exploring the usage of digital technologies for construction project management. *Planning Malaysia*, *19*(3), 13–22.

Wang, K., Guo, F., Zhang, C., Rashidi, M., Hao, J., & Schaefer, D. (2022). Digital technology in architecture, engineering, and construction (AEC) industry: Research trends and practical status toward construction 4.0. In *Construction research congress 2022* (pp. 983–992). https://doi.org/10.1061/9780784483978.100

Wang, M., Wang, C. C., Sepasgozar, S., & Zlatanova, S. (2020). A systematic review of digital technology adoption in off-site construction: Current status and future direction towards industry 4.0. *Buildings*, *10*(11), 204.

Yevu, S. K., Yu, A. T. W., & Darko, A. (2021). Digitalization of construction supply chain and procurement in the built environment: Emerging technologies and opportunities for Sustainable Processes. *Journal of Cleaner Production*, *322*, 129093.

PART 2

ENVIRONMENTAL ISSUES AND TECHNOLOGY

GREEN GROWTH STRATEGIES: EXPLORING THE ROLE OF ENVIRONMENTAL TAXATION IN PROMOTING SUSTAINABLE DEVELOPMENT OF HEAVILY POLLUTING ENTERPRISES

Ningyu Zhai and Scarlett Ruopiao Zhang

Macau University of Science and Technology, Macao

ABSTRACT

In developing countries, rapid industrial growth frequently results in companies with high pollution levels, which in turn exhibit characteristics such as elevated emissions, increased energy consumption and overcapacity. In order to promote sustainable development among these heavily polluting firms, it is essential to implement a system of incentives and penalties that encourages environmentally responsible behaviour. China's environmental protection tax has replaced the previous pollution discharge fee (PDF) system. This tax aims to guide enterprises towards continuous adjustments and improvements in their production methods, increased investments in green technology, adoption of environmentally friendly production methods, reduced pollutant emissions and promotion of high-quality development. This chapter analyses how China's Environmental Protection Tax Law, enforced in 2018, affects the sustainable development capabilities of A-share listed companies in China. We utilise a difference-in-differences (DiD) model and measure total factor productivity (TFP) to quantify the impact of the tax law on these enterprises. TFP is a key indicator used to measure the effectiveness of resources utilised by enterprises in the production process. Our empirical analysis provides compelling evidence that the implementation of environmental protection taxes has significantly enhanced the TFP of heavily polluting enterprises. Importantly, the impact of

Social Responsibility, Technology and AI
Developments in Corporate Governance and Responsibility, Volume 23, 93–109
Copyright © 2025 Ningyu Zhai and Scarlett Ruopiao Zhang
Published under exclusive licence by Emerald Publishing Limited
ISSN: 2043-0523/doi:10.1108/S2043-052320240000023005

these taxes is more pronounced for state-owned enterprises (SOEs) in comparison to their private counterparts in this sector. These findings offer valuable insights for policymakers in developing countries as they consider the design of environmental protection tax systems and supportive measures to promote sustainable development of companies with significant environmental impacts.

Keywords: Sustainable development; Total factor productivity (TFP); environmental tax; green growth; sustainable development

1. INTRODUCTION

Sustainable development is a fundamental aspect of numerous international policy agendas, emphasising the need to bring together economic, social and environmental dimensions to guarantee a better quality of life for present and future generations (Parris & Kates, 2003). In recent years, the concept of green growth strategies has gained prominence as a way to address pressing issues such as climate change, depletion of natural resources and biodiversity loss (Bartelmus, 2013). Green growth promotes the creation of environmentally sustainable and socially inclusive economic growth.

Environmental pollution remains a major concern worldwide, particularly in heavily polluting industries (Shapiro & Walker, 2018). In recent years, many developing countries have been searching for ways to balance economic development with sustainable, green development. With the ever-increasing threat of climate change, it has become imperative to find solutions that not only improve the economy but also protect the environment. Governments and policymakers have been implementing various environmental regulations to tackle this issue, including environmental taxes. For example, due to rapid industrialisation and urbanisation, China has struggled with shockingly high levels of pollution over the past few decades, leading to severe ecological consequences and health hazards (Zhang & Wen, 2008). The government has implemented various policies, such as the pollution discharge fee (PDF) system and recently the environmental tax, which became effective in 2018 (Liu et al., 2022). The shift from PDF to environmental taxes aims to strengthen polluters' responsibility and promote sustainable development (Li & Masui, 2019).

Heavy pollution industries (HPIs), such as coal mining, steel and chemical manufacturing, are major contributors to global air and water pollution, resource depletion and environmental degradation (Wardekker et al., 2010). Their continuous emissions release a tremendous amount of pollutants into the environment, thereby affecting the ecological balance and human health. As such, there is an urgent need to restructure HPIs and implement measures that promote sustainable development. To combat these environmental issues, China introduced the PDF system in 1979, wherein polluters must pay fees based on the amount of pollutants they produce (Wang & Wheeler, 2005). The PDF system has undergone several reforms since its introduction, and it is based on the 'polluter pays' principle, which aims to internalise the external expenses of pollution by imposing fees on those responsible for pollution (Zahar, 2018). The government determines the types of pollutants, fee rates and collection methods and regularly reviews them. The fees collected are used to finance environmental conservation and pollution control projects (Wu & Tal, 2018). However, the PDF system encounters several challenges that limit its effectiveness. For instance, the fee rates are too low to incentivise polluters to change their behaviour (Wu & Tal, 2018). Additionally, the absence of proper monitoring and enforcement mechanisms renders the system less effective (Zheng & He, 2022).

As a response to the limitations of the PDF system, China's government implemented the Environmental Tax Law in 2018, marking a shift towards a tax-based policy aimed at enhancing environmental governance (Liu et al., 2022). According to Xue et al. (2022), the Chinese environmental tax system aims to shift from a command-and-control regulatory approach to a more market-based instrument, such as taxation. The tax law aimed at reducing air and water pollution, solid waste and noise pollution by levying a tax based on the level of emissions (Ministry of Finance, 2018).

The transition to an environmental tax policy is seen as an opportunity to better regulate pollution and promote sustainable development. In their study, Wang and Yu (2021) identified several challenges that the Environmental Tax Law encountered during its implementation, such as unclear tax jurisdiction, potential revenue declines for local governments and weak third-party supervision. They proposed improvements in tax design, better coordination among government institutions and more effective enforcement mechanisms to overcome these obstacles. Moreover, Guo et al. (2022) conducted an empirical analysis on the environmental tax's effectiveness in reducing pollution levels and found that the tax implementation had brought about significant and positive changes in some regions. However, they also underlined the importance of considering regional economic and environmental differences to maximise the tax policy's impact.

This chapter investigates the impact of China's Environmental Protection Tax Law, implemented in 2018, on the sustainable development capabilities of A-share listed heavily polluting enterprises in China. Utilising a difference-in-differences (DiD) model and measuring the effect through total factor productivity (TFP), we assess the influence of the tax law on these enterprises from 2015 to 2021. Empirical evidence demonstrates that the law has significantly enhanced the TFP of heavily polluting enterprises, with more pronounced effects on state-owned enterprises (SOEs) than private entities. These findings offer valuable insights for policymakers in developing nations concerning the design of environmental protection tax systems and support measures targeted at promoting sustainable development for companies with considerable environmental impact. The results indicate that environmental protection tax systems can serve as an effective means of fostering sustainable development in heavily polluting enterprises, particularly in the case of SOEs. Policymakers in developing countries can glean insights from this analysis into the design and implementation of environmental tax laws that encourage sustainable practices and minimise ecological harm. Furthermore, regulators can devise strategic support measures and incentives for compliance, stimulating more businesses to transition towards environmentally friendly models. Heavily polluting enterprises, both state-owned and private, can benefit from comprehending the impact of environmental tax laws on their sustainable development capabilities. By adopting eco-friendly practices and technologies, these companies can enhance their TFP, which can subsequently have a positive influence on their overall performance and competitiveness in the long term. Moreover, this study can help managers to inform and justify changes in their business operations and investments that align with environmental sustainability objectives. By understanding the potential benefits of adopting more sustainable practices, companies can ultimately improve their sustainable development capabilities and long-term competitiveness.

2. ENVIRONMENTAL TAX AS A GREEN-GROWTH STRATEGY TOWARDS SUSTAINABLE DEVELOPMENT

The increasing global awareness of climate change and environmental degradation is driving the need for effective policy interventions to encourage sustainable development (Jabareen, 2008; Mitlin, 1992). Environmental tax, also known as the 'Pigouvian tax' after the British scholar Pigou who proposed it, is a tax targeting individuals and organisations that exploit environmental resources, causing damage and pollution, with the aim of promoting environmental and ecological protection. This type of tax may also be referred to as an 'ecotax' or a 'green tax' (Barnett, 1980; Pigou, 1927). By imposing taxes on harmful activities or on the goods and resources that generate pollution, governments can incentivise industries and consumers to adopt cleaner technologies and greener practices. Additionally, revenue generated from environmental taxation can finance investment in renewable energy, public transportation and other environmental initiatives. Environmental taxes have become an essential tool for governments to internalise the environmental and social costs associated with pollution and the use of natural resources (Baumol & Oates, 1988). Environmental taxes are based on the notion that economic agents causing pollution must bear the costs of their actions (Bosquet, 2000). In principle, such taxes encourage businesses and consumers to be more aware of their environmental impact and to adopt cleaner technologies and practices, thereby reducing pollution and contributing to sustainable development (Fullerton & Metcalf, 2001). For instance, research conducted by Lanoie et al. (2011) found that implementing environmental regulations in companies could result in a phenomenon known as 'creativity squeeze', ultimately reducing financial performance. Conversely, the 'Porter hypothesis' (Lanoie et al., 2008; Porter & Van der Linde, 1995; Zhang, 2021) suggests that environmental regulations can promote innovation within companies.

On the other hand, productivity is a crucial concept in economic research that has evolved over time. Initially, scholars predominantly focused on the productivity of a single input, labour. However, Solow (1957) pioneered the notion of

TFP, which encompassed a broader understanding of productivity. TFP posits that output growth and technological advancements can surpass the input factors (capital, labour, etc.) in the production process, leading to a residual surplus after accounting for the contributions of other production factors. As Chou et al. (2014) pointed out, TFP is grounded in neoclassical economic growth theory and serves as an indicator to measure the production process efficiency and the effect of technological innovation on productivity improvement, thereby reflecting the quality of economic growth. In the context of sustainable development, TFP can be seen as a useful tool for assessing whether economic growth is occurring in an environmentally sustainable manner (Shen et al., 2021; Stern, 2004; Zhang, 2021).

Within the academic sphere, there are two primary methods for measuring enterprise-level TFP. The first, proposed by Olley and Pakes (1996), is the Olley and Pakes (OP) method. This approach indirectly measures TFP by substituting enterprise production efficiency with investment efficiency. However, the OP method has its limitations. It presupposes that the amount of investment capital must increase proportionally with enterprise production efficiency and requires positive investment each year. This assumption is not always accurate in practice, as businesses cannot guarantee positive investment annually, which may constrain the sample size for empirical research. To overcome this issue, Levinsohn and Petrin (2003) introduced an alternative method based on the OP approach, known as the Levinsohn and Petrin (LP) method. This method replaces the investment variable with intermediate input, making it more flexible in sample selection. The LP method is no longer constrained by issues arising from missing samples and enables a more adaptable selection of intermediate input proxy variables according to the research direction and sample characteristics. This enhanced approach provides a more accurate and representative measurement of enterprise-level TFP (Zhao et al., 2022).

Ghosh and Pollitt (2019) suggest that TFP can be used to measure the environmental performance of firms in the energy sector. The authors argued that firms with high TFP scores had more environmentally sustainable operations because they were able to deliver more output with fewer inputs. Furthermore, Ghosh and Pollitt (2019) also suggested that TFP can be used to incentivise firms to adopt cleaner technologies and reduce their environmental impact. Another study by Dang and El-Kiran (2019) examined the relationship between TFP and urbanisation in China. The authors concluded that TFP can be used to measure the efficiency of urbanisation processes, which can be an indicator of sustainable development. The authors suggested that improving TFP can lead to more sustainable urbanisation processes and, therefore, help to promote sustainable development. Outreville and Clement (2016) investigated the impact of TFP on sustainable development in the insurance sector. The authors found that TFP can help create value for customers, employees, shareholders and the environment. Furthermore, TFP can encourage insurance companies to adopt more sustainable practices, such as investing in renewable energy.

Traditional economists have often argued that environmental regulations significantly affect the costs and expenses of businesses, leading to a negative impact on productivity and competitiveness. However, Porter's hypothesis suggests that when enterprises adopt suitable environmental regulations, it can accelerate the process of research and development innovation. This, in turn, allows companies to bear the costs of protecting the ecological environment while providing long-term economic stability. To support his argument, Porter proposed two theories: innovation compensation theory and first-mover advantage theory (Luo & Chung, 2013; Porter & Van der Linde, 1995; Rubashkina et al., 2015). The innovation compensation theory posits that when enterprises face constraints due to environmental regulations, they can increase their technological innovation and upgrade their equipment, resulting in a significant improvement in resource utilisation efficiency. This process also leads to the development of new green products that enhance the company's core competitiveness. Consequently, one vital path to achieving a high-quality development strategy is the creation of green innovation products. As enterprises improve their production technology and optimise their processes, the innovative products' benefits will eventually exceed their production costs, thereby increasing the company's TFP (Porter & Van der Linde, 1995; Zhao et al., 2022). On the other hand, the first-mover advantage theory emphasises that the current trend prioritises high-quality economic development over high-speed economic growth. With the rise in living standards, people increasingly demand a higher quality of life, leading to greater environmental awareness and the ingrained concept of green consumption. Consumers tend to favour environmentally friendly green products, and as living standards improve, environmental concerns receive heightened attention. As a result, enterprises need to optimise and upgrade to meet these consumer demands, allowing them to reap better economic and social benefits (Moreira et al., 2023).

Fig. 1 exhibits the complex and multifaceted effects of imposing an environmental tax on the TFP of heavily polluting enterprises. The consequences of

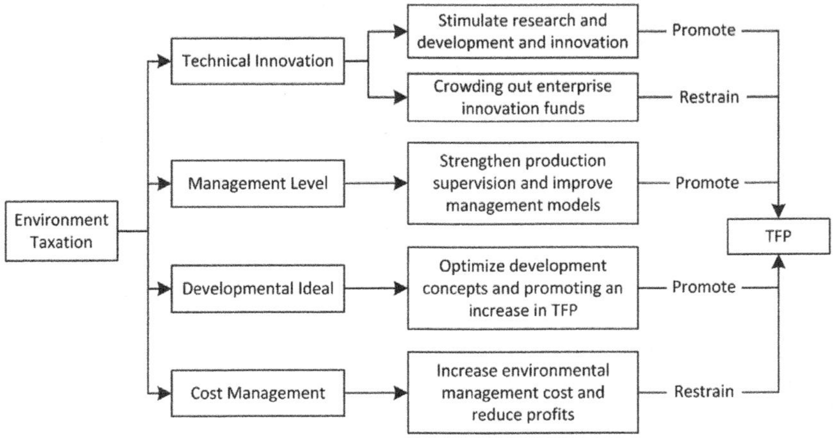

Fig. 1. Multifaceted Impacts of the Environmental Tax on TFP.

levying such a tax are not straightforward, as they can both positively and negatively affect key aspects of the enterprise's operations. On the one hand, an environmental tax may raise environmental management costs, reduce profits and potentially decrease funds for enterprise technological innovation, equipment upgrades and scale expansion, all of which could adversely affect TFP. However, on the other hand, the imposition of such a tax can stimulate research and development innovation, bolster production supervision, improve management models and optimise development concepts, which in turn can positively impact TFP. It is important to acknowledge that different stakeholders may have different prerequisites, and their responses to a sweeping, top-down policy such as an environmental tax may vary significantly. Consequently, the effects of implementing an environmental tax on TFP may differ depending on a range of factors unique to each enterprise's circumstances. Overall, the visual representation in Fig. 1 underscores the various ways in which an environmental tax can affect an enterprise's TFP.

Hamamoto (2006) asserts that environmental regulations can enhance research and development (R&D) investment, leading to an increase in industrial productivity within the manufacturing industry. Similarly, Kivimaa and Kern (2016) argue that effective environmental policies targeting energy conservation and emission reduction are crucial in fostering innovation in firms' technological capabilities, which in turn contributes to the upgrading of the industrial structure. This analysis is carried out from the perspective of technological progress, which posits that environmental regulations increase the cost of pollution control for businesses. As a result, this stimulates companies to adopt innovative technological methods that positively impact their TFP. One way firms can enhance their innovative product optimisation is through improving production technology and achieving cleaner production (Lin & Chen, 2018; Porter & Van der Linde, 1995). This can lead to a significant positive effect on the TFP of companies, especially when the benefits generated by such innovative products are much higher than their production costs (Cai & Ye, 2020; Testa et al., 2011).

Empirical evidence shows the potential of environmental taxes in forcing industries to adopt advanced technology, upgrade facilities and reduce pollutant emissions. For example, Wang et al. (2016) studied the introduction of an environmental tax on air pollutant emissions in the United States and established a significant reduction in emissions levels as a direct consequence. Similarly, Lin and Li (2011) identified a positive impact of the Chinese pollution levy system in reducing water pollution emissions among industrial firms. In a world where environmental protection issues are gaining increased attention, environmental policies are becoming more rigorous, and the prominence of environmental protection taxes is rising. Consequently, businesses are paying closer attention to their performance in areas such as environmental protection, energy-saving and emission reduction. Thus, this study proposes its first hypothesis:

H1. Imposing environmental protection taxes can promote the total factor productivity of heavily polluting enterprises.

In China, SOEs are subject to considerably less stringent government regulation compared to private enterprises (Huang, 2008). Given their partial control and management by the government, SOEs benefit from closer relationships with regulatory authorities and political stakeholders, resulting in lower relationship costs (Huang, 2008). In contrast, private businesses face greater challenges and expenses due to the absence of direct government involvement, forcing them to navigate relationships with various agencies, regulators and stakeholders (Tang et al., 2020). Furthermore, Chinese SOEs possess a stronger capacity to raise capital and are thus able to fund their expansion and operational costs more effectively than private enterprises (Cai & Ye, 2020). These advantages stem from their direct or indirect government ownership and backing, frequently providing them with preferential access to financial resources from state-owned banks and other financial institutions (Huang, 2008; Li & Chen, 2019). Moreover, SOEs enjoy a more abundant cash flow and a greater ability to manage risks, owing to government support and their generally larger scale of operations (Tang et al., 2020).

Beyond financial benefits, Chinese SOEs are often perceived as advocates of the government's interests and are expected to assume greater social responsibility compared to private firms (Huang, 2008). Consequently, they are tasked with spearheading sustainable and high-quality development for other national enterprises (Cai & Ye, 2020). This responsibility leads SOEs to invest more in advanced technologies, standardised management practices and environmental protection initiatives, which in turn enhance their corporate quality and competitive strength (Huang, 2008). However, private enterprises typically grapple with limited resources and weak policy support for business development (Chen & Feng, 2000; Liang et al., 2012). In addition, compliance with environmental regulations is often made more difficult by stringent environmental tax levies, which disproportionately burden private enterprises compared to their state-owned counterparts (Huang, 2008). These challenges can stifle the growth and sustainability of private enterprises, rendering it difficult for them to compete on equal terms with SOEs (Cai & Ye, 2020).

Considering the aforementioned analysis, the following research hypothesis is proposed:

H2. The implementation of environmental protection tax will have a more substantial impact on the total factor productivity of state-owned heavy polluting enterprises compared to non-state-owned heavily polluting enterprises.

3. DATA AND METHODOLOGY

This study focuses on listed companies in China's Shanghai and Shenzhen A-shares from 2015 to 2021. The sample consists of 20,797 observations after screening for invalid data. Table 1 presents the definition of the main variables in the empirical analysis.

Table 1. Variable Definitions.

Variable	Definition
TFP	Firm-level TFP calculated by the LP method.
TREAT	A dummy variable equals to 1 for experimental group and 0 for control group.
PERIOD	A dummy variable equals to 1 for firm-year observation after 2018 and 0 otherwise.
TREAT*PERIOD	A dummy variable equals to 1 for experimental group after 2018 and 0 otherwise.
SIZE	Natural logarithm of total assets in year t.
LEV	Total liabilities on total assets.
CASHFLOW	Cash flow on total assets.
DUAL	A dummy variable equals to 1 if the chairman and general manager are the same and 0 otherwise.
TOP10	The proportion of shares held by the top 10 shareholders.
FIRMAGE	Ln (current year – year of company establishment +1).

In order to investigate the impact of the environmental protection tax on the TFP of heavily polluting companies, this study employs a DiD model. The DiD model enables us to assess whether the policy has influenced firms' TFPs, while minimising the risk of reverse causality given the exogenous nature of the policy. Additionally, the double difference model helps to mitigate endogeneity issues within the model. Thus, we choose the year 2018, when the environmental protection tax was formally introduced, as the time period for the policy's exogenous impact. The model for this study is presented below:

$$\mathrm{TFP}_{i,t} = \beta_0 + \beta_1 \mathrm{Treat}_i * \mathrm{Period}_t + \sum \beta_j X_{i,t} + \lambda_t + \mu_i + \epsilon_{i,t}$$

The subscripts i and t denote enterprise and year, respectively. $\mathrm{TFP}_{i,t}$ represents the TFP of a given enterprise in a given year. Period_t is a dummy variable that takes the value of 1 if the firm-year observation is after 2018, and 0 otherwise. Treat_i is a dummy variable indicating whether the enterprise is a heavy polluter, with 1 representing heavily polluting enterprises (the experimental group) and 0 representing non-heavily polluting enterprises (the control group). The interaction term, Treat_i*Period_t, represents the policy variable interaction. Its coefficient, β_1, quantifies the policy effect. If $\beta_1 > 0$, it suggests that the implementation of environmental protection tax policy effectively improves the TFP of heavily polluting enterprises and promotes their high-quality development. Conversely, if $\beta_1 \leq 0$, it implies a negative effect on the TFP of heavily polluting enterprises, hindering their upgrading and development. $X_{i,t}$ encompasses various control variables that influence the TFP of heavily polluting enterprises. λ_t and μ_i denote year fixed effects (FE) and firm fixed effects (FE), respectively, while $\epsilon_{i,t}$ refers to the random disturbance. This is summarised in Table 2.

Table 2. Summary Statistics.

Variable	Firm-year	Mean	Std. Dev	Min	Max
TFP	20,797	9.152	1.116	5.615	13.64
TREAT	20,797	0.321	0.467	0	1
PERIOD	20,797	0.636	0.481	0	1
TREAT * PERIOD	20,797	0.200	0.400	0	1
SIZE	20,797	22.32	1.284	19.72	26.43
LEV	20,797	0.424	0.201	0.0536	0.906
CASHFLOW	20,797	0.0486	0.0674	−0.180	0.257
TOP10	20,797	0.581	0.148	0.227	0.910
DUAL	20,797	0.298	0.457	0	1
FIRMAGE	20,797	2.973	0.285	2.079	3.611

4. RESULTS AND DISCUSSIONS

Column (1) in Table 3 displays the effect of the environmental tax on TFP for heavily polluting enterprises without the inclusion of control variables. Column (2) highlights the effect of the environmental tax on TFP for heavily polluting enterprises with the control variables included. Both columns imply that the introduction of the environmental tax has significantly positive impacts on the TFP of heavy heavily polluting enterprises. The findings echo Porter's innovation compensation theory that firms strategically react to new regulation by adopting innovative processes and products that reduce pollution and waste, thereby minimising the costs associated with the regulations (Porter & Van der Linde, 1995). Similarly, York and Venkataraman (2010) provide quantitative evidence

Table 3. Test of *H1*.

Variable	TFP (1)	TFP (2)
TREAT * PERIOD	0.050***(0.018)	0.049***(0.014)
SIZE		0.633***(0.017)
LEV		0.031 (0.053)
CASHFLOW		0.877***(0.066)
TOP10		0.119 (0.076)
DUAL		−0.021*(0.011)
FIRMAGE		0.433***(0.128)
_CONS	8.810***(0.010)	−6.403***(0.510)
Firm FE	Yes	Yes
Year FE	Yes	Yes
N	20,797	20,797
Adjusted R^2	0.206	0.471

Note: *,** and *** denote significant at the 10, 5 and 1% levels, respectively.

that firms investing in early-stage green technologies exhibit higher TFP growth rates, as they take advantage of market opportunities ahead of their competitors. Furthermore, Rexhäuser and Rammer (2014) highlight that resource-efficient and eco-innovative firms tend to achieve higher returns on investment than their less-innovative counterparts.

Fig. 2 illustrates a parallel trend analysis. Prior to the implementation of the policy, the TFP index for sample firms depicted considerable fluctuations. However, after the policy was implemented, a positive change in TFP was observed, indicating that the environmental protection tax had a catalysing effect.

A placebo test is also conducted to verify the accuracy of the regression results. We select 2016 as the time node of policy impact, where Treat is used to denote the dummy variables of the experimental and control groups, and Period1 denotes the dummy variables before and after policy implementation. Time before 2016 is taken as 0; otherwise, the value is 1. A new interaction of policy variables is created as item DiD1, and DiD regression is conducted on the sample of enterprises before policy implementation (2015–2017). From Table 4, the estimated coefficient of the policy variable interaction (Did1) is not significant. Thus, if the Environmental Protection Tax Law had taken effect in early 2016, the implementation of the policy would not have had a significant effect on the TFP of heavily polluting enterprises. The placebo test further validates the *H1*.

To test the second hypothesis, we conducted a group regression by dividing the SOEs and private enterprises into two groups. The results of the regression analysis are presented in Table 5. The interaction term coefficient for SOEs is 0.085, which is significant at the 1% level. This finding suggests that the

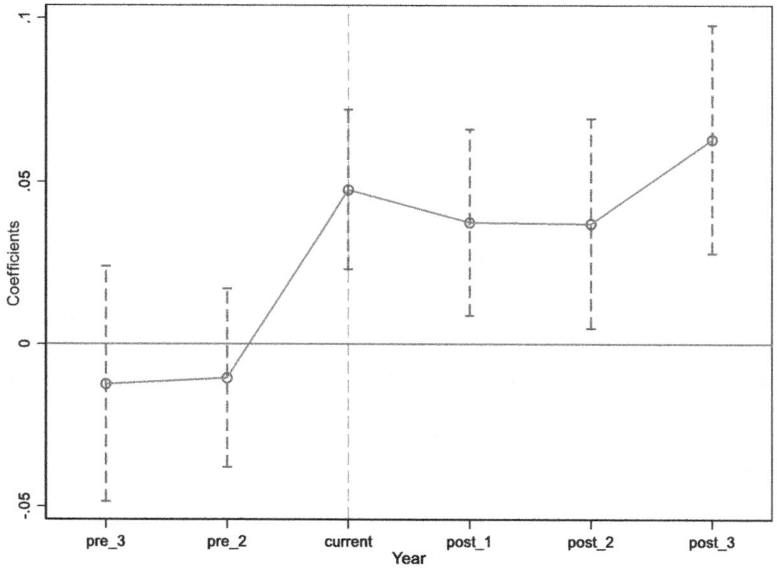

Fig. 2. Parallel Trend Analysis.

Table 4. Placebo Test of *H1*.

Variable	TFP
TREAT* PERIOD1	0.00645 (0.0146)
SIZE	0.530***(0.0334)
LEV	0.0915 (0.0841)
CASHFLOW	0.644***(0.103)
TOP10	0.293**(0.130)
FIRMAGE	0.448*(0.255)
DUAL	−0.0269 (0.0207)
_CONS	−4.302***(0.941)
Firm FE	Yes
Year FE	Yes
N	7,578
Adjusted R^2	0.415

Note: *, ** and *** denote significant at the 10, 5 and 1% levels, respectively.

environmental protection tax can effectively promote the improvement of productivity among state-owned heavy polluters. In contrast, the estimated coefficient of the interaction term for private enterprises is 0.025, which is positive but fails to pass the significance test. This result indicates that the imposition of environmental tax may not have a significant impact on the TFP of private heavy polluting enterprises. Hence, we can confirm the second hypothesis that the environmental tax has a more significant effect on the TFP of state-owned heavy polluting enterprises than their private counterparts.

Table 5. Test of *H2*.

	SOEs	Private Enterprises
Variable	TFP	TFP
TREAT*PERIOD	0.08535***(0.00005)	0.02539 (0.10427)
SIZE	0.66850***(0.00000)	0.62326***(0.00000)
LEV	−0.34225***(0.00318)	0.11376*(0.05875)
CASHFLOW	0.90172***(0.00000)	0.75873***(0.00000)
TOP10	0.08947(0.50542)	0.21406**(0.01612)
FIRMAGE	0.26936***(0.00450)	0.47004***(0.00000)
DUAL	−0.01148 (0.62637)	−0.02240*(0.09159)
_CONS	−6.54274***(0.00000)	−6.34746***(0.00000)
Firm FE	Yes	Yes
Year FE	Yes	Yes
N	6,276	14,521
Adjusted R^2	0.4634	0.4588

Note: *, ** and *** denote significant at the 10, 5 and 1% levels, respectively.

Through the group regression analysis, it is evident that the state-owned and private enterprises react differently to the environmental protection tax. The significant coefficient for SOEs suggests that they respond positively to the imposition of the tax, thereby improving their productivity. On the other hand, the insignificant coefficient for private enterprises indicates that the tax may not be the most effective tool for improving their productivity. These findings highlight the need for differentiated policy mechanisms that cater to the specific needs of different types of enterprises. For instance, policymakers can focus on crafting policies that target private heavy polluters, incorporating other measures beyond the environmental protection tax to promote their productivity. Moreover, the study's findings can help inform future research on pollution control and environmental management policies, particularly in developing countries.

5. CONCLUDING REMARKS

The increasing concern for environmental preservation has led to the adoption of eco-friendly practices across various development sectors. Over recent decades, China has experienced rapid economic development, resulting in significant environmental challenges. As a response, the government implemented the Environmental Protection Tax Law in 2018, targeting pollution by encouraging organisations, particularly heavy-polluting enterprises, to improve their environmental performance. This study evaluates the effectiveness of this tax law in bolstering the sustainable development capabilities of A-share listed companies in China by examining a sample of firms listed on the Shanghai and Shenzhen Stock Exchanges between 2015 and 2021.

Our empirical findings indicate that the implementation of the Environmental Protection Tax Law has led to a substantial improvement in the TFP of heavily polluting enterprises. The impact of the law appears to be more pronounced for SOEs compared to their private counterparts, suggesting that government efforts to promote sustainable development and protection have been successful, particularly among these heavily polluting enterprises.

These findings highlight the efficacy of China's Environmental Protection Tax Law in enhancing the sustainable development capabilities of heavily polluting A-share listed companies. The law has stimulated productivity improvements, especially in SOEs, contributing to the nation's environmental protection and sustainable development objectives. These insights may inform policymakers in developing efficient environmental tax systems that aim to achieve environmental and economic benefits for organisations and society at large, particularly in other developing countries. For instance, environmental taxes can generate revenues that could be allocated to green projects like infrastructure improvements, renewable energy and environmental conservation. This would enable developing countries to invest in sustainable growth and meet their developmental goals. The introduction of environmental taxes in other developing countries may encourage businesses and industries to adopt eco-friendly technologies as they seek to comply with tax regulations and avoid financial penalties.

However, implementing and monitoring environmental taxes can be challenging in developing countries with inefficient or opaque tax administrations. The enforcement of environmental taxes necessitates an efficient and transparent tax administration system capable of effectively identifying and taxing environmental externalities. To overcome these challenges and ensure successful implementation and monitoring of environmental taxes, it is essential to improve institutional capacity and establish transparent, efficient tax administration systems. Moreover, we recommend adopting progressive environmental taxes, with higher earners or larger polluters paying more, to protect small-to-medium-sized businesses from excessive tax burdens.

This chapter explores the implementation of China's Environmental Protection Tax Law and its impact on the sustainable development capabilities of heavily polluting enterprises. While the study reveals improvements in sustainability, it raises the question of whether these industries have become truly sustainable or if the observed changes merely indicate reduced pollution levels and a gradual shift towards environmentally friendly practices. A genuinely sustainable industry should efficiently use resources, mitigate waste, preserve ecosystems and contribute positively to social welfare, among other dimensions. Thus, this chapter contends that industries contributing significantly to pollution are not inherently sustainable, as their practices often lead to environmental degradation and the depletion of natural resources.

Recognising the pressing global climate challenges, it is crucial for developing and less-developed countries to take practical steps to reduce pollution and its associated impacts. The pursuit of economic benefits, if unmanaged responsibly, can result in negative environmental and social consequences. In contrast, a focus on sustainability can foster innovation, resource efficiency and new market opportunities, leading to long-term economic growth. Consequently, implementing higher environmental taxes on polluting industries serves as a policy instrument aimed at incentivising firms to modify their production processes and adopt more sustainable practices. Understanding sustainability requires examining its three interconnected dimensions: economic, social and environmental. This chapter utilises TFP as a measure of sustainable development capabilities, focusing on resource efficiency and effectiveness in the production process. However, sustainable development should also address other facets, such as social equity, cultural preservation and inclusive decision-making processes. Relying solely on TFP and economic analysis may not provide a comprehensive understanding of sustainable development and its relationship with economic growth. Therefore, TFP is only one aspect of the broader sustainability discourse.

A delicate balance between economic benefits and sustainability is necessary. A singular focus on economic benefits may lead to adverse effects on the environment and society, highlighting the importance of incorporating qualitative and interdisciplinary perspectives when evaluating sustainability. The relationship between economic benefit and sustainability can be analysed using methodologies that encompass environmental and social aspects, such as cost–benefit Analysis (adjusting for externalities) or the triple bottom line approach (assessing economic, environmental and social performance). Ultimately, a more inclusive approach, incorporating qualitative and interdisciplinary perspectives alongside economic analysis, is essential for capturing the full spectrum of complexities and nuances involved in true sustainability.

REFERENCES

Barnett, A. H. (1980). The Pigouvian tax rule under monopoly. *The American Economic Review*, *70*(5), 1037–1041.

Bartelmus, P. (2013). The future we want: Green growth or sustainable development? *Environmental Development*, *7*, 165–170.

Baumol, W. J., & Oates, W. E. (1988). *The theory of environmental policy*. Cambridge University Press.

Bosquet, B. (2000). Environmental tax reform: Does it work? A survey of the empirical evidence. *Ecological Economics*, *34*(1), 19–32.

Cai, W., & Ye, P. (2020). 'How does environmental regulation influence enterprises' total factor productivity? A quasi-natural experiment based on China's new environmental protection law. *Journal of Cleaner Production*, *276*, 124105.

Chen, B., & Feng, Y. (2000). Determinants of economic growth in China: Private enterprise, education, and openness. *China Economic Review*, *11*(1), 1–15.

Chou, Y. C., Chuang, H. H. C., & Shao, B. B. (2014). The impacts of information technology on total factor productivity: A look at externalities and innovations. *International Journal of Production Economics*, *158*, 290–299.

Dang, L., & El-Kiran, H. (2019). Urbanization efficiency in China: Total factor productivity-based measurement and sustainable development implications. *The Chinese Economy*, *52*(4), 306–327.

Fullerton, D., & Metcalf, G. E. (2001). Environmental controls, scarcity rents, and pre-existing distortions. *Journal of Public Economics*, *80*(2), 249–267.

Ghosh, R., & Pollitt, M. (2019). Has the energy-environment productivity nexus weakened in OECD countries? *Energy Economics*, *80*, 938–949.

Guo, B., Wang, Y., Zhou, H., & Hu, F. (2022). Can environmental tax reform promote carbon abatement of resource-based cities? Evidence from a quasi-natural experiment in China. *Environmental Science and Pollution Research*, 1–13.

Hamamoto, M. (2006). Environmental regulation and the productivity of Japanese manufacturing industries. *Resource and Energy Economics*, *28*(4), 299–312.

Huang, Y. (2008). *Capitalism with Chinese characteristics: Entrepreneurship and the state*. Cambridge University Press.

Jabareen, Y. (2008). A new conceptual framework for sustainable development. *Environment, Development and Sustainability*, *10*, 179–192.

Kivimaa, P., & Kern, F. (2016). Creative destruction or mere niche support? Innovation policy mixes for sustainability transitions. *Research Policy*, *45*(1), 205–217.

Lanoie, P., Laurent-Lucchetti, J., Johnstone, N., & Ambec, S. (2011). Environmental policy, innovation and performance: New insights on the Porter hypothesis. *Journal of Economics and Management Strategy*, *20*(3), 803–842.

Lanoie, P., Patry, M., & Lajeunesse, R. (2008). Environmental regulation and productivity: Testing the porter hypothesis. *Journal of Productivity Analysis*, *30*, 121–128.

Levinsohn, J., & Petrin, A. (2003). Estimating production functions using inputs to control for unobservables. *The Review of Economic Studies*, *70*(2), 317–341.

Li, P., & Chen, Y. (2019). The influence of enterprises' bargaining power on the green total factor productivity effect of environmental regulation—Evidence from China. *Sustainability*, *11*(18), 4910.

Li, G., & Masui, T. (2019). Assessing the impacts of China's environmental tax using a dynamic computable general equilibrium model. *Journal of Cleaner Production*, *208*, 316–324.

Liang, X., Lu, X., & Wang, L. (2012). Outward internationalization of private enterprises in China: The effect of competitive advantages and disadvantages compared to home market rivals. *Journal of World Business*, *47*(1), 134–144.

Lin, B., & Chen, Z. (2018). Does factor market distortion inhibit the green total factor productivity in China? *Journal of Cleaner Production*, *197*, 25–33.

Lin, B., & Li, X. (2011). The effect of carbon tax on per capita CO2 emissions. *Energy Policy*, *39*(9), 5137–5146.

Liu, G., Yang, Z., Zhang, F., & Zhang, N. (2022). Environmental tax reform and environmental investment: A quasi-natural experiment based on China's Environmental Protection Tax Law. *Energy Economics*, *109*, 106000.

Luo, X. R., & Chung, C. N. (2013). Filling or abusing the institutional void? Ownership and management control of public family businesses in an emerging market. *Organization Science*, *24*(2), 591–613.

Luo, Y., Mensah, C. N., Lu, Z., & Wu, C. (2022). Environmental regulation and green total factor productivity in China: A perspective of Porter's and Compliance Hypothesis. *Ecological Indicators*, *145*, 109744.

Ministry of Finance. (2018). *People's Republic of China Environmental Protection Tax Law*. http://www.mof.gov.cn/zhengwuxinxi/caizhengfagui/shuili10/201801/t20180118_2822079.htm

Mitlin, D. (1992). Sustainable development: A guide to the literature. *Environment and Urbanization*, *4*(1), 111–124.

Moreira, L., Galvão, A. R., Braga, V., Braga, A., & Teixeira, J. (2023). Sustainability as a Gateway to textile international markets: The Portuguese case. *Sustainability*, *15*(5), 4669.

Olley, G. S., & Pakes, A. (1996). The dynamics of productivity in the telecommunications equipment. *Econometrica*, *64*(6), 1263–1297.

Outreville, J. F., & Clement, R. (2016). Total factor productivity and sustainable development in the insurance industry. *Journal of Cleaner Production*, *112*, 3621–3632.

Parris, T. M., & Kates, R. W. (2003). Characterizing and measuring sustainable development. *Annual Review of Environment and Resources*, *28*(1), 559–586.

Pigou, A. C. (1927). The laws of diminishing and increasing cost. *The Economic Journal*, *37*(146), 188–197.

Porter, M. E., & Linde Van der, C. (1995). Green and competitive: Ending the stalemate. *Harvard Business Review*, *73*(5), 120–133.

Rexhäuser, S., & Rammer, C. (2014). Environmental innovations and firm profitability: Unmasking the Porter hypothesis. *Environmental and Resource Economics*, *57*(1), 145–167.

Rubashkina, Y., Galeotti, M., & Verdolini, E. (2015). Environmental regulation and competitiveness: Empirical evidence on the Porter Hypothesis from European manufacturing sectors. *Energy Policy*, *83*, 288–300.

Shapiro, J. S., & Walker, R. (2018). Why is pollution from US manufacturing declining? The roles of environmental regulation, productivity, and trade. *The American Economic Review*, *108*(12), 3814–3854.

Shen, W., Wang, Y., & Luo, W. (2021). Does the Porter hypothesis hold in China? Evidence from the low-carbon city pilot policy. *Journal of Applied Economics*, *24*(1), 246–269.

Solow, R. M. (1957). Technical change and the aggregate production function. *The Review of Economics and Statistics*, 312–320.

Stern, D. I. (2004). Economic growth and energy. *Encyclopedia of Energy*, *2*(00147), 35–51.

Tang, H. L., Liu, J. M., & Wu, J. G. (2020). The impact of command-and-control environmental regulation on enterprise total factor productivity: A quasi-natural experiment based on China's "Two Control Zone" policy. *Journal of Cleaner Production*, *254*, 120011.

Testa, F., Iraldo, F., & Frey, M. (2011). 'The effect of environmental regulation on firms' competitive performance: The case of the building and construction sector in some EU regions. *Journal of Environmental Management*, *92*(9), 2136–2144.

Wang, Y., Han, R., & Kubota, J. (2016). Is there an environmental Kuznets curve for SO2 emissions? A semi-parametric panel data analysis for China. *Renewable and Sustainable Energy Reviews*, *54*, 1182–1188.

Wang, H., & Wheeler, D. (2005). Financial incentives and endogenous enforcement in China's pollution levy system. *Journal of Environmental Economics and Management*, *49*(1), 174–196.

Wang, Y., & Yu, L. (2021). Can the current environmental tax rate promote green technology innovation? Evidence from China's resource-based industries. *Journal of Cleaner Production, 278*, 123443.

Wardekker, J. A., de Jong, A., Knoop, J. M., & van der Sluijs, J. P. (2010). Operationalising a resilience approach to adapting an urban delta to uncertain climate changes. *Technological Forecasting and Social Change, 77*(6), 987–998.

Wu, J., & Tal, A. (2018). From pollution charge to environmental protection tax: A comparative analysis of the potential and limitations of China's new environmental policy initiative. *Journal of Comparative Policy Analysis: Research and Practice, 20*(2), 223–236.

Xue, J., Zhu, D., Zhao, L., & Li, L. (2022). Designing tax levy scenarios for environmental taxes in China. *Journal of Cleaner Production, 332*, 130036.

York, J. G., & Venkataraman, S. (2010). The entrepreneur–environment nexus: Uncertainty, innovation, and allocation. *Journal of Business Venturing, 25*(5), 449–463.

Zahar, A. (2018). Implementation of the polluter pays principle in China. *Review of European, Comparative & International Environmental Law, 27*(3), 293–305.

Zhang, D. (2021). Green credit regulation, induced R&D and green productivity: Revisiting the Porter Hypothesis. *International Review of Financial Analysis, 75*, 101723.

Zhang, K. M., & Wen, Z. G. (2008). Review and challenges of policies of environmental protection and sustainable development in China. *Journal of Environmental Management, 88*(4), 1249–1261.

Zhao, S., Cao, Y., Feng, C., Guo, K., & Zhang, J. (2022). How do heterogeneous R&D investments affect China's green productivity: Revisiting the Porter hypothesis. *Science of the Total Environment, 825*, 154090.

Zheng, H., & He, Y. (2022). How do the China Pollution Discharge Fee Policy and the Environmental Protection Tax Law affect firm performance during the transitional period? *Environmental Science and Pollution Research, 29*(29), 44541–44557.

TECHNOLOGICAL SUSTAINABILITY OF SUPPLY CHAIN MANAGEMENT IN FOOD AND BEVERAGE SECTOR

Zaleekha Aman[a] and Muneer Al Mubarak[b]

[a]*The George Washington University, USA*
[b]*Ahlia University, Bahrain*

ABSTRACT

Over the course of the last 10 years, companies involved in the supply chain have been confronted with a myriad of issues, the most of which can be traced back to modifications in the external environment, such as technical considerations. In addition to the issues that were already present, the recent pandemic generated a new set of challenges for supply chain companies, which had a direct impact on the continuity and sustainability of their businesses. By looking at the ways in which technology is being used to improve the long-term viability of supply chain organisations, this study takes into consideration the changes that were implemented in response to the pandemic, particularly in the food and drink industry. This study was conducted based on a critical literature assessment, and it asks for additional supply chain management research to be conducted in this field. Several ideas have been discussed to better understand the role of technology in the sector. The findings of the study make it clear that the benefits of technological sustainability and ease of use go a long way towards promoting the use of technology and enabling companies to effectively utilise technology within supply chain companies. The study adds to the literature as it integrates technology with the supply chain in the food and beverage sector, a path that is not well researched in the Kingdom of Bahrain.

Keywords: Technological sustainability; food and beverage; supply chain management; integrated technology; Bahrain business

Social Responsibility, Technology and AI
Developments in Corporate Governance and Responsibility, Volume 23, 111–124
Copyright © 2025 Zaleekha Aman and Muneer Al Mubarak
Published under exclusive licence by Emerald Publishing Limited
ISSN: 2043-0523/doi:10.1108/S2043-052320240000023006

1. INTRODUCTION

1.1 Background

Technological sustainability in supply chain management has become the engine of economic growth for countries because of the direct impact it has had on all facets of human existence, especially the economy, society and culture. As a result of these breakthroughs, the world has seen profound and rapid upheavals in recent years. These shifts and modifications are the effect of these adjustments. It is crucial that these countries liberalise their economies and bring modern technological tools and techniques to join the integration of global technological sustainability, as well as increasing the indicators of openness of their economies and reducing the economic turmoil that these countries suffered from to join the integration in global communication (Huang, 2021).

1.2 Definitions of Technology

This chapter will clarify the idea of technology as well as several notions that are related to it. The term technical is one of the relatively new concepts that is concerned with the adoption of contemporary technology in all disciplines, including economics.

The idea of technology, according to Kao et al. (2019), is: The term technology clearly indicates modern technology, but it is more simple and accurate than it, and it is considered one of the most common words in our time, but the more common its use increases, the more ambiguity and confusion in it, and the subject of technology still raises many questions about economists defining an accurate concept of it, and accordingly, there are many visions and concepts that differ around it, including the followings:

- They are the instruments or methods that are utilised for applied scientific reasons and are utilised by man in his work to complete his forces and capabilities, as well as to meet those demands that exist inside the framework of his social, economic as well as historical conditions.
- It is a process or set of processes that allows, through a clear method of scientific research, the improvement of basic techniques and the application of practical knowledge to the development of industrial production.

1.3 The Concept of Technological and Sustainability of Supply Chain Management

It is far more difficult to achieve and maintain long-term success without investing in technological advancements and environmentally responsible practices, so these factors should be prioritised when assessing a company's competitiveness. When businesses adopt ecologically responsible policies and invest in cutting-edge technology, they see increased profits, expanded market opportunities, expanded customer bases and improved profit margins. Incorporating sustainable business practices and technologies into corporate strategies and cultures, investing in these areas, acting on results and frequently evaluating performance are all necessary for this to happen. In recent decades, a novel notion of sustainability has surfaced in a variety of contexts. In the most recent few years, sustainability has been one of the topics that has captured the attention of governments, businesses and academia. The concept of sustainability refers to the effective management of the world's resources to fulfil the requirements of the world's population at the present time while minimising the impact on the ability of future generations to have their requirements met. Management of supply chains is also seen as an essential aspect of sustainable business practices in organisations (Yang et al., 2017).

The concept of sustainable supply chain management has emerged because of the incorporation of the environmental, social and economic dimensions of sustainability into conventional supply chain management practices. The term "sustainable supply chain management" refers to the practice of coordinating the exchange of data, goods and money across businesses in a supply chain. Sustainable development in all its economic, social and environmental dimensions is considered by this style of management, which is in turn based on what customers and other stakeholders want. Companies have, in recent years, begun to adopt the ideas of sustainability due to the actions of non-governmental groups, public awareness and regulatory duties. To produce and distribute goods in the right quantities to the right locations at the right time for the overall cost of the system to be as low as possible while maintaining the achievement of service-level requirements, food and beverage companies employ a set of methodologies known as a supply chain.

1.4 The Research Problem

With the help of the existing literature, the primary issue that has been identified for this research paper is how technological sustainability of supply chain has become an increasing challenge for food and beverage organisations by utilising an appropriate alternative to the basic raw materials available in the country to reduce import costs and avoid delays, which has a positive impact on the recovery of the food and beverage sector and thus resolves crises.

1.5 The Importance of the Study

First, the study has scientific significance because it adds to the body of literature on the topic of technological sustainability and supply chain integration, as well as the impact these factors have on the expansion of food and beverage businesses. It also contributes to the Arab Scientific Library's collection of such literature. Second, the study has practical significance because it is hoped that decision-makers, managers and department heads in the supply chain department of food and beverage companies and others will use the findings to strengthen their own supply chain management practices and address any gaps that have been revealed. In this research paper, we will specifically focus on the technological sustainability of supply chain management in food and beverage manufactures. According to Gloet and Samson (2022), the manufacturers of food and beverages, as well as the supply chains that serve them, continue to face difficulties in the management of sustainable practices. There has been a steady increase in the amount of pressure coming from a variety of stakeholders directed at the sector to support various social and environmental projects. This study's goal is to shed light on the following conundrum: For example, how can food and beverage manufacturers in the Kingdom of Bahrain incorporate technological sustainability principles into their operations and supply chains?

2. LITERATURE REVIEW

2.1 Overview

The World Business Forum (Expo 2020 Dubai) discussed the use of technological sustainability and innovation in the development of knowledge-based economies, Islamic finance, the development of supply chains in the global Islamic economy to keep pace with the digitisation of the financial world, renewable energy and cooperation opportunities that support the transition of the two regions towards low- and zero-carbon energy, halal products, securing the food supply chain and entrepreneurship. On the other hand, the topics discussed the degree to which the economies of the Gulf and the ASEAN region are integrated with one another in several ways, the most important of which is agriculture and the provision of food. The economies of the Gulf Cooperation Council (GCC) countries depend on importing more than 80% of their food requirements to meet the requirements of the local market, whereas agriculture is a major economic driver for many of the ASEAN economies.

The delegates will discuss the potential for increased cooperation in maintaining food security, as well as the ways in which agricultural technological sustainability can advance the aims of food security in both regions. Global supply chains and their management and functioning should be reviewed. Those businesses who can successfully adapt their supply chain management to the unpredictable, ever-shifting and technology-driven business climate are the ones that will not only thrive but also survive.

According to the research conducted by Moradi and Kebryaee (2009), technology investment and GDP expansion were analysed for 48 Organisation of Islamic Cooperation (OIC) members between 1995 and 2005. The team concluded that the technique has a substantial, favourable and direct effect on GDP, especially in oil-producing countries. Additionally, the results of the study show that technology sustainability has emerged as a significant economic factor worldwide. The goal of Salahuddin's 2016 research was to find out how the use of technology affected economic growth, financial development and trade openness in 11 South African countries from 1990 to 2012. The researcher concluded that the use of technology has a positive long-term effect on economic growth in the region. The study's results showed that using the internet will influence economic growth not only during the sample period of the study (1990–2012) but will also have an even bigger effect on economic growth in the region in the years to come (2013–2034).

2.2 Theoretical Foundations

E-Learning, Learning Management System (LMS), Technology Acceptance Model (TAM), and Interpretive Structural Modelling (ISM) are current theories that integrate ideas of technology with supply chain management in the food and beverage industry. Each of them will be discussed in a greater detail below.

2.2.1 E-Learning, Learning Management System (LMS)

Due to the breadth of its applicability, numerous ideas for the concept of an e-learning system have been proposed. E-learning, or electronic learning, refers to the process of developing and implementing learning environments through the application of information and computing technologies as well as various programs (Horton, 2006). Because of this, the utilisation of e-learning systems for technological sustainability among organisations is a starting point for evaluating and then designing technology integration training to improvement the supply chain management, especially in food and beverage organisations. This is done to determine to what extent the organisations adhere to and are satisfied with the use of accessible e-learning systems. Additionally, because of this, the objective of this research is to investigate the attitudes held by supply chain managers in food and beverage companies towards the implementation of e-learning systems as well as their behavioural intentions to do so for the purpose of achieving technological sustainability. This research adds to the existing body of work on the TAM by investigating the link between TAM variables and supply chain managers' perspectives on and plans for using e-learning systems. This research may benefit practitioners who create and promote e-learning systems for technological sustainability, as well as researchers who build and test theories about e-learning systems for technical sustainability.

Electronic markets (EMs) that are based on the internet are currently seeing rapid expansion all over the world. They operate in a variety of markets, facilitate a variety of exchanges of commodities or services with and for numerous types of players, support supply chains and adhere to a variety of business concepts and models to outmanoeuvre their rivals and realise their goals. Most commentators have hypothesised that the field of e-business will eventually be dominated by electronic markets, and that this will be necessary to attain electronic sustainability for all businesses and institutions, particularly those in the food and beverage companies. The concept of numerical economy will be realised in the contemporary and foreseeable future in the form of hyper-connectedness, also known as the expanding interconnectedness of people, institutions and equipment that switch from the network, mobile technology or other internet-connected gadgets. This is a challenge for us in both the present and the future. Because everything is becoming digitised, new intelligent digital networks are being formed, and these networks are fundamentally altering the way in which commerce is managed, optimised, shared and distributed (Taghipour et al., 2021).

The management of supply chains has become an increasingly important aspect in determining competitive advantages in today's market, which is more focused on the consumer. However, given that we have decided to take on the challenge of developing a synchronised supply chain that can compete in the e-economy of the future, the next question is: what specific capabilities do we need to master to achieve technological sustainability in the food and beverage industry? There has been a rise in the prevalence of business models that leverage information systems that cut over traditional organisational boundaries, such as those that link many businesses to their consumers and/or suppliers. The usefulness of these business models is rising as a direct result of this trend. Why not instead raise the question: what efficiencies should the business model be able to concurrently address regarding the "supply chain against supply chain" in the food and beverage sector considering the present digital transformation?

The purchasing and selling of physical and digital items, as well as the provision of services, over the internet is referred to as 'e-commerce'. There are a few different names for what we know as 'e-commerce', including 'online commerce' and 'internet commerce'. The internet's network links enable the delivery of these services online. The four main types of electronic commerce can be defined by the types of participants in the trades and deals. Therefore, the fundamental models of electronic commerce can be broken down into the following categories: The 'B2B electronic marketplace' (EM) is one of these business models, and it is going to be the topic of discussion in this document.

Business-to-Business (B2B) is a form of transaction between businesses such as building materials companies targeting architects and designers as potential customers to do business with. For instance, a building goods firm will target architects and designers as its primary customers for the sale of their wares. Companies that sell to consumers on an individual basis are classified as B2C (business to consumer) enterprises. This format predominates, and one need only look at the thousands of retail establishments offering clothing, footwear and electronics to see this type of business in action (for example Amazon, Zalando, etc.). C2B websites, also known as consumer-to-business websites, are websites in which people give products or services to businesses. This term is most used to refer to traditional websites for freelancers, such as Freelancer, Twago or Adtriboo. C2C stands for 'consumer to consumer' and refers to businesses that allow customers to buy and sell things directly with one another. The best illustration of this would be eBay or any other website that deals in used goods (for example, OLX).

Additional types are occasionally employed as well: The term 'business to government' (B2G) describes transactions involving commercial enterprises and governmental organisations. 'Business-to-government' transactions can also be referred to as 'government-to-consumer' and 'government-to-government' interactions (Government-to-Government). The network is currently utilised extensively by government entities across all levels of the procurement process, including both local and national levels. Mobile commerce, commonly referred to as 'mobile e-commerce' or 'm-commerce', is another key business model that has been growing over the course of the past several years as e-commerce continues to advance and become more sophisticated. Most of the authors that we read and analysed are of the opinion that B2B transactions would eventually be replaced by electronic markets. However, once you cross the threshold, you will rapidly come to the realisation that many online markets are having difficulty attracting a significant number of users or members, a lengthy product list and many different offers on their websites in response to requests to buy or sell items. However, the overall number of transactions that are completed is a significantly smaller number than the number of users.

First, the value proposition that allows competing transactions between suppliers and enables clients to acquire the best possible price is one of the three major drawbacks of using electronic markets. The most recent ideas concerning the relationships between buyers and sellers are seen as having a good outlook. In a broader sense, the market is defined by its extreme anonymity, transparency of information and the relevance of current corporate issues to the market's ever-changing prices. Despite this fact, the plan maximises economic gains by allocating resources efficiently. However, this plan is also astonishingly unrealistic, as it brings the company's profit margins which are equal virtually to zero. Price is not always the most important factor to consider when determining the overall value that is provided by a supplier. Other aspects, such as quality, delivery time and the ability to personalise an item for the consumer, are often more important. Many companies have spent considerable resources over a long period of time managing their supply chain links and/or steadily constructing better and more strategic relationships with their suppliers.

Work alliance product design, sophisticated operation incorporation and ongoing service agreements and contracts are all common outcomes of such collaborations. According to these writers, suppliers can increase the number of buyers they attract with only a negligible increase in the amount of money they spend on marketing, but this advantage is more than offset by the competition over prices. The percentage of vendors who are willing to bid anonymously in high-stakes situations is low. Nonetheless, the highest-quality and most creative vendors abhor price wars. It's fair to say that many internet marketplaces' business process models can best be described as naive over the long haul. Companies that dominate the electronic marketplaces have been in such a rush to become wired that they haven't taken the time to do thorough customer preference research necessary to establish effective strategies or even special offers. This is so since becoming wired is an aim of these businesses. The question of whether technology or electronic marketplaces itself exacerbate antitrust issues appears to be the most crucial.

2.2.2 Technology Acceptance Model (TAM)

When it comes to studying how people react to new technologies, the Technology Adoption Model (TAM) is a tried-and-true strategy that has been used in a wide range of studies. There are almost 36,000 results in Google Scholar citing this approach. In 1989, Fred Davis introduced the TAM as a scientific paradigm based on the idea of rational behaviour analysis (TRA) (Davis, 1989). The Technology Adoption Model (TAM) is a framework for evaluating a user's level of technological adoption by looking at how they interact with the things they buy (Holden & Rada, 2011). Authors like Bienstock and Royne have done extensive research on this idea, and their findings suggest widespread acceptance in many academic disciplines, including consumer behaviour, marketing, management, behavioural psychology and supply chain management (Bienstock & Royne, 2010). When compared to TAM, most acceptance models fail to successfully combine the theoretical frameworks of psychology and technology.

Perceived utility (PU) and perceived ease of use (EOU) are two characteristics that can be used to forecast an employee's adoption and use of new technology in the workplace (PEOU). Perceived usefulness, or PU, is the extent to which an individual thinks their performance in the workplace will improve because of using the system. PU can explain, for instance, if a user thinks the system will help them finish a task faster or not. The perceived ease of use, or PEOU, of a technological tool is the extent to which its usage requires minimal cognitive or physical effort on the part of the user (Venkatesh, 2015). In response to growing criticism levelled against the TAM, it was modified to incorporate new characteristics, including social influence, age and gender, all of which play a role in determining how one intends to behave. The TAM2 model builds on the work of Venkatesh and Davis (2000), who created the TAM. It considers both internal and external social elements that influence a person's behavioural intention to adopt new technology. In 2008, Venkatesh and Bala made some additional improvements and extensions to the model.

The authors Bienstock and Royne (2010) are among those who have argued in favour of using the TAM in supply chain management and logistics because it can assist in determining the connection between user acceptance of the organisation's technology and perceptions of its quality, primarily in terms of how it is perceived by the customers of the company. This is because the model can assist in determining the connection between user acceptance of the organisation's technology and perceptions of its quality because it can assist in determining the connection between user acceptance of the organisation The authors who have been discussed thus far were of the belief that the quality of the logistics service was one of the most significant factors that was directly influenced by the degree to which an organisation embraces new technologies. The authors who were previously mentioned also explained, with the assistance of previous research, that implementing the TAM in the field of supply chain and logistics plays a significant role in enabling organisations to continuously track customer satisfaction each time they implement a new technology or improve technology that is already present within the organisations. This was done in conjunction with the authors of the previously mentioned studies.

2.2.3 Interpretive Structure Modelling (ISM)

The ISM method is a computer-based approach that assists smaller groups in the development of graphical representations of more complicated systems. The fundamental ideas that underlie the technique are investigated, and its application in a variety of activities including technology assessment is developed as a result. Several different implementations of ISM are discussed, and based on these experiences, some observations are made regarding the nature of the ISM process and product as well as how effective it is. It was discovered that ISM gives its users access to a procedure that is both methodical and thorough, allowing them to integrate group judgements into the process of developing 'first-cut' structural models. On the other hand, it was discovered that the method is relatively rigid, and that it may, in some circumstances, stifle the activities that are carried out by groups. There are some suggestions made regarding possible directions for the development of procedures that are less strict.

Using ISM, risk managers can gain a deeper comprehension of the linked structure of hazards inside the supply chain (ISM). Pfohl et al. (2011) have provided examples of ISM. To build subsystems of interdependent elements with matching driving force and reliance, we shall deduce and organise the interdependencies among dangers into a hierarchy. For creating risk-management subsystems, we shall implement this. Using ISM, we were able to determine how various threats to the supply chain relate to one another and then categorise them according to the degree to which they serve as drivers or dependencies. Design, method and strategy were employed to achieve this result. Two case studies were conducted with two German industrial and commercial companies in order to assess both the theoretical results of modelling and the application of those results for actual use. As a result, we can carry out the same test by investigating the situation of food and beverage producers in the Kingdom of Bahrain who are interested in making use of technologically sustainable supply chains.

Findings – ISM is a useful methodology for structuring supply chain risks in a streamlined and decentralised fashion, one that can be implemented sequentially throughout a variety of production phases. To provide the user with an accurate picture of all the needs to be measured and evaluated or the risks to be evaluated, the input of the algorithm must be carefully defined. This is because the result and representation of the ISM are directly proportional to the quality of the input. In conclusion, it has been demonstrated that the supervised process is more trustworthy than the paper-based assessment in situations where this method is desirable. As a result of viewing this model, supply chain managers will be better able to allocate resources such as risk management at later phases of the supply chain process. This model's originality and value lie in the fact that it will aid supply chain managers.

Some problems that might occur in transportation as part of supply chain include delays and disruptions in the delivery of raw materials from other countries especially raw materials coming from long distance countries. Such problems might negatively affect firm's production. Supply chain departments must adopt the use of advanced technology to improve their performance, work and long-term sustainability, while adopting innovative strategies, methods and models. ISM is a qualitative and interpretative strategy that creates solutions for difficult problems through discourses that are based on the structural mapping of intricate linkages between elements. Within the framework of the ISM, a structure of the components is produced as a result, and this structure is dependent on a certain relation type that represents the elements' links to one another. The method facilitates the identification and ordering of the intricate relations that exist between the components of a system, allowing for an investigation into how the components are influenced by one another. ISM has been utilised in the solution of a variety of issues. A complicated issue or the interdependencies between components that need to be investigated are viewed as a complex system (object system) that is either poorly structured or not structured at all. Through modelling, the object system is transformed into a system that is well-defined and representative and is made up of directed graphs (digraph). In addition to the interpretation of the object system in terms of its structure, an interpretation of the object system in terms of its content is also carried out; this is accomplished by completing the digraphs with context (information). The object system, when represented as digraphs, turns into the "fundamental structural model."

The ISM is interpretive, as it relies on group debate to determine the relationship between elements. The methodology is best suited for specialists who understand the problem's background. The approach establishes a framework that creates a comprehensive structure of complex elements based on their relationships, considering all possible pairwise interactions. The method is modelled because digraphs are used to demonstrate both overall structure as well as individual connections between the constituent parts (Agarwal et al., 2007).

2.2.4 Unified Theory of Acceptance and Use of Technology (UTAUT)

The unifying theory of technology acceptance and utilisation is a further significant theoretical framework that helps explain the link between technological sustainability and supply chain management of food and beverage companies. This theory, which has been discussed by various authors and scholars in the existing literature, including Ursavaş (2022), is a unifying theory of technology acceptance and utilisation. According to the authors, this theory incorporates numerous theoretical concepts and perspectives that link new technologies that have emerged in recent years, such as artificial intelligence, communication technologies, cloud computing, robotics and other emerging technologies, into a unified theoretical framework and analyses the impact of such technologies on the performance of business organisations and various international organisations.

This theory also considers the behavioural intentions of the customers and users of such technology to bring about contextual and theoretical similarities with previous theoretical efforts, such as the technology acceptance theories discussed above. This is done to bring about contextual and theoretical similarities with previous theoretical efforts. This theory also considers findings from behavioural theory and social psychology theories to determine the acceptance of new technologies by users in various aspects of an organisation's business operations. The goal of this theory is to determine how users will react to new technologies that are introduced by the organisation to achieve sustainability in supply chain management of food and beverage organisations. According to Marikyan et al. (2021), the success of this theory is dependent on four distinct aspects of performance, each of which is accounted for within the theoretical framework. The aspects of performance that are being questioned are the facilitative conditions, social influence, expected level of effort and expected level of performance. The theory, according to Ursavaş (2022), takes into consideration aspects such as behavioural intention and user behaviour when determining performance expectations, effort expectations, societal influence and enabling circumstances. When conducting this kind of analysis, various aspects of the users, such as their gender, age, level of experience and level of volitional commitment towards the technology, are taken into consideration. Numerous studies have been carried out to investigate how this theory is implemented in a variety of economic activities and industries, and the results of these studies show that it takes all these elements into consideration.

3. DISCUSSION

This study shows the extent to which the commercial success of a company's supply chains is always affected by the degree of implementation of technical sustainability. This is especially true for businesses that are involved in the food and beverage industry. The food and beverage industries are a good example of dynamic industries that face many issues when it comes to the issue of sustainability. These challenges include the effects of climate change, the depletion of resources and the exploitation of people in their supply chains. The reach of customers, special interest groups and other individuals and organisations that exert pressure on food firms in the field of sustainability has risen as a result of globalisation, the rapid expansion of information technology and the proliferation of social media. Many ideas and models have been put forward that we can use to achieve hypotheses and objectives to reach the positive benefit and statistical significance that confirm the relationship between technological sustainability and chronic supply chains implemented on the food and beverage sectors. Such models include E-learning, Learning Management System (LMG), Technology Acceptance Model (TAM), Interpretive Structure Modelling (ISM), and Unified Theory of Acceptance & Use of Technology (UTAUT). This indicates that organisational managers and leaders, as well as technology service providers, have a responsibility to ensure that a high amount of user-friendliness is considered when designing any new technology for supply chain organisations. This is because user-friendliness plays a very important role in contributing to the overall acceptance of the technology.

4. CONCLUSION

According to the findings of the previous investigation, technology designers and makers have an additional responsibility to take into account the issue of sustainability. This is because sustainability also plays a significant part in the acceptability of technology. From a logistics perspective, companies applying technology and supply chain management are not only compatible: their evolution depends largely on technological sustainability and supply chain management. The ISM application has also shown that it can be used as a tool for analysis and decision assistance, which can help promote a more comprehensive understanding of a difficult topic. The use of this approach (e-learning) is appropriate to clarify the problems and risks of supply chains so that they are avoided, avoided and solved in a sophisticated and technological manner to reach the required sustainability. As for the use of the TAM, it helps us to have statistically significant relationships to study the relationship between the use of technology in food and beverage manufacturing companies and the extent to which its use is accepted and achieving sustainability in supply chains in obtaining raw materials with the availability of quality at the lowest prices and quickly.

The environmental, social and economic components of sustainability have been the primary focus of our research, and we have offered examples of practices and best practices from across industries for each of these categories. Companies that successfully adopt sustainability practices across their supply chain and in their operations should be able to generate a distinct competitive advantage for themselves as well as for their partners in the supply chain. Collaboration is essential since there is always the possibility of just passing the expense of sustainability measures onto upstream supply chain partners, which would defeat the purpose of these activities. In conclusion, what was contributed to this research paper is that several strategies that can be applied in the study were put forward to convince companies and institutions to use advanced technology in the food and beverage sector to achieve economic sustainability in the country.

4.1 Study Implications

These findings suggest that to the best of our knowledge, this is the first time that the sustainability practices of food and beverage industries have been reviewed using empirical data. The findings should be of assistance to managers, policymakers, academics and anyone working in this important subject. It is vital to think of technology as an enabler for sustainability because throughout the course of human history, there have always been technical advancements that have the potential to improve society and make processes more efficient. Both the concepts of sustainability and sustainable production, as well as the methodological approach, served as the foundation for the theoretical formulation. It has been demonstrated that businesses who utilise supply chain management strategies and technology attain higher levels of firm performance. According to the findings, technical sustainability practices embedded in effective and continuous supply chain management have an indirect impact on the performance of the organisation as a result of their impact on competitive advantage.

4.2 Study Limitations

The study mainly focuses on food and beverage industry in the Kingdom of Bahrain. Although there was no attempt made to perform a cost–benefit analysis of the many different sustainability techniques that were investigated, this would be an intriguing topic for academic research in the near or far future. This article does not concentrate its discussion on the effects of technology solely on various types of commercial enterprises operating in the first-world countries. Because of the significant challenges that they are currently facing, food and beverage companies will be compelled to respond.

4.3 Future Research

There are many suggestions for future work in the field of technological sustainability in supply chain management in food and beverage sector as follows:

The first suggestion is to find more variables and factors that positively affect the achievement of technological sustainability in the supply chains of food and beverage manufacturing companies. The second proposal is to put forward more ideas on ways to employ technology to increase productivity in supply chains for the growth of food and beverage manufacturers and then reach technological sustainability. The third suggestion is that it is preferable to research more into the technological uses and simplify them for these companies so that they can and be encouraged in their acquisition as they are a reason to reach technological sustainability. Fourth, future research to investigate this issue further across the industries and countries. Finally, we advise future researchers to pay more attention to the practical and applied field of food and beverage manufacturers in the supply chain department while transferring experiences to other companies that are successful in their use of technology so that the country is helped in economic growth and the achievement of the Sustainable Development Goals.

5. RECOMMENDATIONS

- The study recommends the importance of continuing to identify the concept of technological sustainability and the necessity of applying it in competition processes, as the ability of companies to use technology appropriately gives them greater flexibility in facing challenges and crises and knowing the best market opportunities.
- The study also suggests that senior management leaders in food and beverage companies should be made more aware of the significance of supply chain integration as one of the modern core concepts. This is particularly important for suppliers and customers, as they are the ones responsible for providing companies with resources that can achieve excellence and maintain a sustainable competitive advantage.
- The study recommends the need to develop flexible strategies adapted to global changes and crises, in addition to developing alternative plans or programmes that can be resorted to in the event of any change or emergency.
- Finally, it recommends the development of administrative leaders while attracting individuals with competence and experience accumulated through many years of work in the field of supply chain, which enables them to carry out their duties and responsibilities in a manner that achieves the competitive advantage of the company.

REFERENCES

Agarwal, A., Shankar, R., & Tiwari, M. K. (2007). Modeling agility of supply chain. *Industrial Marketing Management, 36*(4), 443–457.

Bienstock, C. C., & Royne, M. B. (2010). Technology acceptance and satisfaction with logistics services. *International Journal of Logistics Management*. https://doi.org/10.1108/09574091011071951

Davis, F. D. (1989). Perceived usefulness, perceived ease of use, and user acceptance of information technology. *MIS Quarterly, 13*(3), 319–340.

Gloet, M., & Samson, D. (2022). Knowledge and innovation management to support supply chain innovation and sustainability practices. *Information Systems Management, 39*(1), 3–18. https://doi.org/10.1080/10580530.2020.1818898

Holden, H., & Rada, R. (2011). Understanding the influence of perceived usability and technology self-efficacy on teachers' technology acceptance. *Journal of Research on Technology in Education, 43*(4), 343–367.

Horton, W. (2006). *e-Learning by Design*. Pfeiffer: John Wiley & Sons, Inc.

Huang, Y. (2021). Technology innovation and sustainability: Challenges and research needs. *Clean Technologies and Environmental Policy, 23*, 1663–1664.

Kao, Y., Nawata, K., & Huang, C. (2019). Systemic functions evaluation based technological innovation system for the sustainability of IoT in the manufacturing industry. *Sustainability, 11*(8), 2342.

Marikyan, D., Papagiannidis, S., & Alamanos, E. (2021). Smart home technologies: Cognitive dissonance perspective. In *Paper presented at British Academy of Management, Lancaster*. United Kingdom. https://www.bam.ac.uk/events

Moradi, M., & Kebryaee, M. (2009). Impact of information and communication technology on economic growth in selected Islamic countries. In *ECOMOD 2009 conference, Faculty of Social Sciences*. University of Ottawa. Ottawa, Canada.

Pfohl, H. C., Gallus, P., & Thomas, D. (2011). Interpretive structural modeling of supply chain risks. *International Journal of Physical Distribution & Logistics Management*. https://doi.org/10.1108/09600031111175816

Taghipour, A., Murat, S., & Huang, P. (2021). E-supply chain management: A review. *International Journal of e-Education, e-Business, e-Management and e-Learning, 11*(2), 51–61.

Ursavaş, Ö. F. (2022). Unified Theory of Acceptance and Use of Technology model (UTAUT). In *Conducting echnology acceptance research in education: Theory, models, implementation, and analysis* (pp. 111–133). Springer International Publishing.

Venkatesh, V. (2015). Technology acceptance model and the unified theory of acceptance and use of technology. *Wiley Encyclopedia of Management*, 1–9.

Venkatesh, V., & Bala, H. (2008). Technology acceptance model 3 and a research agenda on interventions. *Decision Sciences, 39*(2), 273–315.

Venkatesh, V., & Davis, F. D. (2000). A theoretical extension of the technology acceptance model: Four longitudinal field studies. *Management Science, 46*(2), 186–204.

Yang, Z., Sun, J., Zhang, Y., & Wang, Y. (2017). Green, green, it's green: A triad model of technology, culture, and innovation for corporate sustainability. *Sustainability, 9*, 1369.

THE HISTORY AND FUTURE OF CLIMATE CHANGE RESEARCH: WILL NOVEL TECHNOLOGIES FALL VICTIM TO DENIALISM AND CONSPIRACY?

Mirela Panait[a], Răzvan Ionescu[b], Iza Gigauri[c] and Lukman Raimi[d]

[a]*Petroleum-Gas University of Ploiesti, Romania*
[b]*School of Advanced Studies of the Romanian Academy, Romania*
[c]*St. Andrew the First-Called Georgian University, Georgia*
[d]*Universiti of Brunei Darussalam, Brunei*

ABSTRACT

The current relationship between humans and nature is complex and tense. Overexploitation of natural resources, pollution, climate change and biodiversity loss present the main challenges for modern society. In particular, the issue of climate change is being intensely debated, and the interest in protecting natural resources by adopting sustainable practices is growing. Therefore, this chapter examines a brief history and concept of climate change, reviewing relevant theories and authors from Svante Arrhenius and Guy Stewart Callendar to Charles David Keeling and Mikhail Budyko. This chapter explores the first measurements and warnings regarding climate crisis and reviews international treaties and policy development at local, national and global levels. Furthermore, adverse consequences of the climate crisis are described, and ecologism, eco-imperialism and climate change denialism are explained.

Keywords: Climate change; ecosystems; ecologism; denialism; sustainability

Social Responsibility, Technology and AI
Developments in Corporate Governance and Responsibility, Volume 23, 125–142
Copyright © 2025 Mirela Panait, Răzvan Ionescu, Iza Gigauri and Lukman Raimi
Published under exclusive licence by Emerald Publishing Limited
ISSN: 2043-0523/doi:10.1108/S2043-052320240000023007

1. INTRODUCTION

The relationship between the first humans and nature was symbiotic, essential and crucial for species survival for tens of thousands of years. The humans were strictly hunter-gatherers, and they relied completely on natural resources for food, shelter and materials needed for tool-making. Living in harmony with the surrounding environment, the ancestors were deeply connected to the cycles of nature. Hunting and fishing provided them with food, while gathering wild fruits, vegetables and medicinal plants complemented their diet. As human societies evolved and developed, their relationship with nature changed. With the advent of the agricultural revolution in the Neolithic period, humans began cultivating plants and raising animals in a controlled manner, leading to the emergence and development of stable human communities, precursors to the complex human society we know today. This transition had a significant impact on nature, as humans developed new techniques and technologies to shape the surrounding environment into a habitat conducive to their needs, which almost invariably resulted in ecological imbalance. Currently, the relationship between humans and nature is complex and often tense. Overexploitation of natural resources, pollution, climate change and biodiversity loss pose major challenges for modern society in an increasingly apparent manner (Andreea & Victor, 2014; Crowther & Seifi, 2023; Nabaweesi et al., 2023; Panait et al., 2019; Platon et al., 2023; Seifi & Crowther, 2016; Vasile & Balan, 2008). Considering the negative externalities generated by human activity on the environment at international level, there is also a growing interest in conserving and protecting the environment. Moreover, humanity engaged in a race for adopting and promoting sustainable practices in the use of natural resources.

The topic of climate change is intensely debated today. There are diverse opinions and perspectives regarding climate change, including different interpretations of scientific data, assessments of economic and social impacts and discussions about the necessary measures to address this challenge. While a vast majority of the scientific community supports the view that climate change is largely caused by human activities and represents a serious threat to the environment, human health and society, there are voices that contest this opinion, arguing that the anthropogenic impact on the environment is often overestimated and not a cause for concern. Some arguments against the theory of anthropogenic climate change include alternative interpretations of data or a rejection of scientific consensus. Furthermore, climate change is a topic that often generates political, economic and social debates, with strongly polarised positions. There are different opinions regarding the policy and regulatory measures needed to combat climate change, with arguments addressing aspects such as economic costs, national priorities, geopolitical factors or social implications (Khan et al., 2022).

Considering the numerous challenges determined by the negative externalities generated by human activity on the environment, this chapter aims to provide a brief history of scientific thinking on climate change.

2. THE HISTORY OF CLIMATE CHANGE RESEARCH

In 1859, Svante Arrhenius was born in Uppsala, Sweden. He was a Nobel laureate in Chemistry in 1903 and one of the founders of physical chemistry. In 1896, in his work titled 'On the Influence of Carbonic Acid in the Atmosphere on the Earth's Temperature', Arrhenius presented his research and conclusions regarding the link between the concentration of carbon dioxide in the atmosphere and the Earth's temperature. In this work, Arrhenius examined the properties of carbon dioxide (also known as carbonic acid) and its effects on the absorption and re-emission of solar radiation. He used radiation theory to calculate how changes in the concentration of CO2 in the atmosphere could influence the average temperature of the Earth. Arrhenius concluded that variations in the concentration of carbon dioxide in the atmosphere have a direct impact on global temperature. He estimated that halving the amount of carbon dioxide in the atmosphere would trigger an ice age, while doubling the concentration of CO2 could lead to an increase in the Earth's average temperature by approximately 4–5 degrees Celsius (Arrhenius & Holden, 1897). This is due to the capacity of carbon dioxide to act as a greenhouse gas that traps heat inside the atmosphere and contributes to global warming. Arrhenius's research was one of the first attempts to quantify the relationship between greenhouse gases and temperature. It paved the way for further development in climate science and became an important basis for understanding climate change induced by human activities. His work had a significant impact on the field and is considered one of the key contributions to the study of climate change.

The theories proposed by Arrhenius would be demonstrated four decades later by British engineer and inventor Guy Stewart Callendar. In 1938, he published an article titled 'The Artificial Production of Carbon Dioxide and Its Influence on Temperature'. His research, the result of tremendous effort that involved collecting records from 200 meteorological stations worldwide and manually performing calculations, revealed that the global average temperature had increased by 0.3°C over the past 50 years. He also gathered all the estimates of atmospheric carbon dioxide, demonstrated the increasing levels of CO2 and linked it to the burning of coal and fossil fuels. Remarkably, even with his basic methodologies, Callendar's projections of global warming demonstrated a remarkable level of accuracy, aligning closely with modern evaluations. His research was groundbreaking at the time as it provided the first comprehensive analysis of the relationship between CO2 emissions and climate change. He hypothesised that increasing levels of CO2 would lead to the greenhouse effect, causing global warming (Callendar, 1938). Despite initial scepticism from the scientific community, his findings laid the foundation for subsequent studies on anthropogenic climate change. Callendar's work was instrumental in shaping the understanding of the role of greenhouse gases in influencing Earth's climate. From 1938 until his death in 1964, Callendar published 35 scientific articles on global warming, infrared radiation and anthropogenic emissions of carbon dioxide.

Although still relevant today, the works of Arrhenius and Callendar were met with scepticism and largely ignored by the scientific community of their time.

However, their research inspired American scientist Charles David Keeling to closely investigate the atmospheric concentration of carbon dioxide. In his work titled 'The Concentration and Isotopic Abundance of Carbon Dioxide in the Atmosphere', published in 1961, he presents the results of continuous measurements of CO2 concentration carried out at the monitoring station on Mauna Loa in Hawaii, using equipment he designed himself. In his work, Keeling describes for the first time the seasonal variations in atmospheric CO2 concentrations (Keeling, 1960). The data collection at the Mauna Loa observatory, initiated by Keeling in 1958, continues to this day, and the dataset is known as the 'Keeling Curve'. The graph is updated daily and is publicly available on the website of the Scripps Institution of Oceanography at the University of California, San Diego. Unlike the works of Arrhenius and Callendar, which were largely ignored by their contemporaries, the measurements conducted by Keeling received attention. The 1965 Report of the President's Science Advisory Committee on Atmospheric Carbon Dioxide, based in part on Keeling's observations and measurements, was an important document that highlighted concerns about the increasing concentration of CO2 in the atmosphere and its potential to influence Earth's climate. The report drew attention to the risks associated with the accumulation of carbon dioxide in the atmosphere, particularly in relation to global warming and climate change. One of the key points of the report was the recognition that the burning of fossil fuels for different human activities increase in CO2 concentration in the atmosphere.

The report emphasised the need to reduce emissions and find cleaner and more sustainable alternatives in energy production. It also highlighted the importance of continued research and monitoring of carbon dioxide concentration in the atmosphere and its effects on climate and ecosystems. The report emphasised the need to develop models and forecasting methods to better understand climate change and guide environmental protection policies (President's Science Advisory Committee Report on Atmospheric Carbon Dioxide 1965). The 1965 report of the President's Science Advisory Committee represented an important step in raising awareness of the issue of increasing carbon dioxide concentration and its impact on the environment. It contributed to initiating discussions and subsequent actions regarding climate change and environmental protection, serving as a milestone in the evolution of policies and strategies to combat global warming. However, during a period marked by a profound division between the West and the East, it was not only Western researchers who drew attention to the risks of global warming.

The work 'The Effect of Solar Radiation Variations on the Earth's Climate', published in 1969 by Soviet researcher Mikhail Budyko, first described the 'Arctic amplification' effect, which causes average temperatures to increase more at the poles. Budyko hypothesised that a continuation of this trend would lead to accelerated melting of ice caps (Budyko, 1969). One of the key moments in raising awareness of the risks associated with climate change caused by greenhouse gas emissions occurred in 1988. When testifying before the United States Congress, James Edward Hansen, the director of NASA's Goddard Institute for Space Studies, provided evidence indicating that greenhouse gas emissions, notably those arising from the combustion of fossil fuels, played a role in the observed and quantified rise in global temperatures. Hansen underscored the potential gravity of unregulated emissions, warning of severe consequences such as elevated sea levels, heightened occurrences of extreme weather events and disturbances to ecosystems. He advocated for prompt measures to curtail greenhouse gas emissions and mitigate the repercussions of climate change. Hansen's testimony played a significant role in raising awareness and shaping public and political discourse on the issue of climate change. In his testimony, he describes the probability of future climatic extremes as follows:

> Until 1995, which is 7 years in the future, we calculate that the greenhouse effect has altered the probabilities in such a way that four faces of the die will be red. One face is white, representing average conditions from the period 1950–1980, and one face is blue, or cooler than the average from the period 1950–1980. So, one thing we can say is that even in the '90s, with the expected increase in the greenhouse effect, there will be years when the temperature will be lower than normal – probably around 2 years during the '90s. What I want to emphasize is that, in my opinion, at least until 1995, the average person will notice this change in probabilities. They will say, "What's happening here? This die is rigged. We have hotter summers more often than before, and the hottest ones are more intense than they used to be." James Edward Hansen – Testimony to U.S. Congress – 23 June 1988.

James Hansen stepped down from his position as the director of the NASA Goddard Institute for Space Studies in 2013. Since 2014, he has been leading the Climate Science, Awareness, and Solutions Program at the Earth Institute of Columbia University in New York while also being an environmental advocate.

3. INSTITUTIONS, POLICIES AND INITIATIVES IN THE FIELD OF CLIMATE CHANGE

The United Nations Framework Convention on Climate Change (UNFCCC) is an international treaty adopted in 1992 with the aim of addressing climate change and promoting coordinated global actions to reduce greenhouse gas emissions and adapt to the impacts of these changes. The main objectives of the UNFCCC are to establish a framework for international cooperation on climate change, reduce greenhouse gas emissions to prevent dangerous interference with the climate system, promote adaptation to the impacts of climate extremes and the capacity of vulnerable countries to adapt and provide financial and technological assistance to developing countries to achieve the convention's goals. The UNFCCC has been signed by nearly all countries in the world and has over 190 contracting parties. It regularly organises Conference of the Parties (COP) meetings to assess progress in combating climate change and negotiate and adopt relevant decisions and agreements.

One of the most significant outcomes of the UNFCCC was the adoption of the Kyoto Protocol in 1997, which imposed emission reduction commitments on developed countries. Currently, the UNFCCC continues to play a central role in promoting global climate action and facilitating international cooperation to achieve the convention's objectives. The Intergovernmental Panel on Climate

Change (IPCC) was established in 1988, by the United Nations Environment Programme (UNEP) and the World Meteorological Organization (WMO), as an international organisation. The IPCC is tasked with providing policymakers with unbiased and scientifically supported evaluations of climate change, encompassing its potential effects and potential strategies for both mitigation and adaptation. The IPCC brings together thousands of scientists from around the world to review and evaluate the latest climate research. It regularly produces complex assessment reports in order to summarise the state of knowledge on specific aspects of climate change and to offer options for adaptation and mitigation. IPCC reports are considered authoritative and widely recognised as key references for decision-makers, organisations and other stakeholders implicated in the field of climate change. Through its assessments, the Panel provides a scientific basis for understanding the risks and impacts of climate change, as well as for decision-making and policy development at local, national and international levels. The IPCC operates on a consensus-based process, and its reports undergo rigorous review involving experts and governments.

Its work contributes to global efforts to address climate change, including the implementation of the UNFCCC and the Paris Agreement. In 2007, together with former US Vice President Al Gore, the Panel was awarded the Nobel Peace Prize in recognition of their efforts to raise awareness about the dangers of climate change. The AR6 Synthesis Report is the most recent assessment report published by the IPCC in 2023. This report is remarkable taking in account that it presents a comprehensive summary of scientific knowledge on the topic of climate change. The report offers an overview of the current state of the climate situation, including observed changes for specific issues like temperature, precipitation patterns, sea-level rise and impacts on various ecosystems. It assesses the drivers of climate change, such as greenhouse gas emissions and land-use changes, as well as their future scenarios.

Additionally, the report highlights the risks and potential impacts associated with different levels of global warming, underscoring the importance of limiting the rise in global temperatures to a level significantly below 2 degrees Celsius above pre-industrial levels. The report advocates for the intensification of international efforts in order to attain the more ambitious target of limiting the increase to 1.5 degrees Celsius. It also underscores the need for urgent and ambitious actions to reduce greenhouse gas emissions, adapt to climate change and enhance resilience. The report places particular emphasis on international cooperation, categorising it as a critical factor for the successful implementation of coherent environmental policies (IPCC, 2023). The AR6 Synthesis Report aims to provide policymakers, stakeholders and the public with a comprehensive and accessible summary of the current understanding of climate change, its impacts and options for reducing potential risks associated with it. It serves as a scientific-technical tool to guide climate actions and policy development at the global, regional and national levels.

4. FROM ECOLOGISM TO ECO-IMPERIALISM

The term 'Global South' refers to countries that are generally considered less economically developed, primarily located in the southern hemisphere. The concept of the Global South is often used to highlight common socio-economic issues faced by these countries, such as poverty, inequality and limited access to resources. It is a way of classifying nations based on their shared development characteristics and geopolitical position, as opposed to the more economically developed countries of the Global North. Like many other concepts, the term is not universally accepted and can be subject to different interpretations. The term 'Ecological Imperialism' has multiple meanings. Although in this, work it will not be used to explain the effect of European colonial expansion on the environment, the author wants to mention the book 'Ecological Imperialism: The Biological Expansion of Europe, 900–1900' published in 1986 by American environmental historian Alfred W. Crosby Jr. The book examines how European colonisers introduced new species of plants and animals, as well as pathogens, into their colonies worldwide, often significantly disrupting ecosystems and indigenous life. Crosby argues that the colonial success of Europeans was, to some extent, due to their resistance to diseases, a resistance developed in the often unsanitary cities of mediaeval Europe (Crosby, 2004). However, in the context of anthropogenic climate change and the plans and measures of national states and international organisations to counteract its effects, the term 'ecological imperialism' (often referred to as green imperialism or eco-imperialism) has taken on another meaning. In the modern context, as currently used, ecological imperialism refers to the domination or control exerted by more developed or powerful nations or organisations over less developed or vulnerable regions in the name of environmental conservation or sustainability. It involves the imposition of environmental policies, regulations or practices by external actors without sufficient understanding or consideration of local needs and capacities.

The term is often used to criticise situations where environmental initiatives or projects are implemented unilaterally, without the participation or consent of local communities, potentially leading to economic and social disruptions. According to the 1987 Brundtland Report, critical global environmental issues are the results of a mix of factors that target all countries, regardless of the level of development – extreme poverty in Southern countries and unsustainable consumption and production in Northern countries. The report states the necessity for a strategy in order to integrate economic development and environmental preservation Sustainable development is delineated as a form of progress that 'satisfies current needs without jeopardizing the capability of subsequent generations to satisfy their own requirements' (Brundtland, 1987).

Taking in account the debates in 1989, the report was adopted by the United Nations General Assembly, which being aware of the need to integrate environmental aspects in the promotion of economic development decided to organise a UN Conference on Environment and Development. Met with scepticism by representatives of less affluent nations, the report is often regarded as the basis for green imperialism, as discussed in this work. In her 2000 book titled 'Beyond

Eco-Imperialism: A Critique of Environmental Justice on Free Trade', Carmen Gonzales attracted attention that initiatives from the Global North to balance the trade and environmental protection issues must be viewed with circumspection in order to ensure that they promote environmental justice and do not become just another instrument for resource transfer from the South to the North (Gonzalez, 2000). In his 2003 book, 'Eco-Imperialism: Green Power, Black Death', Paul Driessen talks about how humanitarian, social and economic disasters could easily be avoided in poor countries (especially in Africa) if these states had access to inexpensive tools to control famine and diseases, tools that are often denied to them by the West. The author points out that the efficient insecticide dichlorodiphenyltrichloroethane (commonly known as DDT), often associated with a chemical weapon in the Western world and banned by most countries decades ago, remains one of the cheapest and most effective methods to control mosquitoes, the main viral vector of malaria. Additionally, Driessen ironically questions whether people on the brink of extreme hunger would refuse to eat genetically modified wheat, soy or rice if they came from those crops (Driessen, 2007).

An example of a policy seen as promoting climate imperialism is the European Union's Carbon Border Adjustment Mechanism (CBAM). The EU's carbon border adjustment mechanism is a proposed policy designed to address the carbon leakage issue that may occur in case of relocation of companies to countries with less restrictive climate policies. Through this mechanism, global emissions can be kept under control. Through the CBAM, the EU would impose carbon tariffs on certain imported goods based on their carbon footprint, ensuring that foreign producers face similar carbon prices as industries in the EU.

Concerns have been raised about the impact on poorer countries, with worries that they may have limited resources to comply with strict climate policies or invest in cleaner technologies. Additionally, these countries may heavily rely on carbon-intensive industries for economic growth and development. However, proponents of the CBAM argue that it can be designed in a way that takes into account the concerns of poorer countries. They highlight the potential benefits of the revenue generated from the mechanism, which could be used to support climate action and sustainable development initiatives in these countries. Debates surrounding the EU's carbon border adjustment mechanism and its impact on poorer countries are complex, and different stakeholders have divergent opinions.

Ultimately, the effectiveness and fairness of such a mechanism would depend on its design, implementation and consideration of the specific circumstances and needs of developing countries. However, the authors of this work want to emphasise that recent events and scientific consensus have highlighted the fact that poor countries in the Global South are much more vulnerable to the adverse effects of climate change and extreme weather events. Green imperialism can also be viewed as a form of disguised economic protectionism. In 1999, American constitutional and international law professor Jeremy Rabkin published an article titled 'Morgen Die Welt The EU's "Green Imperialism"' in the review of the think tank Institute of Public Affairs, in which he observed that the environmental policies of the European Union gained momentum after the signing of the Single European Act in 1986. Rabkin suggests that countries with higher environmental standards have become concerned about competition from countries where economic competitiveness, to the detriment of environmental protection, is the priority (Rabkin, 1999). The world's poorest countries, which have historically contributed the least to global emissions and climate change, are currently taking the brunt of the climate crisis. COP 28, which took place in Dubai, the United Arab Emirates in 2023, was a controversial one to say the least. However, a landmark deal was struck on the first day of the conference regarding the creation of a fund that would help the world's poorest countries when they are impacted by natural disasters.

5. HABITAT IN PERIL: THE ACCELERATING EFFECTS OF THE CLIMATE CRISIS

In the 1970s, the Club of Rome theorised that economic growth would mean extended pressure on the environment (Meadows et al., 1972). Consequently, the authors of 'The Limits to Growth' predicted impending environmental disaster. Since then, the planet has become warmer due to unsustainable human activities such as fossil fuel, power plants, environmental degradation, deforestation, contamination and emissions putting pressure on the ecosystem and biodiversity. Augmented global warming and increased temperature have transformed countries. On the one hand, temperature rise, droughts, extreme hot weather and fires, and on the other hand, sea-level rise, floods, storms and landslides cause famine, species extinction, environmental alteration, and ultimately, human conflict or wars.

Increasing temperature globally has affected the world and every country in recent years. In 2022, Europe faced the hottest summer at 1.4°C higher than the average, reported by the Copernicus Climate Change Service. In the last few years, Europe and the Arctic experienced rising temperatures leading to severe events such as extreme drought, wildfires and heatwaves (ESOTC, 2023). Temperatures have increased significantly more quickly in the Arctic region than in most other parts of the world. The year 2022 ranked as the sixth hottest year on record for the Arctic, and Svalbard, one of the most impacted Arctic locations, had one of the hottest summers in 2022, as the temperature increased more than 2.5°C above average (ESOTC, 2023).

Due to heat waves, Greece faced wildfires which were followed by intense rainfall causing flooding. In southern Europe, the number of hottest summer days is on the rise, and the number of days with 'no heat stress' is likewise on the decline. Similarly, the number of snow days decreased, and precipitation declined across the continent leading to ice melting in Alpine glaciers. Along with the extreme heatwaves, the summer's below-average precipitation also contributed to a broad and protracted drought that had an impact on a number of industries, including energy, river transportation and agriculture. As a result of the driest year, 63% of Europe's rivers have below-average flows. Hence, the occurrences of wildfire increased in the European countries resulting in the greatest wildfire emissions in summer (ESOTC, 2023).

Wildfires thrived in Canada, which was caused by hot and dry climate. The country saw above-average fire hazard conditions. From April to June 2023, the emissions from the forest fires achieved the maximum amount that has ever been measured in Canada. Overall, 6,400 wildfires were registered in Canada this year, and around 43.43 million acres (17.577 million ha) have been burned producing 327 megatons of carbon emissions, as of September 20.

Moreover, Greenland saw exceptionally harsh conditions, with unusually high temperatures, but rain in September when snow is more common. The average temperature for the month was 8°C higher causing at least 23% of the ice sheet to melt due to heatwaves (ESOTC, 2023).

Extreme weather conditions resulted in catastrophic flooding in Libya forcing approximately 43,000 individuals to be displaced, while more than 11,000 people died. Unprecedented flooding ruined buildings, vehicles, businesses, infrastructure and dams leading to heavy destruction and a humanitarian crisis.

Devastating climate consequences are recorded in China in 2023. The country faced both heat and flood even in the regions previously unimpacted by such weather conditions. As a result, the rice harvest was destroyed, 81 people died, and there was destructive damage to households and communities (McDonell, 2023). Extreme climate change being it drought or flood generates destructive effects for people and countries. It is also confronted with natural disasters that destroy people's lives, cities and villages. The landslide processes in the western part of the country became active, which devastated whole villages and killed people. Hectares of territory turned into a mass of mud. Similarly, abundant rainfall initiated flooding that damaged houses, roads, power lines and injured local residents. In the eastern regions of Georgia, severe thunderstorms and hail ruin plots and crops in dozens of villages each year. In 2022, due to floods, one-third of Pakistan turned out to be under water affecting more than 33 million people. The list of climatic disasters affecting lots of countries is long. Every country encounters extreme loss, which is also reinforced by human intervention such as greedy behaviour of corporations and corruption of governmental bodies enabling rough interference in ecosystems, for instance, cutting down the forests, constructing buildings unsuitable and unallowed places, extracting inert materials from rivers and changing river beds.

5.1 Ecosystems, Health and Lives Affected by Climate

Climate change induces dangerous conditions for human health. Accelerating global warming causes unbearable conditions for human bodies in the Middle East. This summer, the temperature reached 152°F (66.7°C) in Iran. Since the human body can cool itself at 35°C, such a high temperature can be considered fatal. Over the course of the last few years, 60,000 people were killed each year due to natural disasters (Wiranata & Simbolon, 2021).

Moreover, climate change accelerates mental-related problems, anxiety and stress. Natural disasters give rise to post-traumatic disorder and psychological dysfunction (Abbass et al., 2022). Not only does media news about the catastrophes induce prolonged stress but living in areas disposed to flooding with the lack of proper infrastructure generates additional fear and worries (Abbass et al., 2022). Mental health issues are amplified in communities that have experienced natural disasters.

In addition, climate change affects almost all sectors of the economy and society. Agriculture becomes vulnerable, and food supply is threatened (Abbass et al., 2022). Natural resources, especially water, become scarce, insect disease outbreaks are provoked by warm temperatures and the loss of glaciers and increase of mercury contamination endanger plants. In China, for example, crop production is impacted by climatic disasters. The country is gravely harmed due to its dense population, unfavourable ecological conditions and climate change. Millions of people were affected by different climatic disasters in 2016, not to mention the economic harm as a consequence (Xie et al., 2020).

In a similar way, the magnitude of climate impact alters ecosystems as species may change microhabitat and activity (Bates et al., 2014). Species either adapt to the altered environment or move. The best chances to survive are those species that have abilities to adjust to the changed ecosystems (Bates et al., 2014). Accordingly, biodiversity is endangered due to the increasing temperature, droughts, floods as well as the spread of pest species (Abbass et al., 2022). Forests are basic resource for over 1.6 billion people worldwide (Sunderlin et al., 2005). The livelihoods of those people who rely on forest resources for are severely influenced by climate disruptions (Brown et al., 2014). Furthermore, the tourism industry is affected exceedingly as the climate is an important enabler of tourism destinations. The weather plays a key role in attracting tourists in particular countries (Abbass et al., 2022; Surugiu et al., 2012). Also, the coastal ecosystem is in danger and is becoming an unfavourable destination for tourists.

Thus, climate change and its consequences are the most pressing contemporary challenges requiring joint efforts by many actors to alleviate them (Apostu et al., 2023; Gigauri & Vasilev, 2022; Panait et al., 2023). The severity of the problem is confirmed by the fact that the United States, in 2023, proclaimed to allocate US 3.5 billion funds for projects aiming at removing carbon dioxide from the air. Moreover, scientists are researching how Earth can be kept cool by making the stratosphere lighter using solar geoengineering (MacMartin et al., 2022). Such strategies can prevent the temperature from rising too high. However, solar radiation modification is a theoretical approach requiring more research and experiments to understand its results globally. Today, geoengineering is an expensive approach, its implementation is still far away and its use may have potential risks. For example, intrusion into climate systems can trigger unexpected consequences for some regions, while helping others.

6. THE RISE OF DENIALISM AND CONSPIRACY: IS PUBLIC PERCEPTION BEING MANIPULATED?

At the global level, especially in developed countries, there is overwhelming scientific evidence confirming that irresponsible human actions and unsustainable industrial activities related to the burning of fossil fuels are causing significant changes in the Earth's climate system (Conversi et al., 2023). However, small, vocal, right-wing and influential minority groups and activists continue to contest the climate consensus ideologically, politically and intellectually, a phenomenon referred to in the climate literature as denialism (Clarke et al., 2019; Żuk & Żuk, 2021). Climate change denial is a complex and multifaceted phenomenon. There are several definitions for this phenomenon. Climate change denial is based on the ideological resistance against the scientific consensus on both global warming and the negative externalities of climate change based on cherry-picking data, echo-chamber comments and promoting conspiracy theories. This denial is substantiated on the influence of economic interests that focus more on climate politics than scientific facts (Jacques & Knox, 2016; Walter et al., 2018). In addition, denialism refers to rejection or scepticism of the widely accepted scientific consensus that human activities, primarily fossil fuel burning and deforestation, contribute to global climate change and its negative impacts (Walter et al., 2018; Washington, 2013).

Denialism is devastating because it hinders the efforts of global stakeholders and nations to combat climate change. It also undermines public trust in scientific knowledge and poses significant risks to human well-being and the environment if propaganda is left unchecked (Uscinski & Olivella, 2017). By identifying and addressing the underlying factors that drive denialism, we can promote a more informed and constructive dialogue about climate change and work towards effective solutions. In the United States, the climate denial movement is a mix of ideological small-government conservatives, libertarians and laissez-faire believers who claim the defence of the American way of life as their mission, but their intent is to prevent government regulation of their fossil fuels and reckless operational activities that threaten the planet (Collomb, 2014; McCright et al., 2016). The most powerful tools of the denialists in the United States are warmongering nationalism and political propaganda (Abudu et al., 2023; Conversi et al., 2023). In recent years, many stakeholders have decided to address the climate crisis and fight fossil fuel propaganda in a different way: by protesting in a very public and visible manner. Organisations such as Just Stop Oil, Extinction Rebellion and Scientist Rebellion, just to name a few, have made it their mission to draw attention to the fact that the world is running out of time in the fight against climate change. The fossil fuel-backed disinformation machine has been quick to label them as eco-anarchists and eco-extremists, looking to disrupt the world's way of life. And while most climate protesters are young people who have a very good understanding of the future that lies ahead in a 'business as usual' climate scenario, it is refreshing to see that many elders are also taking to the streets in protest against habitat destruction. In 2020, during a climate protest in London, Extinction Rebellion members Sue, a 77-year-old priest, and Arnold, a 92-year-old retired teacher, were arrested. When interviewed during the protest, Arnold stated that 'the science is clear' on climate change. This goes to show that as long as you fight disinformation and make sure that people know the truth about the climate crisis and its causes, it is much easier to inspire them to take action.

6.1 Types of Denialism

Denialism is not associated with any particular nation or ideological group but has over time attracted active adherents and prominent figures in various countries around the world. Their antagonistic viewpoints are diverse, but the common features of their climate change denial can be divided into five perspectives as depicted in Fig. 1.

The first type is denial of the scientific consensus on climate change and its associated consequences. People with this perspective often dispute the widespread consensus among climate scientists and environmentalists that climate change is real and is caused primarily by irresponsible human actions and unsustainable industrial activities by global corporations. In several cases, such climate change deniers challenge the scientific consensus by arguing that fluctuations in Earth's temperature are natural and not influenced by human activities, despite extensive scientific evidence to the contrary.

Others may downplay the severity of climate change, claiming that it is not as urgent or severe as experts suggest. These viewpoints are often at odds with the overwhelming body of scientific research and evidence supporting the reality of human-caused climate change (Walter et al., 2018; Washington, 2013).

The second type of denial has its roots in conspiracy theories. Conspiracy theories often arise in response to complex or uncertain issues and provide those who espouse them with a sense of control or understanding. In the case of climate change denial, conspiracy theories are often used to cast doubt on the motives and integrity of scientists and institutions involved in climate research. Spreading conspiracy theories is a common tactic of climate change deniers who believe climate change is a hoax designed by climate scientists, environmentalists and

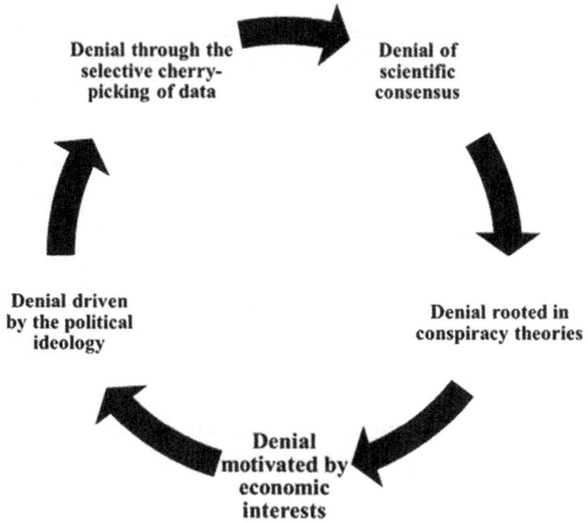

Fig. 1. Climate Change Denial Views. *Source:* Authors based on international literature.

policymakers to manipulate and deceive people about the devastating effects of climate change, or part of it a vast conspiracy aimed at manipulating data, disseminating data and deceiving the public in order to secure research funding or advance a political agenda. These conspiracy theories not only undermine the credibility of the scientific community but also divert attention from the clear evidence supporting human-caused climate change (Haltinner & Sarathchandra, 2018). Therefore, conspiracy theories that suggest widespread collusion among scientists are not only unfounded but also undermine public trust in the scientific enterprise.

The third type of denialism is related to the economic interests of powerful interest groups that stand to lose in combating climate change. For example, the fossil fuel industry has a significant financial interest in maintaining the status quo and avoiding regulations that would restrict its operations or require costly emissions reductions. In other words, subtle and radical denial of climate change is often linked to the economic interests of a few powerful and faceless interest groups. In most cases, this form of denial is encouraged and supported by major carbon polluters, oil and gas companies that rely on fossil fuels and multinational corporations that contribute heavily to greenhouse gas emissions (Gunderson et al., 2020). To make climate change denial viral and visible, these corporate beneficiaries and their companies generously fund denialist organisations or think tanks that produce and disseminate misleading information about climate change. By sowing doubt and confusion, these interest groups seek to protect their profits and delay the transition to cleaner and more sustainable energy sources. It is worth noting that not all individuals or organisations challenging the climate change consensus are directly influenced by economic interests. Some may hold different perspectives based on their interpretation of the evidence or ideological beliefs. However, the influence of powerful interest groups cannot be ignored when understanding the broader context of denialism.

The fourth type of denial is driven by the political ideology of embittered activists, individuals and groups, including those who oppose government regulations or international agreements to combat climate change. In some cases, denialism is accompanied by a broader scepticism of government intervention or a distrust of international institutions. Individuals who hold these ideological positions may be more inclined to reject the scientific consensus on climate change and view it as a means of expanding state control or undermining national sovereignty. Furthermore, some denialism is driven by the political ideology of certain embittered activists, individuals and groups with left-wing political ideologies, as well as those who oppose government regulations or international agreements to combat climate change. Political ideologies can shape a person's perception of climate change and lead them to reject scientific evidence that is inconsistent with their pre-existing beliefs. This ideological divide is evident in the political rhetoric surrounding climate change, with conservatives and liberals often holding different views on the issue. However, it is important to recognise that climate change is a global challenge that requires bipartisan collaboration and collective action.

The fifth type of denial is data cherry-picking, a phenomenon that describes deniers in both developed and developing countries who selectively use subjective data or anecdotal evidence collected in a few places to challenge the idea that global temperatures are rising or that extreme weather events are linked to climate change (Tynkkynen & Tynkkynen, 2018; Wyatt & Brisman, 2017). These cherry-picking deniers avoid reputable scientific sources and institutions but selectively choose information or studies that support their preconceived notions while ignoring the abundant evidence pointing to human-caused climate change (Yagodin, 2021). By selectively focusing on false, discrete, unscientific outliers or minor uncertainties in scientific research, these deniers attempt to create doubt, distort science and undermine consensus opinion (McGarity & Wagner, 2010). Sometimes, they highlight short-term temperature fluctuations or specific regions where warming has been less pronounced to argue that global warming is not occurring or is not caused by human activity – an approach that ignores the long-term trends and the overwhelming evidence that clearly demonstrates the negative impact of greenhouse gas emissions on the climate system (Oreskes, 2018).

In terms of impacts, climate change denial, characterised by doubt and misinformation, has serious social, political and environmental consequences. It is hampering efforts to combat climate change, delaying key policies and investments in renewable energy while undermining support for international agreements to reduce emissions. Denial also endangers public health and safety by underestimating the risks of climate change, hindering protective measures against extreme weather events and sea level rise and leading to human suffering and economic losses. Effectively combating climate change denial requires a multifaceted approach that addresses its motivations and misinformation. Scientists, policymakers and educators must communicate the extensive evidence on climate change and counter misinformation.

Promoting open discussions that encourage critical thinking, evidence-based reasoning and respectful debate can bridge ideological gaps and improve understanding of climate change. It is important to understand that the scientific consensus is based on decades of research, multiple lines of evidence and rigorous peer review, and not on a single study. Deniers distort this consensus through the selective use of data, leading to confusion and misunderstanding among the public. In summary, unaddressed climate change denial poses significant challenges, hinders climate action and endangers society. Addressing this issue requires a comprehensive strategy that includes informed public discourse and accurate information dissemination, which is critical to mitigating the impacts of and adapting to climate change.

7. CONCLUSIONS

Despite the controversies often surrounding the subject, anthropogenic climate change remains a scientifically proven reality, quantified and measured by researchers worldwide and increasingly felt by the global population. From the devastating floods in Pakistan and the historic drought in Europe in 2022, to the unprecedented wildfires that continue to ravage a significant portion of the Canadian boreal forest at the time of writing this work, the frequency, severity and magnitude of extreme weather events continue to be amplified by human activities.

Along with the evolution of human societies evolved, their harmonious coexistence with nature has changed, causing an imbalance in ecosystems. Unsustainable activities lead to environmental degradation, threatening life on Earth. In this regard, sustainable development and social responsibility actions undertaken by organisations of all types in both developed and emerging economies should be strengthened. Environmental damage can be mitigated through addressing climate crises and maintain the natural environment. The concerted efforts around the world are required as the climate is a common resource.

Although numerous global environmental initiatives exist, they lack genuine decision-making will that translates into coherent actions, which are the only ones that can prevent a dystopian future where human society loses its capacity for initiative, becomes overwhelmed and can only react, invariably late, to increasingly frequent and severe climate disasters. Although existential in nature for the human habitat, the subject of climate change is often used in a subversive and diversionary manner in the pursuit of material profit or ephemeral power.

The future research will need to focus on identifying and gaining a deeper understanding of the effect that international regulations in the field of climate change, which are likely to become increasingly stringent, will have on economic relationships and public perception.

REFERENCES

Abbass, K., Qasim, M. Z., Song, H., Murshed, M., Mahmood, H., & Younis, I. (2022). A review of the global climate change impacts, adaptation, and sustainable mitigation measures. *Environmental Science and Pollution Research, 29*(28), 42539–42559. https://doi.org/10.1007/s11356-022-19718-6

Abudu, H., Wesseh, P. K., Jr., & Lin, B. (2023). Does political propaganda matter in climate change? Insights from the United States of America. *Journal of Management Science and Engineering, 8*(3), 386–397.

Andreea, C., & Victor, P. (2014). Sustainable development paradigm–synopsis. *Annals of the University of Oradea, Economic Science Series, 23*(1).

Apostu, S. A., Gigauri, I., Panait, M., & Martín-Cervantes, P. A. (2023). Is Europe on the way to sustainable development? Compatibility of green environment, economic growth, and circular economy issues. *International Journal of Environmental Research and Public Health, 20*(2), 1078. https://doi.org/10.3390/ijerph20021078

Arrhenius, S., & Holden, E. S. (1897). On the influence of carbonic acid in the air upon the temperature of the earth. *Publications of the Astronomical Society of the Pacific, 9*(54), 14–24. http://www.jstor.org/stable/40670917

Bates, A. E., Pecl, G. T., Frusher, S., Hobday, A. J., Wernberg, T., Smale, D. A., Sunday, J. M., Hill, N. A., Dulvy, N. K., Colwell, R. K., Holbrook, N. J., Fulton, E. A., Slawinski, D., Feng, M., Edgar, G. J., Radford, B. T., Thomspon, P. A., & Watson, R. A. (2014). Defining and observing stages of climate-mediated range shifts in marine systems. *Global Environmental Change, 26*, 27–38. https://doi.org/10.1016/j.gloenvcha.2014.03.009

Brown, H. C. P., Smit, B., Somorin, O. A., Sonwa, D. J., & Nkem, J. N. (2014). Climate change and forest communities: Prospects for building institutional adaptive capacity in the Congo Basin forests. *Ambio*, *43*, 759–769. https://doi.org/10.1007/s13280-014-0493-z

Brundtland, G. H. (1987). *Our common future: Report of the world commission on environment and development*. UN-Dokument A/42/427, Geneva.

Budyko, M. I. (1969). The effect of solar radiation variations on the climate of the Earth. *Tellus*, *21*(5), 611–619.

Callendar, G. S. (1938). The artificial production of carbon dioxide and its influence on temperature. *Quarterly Journal of the Royal Meteorological Society*, *64*, 223–240. https://doi.org/10.1002/qj.49706427503

Clarke, E. J., Ling, M., Kothe, E. J., Klas, A., & Richardson, B. (2019). Mitigation system threat partially mediates the effects of right-wing ideologies on climate change beliefs. *Journal of Applied Social Psychology*, *49*(6), 349–360.

Collomb, J. (2014). The ideology of climate change denial in the United States. *European Journal of American Studies*, *9*. https://doi.org/10.4000/EJAS.10305

Conversi, D., Hassan, C., & Posocco, L. (2023). From climate change denial to war-mongering nationalism. *Culture Della Sostenibilità*, *31*(1), 99–122.

Crosby, A. W. (2004). *Ecological imperialism: The biological expansion of Europe, 900–1900*. Cambridge University Press.

Crowther, D., & Seifi, S. (2023). The many facets of sustainability. *The Complexities of Sustainability*, 1–21. https://doi.org/10.1142/9789811258756_0001

Driessen, P. (2007). *Eco-imperialism green power, black death*. Academic Foundation.

ESOTC. (2023). *Extreme heat, widespread drought typify European climate in 2022*. European state of the climate 2022. https://climate.copernicus.eu/extreme-heat-widespread-drought-typify-european-climate-2022. Accessed on September 22, 2023.

Gigauri, I., & Vasilev, V. (2022). Corporate social responsibility in the energy sector: Towards sustainability. In S. A. R. Khan, M. Panait, F. Puime Guillen, & L. Raimi (Eds.), *Energy transition. Industrial ecology*. Springer. https://doi.org/10.1007/978-981-19-3540-4_10

Gonzalez, C. G. (2000). Beyond eco-imperialism: An environmental justice critique of free trade. *Denver Law Review*, *78*, 979.

Gunderson, R., Stuart, D., & Petersen, B. (2020). The fossil fuel industry's framing of carbon capture and storage: Faith in innovation, value instrumentalization, and status quo maintenance. *Journal of Cleaner Production*, *252*, 119767.

Haltinner, K., & Sarathchandra, D. (2018). Climate change skepticism as a psychological coping strategy. *Sociology Compass*, *12*(6), e12586.

IPCC. (2023). Climate change 2023: Synthesis report, summary for policymakers. In H. Lee & J. Romero (Eds.), *Contribution of Working Groups I, II and III to the Sixth Assessment Report of the Intergovernmental Panel on Climate Change*. IPCC.

Jacques, P., & Knox, C. (2016). Hurricanes and hegemony: A qualitative analysis of micro-level climate change denial discourses. *Environmental Politics*, *25*, 831–852. https://doi.org/10.1080/09644016.2016.1189233

Keeling, C. D. (1960). The concentration and isotopic abundances of carbon dioxide in the atmosphere. *Tellus*, *12*, 200–203. https://doi.org/10.1111/j.2153-3490.1960.tb01300.x

Khan, S. A. R., Panait, M., Guillen, F. P., & Raimi, L. (2022). *Energy transition*. Springer.

MacMartin, D. G., Visioni, D., Kravitz, B., Richter, J., Felgenhauer, T., Lee, W. R., Morrow, D. R., Parson, E. A., & Sugiyama, M. (2022). Scenarios for modeling solar radiation modification. *Proceedings of the National Academy of Sciences*, *119*(33). https://doi.org/10.1073/pnas.2202230119

McCright, A. M., Marquart-Pyatt, S. T., Shwom, R. L., Brechin, S. R., & Allen, S. (2016). Ideology, capitalism, and climate: Explaining public views about climate change in the United States. *Energy Research & Social Science*, *21*, 180–189.

McDonell, S. (2023). China's summer of climate destruction. https://www.bbc.com/news/world-asia-china-66616699. Accessed on September 22, 2023.

McGarity, T. O., & Wagner, W. E. (2010). *Bending science: How special interests corrupt public health research*. Harvard University Press.

Meadows, D. H., Meadows, D. L., Randers, J., & Behrens III, W. W. (1972). *The Limits to growth*. Club of Rome.

Nabaweesi, J., Kigongo, T. K., Buyinza, F., Adaramola, M. S., Namagembe, S., & Nkote, I. N. (2023). Investigating the modern renewable energy-environmental Kuznets curve (REKC) hypothesis for East Africa Community (EAC) countries. *Technological Sustainability*. https://doi.org/10.1108/TECHS-09-2023-0037

Oreskes, N. (2018). *The scientific consensus on climate change: How do we know we're not wrong?* (pp. 31–64). Springer International Publishing.

Panait, M., Gigauri, I., Hysa, E., & Raimi, L. (2023). Corporate social responsibility and environmental performance: Reporting initiatives of oil and gas companies in central and eastern Europe. In C. Machado & J. Paulo Davim (Eds.), *Corporate governance for climate transition* (pp. 167–186). Springer International Publishing. https://doi.org/10.1007/978-3-031-26277-7_6

Panait, M., Voica, M. C., & Rădulescu, I. (2019). Approaches regarding environmental Kuznets curve in the European Union from the perspective of sustainable development. *Applied Ecology and Environmental Research*, *17*(3).

Platon, V., Pavelescu, F. M., Surugiu, M., Frone, S., Mazilescu, R., Constantinescu, A., & Popa, F. (2023). Influence of eco-innovation and recycling on raw material consumption; econometric approach in the case of the European union. *Sustainability*, *15*(5), 3996.

Rabkin, J. (1999). Morgen Die Welt: The EU's' green imperialism. *Review-Institute of Public Affairs*, *51*(3), 8.

Seifi, S., & Crowther, D. (2016). Managing with depleted resources. In *Corporate responsibility and stakeholding* (pp. 67–86). Emerald Publishing Limited.

Sunderlin, W. D., Angelsen, A., Belcher, B., Burgers, P., Nasi, R., Santoso, L., & Wunder, S. (2005). Livelihoods, forests, and conservation in developing countries: An overview. *World Development*, *33*(9), 1383–1402. https://doi.org/10.1016/j.worlddev.2004.10.004

Surugiu, C., Surugiu, M. R., Breda, Z., & Dinca, A. I. (2012). An input-output approach of CO2 emissions in tourism sector in post-communist Romania. *Procedia Economics and Finance*, *3*, 987–992.

Tynkkynen, V. P., & Tynkkynen, N. (2018). Climate denial revisited: (Re) contextualising Russian public discourse on climate change during Putin 2.0. *Europe-Asia Studies*, *70*(7), 1103–1120.

Uscinski, J., & Olivella, S. (2017). The conditional effect of conspiracy thinking on attitudes toward climate change. *Research & Politics*, *4*. https://doi.org/10.1177/2053168017743105

Vasile, V., & Balan, M. (2008). Impact of greenhouse effect gases on climatic changes. Measurement indicators and forecast models. *Annales Universitatis Apulensis - Series Oeconomica*, *2*(10), 1–19.

Walter, S., Brüggemann, M., & Engesser, S. (2018). Echo chambers of denial: Explaining user comments on climate change. *Environmental Communication*, *12*, 204–217. https://doi.org/10.1080/17524032.2017.1394893

Washington, H. (2013). *Climate change denial: Heads in the sand*. Routledge.

Wiranata, I. J., & Simbolon, K. (2021). Increasing awareness capacity of disaster potential as a support to achieve sustainable development goal (sdg) 13 in lampung province. *Jurnal Pir: Power in International Relations*, *5*(2), 129–146. https://doi.org/10.22303/pir.5.2.2021.129-146

Wyatt, T., & Brisman, A. (2017). The role of denial in the 'Theft of Nature': Comparing biopiracy and climate change. *Critical Criminology*, *25*, 325–341.

Xie, W., Huang, J., Wang, J., Cui, Q., Robertson, R., & Chen, K. (2020). Climate change impacts on China's agriculture: The responses from market and trade. *China Economic Review*, *62*, 101256. https://doi.org/10.1016/j.chieco.2018.11.007

Yagodin, D. (2021). Policy implications of climate change denial: Content analysis of Russian national and regional news media. *International Political Science Review*, *42*(1), 64–77.

Żuk, P., & Żuk, P. (2021). On the socio-cultural determinants of polish entrepreneurs' attitudes towards the development of renewable energy: Business, climate skepticism ideology and climate change. *Energies*, *14*(12), 3418.

INTERNET OF THINGS IN WATER DISTRIBUTION SYSTEMS

Ahmed Ali Alkuwaiti[a] and Muneer Al Mubarak[b]

[a]*The George Washington University, USA*
[b]*Ahlia University, Bahrain*

ABSTRACT

This chapter aims to identify the important role of using the Internet of Things (IoT) technology in water distribution systems. It focuses on the features of this technology and how it facilitates data collection, communications, system control, condition monitoring, etc. It shows how these features can provide better system understanding and securely enable reliable and timely data. Additionally, IoT offers advanced solutions in smart metering and leak detection, aiding water sustainability and conservation measures by reducing water losses. Through the literature, the features and investment opportunities of IoT are discussed. This study illustrates the prospect, applicability, benefits, and adaptability of IoT to meet the requirements of most industries. Conclusively, the literature reviewed indicate that the deployment of IoT in the water industry is financially justified as it increases the utility's revenue by connecting customers, minimizing losses and enabling timely monitoring. IoT technologies are found in every industry nowadays, yet it is considered relatively new in the power and water supply sectors. However, the findings and research conducted in this field confirmed the financial return and capabilities it grants, enriching such industries to prosper and keep up with the uprising limited natural resources crisis through technological advancement. This study presents the benefits of implementing IoT in water supply networks, by discussing its features, cost of implementation, return on investment and the need for such advancements to sustain our natural resources.

Keywords: Internet of Things; Industry 4.0; water distribution network; system understanding; water industry

Social Responsibility, Technology and AI
Developments in Corporate Governance and Responsibility, Volume 23, 143–159
Copyright © 2025 Ahmed Ali Alkuwaiti and Muneer Al Mubarak
Published under exclusive licence by Emerald Publishing Limited
ISSN: 2043-0523/doi:10.1108/S2043-052320240000023008

1. INTRODUCTION

Internet of Things (IoT) is considered a shift in the field of information technology. There is no accepted or common definition for the IoT as it includes many components and appears in many fields. According to Kramp et al. (2013), it can be defined as an open and comprehensive network of intelligent objects that can auto-organise and share information, data, and resources, reacting and acting in the face of situations and changes in the environment. The IoT as a term can be divided into two segments. First, the internet is the known global interconnected computer network connected by a broad array of electronic, wireless and optical networking technologies. On the other hand, 'Things' can be objects or persons. As it exceeds electronic devices that are connected to the internet, as living things, electronic and non-electronic objects are included (Madakam et al., 2015). IoT played a significant role in Industry 4.0 and is expected to thrive and provide a spawn of new opportunities in many fields in Industry 5.0. As today many industries are being mixed providing further facilities, features, control and monitoring. As all industries are relying heavily on data collection and analysis (Lampropoulos et al., 2019). Nevertheless, there are various industries and applications with minimum or limited IoT utilisation such as water distribution networks (Anandhavalli et al., 2018). Currently, utilities are starting to invest more in IoT implementations, trying to furnish the infrastructure to allow more timely and reliable water supply/consumption data aiding the conservation and sustainability of water resources.

1.1 IoT Architecture

There is no uniform model or standards to be followed to construct an IoT. In other words, IoT is a network that can be designed or furnished according to requirements and applications. The IoT was inspired by members of the Radio Frequency Identification (RFID) community, as first the idea of an internet address or identifying a tagged object arose. This was aided by RFID and NFC technologies. Tagging technologies furnished the way to IoT as it has various forms that can be utilised in one or multiple systems/networks. RFID, NFC, barcoding and sensors are all technologies that make connecting objects to a fixed network or a control system possible. Moreover, the same technologies allowed remote communication and control through two-way communications (Singhania, 2015).

1.2 Radio Frequency Identification (RFID)

This system allows objects or persons to be identified wirelessly through radio waves. It is an old technology that was used first during the Second World War for military applications. This technology relies on the power supply of an object as it classifies into three provisions: Active, Passive and Semi Passive. In general, RFID is assembled by the following main components: tag, reader, antennas, controller and servers. Reliability, low cost, accuracy and security are all features provided by this technology and justify the wide range of applications deploying this technology (Madakam et al., 2015).

1.3 Internet Protocol (IP)

This protocol was developed first in the 1970s, as a primary network protocol used on the internet. Its principal is to communicate and transfer diagrams across the network boundaries. There are two versions of this protocol IPv4 and IPv6 and each defines the address differently (Madakam et al., 2015).

1.4 Barcode

Simply this technology is just another form of encoding numbers and letters using a combination of bars with different spacing and sizes. From the barcode technology the commonly used quick response codes arose, these codes are illustrated by a matrix of barcodes, and it was first used in the automotive industry in Japan. Barcodes were initially used to store numbers or define an object serial or description. However, nowadays QR codes are used widely due to their easy accessibility and storage capacity. Barcodes have three stored data types, Alphanumerical, Numeric, and two dimensional, and all are usually read by machines using laser scanners or cameras (Madakam et al., 2015).

1.5 Wireless Fidelity (Wi-Fi)

This networking technology enables computers and devices to communicate wirelessly. The initial models or Wi-Fi networks used has low data transfer speed compared to the current existing networks. Today Wi-Fi is integral in the modern world as it connects everybody to everything and we can find it at home, work, schools, etc. (Madakam et al., 2015).

1.6 Bluetooth

It is a technology that works with short-range radio signals that do not require wires or cables to connect the devices. It was first used in mobile communications as it was the product of a project held in Ericson Mobile Communication company. It is considered a personal network 'PAN'. This technology allows two or more devices to communicate various types of data such as text, videos, pictures, etc. Today, most of our appliances and devices support this technology and can be connected and communicate through it (Madakam et al., 2015).

1.7 Near Field Communication (NFC)

NFC is known for communicating and controlling devices in your surroundings. It uses a set of short-range wireless technology. It shares similar features with Bluetooth. However, NFC is capable to be operating in a harsh environment, providing easier connections among devices, and allowing connections among more distant devices (does not require line of site communication). It is a relatively cheap technology with low-power demands (Madakam et al., 2015).

1.8 Actuators

These are devices that convert several types of energies into mechanical motion. It can be powered by electrical currents, hydraulic fluid and air. Commonly, actuators are used in industrial applications where mechanical motion is needed, as they allow remote control of devices and some processes (Madakam et al., 2015).

1.9 Wireless Sensor Network (WSN)

It is a network that includes various devices with sensors to collaboratively enable physical or environmental conditions monitoring. Sensors are used to monitor certain variables such as temperature, motion, etc. This condition monitoring is done through multiple sensors depending on the application to communicate changes or undesired conditions once detected (Madakam et al., 2015). All technologies described are enablers of IoT, where a combination of two or more are utilised to attain the required outcome. This research aims to discuss the application of IoT in water distribution systems and flow metres and what are the benefits of this technology to this industry. Thus, to understand the need for such applications water scares are described emphasising the need for enhancement in that industry.

1.10 Water Scares

With the global water scares rising and with considerations to how water is for our well-being and economical sustainability, utilities are pursuing all measures to sustain water resources. Improving water network management and balance models is a known widely used approach followed to target the reduction of water losses, and conserving water consumption in all sectors (Yasin et al., 2021). The World Economic Forum ranked water among the top 10 global risks (World Economic Forum, 2017). Furthermore, the International Water Association (IWA) estimates that there is a 40% gap between the supply and demand of water (IWA, 2016). Most developed countries are considering water as the future oil due to the limited natural resources and the increasing demand caused by the population increase, economic growth and industrial demands (Suri et al., 2022). Water loss varies in networks, where each type has several contributing factors (AL-Washali et al., 2020; Farley, 2003). These losses differ regionally and from one area to the other, depending on how developed the network is and how efficiently the utility is managing its resources (IWA Water Loss Specialist Group, 2016).

1.11 Water Flow Metres

A water flow metre is a device that measures the amount of water consumed by consumers (residential, commercial, industrial and agricultural) (D. Anandhavalli et al., 2018). Water utilities consider metres an integral component of their system as they calculate the amount of water consumed per service point. In other words, metres are decisive in terms of revenue (Mendoza & Benavides-Muñoz, 2021). Usually, metre readings are obtained once per month to calculate the total water consumed and issue the bills accordingly. This process is done manually, where metre readers visit each service point to collect these data (Charalambous et al., 2014).

1.12 Study Contributions and Objectives

This research aims to discuss the induction of IoT technologies in the water distribution sector, as it is where most of the water losses occur (from water production to consumers). The study provides literature augmenting the premise of IoT benefits in various sectors and in water distribution systems. By discussing the prospects of IoT in the water sector and how it might aid the measures followed to sustain this resource by presenting real-time data and the ability to remotely control and gather data, saving labour costs as their field service is no longer required.

1.13 Research Scope

This research covers issues such as the degree of flexibility of IoT technologies, in terms of the ability to be introduced to different industries, potentials and benefits attained from IoT implementation in the water supply system, and reflection on the implementation and deployment of IoT technologies in existing water supply systems. It discusses the current implementation of IoT in this application around the world. Furthermore, the research considers the advantages of the induction of IoT in water distribution networks, in terms of revenue, and real-time data.

2. LITERATURE REVIEW

The Term IoT was first referred to by the technology pioneer Kevin Ashton in 1999, stating that it is a system with objects connected to the internet by various gadgets (Singhania, 2015). Generally, IoT refers to a system where connectivity and communications are not limited to networks; it expands and provides technologies to connect various things and objects (Farooq et al., 2015); doing so with minimal human interaction or intervention. Thus, IoT is many technologies, modems and gadgets employed to attain the goal of connecting objects or things in one system and furnishing the ability for precise and larger datasets (Rad & Ahmada, 2017).

IoT provides promising social and economic benefits when applied, that aid in controlling, monitoring and evaluating systems and attain further growth. Currently, it is used heavily in monitoring water quality, healthcare, sustainable agriculture and environmental management (Boyle et al., 2013). Not only industrialised or developed countries are deploying IoT technologies. Developing countries are interested in the deployment of IoT, due to its promising benefits and role in effective management (Maroli et al., 2021). The technological changes caused by the evolution of information and communication technologies are availed by IoT, as it interconnected hardware and software components thriving with the supply chain network (Oláh et al., 2020).

2.1 IoT and Industry 4.0

The technological changes caused by the evolution of information and communication technologies expanded the utilisation of IoT and made it known to many industries. The significance of IoT in Industry 4.0 is unmeasured, where it can be defined by how easy our lives are today compared to the initial stages of Industry 4.0. Furthermore, ever since the Industrial Revolution, the advancement of technology has been driven by the need for more efficient processes and more productivity. Nowadays, the need for these technologies extends towards sustainability, data analysis, less human intervention and rising to the recent energy and resources challenges (Lampropoulos et al., 2019). Today, due to technological advancements smart devices are everywhere, and the uprising need for devices that can interconnect and communicate within a network. Moreover, the technological evolution and the increasing need for smart devices resulted in decreasing the size of objects, devices and gadgets, while increasing their processing power, features and storage capabilities (Farooq et al., 2015).

Consequently, devices today are equipped with implanted systems to enable communication and coping with the current industrial and application requirements, systems allowing sensing, actuating, data storage and retrieval and processing. Furthermore, the industrial IoT not only enables communication, but also aims to transform devices and processes through optimisation, self-customisation, self-cognition and self-maintainability (Mohammadi et al., 2019). Thus, the magnitude of offerings and benefits of the IoT not only ensures network interconnected devices but extends to more advanced applications, easier operations and longer lifespans (Lampropoulos et al., 2019). IoT is not limited to industrial purposes only, where the IoT is improving our life quality for end users and laying the grounds for general-purpose operations (Akpakwu et al., 2017).

The domains where the IoT is implemented or applied are numerous; a survey was conducted by Atzoria et al. (2010) to categorise IoT applications as follows:

Healthcare domain: including identification of pharmaceuticals, equipment, etc., tracking, data collection, sensors and monitoring devices, authentication, etc.

Smart environment domain: comfortable households/workplaces, industrial plants, smart libraries, smart museums, shopping malls, gyms, etc.

Transportation and logistics domain: involving mobile tracking, assisted driving environment monitoring, GPS, mapping, etc.

Personal and social domain: the application in this domain includes social networking, queries, historical data, losses, and thefts.

Futuristic domain: involving city information models, robotics services, etc.

2.2 IoT Design Requirements

IoT design differs according to the network size, criticality of the application and the number of interconnected devices, networks or processes. However, there are main requirements to be considered when deploying or constructing a network such as the operability, lifespan, deployment cost, coverage area, number of interconnected devices and security. Akpakwu et al. (2017) presented the main considered requirements of IoT as follows:

2.2.1 Low Device Cost

Compared to mobile networks (broadband), communication within an IoT is expected to be low given that most devices are connected with minimal if not zero subscription fees. Additionally, the device's complexity is significantly contributing to the ability to utilise the device in numerous industries, markets and applications.

2.2.2 Low Deployment Cost

To enable IoT applications, the cost of capital investment or capital expenditure and the operational and maintenance costs should be low. This is aided by utilising already laid networks to enable connectivity and making devices adaptable to interconnect with these networks.

2.2.3 Long Battery Life

One of the most important aspects of the IoT concept is energy efficiency. As most devices are powered by a built-in battery and expected to be operating for a long period, it is expected that these devices can operate and provide real-time data when needed for the longest possible period with minimum power consumption. This ensures minimum human intervention and the need to reconnect devices after replacing them or recharging the power source. This concept must be ensured on both hardware and software as the programming or the intervals where a device is communicating plays a major role in how energy efficient the device is.

2.2.4 Extended Coverage

The coverage area is a key design requirement for massive applications such as smart cities and smart metring. In such applications, devices are installed in various locations with different installation parameters and orientations, and devices such as electricity and water metres, and elevators can be indoors with very low coverage.

2.2.5 Security and Privacy

In any network or communication among devices, security and privacy are integral to the design and most industries consider it as one of the main aspects of their design. As the communicated information is usually confidential and critical, without security or privacy, interconnected devices can be corrupted or operated by outer or unauthorised users. Furthermore, these devices store some classified information or identity-revealing information which is considered high risk if accessed by others.

2.2.6 The Massive Number of Devices Support

The number of smart devices that are connected to IoT cellular technologies is increasing rapidly and is expected to increase further in Industry 5.0. Thus, cellular stations and networks will be highly dense as the number of devices is increasing rapidly and IoT technologies are invading every industry and application in our modern world.

2.3 Existing IoT Communication Technologies

As stated earlier, there are no unified solutions or technology to interconnect or construct an entire network. All IoT solutions combine a mixture of communication technologies that are employed to cope with all types of devices and achieve massive IoT. In general, connectivity is achieved by combining both fixed and short-range communication standards in most applications (Atzoria et al., 2010). One of the traditional networks is the Low-Power Wide-Area Network (LPWAN), which is widely used due to the features it provides such as high energy efficiency, channelled bandwidth, wide coverage area, low power consumption and data rates. This technology represents the possibility of interconnecting devices, gadgets, sensors and controllers to the internet without the need for Wi-Fi or cellular networks as per the traditional methods of networking. Many known technologies are increasing in the market to accommodate all industries and application requirements such as Ingenue RPMA, SigFox, LoRa, LoRaWan, Radio Modems, NB-IoT, M-IoT, etc. These technologies enabled the concepts of smart buildings, smart cities, asset monitoring and smart agriculture. However, these technologies can be categorised into long-range networks, short-range networks and cellular technologies (Akpakwu et al., 2017).

Long-Range Networks:

LPWA technologies are promising due to their ability to provide long-range connectivity and low-power solutions for the IoT applications. There are several known technologies deploying LPWAN as follows:

2.3.1 LoRa

It is an emerging technology providing long-range communications with low-power demands. It is commonly used for wide coverage area networks depending on the concept of star-to-star network topology, where interconnected devices are communicating through a single-hop connection to the LoRa gateway. Moreover, it supports two-way communications making it resourceful for smart cities and rural areas communications. Simply, its communications model consists of servers, gateways, device nodes and a remote terminal as shown in Fig. 1. It can achieve up to 15 km of communications in urban environments without a clear line of sight.

2.3.2 Sigfox

It offers end-to-end connectivity solutions based on ultra-narrowband. It is deployed by proprietary base stations that are connected to servers using

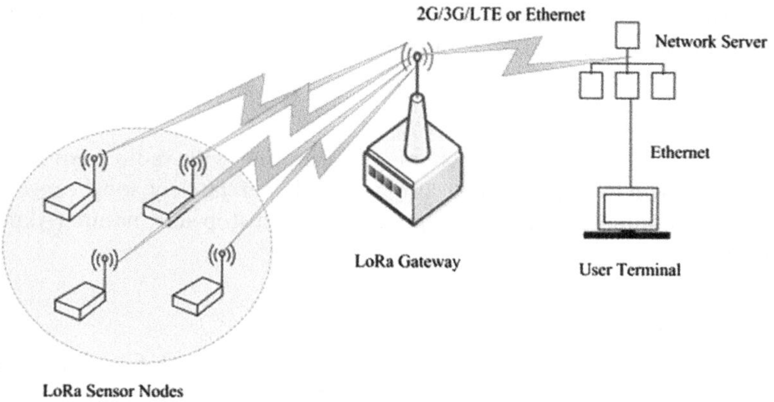

Fig. 1. LoRa Network Architecture, as Retrieved From (Akpakwu et al., 2017).

IP-based networks. Moreover, Sigfox communications require a line of sight between devices and receivers, as shown in Fig. 2. The provided coverage range varies depending on the area; it can reach up to 50 km in rural areas and 10 km in urban areas (Gomez et al., 2019).

2.3.3 Weightless

It was introduced by Weightless Special Interest Group, as a wireless technology complying with LPWA standards and providing its solution on three bases, Weightless-W, Weightless-N, and Weightless-P. All solutions are capable to serve various ranges with low energy consumption and for both licenced and licence-free spectrums. Weightless technology uses cognitive radio and TV

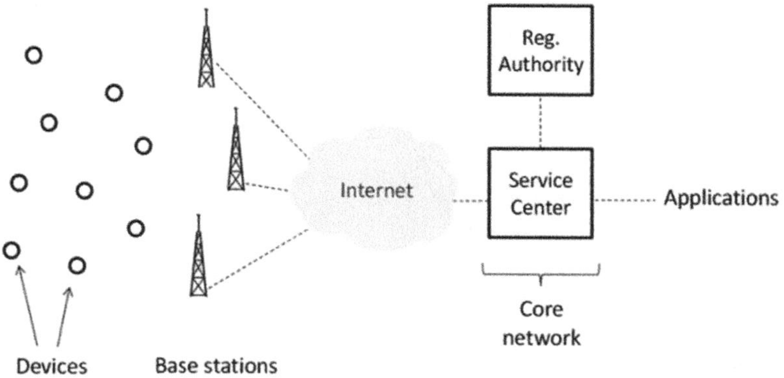

Fig. 2. Sigfox Network Architecture, as Retrieved From Gomez et al. (2019).

white-space bands as opportunistic users without any interference (Akpakwu et al., 2017). This architecture is displayed in Fig. 3.

2.3.4 DASH7

It was inspired by the RFID technology, operating with radio frequency 433 MHz band with low power consumption and in relatively long range. This technology is suitable for low-rate applications with stop-start nature (Akpakwu et al., 2017).

2.3.5 INGENU-RPMA

This technology is known for its flexibility, unlike other LPWA technologies. As it operates with Random Phase Multiple Access (RPMA), Direct Sequence Spread Spectrum (DSSS) makes it useful for uplink communication and allows multiple transmitters to share one slot while communicating without overlapping due to the random offset delay (Akpakwu et al., 2017).

2.4 Introducing the IoT to Water Distribution Systems

Is the implementation of the IoT Technology feasible? What are the expected outcomes of benefits attained from deploying such technologies in this industry? How does IoT provide modern cost-efficient solutions for the water distribution industry? What is the feedback of countries or utilities implementing full or partially IoT networks in their systems? These are all questions that might be rising when discussing the induction of such technologies in this field. Like many

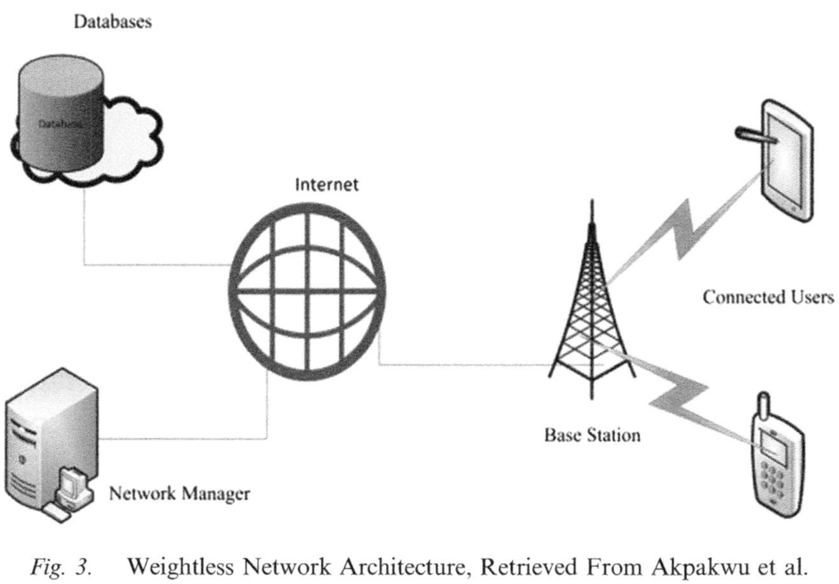

Fig. 3. Weightless Network Architecture, Retrieved From Akpakwu et al. (2017). Used under Creative Commons Licence courtesy of IEEE.org.

industries in our modern world, the water industry was introduced to the IoT technologies to overcome the shortcomings in this field and improve its applications and sustainability. Driven by the solutions, low deployment cost and expected benefits in addition to the low deployment cost compared to gains, IoT invaded all applications and industries, and with water being a globally scarce resource, the necessity to sustain and improve the management of this vital resource dictates the implementation of up-to-date technologies (Thiemann et al., 2011).

Having interconnected sensors that provide sufficient and real-time data can tackle and help to overcome the challenges of insufficient management in the water distribution industry. IoT is a promising solution that can improve the monitoring and control of aspects such as water quality, natural resources level and availability and water losses. Electrical conductivity sensors and fluoride sensors are an example of sensors implemented to monitor and control water parameters and ensure that the supplied water is fitting the standard quality; these sensors are connected and provide data through cloud computing, thus providing remote access to these parameters and allowing remote intervention when needed. One of the major issues in the water distribution networks around the world is water losses (Al-Maskati, 2011). Water losses are caused by numerous factors and are classified into apparent and real losses (Mastaller & Klingel, 2017). The IWA provided a water balance model to aid utilities to improve their management strategies, detecting the water losses and tackling wasted water causations (Non-Revenue Water) (Liemberger & Farley, 2005). Furthermore, according to Al-Maskati (2011), water management can be enhanced by investing in technologies enabling leak prevention and detection methods. Through IoT technologies, water supply management is improved by ensuring better data collection, storage, managing distribution network and water treatment (Zenga et al., 2020).

Water supply is a global concern nowadays, yet countries around the world vary in terms of the challenges encountered. Form abundance of natural renewable sources, infrastructure, level of network development, geographical conditions, population, technological capabilities and economy are all factors deciding the level of risk (Maroli et al., 2021). The sustainable management for water distribution is confronted with many external factors such as climate change, water deficiency, rapid population growth and condensed urban areas. Utilities are increasing the imposed water tariffs to overcome arising challenges and to cover the cost and investments induced in their management strategies covering the monitoring of non-revenue water which has a significant impact on the amount of water lost in the network (Maroli et al., 2021). To overcome these arising and changing challenges, water utilities are taking all measures and investments to achieve sustainable water management and this goal is considered a critical strategic approach for water utilities (Al-Maskati, 2011). Currently, the estimates indicate that there is a 40% gap between supply and demand globally according to the IWA. This emphasises the need for proper water management to keep up with the increasing gap, a solution that can be provided by modern-day technologies such as the IoT (Boyle et al., 2013).

Consequently, water utilities around the world are implementing new technologies and strategies rather than the traditional supply-oriented role. These strategies include measuring management of demand rates, metering accuracy and data, loss detection and prevention, pricing, regulations and education. Therefore, in order for these strategies to achieve the desired outcome, accurate, reliable and adequate data is needed to conduct analysis and present a cost-effective interpretation, improving the level of services provided, reducing water losses, targeting shortcomings, and solving it proactively, credibility, more accurate bills, data justified investments and planning and improving customers satisfaction (Boyle et al., 2013). Timely data lay the ground for involving and engaging individuals in the process of sustaining water. The access to such data will make consumers feel more responsible on an individual level rather than relying on the utilities and government to take these measures through regulations.

2.5 Smart Metring

The introduction of IoT and the concept of interconnected devices made it necessary for water distribution apparatus, gadgets and devices to have the capability to interconnect (Boyle et al., 2013). Water flow metres are considered the end point of the distribution network, as it is the point where the utility demarcation ends, consumption calculates and revenue is attained from the utility end (Charalambous et al., 2014; Van Zyl, 2011). Moreover, smart metring allows remote monitoring and data retrieval for utilities, providing real-time or near-real-time data for proper monitoring (Lee et al., 2021).

The introduction of smart water metres was inspired by the implementation of similar technologies in both electricity and gas metres. Up until the recent decade the implementation of smart metres was considered tentative due to the cost of such devices and constructing the network. According to Boyle et al. (2013), as of 2009 projects deploying the smart metring concepts illustrated only 18% of the globe considering the vast opportunities and solutions provided by this technology, utilities are more attracted to smart metring due to its ability to reduce labour cost, whereas the traditional data collection methods impose sending one worker to the field to obtain data. Generally, metre readings are to be obtained at least once every month for bill issuing purposes which require a large workforce to complete this task monthly considering a large number of metres in urban areas and the few far numbers of metres in rural areas. The attention gained by the smart metres from all utilities has various factors far from reducing labour costs. It provides the utility with reliable real-time data (aiding in loss control and reduction), and it helps them better understand consumption behaviours (Van Zyl, 2011).

2.5.1 Metring Technologies

The range of technologies implemented following different principles to record water consumption is abundant in the market. There is the classical metre employing mechanical displacement methods to capture the water velocity

(Mishra, 2020). Where on the other hand, we have relatively modern technologies to serve the same purpose more accurately implementing Faraday's electromagnetic metres and the Ultrasonic flow metres (Mishra, 2020). However, metre prices vary according to their accuracy class, metrology, size, applications and other factors (International Organization of Legal Metrology, 2013). Therefore, commonly utilities select the type of metre according to the application, environment, required accuracy, and amount of water supplied (Arregui De La Cruz et al., 2015). However, the recent changes in the industry changed how utilities are considering and choosing their metres. As smart metring provided a new spectrum of requirements for the application, nowadays, utilities are considering more advanced features compared to the old physical requirements. Today, the interval of data obtained, customer nature, the development of the network and the water risk rate dictate the metre selection process (Brinkley et al., 2020).

2.5.2 Automated Metre Readings (AMR) and Advanced Metring Infrastructure (AMI)

Both networks are serving the purpose of smart metring, where both concepts describe the data collection and communication methods. The differences between AMI and AMR are in the level of sophistication of measurement, control and operability. AMR relies on the public networks such as General Packet Radio Service (GPRS) and Global System for Mobile Communications (GSM) or private radio transmission. This is done by smartening the current existing metres with modems or gadgets to communicate the metre data. However, AMI serves the same purpose of enabling metres to communicate and interconnect in a given network and it allows two-way communication enabling the utility to remotely control metres. AMI provide a more complete solution so called a fully-fledged AMI, including smart metres, receivers, servers and data presentation and analysis software (Boyle et al., 2013). AMI Process is shown in Fig. 4.

3. DISCUSSION

According to IWA Water Loss Specialist Group (2016), the introduction of new technologies improves the utility's ability to minimise water losses. Al-Maskati (2011) suggested that countries with higher water risks and limited water

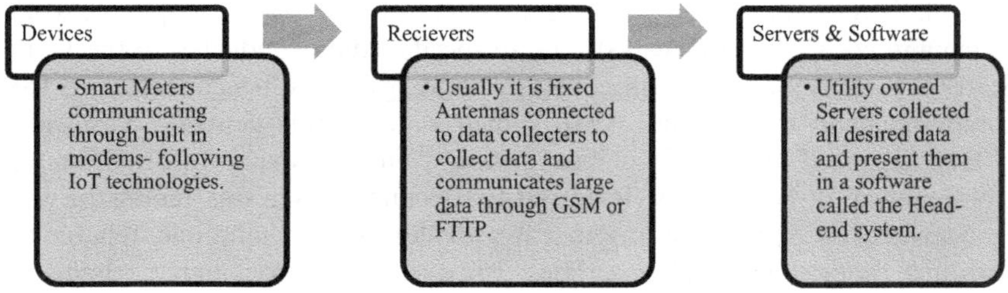

Fig. 4. AMI Process of Data Communications.

resources should invest more in water management technologies, as this will help reduce water losses and provide better management of the system in general. Criminisi et al. (2009) and Arregui et al. (2009) found that metre errors and inaccuracies are the main cause of apparent losses in the water network and have a significant impact on both the utility's credibility and revenue. Van Zyl (2011) emphasised in detail the number of inaccuracies and errors that can be generated by metres. Mastaller and Klingel (2017) illustrated the role of the IWA water balance model, by stating the knowledge and understanding it provides to water utilities. Moreover, he discussed how the induction of strategies such as district-metred areas and leak detection sensors can help mitigate water losses. Before the introduction of the IoT technologies to the water supply industry, Davis (2005) presented the economic impact of failure occurring on the most integral devices in the network in terms of revenue which is flow metres and how the early detection of defects in metres can help the utility reduce its water and revenue losses. Brinkley et al. (2020) discussed the metres and customers type who are more possible to cause losses in the networks due to the total consumed water quantities annually.

Moreover Brinkley et al. (2019) illustrated the financial impact of replacing inaccurate or defective metres in timely manner and how it might increase the revenue of the utility while considering the metre replacement costs. While Viyakesparan (2012) conducted a study in New Zealand suggesting that attending to metres inaccuracies and replacing them will provide payback on the investment within one year considering the water losses and replacement costs. Akpakwu et al. (2017) described the variety of technologies available to interconnect devices through IoT and what are the benefits and potential solutions it provides once introduced to a concerned industry. Farooq et al. (2015) proposed the flexibility of IoT technologies and how they serve numerous industries and applications to thrive and enhance their overall performance and operability. Lampropoulos et al. (2019) illustrated the impact of the IoT technologies on Industry 4.0 and its induction of merely all applications in our world, emphasising on the potential improvements it avails an industry once implemented.

Singhania (2015) provided an overview of the uses of the IoT and what are the challenges rising in our modern interconnected world. Moreover, it depicts the role of such technologies in providing reliable data for industries, service providers and users. Zenga et al. (2020) showed a framework model of implementing IoT in water networks management, describing how it can aid utilities in better understanding their systems given that this technology is going to provide remote control, better monitoring and sustainability to the water supply networks. Thiemann et al. (2011) provided a more specific study conducted in the United States – Kansas City, through conclusive findings of the benefits attained from deploying smart metring and AMI in their water supply network. Yasin et al. (2021) discussed the opportunities arising from deploying Information and Communication Technology (ICT) and IoT technologies in smartening the water management system, suggesting that it provides modern solutions, reliable and real-time data and guides utilities to overcome encountered challenges. Anandhavalli et al. (2018) detected that having accessible and real-time data showing water consumption and usage can help in consumers interaction in the process of water sustainability as it can increase the awareness of consumers and motivate them to share the responsibility of water sustainability with the government and water utilities.

4. CONCLUSION

IoT can be applied in many areas such as healthcare, smart environment, transportation and logistics, social networking and robotics. However, its implementations in fields such as water distribution networks are considered intermediate globally. Despite water global scares and the necessity of conjoined efforts to minimise the water losses and conserve it through timely precises data allowing better control over distribution networks and consumption behaviour. IoT implementations will provide the utilities with reliable data to address their efforts and guide the future investments. While on the other hand, it will enable the engagement of individuals in the process of sustaining water. The access to such data will make consumers feel more responsible on an individual level rather than being forced to conserve water through regulations and higher tariffs. This was achieved in other utilities such as power and gas, where the consumption behaviour was more conservative after the introduction of smart metres providing timely and precise data for both the utility and the consumer.

The findings discussed in this research implicated the necessity of further investments in the introduction of IoT to water supply networks. Demonstrating that this technology has prospect to thrive with this industry and help sustaining it further. All studies reviewed emphasised the role and benefits of IoT in terms of improving the management of resources and enhancing the operability of the discussed industry. Financially, the investment of deploying IoT in the water distribution networks is justified given the solutions it provides to minimise the amount of water losses and the opportunities enabled from reliable and real-time data, involvement of all parties in the decision-making process and offering more control and operability with lower costs.

4.1 Study Limitations

This study is limited to reflecting on literature to discuss IoT technologies and its application in various industries in general and water distribution in detail. This, however, describes the potential opportunities of IoT in water networks without studying an actual application on a regional basis. As this will provide actual data to be discussed illustrating the enhancement IoT provides to such industry in terms of financial return and operability. Further, if a case study was referred to, the results and findings of it will provide actual insights on how the implementation process of IoT is achievable. Providing the ability to study how such technology is deployed from others experience and enabling a set of general recommendations to be followed by any utility interested in this technology.

4.2 Future Studies

Nowadays, IoT applications in water network are widely appealing. Thus, similar studies are encouraged by many governments given that water is listed among the top 10 global risks, and most countries are taking all necessary measures to sustain water resources. Arabian gulf countries are highly interested by such studies, due to the high water scares and the partial or full deployment of IoT in their power and water sectors. A comparative joined study among all six countries will provide abundance of knowledge, given that all countries have good experiences and set of data to be analysed to justify the direction of their investments in such technology.

REFERENCES

Akpakwu, G. A., Silva, B. J., & Abu-Mahfouz, A. M. (2017). A survey on 5G networks for the internet of things: Communication technologies and challenges. *IEEE Access*, *6*, 3619–3647.

Al-Maskati, H. H. (2011). *Water demand management: A case study in Bahrain*. Loughborough University.

AL-Washali, T., Sharma, S., Lupoja, R., AL-Nozaily, F., & Haidera, M. (2020). Assessment of water losses in distribution networks: Methods, applications. *Resources, Conservation and Recycling*, *152*. https://www.sciencedirect.com/science/article/pii/S0921344919304215#section-cited-by

Anandhavalli, D., Sangeetha, K., Dharshini, V. P., & Fathima, B. L. (2018). Smart meter for water utilization using IoT. *International Research Journal of Engineering and Technology*, *5*(4), 1002–1005.

Arregui De La Cruz, F., Balaguer Garrigós, M., Soriano Olivares, J., & García-Serra García, J. (2015). Quantifying measuring errors of new residential water meters considering different consumption patterns. *Urban Water Journal*, 463–475.

Arregui, F., Martinez, B., Soriano, J., & Parra, J. (2009). Tools for improving decision making in water meter management. *Water Loss* Cape Town.

Atzoria, L., Ierab, A., & Morabitoc, G. (2010). The internet of things: A survey. *Computer Networks*, *54*(15), 2787–2805.

Boyle, T., Giurco, D., Mukheibir, P., Liu, A., Moy, C., White, S., & Stewart, R. (2013). Intelligent metering for urban water: A review. *Water*, *5*, 1052–1081.

Brinkley, M., Ilemobade, A. A., & Ncube, M. (2019). Water meter replacement and its impact on water consumption utility, revenue and payback period. *Journal of the South African Institution of Civil Engineers*, 2–9.

Brinkley, M., Ilemobade, A., & NCUBE, M. (2020, September 3). Water meter replacement and its impact on water consumption, utility revenue, and payback periods. *Journal of the South African Institution of Civil Engineers*, 2–9.

Charalambous, B., Foufeas, D., & Petroulias, N. (2014). Leak detection and water loss management. *Water Utility Journal*, 25–30.

Criminisi, A., Fontanazza, C. M., Freni, G., & Loggia, G. L. (2009). Evaluation of the apparent losses caused by water meter under-registration in intermittent water supply. *Water Science and Technology: A Journal of the International Association on Water Pollution Research*, *60*(9), 2373–2382. https://doi.org/10.2166/wst.2009.423

Davis, S. E. (2005). Residential water meter replacement economics. In *IWA Leakage Conference* (pp. 1–10). IWA. Lisbon.

Farley, M. (2003). Non revenue water - international best practice for assessment, monitoring and control. In *12th Annual CWWA Water, Wastewater & Solid Waste Conference. Bahamas: Caribbean Water and Wastewater Association*. https://prowat2.pbworks.com/f/WS1+-+Non+Revenue+water+-+Best+Practice+for+assessment,+monitoring+and+control.pdf

Farooq, M., Waseem, M., Mazhar, S., Khairi, A., & Kamal, T. (2015). (IoT), A review on internet of things. *International Journal of Computer Applications*, *113*(1), 1–7.

Gomez, C., Veras, J. C., Vidal, R., Casals, L., & Paradells, J. (2019). A Sigfox energy consumption model. *Sensors*, *19*(3), 681–702.

International Organization of Legal Metrology. (2013). *Water meters for cold potable water and hot water. Part 1: Metrological and technical requirements*. International Organization of Legal Metrology.

IWA. (2016). *Guidance notes on apparent losses and water loss reduction planning*. IWA.

IWA Water Loss Specialist Group. (2016). *Guidance notes on apparent losses and water loss reduction planning*. International Water Association.

Kramp, T., Kranenburg, R. v., & Lange, S. (2013). Introduction to the internet of things. In *Enabling things to talk* (pp. 1–10). Springer.

Lampropoulos, G., Siakas, K., & Anastasiadis, T. (2019). Internet of things in the context of Industry 4.0: An overview. *International Journal of Entrepreneurial Knowledge*, *7*(1), 4–19.

Lee, J., Choi, W., & Kim, J. (2021). A cost-effective CNN-LSTM-Based solution for predicting faulty remote water meter reading devices in AMI systems. *Sensors*, *21*, 1–21.

Liemberger, R., & Farley, M. (2005). Developing a non-revenue water reduction strategy Part 1: Investigating and assessing water losses. *Water Science and Technology: Water Supply*, *5*, 41–50.

Madakam, S., Ramaswamy, R., & Tripathi, S. (2015). Internet of things (IoT): A literature review. *Journal of Computer and Communications*, *3*, 164–173. https://doi.org/10.4236/jcc.2015.35021

Maroli, A. A., Narwane, V. S., Raut, R. D., & Narkhede, B. E. (2021). Framework for the implementation of an Internet of Things (IoT)-based water distribution and management system. *Clean Technologies and Environmental Policy*, 271–283.

Mastaller, M., & Klingel, P. (2017). Adapting the IWA water balance to intermittent water supply and flat-rate tariffs without customer metering. *Journal of Water, Sanitation and Hygiene for Development*, 396–406.

Mendoza, A. A., & Benavides-Muñoz, H. (2021). Evaluation of domestic water measurement error: A case study. *Journal of Water Supply: Research and Technology*, 217–225.

Mishra, D. S. (2020). *Advisory on water meters, instrumentation & SCADA*. Central Public Health and Environmental Engineering Organization.

Mohammadi, V., Rahmani, A. M., Darwesh, A. M., & Sahafi, A. (2019). Trust-based recommendation systems in internet of things: A systematic literature review. *Human-centric Computing and Information Sciences*, 2–61.

Oláh, J., Aburumman, N., Popp, J., Khan, M. A., Haddad, H., & Kitukutha, N. (2020). Impact of Industry 4.0 on environmental sustainability. *Sustainability*, *12*, 1–21.

Rad, B. B., & Ahmada, H. A. (2017). Internet of things: Trends, opportunities, and challenges. *International Journal of Computer Science and Network Security*, *17*(7), 89–95.

Singhania, V. (2015). *The internet of things: An overview understanding the issues and challenges of a more connected world.* internet society.

Suri, A., Al-Hadrami, A., Sarea, A., & ElAsad, A. (2022). Dubai Electricity and Water Authority (DEWA): A case study on sustainability. *Journal of Business and Socio-economic Development*. https://doi.org/10.1108/JBSED-08-2022-0084

Thiemann, R., Haas, J., & Schlenger, D. (2011). Reaping the benefits of AMI: A Kansas city case study. *Journal American Water Works Association*, *103*(4), 38–41.

Van Zyl, K. (2011). *Introduction to integrated water meter management*. Water Research Commission.

Viyakesparan, J. (2012). Maximising revenue for – Meter replacement strategy replacement strategy. *Water*, 10–29.

World Economic Forum. (2017). *The Global Risks Report 2017*. World Economic Forum.

Yasin, H. M., Zeebaree, S. R., & Sadeeq, M. A. (2021). IoT and ICT based smart water management, monitoring and controlling system: A review. *Asian Journal of Research in Computer Science*, *8*(2), 42–56.

Zenga, S., Du, H., & Xiaac, J. (2020). Development of an interface-oriented add-in modeling framework for integrated water system simulation and its application. *Environmental Modelling & Software*, 134.

PART 3

SOCIAL CHALLENGES FROM TECHNOLOGY

FEMALE ENTREPRENEURSHIP FACING ARTIFICIAL INTELLIGENCE IN THE EUROPEAN UNION COUNTRIES

Aleksandra Gaweł

Poznan University of Economics and Business, Poland

ABSTRACT

Artificial intelligence (AI) carries the risk of widening gender inequalities due to the digital divide, while simultaneously promising to equalise the situation for women through the gender digital dividend. The conflicting findings from previous studies justify the need to investigate the gendered aspects of Artificial Intelligence (AI) diffusion. Specifically, the aim of this chapter is to understand the relationship between female entrepreneurship and the adoption of AI technologies within business contexts at the macroeconomic level. To achieve this, cluster analyses are conducted for the European Union (EU) countries. The results indicate an inverted U-shaped pattern in the relationship between the level of female entrepreneurship and the diffusion of AI technology in business. In the EU countries belonging to clusters with the highest level of AI diffusion, female entrepreneurship is at a moderate level, while in the EU countries with the lowest level of intelligent transformation, both extremes are observed: the highest and the lowest levels of female entrepreneurship. The variety of patterns in female entrepreneurship and AI technology spread in the EU countries implies the complex and multidimensional nature of the interrelationship, and, thus, it indicates the need for diverse, country-specific policies and practices to reach the intelligent transformation with respect to more equal society.

Keywords: Female entrepreneurship; diffusion of artificial intelligence; gender digital divide; gender digital dividend; cluster analysis

Social Responsibility, Technology and AI
Developments in Corporate Governance and Responsibility, Volume 23, 163–182
Copyright © 2025 Aleksandra Gaweł
Published under exclusive licence by Emerald Publishing Limited
ISSN: 2043-0523/doi:10.1108/S2043-052320240000023009

1. INTRODUCTION

Artificial Intelligence (AI) is widely regarded as the technology of the future. The intelligent transformation, involving the diffusion of AI technology from developers to enterprises, changes companies' business models and necessitates an understanding of its enablers and obstacles (Wang et al., 2022). Despite the potential benefits of AI, there are also risk factors associated with intelligent transformation, as AI may lead to unemployment, inequality and inhuman outcomes (Moon, 2023). The deepening of socio-economic inequalities is considered one of the threats posed by AI (Wach et al., 2023). These concerns raise a fundamental question: will AI contribute to fostering a more just and equal society, or will it exacerbate various forms of social and economic disparities.

This chapter focuses on the gendered perspective of AI, as there are conflicting arguments about the effect of digitalisation on women's professional development, distinguishing between the digital gender dividend or the digital gender divide (Chen et al., 2021). Specifically, the goal of this chapter is to recognise the relationship between female entrepreneurship and the diffusion of the adoption of AI technologies within business contexts at the macroeconomic level. As the widespread of AI technologies affects all businesses, no matter whether digital or traditional, this study explores the interrelationships between AI and female entrepreneurship, regardless of their activity in the digital or traditional realm.

Understanding how female entrepreneurship responds to AI is crucial for the following reasons. Despite the ongoing progress towards achieving gender equality (as manifested in Sustainable Development Goal 5), entrepreneurship remains one of the domains where a persistent gender gap exists across time and space. Entrepreneurship is a gendered phenomenon, with men significantly more likely to establish and run their businesses than women (Mustafa & Treanor, 2022). In the European Union (EU) countries, women account for approximately 30% of entrepreneurs (Dilli & Westerhuis, 2018; Ughetto et al., 2020).

Furthermore, despite the progress in gender equality, a digital gender divide persists (Lechman & Popowska, 2022; Picatoste et al., 2023; Sánchez-Rivero et al., 2023; Vimalkumar et al., 2021; Yeganehfar et al., 2018). This divide stems from the under-representation of women in the information and communication technology (ICT) sector (in formal roles as ICT specialists and ICT graduates, as in the EU countries, women account for about 20% of employed ICT specialists and students enroled in tertiary education) and the comparatively lower digital proficiency of women relative to men (in informal capacities). The design, creation and implementation of AI technologies require digital competence (Hidalgo et al., 2020).

All these arguments raise concerns about how women entrepreneurs navigate the business environment in the era of AI. Specifically, the research question in this chapter is whether the widespread use of AI becomes another barrier for women entering entrepreneurship due to the gender digital divide. Or rather, since AI technologies are intended to assist humans in their business endeavours, could the widespread adoption of AI serve as an enabling factor for women to venture into entrepreneurship? The scarcity and fragmentation of research on digital female entrepreneurship (Alhajri & Aloud, 2023), together with the significance of addressing gender and digital equality (Picatoste et al., 2023), justifies undertaking the research.

The remainder of this chapter is the following. The discussion on the gendered perspective of entrepreneurship during the digitalisation, including the intelligent transformation, is followed by the presentation of the research method and results. This chapter is concluded with a discussion and implications.

2. THE GENDER PERSPECTIVE OF ENTREPRENEURSHIP IN DIGITALISATION

Gender equality, driven by women's empowerment (Freeman & Svels, 2022), recognises the equal rights for fair treatment of all individuals, thus, benefiting society by allowing full and equal participation. The progress in achieving gender equality has been made (Bilan et al., 2020; Madsen & Scribner, 2017; Soare et al., 2022); however, there are still some existing aspects of gender disparities that require resolution.

The significant aspect of gender disparity is the gender wage gap (Amado et al., 2018; Coron, 2020; Lips, 2013), which refers to the consistently lower female earnings, compared to male, for performing similar tasks. What is the main concern about the gender wage gap is its persistence despite the fundamental principle in contemporary societies of providing equitable compensation for equivalent work (Amado et al., 2018). The digitalisation of an economy, as the main development trend, does not significantly reduce gender disparities in wages (Zhang, Tian, et al., 2023); in the ICT sector the gender wage gap is approximately 19% (Di Vaio et al., 2023).

Another aspect of gender inequalities is related to women's participation in certain sectors or occupations. The primary labour markets are characterised by their favourable earnings, working conditions, career prospect, etc., compared to secondary sectors, with women being under-represented in primary sectors and over-represented in secondary ones (Damelang & Ebensperger, 2020; Jamali et al., 2008; Mora & Muro, 2015; Symeonaki & Filopoulou, 2017). A significant facet of gender disparity is female under-representation in influential roles such as senior management (Lewellyn & Muller-Kahle, 2020; Madsen & Scribner, 2017; Soare et al., 2022), parliamentary members (Alexander et al., 2016) and entrepreneurship (Gaweł & Mińska-Struzik, 2023; Hägg et al., 2022; Ughetto et al., 2020).

Entrepreneurship is a gendered phenomenon from the quantitative perspective, with men significantly more likely to establish and run their businesses than women (Mustafa & Treanor, 2022) – in the EU countries women on average account for 30% of entrepreneurs (Dilli & Westerhuis, 2018; Ughetto et al., 2020) – and from the qualitative perspective, as female-led businesses are mostly smaller and less profitable than male-led (Reichborn-Kjennerud & Svare, 2014). The cultural perception of stereotypical entrepreneurs associates them with masculinity, primarily that of a white adult male (Jones et al., 2019; Williams & Patterson, 2019).

The uniqueness of the situation of women entrepreneurs with their specific limitations is recognised, along with the need to look for incentives to enter entrepreneurship as a possible manner of gaining empowerment and professional independence (Xu et al., 2023). A significant heterogeneity between men and women is observed regarding the influence of financial literacy and digital skills on the likelihood of becoming an entrepreneur (Oggero et al., 2020). Female entrepreneurs are less likely to attract external financial capital as compared to male entrepreneurs, with the penalising effect of stigma from previous business failures (Morazzoni & Sy, 2022; Pistilli et al., 2022).

Typically, the internal and external factors impacting individual decision to become an entrepreneurship are recognised (Dileo & García Pereiro, 2019; Saunoris & Sajny, 2017), as well as necessity-driven and opportunity-driven factors (Angulo-Guerrero et al., 2017; Nikolaev et al., 2018; Reissová et al., 2020). In the context of women, predictors of female entrepreneurship are recognised among gender-neutral factors similar to those of all entrepreneurs (Holmén et al., 2011), as well as among female-specific factors that reflect their unique circumstances (Dutta & Mallick, 2018; Gaweł & Mroczek-Dąbrowska, 2022; Pérez-Pérez & Avilés-Hernández, 2016). Digitalisation, including intelligent transformation, can be reflected in these aspects of being a potential predictor of female entrepreneurship.

Digitalisation is causing a profound transformation in the business environment (Almansour, 2023; Bansal et al., 2023; Chatterjee et al., 2022). Therefore, digital transformation, including AI technology, impacts business strategies and policies enabling firms to leverage technology for competitiveness (Zhai et al., 2023). The strategic changes brought about by the digitalisation resulted in the notion of digital entrepreneurship, referring to all entrepreneurial activities transferred to the digital sphere (Kraus et al., 2018; Zhai et al., 2023). From this perspective, digitalisation can be treated as a potential external predictor of female entrepreneurship impacting both the market functioning and internal processes of companies.

Coined by computer scientist John McCarthy in 1954, AI pertains to the capacity of an information system to exhibit actions, learning, comprehension and perception (Mariani et al., 2023). AI comprises a range of cognitive technologies, encompassing, for example machine learning or natural language processing (Kuziemski & Misuraca, 2020). AI helps to optimise resources, streamline production, facilitate organisational change, simplify decision-making in uncertainty and reshape business models (Malodia et al., 2023; Zhang, Jin, et al., 2023). Intelligent transformation, which encompasses the spread of AI technology from developers to enterprises, entails adopting AI to change business models towards processes of self-learning, self-optimisation, self-configuration and self-diagnosis (Wang et al., 2022). AI applications mitigate business risks, enhance capabilities and improve efficiency of companies (Drydakis, 2022).

Not only is AI believed to influence organisational resources but it can also extend its positive, long-term benefits to employee's well-being, work–life balance and engagement (Almansour, 2023). The development of AI services is gradually displacing human service providers, resulting in the fusion of products and services (Baek et al., 2023). There are also some wider, societal aspects of the diffusion of AI. For example, through automation, control over physical space, necessary resources and information, AI can be used to enforce citizen control (Kuziemski & Misuraca, 2020).

As AI influences various aspects of life, there is an urgent need to comprehend the novel socio-economic landscapes resulting from its widespread integration (Kuziemski & Misuraca, 2020). This chapter addresses this need and undertakes the investigation on how AI affects female entrepreneurship. The literature review presents contrasting viewpoints on the impact of digitalisation and AI on female entrepreneurship. While the current gender digital divide presents a potential risk of exacerbating gender disparities in entrepreneurship, there is also a perspective that gender digital dividend could hinder the rapid dismantling of gender-related obstacles in entrepreneurship, thereby narrowing the gap.

Digital skills and competences are needed to take advantage of new technologies (Hidalgo et al., 2020). From this perspective, the existence of the gender digital divide (Sánchez-Rivero et al., 2023; Vimalkumar et al., 2021) is a concerning aspect of digitalisation and its impact on female entrepreneurship. The concept of the digital divide, referring to the unequal access to and utilisation of ICT, has developed across three tiers: the first level involves ICT connectivity, the second level encompasses skills and competencies in the use of ICT, and the third level gauges the outcomes arising from the utilisation of the internet (Hidalgo et al., 2020). These three aspects of digital divide are also analysed in the context of gender gap (Picatoste et al., 2023).

Women are recognised as having limited access to digital technologies and infrastructure (Pawluczuk et al., 2021; Yeganehfar et al., 2018). In the context of formal skills and competences, the under-representation of females in the ICT workforce, among Science, Technology, Engineering and Mathematics (STEM) graduates, and at the university-level ICT education is widely observed (Lechman & Popowska, 2022; Patterson et al., 2021; Sattari & Sandefur, 2019; Yeganehfar et al., 2018). According to the data from Eurostat, the statistical office of the European Union, in the EU countries, women account for approximately 20% of employed ICT specialists and students enroled in tertiary education.[1] Additionally, the gender pay gap in the ICT sector is also recognised (Di Vaio et al., 2023). The under-representation of females persists despite the absence of gender-related disparities in STEM academic achievements when considering STEM subject scores, implying rather the stereotypical nature of gender bias and discrimination (Ho et al., 2020). The lower level of digital knowledge and interests, as well as male domination, are the examples of challenges for women operating in digital economic activities (Islam et al., 2023). This aspect of gender disparities in digital

[1]https://ec.europa.eu/eurostat/databrowser/product/page/EDUC_UOE_ENRT03__custom_7186289, https://ec.europa.eu/eurostat/databrowser/view/ISOC_SKS_ITSPS__custom_7162008/default/table, Accessed on 15 August 2023.

competencies can be treated as the individual level predictor of female entrepreneurship.

A common stereotype of males being more capable to STEM (Ho et al., 2020) might also lead to the fact that, compared to women, men more frequently undertake tasks that require 'skills of the future' related to STEM or ICT (Egana-delSol et al., 2022). In addition, ICT specialists are more prevalent in companies with male managers (Sánchez-Rivero et al., 2023). The ICT start-ups demonstrate a limited range of diversity in their workplace, predominantly being founded by young, single, well-educated and middle-class white males (Ferratti et al., 2021).

A consequence of gender stereotypes in the ICT sector is unequal gender participation in the development, implementation and use of ICT (Oleksy et al., 2012; Young et al., 2023), which results in bias in data, algorithms and applications of AI (Allen & Masters, 2020; Lauterbach, 2019; Liang et al., 2021). As men are the mostly likely to get position of AI developers, not women, algorithms of AI are developed being biases towards male perspective, not taking into account female perspective (Cachat-Rosset & Klarsfeld, 2023). By doing so, AI algorithms are also known to cause bias and disadvantageous at the user's side (Liang et al., 2021; Lütz, 2022). In consequences, women are less likely to meet all criteria developed by AI applications when applying for jobs (Kim & Heo, 2022; Kshetri, 2021).

The explanation for the gender digital divide lies in gender stereotypes and the process of gender socialisation, which discourages women from engaging with digital technologies (Sánchez-Rivero et al., 2023). In this context, the importance of training to develop women's digital skills is highlighted in the discussion on bridging the digital divide (Zhang, Tian, et al., 2023), as a factor helping to overcome social stereotypes. In fact, in female entrepreneurship in digital transformation two stereotypes overlap: both of entrepreneurship (Jones et al., 2019; Williams & Patterson, 2019) and the ICT sector (Ho et al., 2020) as stereotypically associated with men. As the impact of entrepreneurs' digital self-efficacy on company digitalisation has been demonstrated (Malodia et al., 2023), the gender digital divide can diminish the digital self-efficacy of female entrepreneurs, consequently impeding the pace of digitalisation within their businesses. Gender-related digital stereotypes can serve as external factors that influence societal norms and their impact on female entrepreneurship.

Access to funding for implementing digital technologies is another obstacle to achieving successful digital and intelligent transformation (Abaddi & AL-Shboul, 2023; Islam et al., 2023). Since female entrepreneurs face fewer opportunities to attract external funds (Pistilli et al., 2022), this barrier can play a significant role in sustaining gender gap in entrepreneurship with the advancement of AI technologies.

Given that the absence of digital competences is proven to be a significant barrier in the integration of AI into the business operations (Wang et al., 2022), the gender digital divide can be an important obstacle for women when establishing and running their own business both directly, by limiting the intelligent transformation of female-led ventures, and indirectly, by diminishing their capacity to engage in collaborative efforts within the intelligent environment. In this context, the gender digital divide can reduce the level of female entrepreneurship.

However, according to the theory of occupational choice, entrepreneurship is sometimes perceived as an alternative occupational choice to wage employment (Capelleras et al., 2019; Pardo & Ruiz-Tagle, 2017). As AI advances, concerns about the future of employment are also on the rise (AlQershi et al., 2023; Egana-delSol et al., 2022). AI algorithms used in human resource management are often biased when job applications are analysed in a way that discriminates against women (Kim & Heo, 2022; Kshetri, 2021). Women face a higher risk of automation due to workplace digitalisation compared to men (Egana-delSol et al., 2022). Being excluded or at the risk of exclusion from the wage employment due to the gender digital divide can serve as a necessity-driven motivation to establish one's own company. This may increase the level of female entrepreneurship, particularly in traditional sectors rather than digital-intensive ones.

There are also findings and arguments suggesting that the process of digitalisation can contribute to promoting greater gender equality and a more unbiased approach to conducting business, thereby overcoming traditional gender barriers and acting as a gender digital dividend (Di Vaio et al., 2023; Gaweł & Mińska-Struzik, 2023; Leong et al., 2022; McAdam et al., 2020; Ughetto et al., 2020). It has been shown that women benefit more from digital transformation compared to men through an increase in employment opportunities for women (Aly, 2022). Digitalisation supports women in their professional careers through its impact on achieving gender equal culture in the workplace (Chen et al., 2021). A new business culture marked by the democratisation of access to resources and the overcoming of traditional entry barriers may increase the number of female entrepreneurs on the internet (Ughetto et al., 2020). There is also evidence that the digital readiness of an economy positively affects women's involvement in entrepreneurship (Moeini Gharagozloo et al., 2023).

The digitalisation of their businesses should support women in fulfiling their business and family roles through more flexible working hours, in reaching the market more easily, and lowering the costs of operations (Alhajri & Aloud, 2023). For example, when considering conversational AI, which enables seamless and natural interactions between humans and computers (Mariani et al., 2023), it can facilitate gender-neutral conversations unlike interpersonal interactions that might be influenced by gendered norms and stereotypes. Digitalisation, including blockchain technology, can support women in financial markets by eliminating the need for physical currency and enhancing access to credit and markets (Di Vaio et al., 2023).

The gender digital dividend can serve as an opportunity-driven motivation for women to enter entrepreneurship. Digitalisation, including the diffusion of AI technologies, can create new opportunities for women to run business more independently and in a more gender-neutral manner, thus gaining a competitive advantage. This may increase the level of female entrepreneurship.

3. METHOD

With all these overlapping and often contradictory arguments in mind, the research aims to investigate the problem whether the diffusion of AI is another obstacle for women entering entrepreneurship or rather the enabler. The cluster analysis is conducted at the macroeconomic level using data from the EU countries. The choice of the EU member states is motivated by their shared institutional background. Despite their national diversity, the EU countries share common values and norms, rooted in the EU institutional environment.

The following 27 countries, all members of the European Union, are included in the research: Austria, Belgium, Bulgaria, Croatia, Cyprus, Czechia, Denmark, Estonia, Finland, France, Germany, Greece, Hungary, Ireland, Italy, Latvia, Lithuania, Luxembourg, Malta, the Netherlands, Poland, Portugal, Romania, Slovakia, Slovenia, Spain and Sweden. The data encompassing female entrepreneurship and the adoption of the AI within companies is utilised to identify the clusters of countries that share similarities within the cluster and distinctions from other clusters in these aspects. All data used in the research are secondary data, sourced in an open-accessed European Statistical Office EUROSTAT database for the year 2021. The choice of the year of study (2021) is motivated by the availability of data on the use of AI in companies. All data used in the research, together with their descriptive statistics, are explained in Table 1.

Female entrepreneurship is understood in this research as the share of women among self-employed. In 2021, the EU national average shows that women account for about 32% of entrepreneurs, oscillating between the minimum value of 23.5% and the maximum value of 40.8%. The diversity of EU countries in the spread of business use of AI is even greater. On average, 8.1% of companies in the European Union use at least one AI technology, ranging from 1.4% to 23.9% depending on a country; while on average 5.9% of them use AI for at least one business purpose, varying between 1.1% and 16.4% depending on a country.

Among the AI technologies, AI technology aimed at robotic process automation and AI technology for written language analysis are most often used by companies operating in the EU countries. AI technology dedicated to automating processes is used by an average of 3.2% of companies in the European Union (depending on the country, it ranges from 0.7% to 16.9%), while AI text mining technology is used by 3% of companies (with differences between countries from 0.4% to 10%). The least widespread AI technology is technology that enables the physical movement of machines, which is used by an average of 1% of companies in the European Union, ranging from 0.1% to 3.6% depending on the country.

Looking at the business purposes, AI technology focused on ICT security is the most widespread, as on average 2.3% of EU companies use this technology, with differences between countries from 0.5% to 8%. The second most explored area of AI use is marketing and sales – 2.2% of companies in the European Union use AI technologies for this purpose. AI technology dedicated to human resources management is the least used, as on average 0.8% of EU companies implement AI in this area of operation, ranging from 0% to 3% of companies depending on the country.

Table 1. Variables' Operationalisation and Their Descriptive Statistics for the EU Countries in 2021.

Acronym	Variable Explanations	Mean	Standard Deviation	Minimum Value	Maximum Value
Female entrepreneurship (FEE)	*Share of women among self-employed, aged 20–64, in %.*	32.563	4.841	23.502	40.816
AI one tech	*'Share of enterprises using at least one of the AI technologies, in %'.*	8.085	5.350	1.400	23.900
AI one purpose	*'Share of enterprises using AI technologies for at least one of the purpose, in %'.*	5.919	4.052	1.100	16.400
AI text mining	*'Share of enterprises using AI technologies performing analysis of written language (text mining), in %'.*	3.026	2.511	0.400	10.000
AI speech recognition	*'Share of enterprises using AI technologies converting spoken language into machine-readable format (speech recognition), in %'.*	1.744	1.104	0.400	4.500
AI natural language generation	*'Share of enterprises using AI technologies generating written or spoken language (natural language generation), in %'.*	1.448	1.121	0.100	5.100
AI images recognition	*'Share of enterprises using AI technologies identifying objects or persons based on images, in %'.*	2.356	1.564	0.400	7.600
AI machine learning for analysis	*'Share of enterprises using machine learning for data analysis, in %'.*	2.726	2.021	0.500	8.800
AI robotic process automation	*'Share of enterprises using AI technologies automating different workflows or assisting in decision-making (AI-based software robotic process automation), in %'.*	3.189	3.261	0.700	16.900
AI physical movement	*'Share of enterprises using AI technologies enabling physical movement of machines via autonomous decisions based on observation of surroundings, in %'.*	0.956	0.783	0.100	3.600
AI marketing or sales	*'Share of enterprises using AI technologies for marketing or sales, in %'.*	2.152	1.593	0.500	6.700
AI production processes	*'Share of enterprises using AI technologies for production processes, in %'.*	1.815	1.198	0.400	4.900
AI business administration processes	*'Share of enterprises using AI technologies for organisation of business administration processes, in %'.*	2.022	1.590	0.400	6.400
AI management	*'Share of enterprises using AI technologies for management of enterprises, in %'.*	1.563	1.778	0.200	9.000
AI logistics	*'Share of enterprises using AI technologies for logistics, in %'.*	0.900	0.788	0.300	3.800

(Continued)

Table 1. *(Continued)*

Acronym	Variable Explanations	Mean	Standard Deviation	Minimum Value	Maximum Value
AI ICT security	*'Share of enterprises using AI technologies for ICT security, in %'.*	2.296	1.887	0.500	8.000
AI HRM	*'Share of enterprises using AI technologies for human resources management or recruiting, in %'.*	0.796	0.787	0.000	3.000

Source: Own based on methodology and data from Eurostat.

The diversity of EU countries, both in terms of women's entrepreneurship and the diffusion of AI technologies, justifies grouping them into clusters with similar characteristics within each cluster and different from other clusters. Through the use of cluster analysis, different patterns of female entrepreneurship and the spread of AI are to be uncovered. The k-means clustering method is used, with the number of clusters determined by Ward's minimum variance technique, assuming the significance level of $p < 0.05$.

As there are data on three aspects of the AI technology diffusion (the general aspect of AI diffusion, the usage of diverse AI technologies and the use of AI for different business purposes), the cluster analyses are conducted on these three aspects. The first cluster analysis is grounded in data concerning female entrepreneurship and the overall extent of AI adoption within companies. The second cluster analysis is founded on data related to female entrepreneurship and detailed measures regarding AI technologies. The third clustering is based on data on female entrepreneurship and AI application for various business purposes.

4. RESULTS

4.1 General Aspects of AI Diffusion

In the first cluster analysis, three variables are taken to identify the clusters for the EU countries: female entrepreneurship (FEE), the share of companies using at least one AI technology (AI one tech) and the share of companies using AI technology for at least one purpose (AI one purpose). Based on these three variables, while using the k-means clustering method (Table 2), three clusters of EU countries are identified.

Looking at the descriptive statistics of these clusters (Table 3), cluster# 1 is characterised by the highest level of female entrepreneurship (on average in countries belonging to cluster# 1, women account for 36.4% of entrepreneurs), while cluster# 2 by the lowest (28.2% of entrepreneurs are women). The level of AI diffusion is relatively low, significantly lower than in cluster# 3, with, on average, 6.7% of companies using at least one AI technology and 4.4% using at least one business purpose in cluster# 1, and with 5.7% of companies using at least one AI technology and 4.2% using at least one business purpose in

Table 2. The Between and Within Cluster Variance for Female Entrepreneurship, and General Aspects Of AI Diffusion Based on the EU Countries' Data in 2021.

Variable	Between Clusters	Df	Within Clusters	df	*F*-value	*p* Value
FEE	376.479	2	232.839	24	19.403	0.000010
AI one tech	426.609	2	317.545	24	16.122	0.000036
AI one purpose	313.291	2	113.610	24	33.091	0.000000

Source: Own based on data from Eurostat.

Table 3. Descriptive Statistics of Clusters Based on Female Entrepreneurship and General Aspects of AI Diffusion Based on the EU Countries' Data in 2021.

	Cluster# 1 (*N* = 11)		Cluster# 2 (*N* = 11)		Cluster# 3 (*N* = 5)	
Variable	*M*	SD	*M*	SD	*M*	SD
FEE	36.449	2.806	28.239	2.927	33.528	4.135
AI one tech	6.745	3.594	5.664	3.131	16.360	4.754
AI one purpose	4.418	1.842	4.173	2.078	13.060	3.022

Source: Own based on data from Eurostat.

Note: M – mean value, SD – standard deviation.

cluster# 2. The last identified cluster# 3 is characterised by a moderate level of female entrepreneurship compared to other two clusters (women account for 33.5% of entrepreneurs) and the highest level of the AI diffusion, as, on average, 16.4% of companies in the countries belonging to cluster# 3 utilise at least one AI technology and 13% of them explore AI technology for at least one business purpose (Table 4).

4.2 Female Entrepreneurship and the Diffusion of AI Technologies

In the second approach to cluster research, i.e. identifying the clusters, data on female entrepreneurship (FEE) and on the diffusion of various AI technologies among enterprises operating in the EU countries is used. Specifically, the following are considered: AI technologies for the analysis of written language (AI text mining), for converting spoken language into machine-readable format (AI speech recognition), for generating written or spoken language (AI natural language generation), for identifying objects or persons based on images (AI images recognition), for machine learning for data analysis (AI machine learning for analysis), for automating different workflows or assisting in decision-making (AI robotic process automation) and for enabling the physical movement of machines (AI physical movement). While using the k-means clustering method, the variable presenting the diffusion of AI technology identifying objects or persons based on images (AI images recognition) proved to be statistically significant in grouping countries. Thus, it was withdrawn and the k-means clustering method was

Table 4. The Between and Within Cluster Variance for Female Entrepreneurship and the Diffusion of AI Technologies Based on the EU Countries' Data in 2021.

Variable	Between Clusters	Df	Within Clusters	df	*F*-value	*p* Value
FEE	425.839	2	183.479	24	27.851	0.000001
AI text mining	46.421	2	117.571	24	4.738	0.018439
AI speech recognition	7.607	2	24.060	24	3.794	0.037009
AI natural language generation	11.448	2	21.200	24	6.480	0.005621
AI machine learning for analysis	49.530	2	56.682	24	10.486	0.000534
AI robotic process automation	199.296	2	77.211	24	30.974	0.000000
AI physical movement	9.168	2	6.758	24	16.279	0.000034

Source: Own based on data from Eurostat.

repeated with one variable less. This allowed us to identify three clusters of EU countries (Table 4).

The descriptive statistics on FEE and on the diffusion of different AI technologies among enterprises operating in the EU countries in the identified clusters are presented in Table 5. Cluster# 1 is characterised by the highest representation of women among entrepreneurs (on average 36.6%), and relatively low levels of all AI technologies' diffusion, and the lowest level of diffusion of AI technologies for generating written or spoken language. Cluster# 2 is the one with the lowest participation of females in entrepreneurship (on average, women account for 28.3% of entrepreneurs in the countries belonging to this cluster), and with the lowest diffusion of almost all AI technologies (0.6%–2.1% of companies using various AI technologies). In countries belonging to cluster# 3, the level of spread of all AI technologies is the highest (from 2.9% to 12.8% of companies in countries belonging to this cluster use AI technologies, depending on the type of technology). At the same time, the level of female entrepreneurship in the

Table 5. Descriptive Statistics of Clusters Based on Female Entrepreneurship and the Diffusion of AI Technologies Based on the EU Countries' Data in 2021.

	Cluster# 1 (*N* = 13)		Cluster# 2 (*N* = 12)		Cluster# 3 (*N* = 2)	
Variable	*M*	SD	*M*	SD	*M*	SD
FEE	36.575	2.735	28.322	2.806	31.937	2.667
AI text mining	3.508	2.884	1.883	1.110	6.750	2.051
AI speech recognition	1.862	1.248	1.342	0.678	3.400	0.566
AI natural language generation	1.254	0.698	1.275	1.031	3.750	1.909
AI machine learning for analysis	2.569	1.579	2.108	1.450	7.450	1.909
AI robotic process automation	2.685	1.418	2.142	1.302	12.750	5.869
AI physical movement	0.992	0.591	0.592	0.380	2.900	0.990

Source: Own based on data from Eurostat.

Note: M – mean value, SD – standard deviation.

countries in this cluster is moderate; on average, 31.9% of entrepreneurs are women.

4.3 Female Entrepreneurship and the Diffusion of AI Purposes

In the last clustering, FEE is considered together with the diffusion of various purposes of the business use of AI technologies', including the use for marketing or sales, production processes, business administration processes, management, logistics, ICT security and human resource management. The introduction of k-means cluster method allows to identify three clusters of EU countries (Table 6).

The descriptive statistics of the clusters (Table 7) show the diversity of the clusters. In the countries belonging to cluster# 1, the level of female

Table 6. The Between and Within Cluster Variance for Female Entrepreneurship and the Diffusion of AI Purposes Based on the EU Countries' Data in 2021.

Variable	Between Clusters	Df	Within Clusters	Df	*F*-value	*p* Value
FEE	398.586	2	210.732	24	22.697	0.000003
AI marketing or sales	49.707	2	16.241	24	36.728	0.000000
AI production processes	26.826	2	10.509	24	30.633	0.000000
AI business administration processes	43.708	2	22.039	24	23.799	0.000002
AI management	42.639	2	39.564	24	12.933	0.000155
AI logistics	10.570	2	5.570	24	22.773	0.000003
AI ICT security	27.977	2	64.633	24	5.194	0.013353
AI HRM	9.586	2	6.524	24	17.632	0.000019

Source: Own based on data from Eurostat.

Table 7. Descriptive Statistics of Clusters Based on Female Entrepreneurship and the Diffusion of AI Purposes Based on the EU Countries' Data in 2021.

	Cluster# 1 (N = 11)		Cluster# 2 (N = 12)		Cluster# 3 (N = 4)	
Variable	*M*	SD	*M*	SD	*M*	SD
FEE	36.449	2.806	28.322	2.806	34.600	3.889
AI marketing or sales	1.382	0.517	1.783	0.992	5.375	0.957
AI production processes	1.327	0.557	1.467	0.754	4.200	0.622
AI business administration processes	1.673	0.914	1.333	0.713	5.050	1.642
AI management	1.082	0.477	1.000	0.739	4.575	3.229
AI logistics	0.655	0.305	0.625	0.317	2.400	1.086
AI ICT security	1.582	0.914	2.1667	2.100	4.650	1.609
AI HRM	0.555	0.250	0.542	0.610	2.225	0.776

Source: own based on data from Eurostat.

Note: M – mean value, SD – standard deviation.

entrepreneurship is the highest, as, on average, women account for 36.4% of entrepreneurs. However, the level of use of AI technologies for different business purposes is relatively low here, ranging from 0.6% to 1.7% of companies exploring AI technologies, depending on the business purpose. Cluster# 2 is also characterised by a low level of prevalence of the use of AI technologies for business purposes, as between 0.5% and 2.2% of companies use them, depending on the purpose. In this cluster, the level of female entrepreneurship is the lowest, as women represent 28.3% of entrepreneurs. In cluster# 3, the spread of AI technology use for business purposes is the highest, with 2.2%–5.4% of companies using AI technology depending on the purpose. This cluster is also characterised by moderate levels of female entrepreneurship, accounting for 34.6% of entrepreneurs.

5. DISCUSSION AND IMPLICATIONS

The cluster analysis shows a relationship between the female entrepreneurship level and the diffusion of AI technology in business, with an inverted U-shaped pattern. Three clusters of the EU countries are identified in all three research attitudes. Regardless of the attitude towards the measures of AI diffusion, the similar patterns are discovered. A relatively low level of diffusion of AI technology occurs in two clusters of countries, where one of these clusters is characterised by a relatively low level of female entrepreneurship, while the other cluster has a relatively high level of female entrepreneurship. The highest level of the utilisation of AI technology is observed in the third cluster of countries, exhibiting a moderate level of female entrepreneurship.

The discovery of an inverted U-shaped relationship between female entrepreneurship and the diffusion of AI technology in business sheds new light on the previously conflicting results. Both concerns rooted in the gender digital divide (Lechman & Popowska, 2022; Patterson et al., 2021; Pawluczuk et al., 2021; Sánchez-Rivero et al., 2023; Sattari & Sandefur, 2019; Vimalkumar et al., 2021; Yeganehfar et al., 2018), regarding the possible deepening of the gender gap in entrepreneurship within the context of digital and intelligent transformation, and the belief in the gender equalising effect of digitalisation (Aly, 2022; Chen et al., 2021; Di Vaio et al., 2023; Leong et al., 2022; McAdam et al., 2020; Ughetto et al., 2020), might be correct, as it appears that this relationship is multidimensional and dependent on the level of AI diffusion.

There is a need for diverse policies and practices due to the variety of patterns in female entrepreneurship and the spread of AI technology in EU countries. The integration of the female perspective into the diffusion of AI is needed to explore the AI technology for the sake of a more sustainable society. Risk factors that could potentially exclude women from entrepreneurship due to AI technology exist and must be pre-emptively addressed as AI continues to advance. Nonetheless, there are instances of countries successfully managing both the implementation of AI and the attraction of women to entrepreneurship.

The results of the research contribute to a better understanding of intelligent transformation and its societal impacts. The inverted U-shaped pattern of the interrelationship between the spread of AI technologies in business and female entrepreneurship sheds light on the multidimensional and country-specific nature of the diffusion of AI, and, most likely, of digitalisation as well. Given that the progress of intelligent transformation can lead to both the deepening and equalising of the gender gap in entrepreneurship, there is a need for social awareness and efforts to ensure that intelligent transformation benefits all, fostering more equal and just societies. The results of clustering indicate the need of country-specific actions supporting different social groups in the digital transformation, as recommended by Egana-delSol et al. (2022).

The results also contribute to the theory of entrepreneurship, particularly in explaining the gender gap in entrepreneurship. Women entrepreneurs are embedded within the social and business context, influenced by external factors in the entrepreneurial environment. The importance of the diffusion of AI technology as an external factor resulting in women's engagement in entrepreneurship is indicated. The results of cluster analyses show the diverse responses of women entrepreneurs to the diffusion of AI, advocating for a more contextual and country-specific understanding of the impact of external factors on women's decisions to become entrepreneurs.

To fully benefit from intelligent transformation, the digital divide should be reduced. In line with the recommendation for specific policy action to reduce the digital divide (Hidalgo et al., 2020), the results imply the need for training and education programmes dedicated to female entrepreneurs and to all entrepreneurs with a lower level of digital competences. Training programmes should focus on empowering under-represented groups with limited digital exposure, such as female entrepreneurs, by enhancing their digital skills and competence in utilising AI technologies for their businesses. These programmes should aim not only to raise the level of digital knowledge and skills but also to address and overcome gender digital stereotypes.

Other ways to reduce the gender digital divide and overcome gender-related obstacles in intelligent transformation can involve providing consulting and implementation services tailored to the utilisation of AI technology for female entrepreneurs and all entrepreneurs with lower levels of digital competence. Promoting knowledge and awareness of the possibilities of using AI in business, especially for female entrepreneurs and those with lower levels of digital competence, can also be supportive. An inclusive, easy-to-implement and user-friendly AI application can help reduce competency barriers in the adoption of AI as well.

REFERENCES

Abaddi, S., & AL-Shboul, M. A. (2023). "Revealing the hidden" – Challenges facing early digital entrepreneurs in Jordan. *Management & Sustainability: An Arab Review*. https://doi.org/10.1108/MSAR-02-2023-0011

Alexander, A. C., Bolzendahl, C., & Jalalzai, F. (2016). Defining women's global political empowerment: Theories and evidence: Measuring women's global political empowerment. *Sociology Compass*, *10*(6), 432–441. https://doi.org/10.1111/soc4.12375

Alhajri, A., & Aloud, M. (2023). Female digital entrepreneurship: A structured literature review. *International Journal of Entrepreneurial Behavior and Research*. https://doi.org/10.1108/IJEBR-09-2022-0790

Allen, R., & Masters, D. (2020). Artificial Intelligence: The right to protection from discrimination caused by algorithms, machine learning and automated decision-making. *ERA Forum*, *20*(4), 585–598. https://doi.org/10.1007/s12027-019-00582-w

Almansour, M. (2023). Artificial intelligence and resource optimization: A study of Fintech start-ups. *Resources Policy*, *80*, 103250. https://doi.org/10.1016/j.resourpol.2022.103250

AlQershi, N., Saufi, R. B. A., Yaziz, M. F. B. A., Permarupan, P. Y., Muhammad, N. M. N., Yusoff, M. N. H. B., & Ramayah, T. (2023). The threat of robots to career sustainability, and the pivotal role of knowledge management and human capital. *Journal of Innovation & Knowledge*, *8*(3), 100386. https://doi.org/10.1016/j.jik.2023.100386

Aly, H. (2022). Digital transformation, development and productivity in developing countries: Is artificial intelligence a curse or a blessing? *Review of Economics and Political Science*, *7*(4), 238–256. https://doi.org/10.1108/REPS-11-2019-0145

Amado, C. A. F., Santos, S. P., & São José, J. M. S. (2018). Measuring and decomposing the gender pay gap: A new frontier approach. *European Journal of Operational Research*, *271*(1), 357–373. https://doi.org/10.1016/j.ejor.2018.05.023

Angulo-Guerrero, M. J., Pérez-Moreno, S., & Abad-Guerrero, I. M. (2017). How economic freedom affects opportunity and necessity entrepreneurship in the OECD countries. *Journal of Business Research*, *73*, 30–37. https://doi.org/10.1016/j.jbusres.2016.11.017

Baek, C. H., Kim, S.-Y., Lim, S. U., & Xiong, J. (2023). Quality evaluation model of artificial intelligence service for startups. *International Journal of Entrepreneurial Behavior & Research*, *29*(4), 913–940. https://doi.org/10.1108/IJEBR-03-2021-0223

Bansal, A., Panchal, T., Jabeen, F., Mangla, S. K., & Singh, G. (2023). A study of human resource digital transformation (HRDT): A phenomenon of innovation capability led by digital and individual factors. *Journal of Business Research*, *157*, 113611. https://doi.org/10.1016/j.jbusres.2022.113611

Bilan, Y., Mishchuk, H., Samoliuk, N., & Mishchuk, V. (2020). Gender discrimination and its links with compensations and benefits practices in enterprises. *Entrepreneurial Business and Economics Review*, *8*(3), 189–204. https://doi.org/10.15678/EBER.2020.080311

Cachat-Rosset, G., & Klarsfeld, A. (2023). Diversity, equity, and inclusion in artificial intelligence: An evaluation of guidelines. *Applied Artificial Intelligence*, *37*(1), 2176618. https://doi.org/10.1080/08839514.2023.2176618

Capelleras, J.-L., Contin-Pilart, I., Larraza-Kintana, M., & Martin-Sanchez, V. (2019). Entrepreneurs' human capital and growth aspirations: The moderating role of regional entrepreneurial culture. *Small Business Economics*, *52*(1), 3–25. https://doi.org/10.1007/s11187-017-9985-0

Chatterjee, S., Chaudhuri, R., Vrontis, D., & Thrassou, A. (2022). SME entrepreneurship and digitalization – The potentialities and moderating role of demographic factors. *Technological Forecasting and Social Change*, *179*, 121648. https://doi.org/10.1016/j.techfore.2022.121648

Chen, F., Liu, Z., Cui, W., Han, S., & Jiang, N. (2021). The impact of digital transformation on female career development: Dividends or divide? An empirical analysis based on the World Bank Survey Data on Chinese manufacturing companies. *Asia Pacific Journal of Human Resources*. https://doi.org/10.1111/1744-7941.12318

Coron, C. (2020). What does "gender equality" mean? Social representations of gender equality in the workplace among French workers. *Equality, Diversity and Inclusion: An International Journal*, *39*(8), 825–847. https://doi.org/10.1108/EDI-06-2019-0185

Damelang, A., & Ebensperger, S. (2020). Gender composition of occupations and occupational characteristics: Explaining their true relationship by using longitudinal data. *Social Science Research*, *86*, 102394. https://doi.org/10.1016/j.ssresearch.2019.102394

Di Vaio, A., Hassan, R., & Palladino, R. (2023). Blockchain technology and gender equality: A systematic literature review. *International Journal of Information Management*, *68*, 102517. https://doi.org/10.1016/j.ijinfomgt.2022.102517

Dileo, I., & García Pereiro, T. (2019). Assessing the impact of individual and context factors on the entrepreneurial process. A cross-country multilevel approach. *The International Entrepreneurship and Management Journal*, *15*(4), 1393–1441. https://doi.org/10.1007/s11365-018-0528-1

Dilli, S., & Westerhuis, G. (2018). How institutions and gender differences in education shape entrepreneurial activity: A cross-national perspective. *Small Business Economics*, *51*(2), 371–392. https://doi.org/10.1007/s11187-018-0004-x

Drydakis, N. (2022). Artificial intelligence and reduced SMEs' business risks. A dynamic capabilities analysis during the COVID-19 Pandemic. *Information Systems Frontiers*, *24*(4), 1223–1247. https://doi.org/10.1007/s10796-022-10249-6

Dutta, N., & Mallick, S. (2018). Enabling women entrepreneurs: Exploring factors that mitigate the negative impact of fertility rates on female entrepreneurship: Enabling women entrepreneurs: Exploring factors that mitigate the negative impact of fertility rates on female entrepreneurship. *Kyklos*, *71*(3), 402–432. https://doi.org/10.1111/kykl.12175

Egana-delSol, P., Bustelo, M., Ripani, L., Soler, N., & Viollaz, M. (2022). Automation in Latin America: Are women at higher risk of losing their jobs? *Technological Forecasting and Social Change*, *175*, 121333. https://doi.org/10.1016/j.techfore.2021.121333

Ferratti, G. M., Sacomano Neto, M., & Candido, S. E. A. (2021). Controversies in an information technology startup: A critical actor-network analysis of the entrepreneurial process. *Technology in Society*, *66*, 101623. https://doi.org/10.1016/j.techsoc.2021.101623

Freeman, R., & Svels, K. (2022). Women's empowerment in small-scale fisheries: The impact of Fisheries Local Action Groups. *Marine Policy*, *136*, 104907. https://doi.org/10.1016/j.marpol.2021.104907

Gaweł, A., & Mińska-Struzik, E. (2023). The digitalisation as gender equaliser? The import and export of digitally delivered services in shaping female entrepreneurship in European countries. *International Journal of Gender and Entrepreneurship*. https://doi.org/10.1108/IJGE-08-2022-0141

Gaweł, A., & Mroczek-Dąbrowska, K. (2022). Gender pay gap in explaining female entrepreneurship – Industry perspective of selected European countries. *International Journal of Manpower*, *43*(9), 42–59. https://doi.org/10.1108/IJM-12-2020-0554

Hägg, G., Politis, D., & Alsos, G. A. (2022). Does gender balance in entrepreneurship education make a difference to prospective start-up behaviour? *Education + Training*. https://doi.org/10.1108/ET-06-2021-0204

Hidalgo, A., Gabaly, S., Morales-Alonso, G., & Urueña, A. (2020). The digital divide in light of sustainable development: An approach through advanced machine learning techniques. *Technological Forecasting and Social Change*, *150*, 119754. https://doi.org/10.1016/j.techfore.2019.119754

Ho, M.-T., La, V.-P., Nguyen, M.-H., Pham, T.-H., Vuong, T.-T., Vuong, H.-M., Pham, H.-H., Hoang, A.-D., & Vuong, Q.-H. (2020). An analytical view on STEM education and outcomes: Examples of the social gap and gender disparity in Vietnam. *Children and Youth Services Review*, *119*, 105650. https://doi.org/10.1016/j.childyouth.2020.105650

Holmén, M., Min, T. T., & Saarelainen, E. (2011). Female entrepreneurship in Afghanistan. *Journal of Developmental Entrepreneurship*, *16*(03), 307–331. https://doi.org/10.1142/S1084946711001860

Islam, M. A., Hossain, M. S., Pullen, E., & Rahman, M. (2023). Unlocking the potential of women in a male dominated society: Key challenges and solutions in integrating women in digital economic activities. *Business Strategy & Development*, *bsd2*, 255. https://doi.org/10.1002/bsd2.255

Jamali, D., Sidani, Y., & Kobeissi, A. (2008). The gender pay gap revisited: Insights from a developing country context. *Gender in Management: International Journal*, *23*(4), 230–246. https://doi.org/10.1108/17542410810878059

Jones, S., Martinez Dy, A., & Vershinina, N. (2019). 'We were fighting for our place': Resisting gender knowledge regimes through feminist knowledge network formation. *Gender, Work and Organization*, *26*(6), 789–804. https://doi.org/10.1111/gwao.12288

Kim, J.-Y., & Heo, W. (2022). Artificial intelligence video interviewing for employment: Perspectives from applicants, companies, developer and academicians. *Information Technology & People*, *35*(3), 861–878. https://doi.org/10.1108/ITP-04-2019-0173

Kraus, S., Palmer, C., Kailer, N., Kallinger, F. L., & Spitzer, J. (2018). Digital entrepreneurship: A research agenda on new business models for the twenty-first century. *International Journal of Entrepreneurial Behavior & Research*. https://doi.org/10.1108/IJEBR-06-2018-0425

Kshetri, N. (2021). Evolving uses of artificial intelligence in human resource management in emerging economies in the global South: Some preliminary evidence. *Management Research Review*, *44*(7), 970–990. https://doi.org/10.1108/MRR-03-2020-0168

Kuziemski, M., & Misuraca, G. (2020). AI governance in the public sector: Three tales from the frontiers of automated decision-making in democratic settings. *Telecommunications Policy*, *44*(6), 101976. https://doi.org/10.1016/j.telpol.2020.101976

Lauterbach, A. (2019). Artificial intelligence and policy: Quo vadis? *Digital Policy, Regulation and Governance*, *21*(3), 238–263. https://doi.org/10.1108/DPRG-09-2018-0054

Lechman, E., & Popowska, M. (2022). Overcoming gender bias in the digital economy. Empirical evidence for European countries. *Gender, Technology and Development*, *26*(3), 404–436. https://doi.org/10.1080/09718524.2022.2127064

Leong, C., Tan, F. T. C., Tan, B., & Faisal, F. (2022). The emancipatory potential of digital entrepreneurship: A study of financial technology-driven inclusive growth. *Information & Management*, *59*(3), 103384. https://doi.org/10.1016/j.im.2020.103384

Lewellyn, K. B., & Muller-Kahle, M. I. (2020). The corporate board glass ceiling: The role of empowerment and culture in shaping board gender diversity. *Journal of Business Ethics*, *165*(2), 329–346. https://doi.org/10.1007/s10551-019-04116-9

Liang, T.-P., Robert, L., Sarker, S., Cheung, C. M. K., Matt, C., Trenz, M., & Turel, O. (2021). Artificial intelligence and robots in individuals' lives: How to align technological possibilities and ethical issues. *Internet Research*, *31*(1), 1–10. https://doi.org/10.1108/INTR-11-2020-0668

Lips, H. M. (2013). The gender pay gap: Challenging the rationalizations. Perceived equity, discrimination, and the limits of human capital models. *Sex Roles*, *68*(3–4), 169–185. https://doi.org/10.1007/s11199-012-0165-z

Lütz, F. (2022). Gender equality and artificial intelligence in Europe. Addressing direct and indirect impacts of algorithms on gender-based discrimination. *ERA Forum*, *23*(1), 33–52. https://doi.org/10.1007/s12027-022-00709-6

Madsen, S. R., & Scribner, R. T. (2017). A perspective on gender in management. *Cross Cultural & Strategic Management*, *24*(2), 231–250. https://doi.org/10.1108/CCSM-05-2016-0101

Malodia, S., Mishra, M., Fait, M., Papa, A., & Dezi, L. (2023). To digit or to head? Designing digital transformation journey of SMEs among digital self-efficacy and professional leadership. *Journal of Business Research*, *157*, 113547. https://doi.org/10.1016/j.jbusres.2022.113547

Mariani, M. M., Hashemi, N., & Wirtz, J. (2023). Artificial intelligence empowered conversational agents: A systematic literature review and research agenda. *Journal of Business Research*, *161*, 113838. https://doi.org/10.1016/j.jbusres.2023.113838

McAdam, M., Crowley, C., & Harrison, R. T. (2020). Digital girl: Cyberfeminism and the emancipatory potential of digital entrepreneurship in emerging economies. *Small Business Economics*, *55*(2), 349–362. https://doi.org/10.1007/s11187-019-00301-2

Moeini Gharagozloo, M. M., Forghani Bajestani, M., Moeini Gharagozloo, A., Amini Sedeh, A., & Askarzadeh, F. (2023). The role of digitalization in decreasing gender gap in opportunity driven entrepreneurship. *Information Technology for Development*, 1–20. https://doi.org/10.1080/02681102.2023.2237470

Moon, M. J. (2023). Searching for inclusive artificial intelligence for social good: Participatory governance and policy recommendations for making AI more inclusive and benign for society. *Public Administration Review*, 13648. https://doi.org/10.1111/puar.13648

Mora, J. J., & Muro, J. (2015). Labor market segmentation in a developing country. *The Indian Journal of Labour Economics*, *58*(3), 477–486. https://doi.org/10.1007/s41027-016-0024-5

Morazzoni, M., & Sy, A. (2022). Female entrepreneurship, financial frictions and capital misallocation in the US. *Journal of Monetary Economics*, *129*, 93–118. https://doi.org/10.1016/j.jmoneco.2022.03.007

Mustafa, M., & Treanor, L. (2022). Gender and entrepreneurship in the new era: New perspectives on the role of gender and entrepreneurial activity. *Entrepreneurship Research Journal*, *12*(3), 213–226. https://doi.org/10.1515/erj-2022-0228

Nikolaev, B. N., Boudreaux, C. J., & Palich, L. (2018). Cross-country determinants of early-stage necessity and opportunity-motivated entrepreneurship: Accounting for model uncertainty. *Journal of Small Business Management*, *56*, 243–280. https://doi.org/10.1111/jsbm.12400

Oggero, N., Rossi, M. C., & Ughetto, E. (2020). Entrepreneurial spirits in women and men. The role of financial literacy and digital skills. *Small Business Economics*, *55*(2), 313–327. https://doi.org/10.1007/s11187-019-00299-7

Oleksy, W., Just, E., & Zapedowska-Kling, K. (2012). Gender issues in information and communication technologies (ICTs). *Journal of Information, Communication and Ethics in Society*, *10*(2), 107–120. https://doi.org/10.1108/14779961211227010

Pardo, C., & Ruiz-Tagle, J. (2017). The dynamic role of specific experience in the selection of self-employment versus wage-employment. *Oxford Economic Papers*, *69*(1), 189–212. https://doi.org/10.1093/oep/gpw047

Patterson, L., Varadarajan, D. S., & Saji Salim, B. (2021). Women in STEM/SET: Gender gap research review of the United Arab Emirates (UAE) – A meta-analysis. *Gender in Management: An International Journal*, *36*(8), 881–911. https://doi.org/10.1108/GM-11-2019-0201

Pawluczuk, A., Lee, J., & Gamundani, A. M. (2021). Bridging the gender digital divide: An analysis of existing guidance for gender digital inclusion programmes' evaluations. *Digital Policy, Regulation and Governance*, *23*(3), 287–299. https://doi.org/10.1108/DPRG-11-2020-0158

Pérez-Pérez, C., & Avilés-Hernández, M. (2016). Explanatory factors of female entrepreneurship and limiting elements. *Suma de Negocios*, *7*(15), 25–31. https://doi.org/10.1016/j.sumneg.2015.12.004

Picatoste, X., Mesquita, A., & González-Laxe, F. (2023). Gender wage gap, quality of earnings and gender digital divide in the European context. *Empirica*, *50*(2), 301–321. https://doi.org/10.1007/s10663-022-09555-8

Pistilli, L., Paccagnini, A., Breschi, S., & Malerba, F. (2022). Gender bias in entrepreneurship: What is the role of the founders' entrepreneurial background? *Journal of Business Ethics*. https://doi.org/10.1007/s10551-022-05275-y

Reichborn-Kjennerud, K., & Svare, H. (2014). Entrepreneurial growth strategies: The female touch. *International Journal of Gender and Entrepreneurship*, *6*(2), 181–199. https://doi.org/10.1108/IJGE-04-2013-0043

Reissová, A., Šimsová, J., Sonntag, R., & Kučerová, K. (2020). The influence of personal characteristics on entrepreneurial intentions: International comparison. *Entrepreneurial Business and Economics Review*, *8*(4), 29–46. https://doi.org/10.15678/EBER.2020.080402

Sánchez-Rivero, M., Gutiérrez-Fernández, M., Fernández-Torres, Y., & Gallego-Sosa, C. (2023). A gender-oriented analysis of digital skills and ICT use intensity in tourism companies in Extremadura (Spain). *Gender in Management: An International Journal*. https://doi.org/10.1108/GM-04-2022-0147

Sattari, N., & Sandefur, R. L. (2019). Gender in academic STEM: A focus on men faculty. *Gender, Work and Organization*, *26*(2), 158–179. https://doi.org/10.1111/gwao.12249

Saunoris, J. W., & Sajny, A. (2017). Entrepreneurship and economic freedom: Cross-country evidence from formal and informal sectors. *Entrepreneurship & Regional Development*, *29*(3–4), 292–316. https://doi.org/10.1080/08985626.2016.1267806

Soare, T.-M., Detilleux, C., & Deschacht, N. (2022). The impact of the gender composition of company boards on firm performance. *International Journal of Productivity and Performance Management*, *71*(5), 1611–1624. https://doi.org/10.1108/IJPPM-02-2020-0073

Symeonaki, M., & Filopoulou, C. (2017). Quantifying gender distances in education, occupation and employment. *Equality, Diversity and Inclusion: An International Journal*, *36*(4), 340–361. https://doi.org/10.1108/EDI-11-2016-0106

Ughetto, E., Rossi, M., Audretsch, D., & Lehmann, E. E. (2020). Female entrepreneurship in the digital era. *Small Business Economics*, *55*(2), 305–312. https://doi.org/10.1007/s11187-019-00298-8

Vimalkumar, M., Singh, J. B., & Gouda, S. K. (2021). Contextualizing the relationship between gender and computer self-efficacy: An empirical study from India. *Information and Management*, *58*(4), 103464. https://doi.org/10.1016/j.im.2021.103464

Wach, K., Duong, C. D., Ejdys, J., Kazlauskaitė, R., Korzynski, P., Mazurek, G., Paliszkiewicz, J., & Ziemba, E. (2023). The dark side of generative artificial intelligence: A critical analysis of controversies and risks of ChatGPT. *Entrepreneurial Business and Economics Review*, *11*(2), 7–30. https://doi.org/10.15678/EBER.2023.110201

Wang, J., Lu, Y., Fan, S., Hu, P., & Wang, B. (2022). How to survive in the age of artificial intelligence? Exploring the intelligent transformations of SMEs in central China. *International Journal of Emerging Markets*, *17*(4), 1143–1162. https://doi.org/10.1108/IJOEM-06-2021-0985

Williams, J., & Patterson, N. (2019). New directions for entrepreneurship through a gender and disability lens. *International Journal of Entrepreneurial Behavior & Research*, *25*(8), 1706–1726. https://doi.org/10.1108/IJEBR-12-2017-0499

Xu, L., Parboteeah, K. P., & Fang, H. (2023). Jump to platform faster? Gender, institutional change, and pre-entrant entrepreneurial attempt. *New England Journal of Entrepreneurship*. https://doi.org/10.1108/NEJE-06-2022-0040

Yeganehfar, M., Zarei, A., Isfandyari-Mogghadam, A. R., & Famil-Rouhani, A. (2018). Justice in technology policy: A systematic review of gender divide literature and the marginal contribution of women on ICT. *Journal of Information, Communication and Ethics in Society*, *16*(2), 123–137. https://doi.org/10.1108/JICES-06-2017-0038

Young, E., Wajcman, J., & Sprejer, L. (2023). Mind the gender gap: Inequalities in the emergent professions of artificial intelligence (AI) and data science. *New Technology, Work and Employment*, 12278. https://doi.org/10.1111/ntwe.12278

Zhai, Y., Yang, K., Chen, L., Lin, H., Yu, M., & Jin, R. (2023). Digital entrepreneurship: Global maps and trends of research. *Journal of Business & Industrial Marketing*, *38*(3), 637–655. https://doi.org/10.1108/JBIM-05-2021-0244

Zhang, C., Tian, X., Yang, X., Xu, B., & Li, Q. (2023). The iron-out effect of digital economy: A discussion on gender wage rate discrimination for working hours. *Journal of Business Research*, *156*, 113399. https://doi.org/10.1016/j.jbusres.2022.113399

Zhang, Z., Jin, J., Li, S., & Zhang, Y. (2023). Digital transformation of incumbent firms from the perspective of portfolios of innovation. *Technology in Society*, *72*, 102149. https://doi.org/10.1016/j.techsoc.2022.102149

UNDERSTANDING THE LOCATION OF WOMEN IN SCIENCE THROUGH FEMINIST LENS

Astha Jaiswal[a] and Dinesh Kumar[b]

[a]*Manipal University, India*
[b]*Shree Rangniketan Foundation, India*

ABSTRACT

This chapter overviews and briefly presents the literature concerning women and science from the field of feminist science studies (FSS). A major and time-consuming challenge encountered during the process of this review was organising the highly varied subtopics into meaningful categories. For the sake of easy understanding, we begin the study by describing the field of science and technology study (STS) and then we move on to discuss the origin of FSS and major strands of intersection between science and feminist epistemology.

Keywords: Feminist science; science and technology study; women and science; feminist epistemology; intersectional science

1. INTRODUCTION: THE FEMINIST QUESTIONS IN SCIENCE

For most of us, science occupies an exalted position in our minds, a holy cow that we cannot question about. We are accustomed to view science as objective and rational, hence an infallible and fool proof method to investigate and understand the world around us. Mainstream practitioners of science claim that science and results of science are non-discriminatory and universal. They also denigrate feminist studies of science as being ‘not scientific’. Feminist science studies (FSS) question this claim of science to being discrimination free and neutral. It is naive to think that science or scientific methodology as practised today is above criticism.

Social Responsibility, Technology and AI
Developments in Corporate Governance and Responsibility, Volume 23, 183–202
Copyright © 2025 Astha Jaiswal and Dinesh Kumar
Published under exclusive licence by Emerald Publishing Limited
ISSN: 2043-0523/doi:10.1108/S2043-052320240000023010

The origin of feminist discourses on science cannot be understood in isolation. Most early and important discourses within the feminist epistemology of science were spread out sporadically across a myriad of disciplines within the multidisciplinary field of science and technology studies (STS), described the coming paragraph.

2. SCIENCE AND TECHNOLOGY STUDIES (STS)

Science and technology study, also known as science, technology and society (STS), is a multidisciplinary field that aims to study science and how science works (Biagioli, 1999). It aims to examine the social construction of scientific knowledge and technological innovation by situating scientific expertise and scientific knowledge production in the context of a variety of disciplines. Primarily, discourses in science studies critique the traditional or mainstream understandings of science as a rational activity and also bring to light different ways in which science is constructed as a social activity. Using insights from a variety of disciplines such as sociology, politics, cultural and geographical studies, psychology, etc. and a variety of methods, science studies scholarship analyses the social construction of scientific knowledge – the production, representation, organisation and reception of scientific knowledge seeks to situate it in the broader social, cultural, historical and philosophical contexts. The Structure of Scientific Revolutions by Thomas S. Kuhn's was the work to have most definitely defined the field of science studies (Daston, 2009).

In the following paragraphs, we explain the origin and relevance of FSS and provide description of various strands of FSS.

3. FEMINIST SCIENCE STUDIES (FSS)

The field of FSS took off from the theoretical foundations set by early science critiques within the field of STS. FSS cannot be defined and confined to disciplinary boundaries. Having evolved independently and sporadically across myriad and diverse subjects, the body of work comprising FSS is rather heterogeneous and amorphous, with no set limits or boundaries. Similarly, the methods and approaches employed within the feminist epistemology of science are varied and cannot be categorised under a single label.

Though not clustered under the umbrella of 'feminist science studies', the foundational ideas of the field can be traced back to the last phase of the women's movement. Not surprisingly, early feminist works on science were inspired by the women liberation movement and were examinations into the status of women in sciences.

The ground field of FSS consists of strong critiques of and different perspectives on science and its methods. According to Subramaniam (2009), the foundational body work of FSS, the feminist critique of science, was primarily set and developed by the western women scientists. These critiques questioned the cultural and professional practices of science and called for an understanding of science as a socially, culturally and politically embedded set of practices Subramaniam (2009). Historically, modern FSS can be traced back to Carolyn Merchant's 'The Death of Nature (1980)' (Subramaniam, 2009). The field, set with the groundbreaking works by Bleier (1984), Haraway (1988) and Hubbard (1990), Keller (1985), Longino (1990) and Schiebinger (1991), has developed into an independent and distinct mode of inquiry, providing original theoretical frameworks for critiques of established perspectives in science.

Feminist studies do not just focus on gender but also expose other issues of inequalities and exclusions based on sexuality, class, race, disability, colonialism and post-colonialism. The fundamental question that FSS ask is how science has contributed to create and sustain these differences (Subramaniam, 2009).

Mainstream practitioners of STS often have disapproved of feminist perspectives on science. There is a tendency on part of the mainstream STS practitioners to view feminist STS as merely an effort to get more women in science (Whelan, 2001). However, issue of location and number of women in science is only a part of the feminist engagements on science. Feminist science scholars have discussed various issues such as history of women in science, exclusion and marginalisation of women in science, locational and equity issues for women in science, the experience of women in science, the effects of science and its products on women, analysing and critiquing the gendered nature of science and feminist theories of scientific ideas, practices and knowledge. The scope of feminist studies of science has now expanded to include other criteria of exclusion such as race, class, sexuality and disability.

Feminist considerations and critiques on science can be broadly categorised into the following groups:

3.1 Problematic Foundational Claims of Science

Feminist science scholars were the first to critique the scientific culture and question the foundational binaries of science. It was Griffin (2015) and Merchant (1979) who first explored the science/nature binary created by science and elaborated on the construction of nature and environment by science. Where Griffin's work analysed how patriarchal western philosophy and religion have used language and science to gain power over both women and nature by identifying women with earth, Merchant's work was a critical historical investigation revealing the historic connection between the domination of nature and subjugation of women by science. According to Merchant (1979), social and ecological changes witnessed in current times were due to images of nature associated with the Scientific Revolution. The atomising, objectifying and dissecting nature of science resulted in the formation of a mechanistic cosmology replacing the pre-modern, organic view of a feminine natural world giving way to viewing of nature as an inert matter, to be exploited, manipulated and controlled by humans (Merchant, 1979).

Beginning with the early feminist critiques on science, feminist science scholars explored the scientific discourse and unearthed several binaries existing within scientific discourse such as rational/irrational, objective/subjective, femininity/masculinity, specificity/universalism, science/nature, pure/constructed and sex/gender. Hubbard (1990) has opined that the binaries defined by science such as rational/irrational, objective/subjective and pure/constructed values of science have been created by the privileged, educated white men who were the ones to do science. Further explorations on binaries in science were done by Haraway (1989) who provided an analysis of gendered and racially biased metaphors and narratives prevalent in primatology.[1]

3.2 Masculine Nature of Science

Keller (1985), an American feminist and bio-physicist, was one of the earliest critiques of modern science who argued that science was a masculine enterprise in its structure, epistemology and methodology. According to her, more than any other social enterprise, science is more inherently masculine in nature. The masculine bias of science begins with the dichotomy between sciences and social sciences. While science is said to be objective, based on hard facts, logic and rationalism, social sciences are said to be subjective, based on feelings and interpretations (Hesse-Biber & Yaiser, 2004).While the masculine is hard and logical, the feminine is soft and emotional – the gender metaphor is clear sexual (Hesse-Biber & Yaiser, 2004).

Harding (1986), Haraway (1989) and Longino (1990) have provided strong and clear critiques on the andro-centrism of science, challenging the intellectual and social foundations of scientific thought, providing evidence for masculine bias in science.[2]

Longino and Doell (1983) have provided evidence of masculine bias within evolutionary and endocrinological research.[3,4] Irigaray (2005) showed how scientific language was not neutral, and the logic of scientific language was sexed.

The feminist writings of 1960s and 1970s played a crucial role in bringing to light the androcentric knowledge construction within and across disciplines (Hesse-Biber & Yaiser, 2004). More and more work came out showing how research was explicitly androcentric, how women were simply missing from mainstream bodies of knowledge.

At the same time, the positivistic nature of sciences and social sciences that stipulates that world is ordered, predictable and measurable was being questioned. The feminists considered subjective or the lived experiences an important component of research.

Dugdale (1985) has outlined three approaches to in which science could be masculine. Firstly, feminist studies contest stories propagated by science as to what is to be counted as natural. Secondly, they challenge science's masculine culture, shaped by men, where values such as competitiveness, 'cold', 'hard', reason, aggressiveness and arrogant self-confidence are positively valued and are taken as criteria for success. Such a masculine ethos of science exerts a selection pressure which continues to favour entry and advancement of men socialised into such behaviour patterns (Dugdale, 1985). Thirdly, the masculinity of science is reflected in the foundational values of science such as objectivity, neutrality and universality.

Haraway (1989) has shown through her study of metaphors and narratives in primatology the tendency in scientific language to masculinise the stories about 'reproductive competition and sex between aggressive males and receptive females [that] facilitate some and preclude other types of conclusions'.

FSS have brought to light how theories laying claim to 'universality' and 'neutrality' are actually not inclusive representation of humanity but biased and based on a lopsided norm of white male. What is claimed to be 'universal' is actually based on only a small and selective portion of a population. Gilligan (1982), for example, has criticised mainstream theories of psychological development as being male-centric in approach.

Similarly, the positivist objective rationality of science is seen by feminist scholars as being masculine in ethos. This masculine ethos of science, scholars claim (Rose, 1994), makes science unattractive to women.

Eco feminist works consist of critiques on the modern western science from a composite view of ecology and feminism. Shiva (1988), a physicist and an environmentalist, has criticised the social forestry programmes and green revolution projects in India as being products of masculine, reductionist science, leading to uprooting of women as well as destruction of environment.

3.3 Scientific Meritocracy, Excellence and Productivity

The scientific concepts of meritocracy and excellence are also open to challenge. Academic excellence and meritocracy supposed to be a universal and unbiased standard of merit are hardly so. Decisions taken in allocation of funds and resources in academic institutions are influenced by several factors such as biases about race, sex, age, geographic location of a university. Van den Brink and Benschop (2012) have argued that academic excellence is a social construct that is inherently gendered. Based on an empirical study conducted in the Netherlands, they have shown how gender is practised in the evaluation of professorial candidates, to produce inequalities in the construction of excellence, resulting in bias in favour of men and against women.

Similarly, feminist writers (Schiebinger, 1991) have problematised the notion of productivity and showed how it was linked to social perceptions. Schiebinger (2001) has pointed to the fact that women employed different standards for publication than men. While women focused on thorough and comprehensive research and were less strategic, men were strategic in getting more number of papers published. It has been reported that men's citation rates were higher as they published more papers. But when considered paper-wise, women were cited almost the same or better than men.

3.4 Construction of Scientific Knowledge

A central focus of FSS is how scientific knowledge, claimed to be objective and neutral, is actually socially and culturally constructed inside and outside the laboratory. Another major point of departure for feminist studies in science is how this knowledge is applied to the lives and bodies of women. As previously seen, several authors such as Harding (1991), Haraway (1989), Longino and Doell (1983) and others have shown that knowledge produced and meanings construed by science are constructed.

Feminist studies have pointed out that science cannot be separated from the person doing science (Tuana, 1988). Since subjectivity can never be removed, knowledge produced is embedded in a certain context and culture.

Sur (2011) has pointed out how the theories of biological differences, evolutionary theory coupled with eugenics and sophisticated psychological tests to measure intellectual quotient have time and again legitimised a social order rooted in sexism, racism and colonialism. The persistent efforts of women scientists within the gamut of science to expose, debunk these faulty experiments, intentional manoeuvring of data and gaps in methodology therein, have changed the situation to a great extent. The creative interventions by women scientists in the conceptualisation and design of experiments have to be viewed as critiques of the gender, race, class bias that permeates the very methodology of science.

Martin (1991) has explored how medical language is sexist in describing women's bodies and processes of reproduction. For example, in 'The Egg and the Sperm: How Science Has Constructed a Romance Based on Stereotypical Male-Female Roles' (1991), Emily Martin shows how scientists have superimposed cultural sex stereotypes onto the process of fertilisation, resulting in sexist descriptions of cell and molecular interactions, the physiology of fertilisation, as well as lopsided research questions and priorities. Similarly, Tuana's work (1988) analyses theories of reproduction from the time of Aristotle and provides evidence that science has always managed to produce biological explanations to validate ritualistic societal treatment of women as inferior. Donna Haraway explores in *Primate Vision: Gender, Race, and Nature in the World of Modern Sciences (1989)* how scientific findings in primatology have been deeply constructed by gendered and racialised notions.

Halpin (1989) equates scientific objectivity to the process of 'othering' by the scientists, who have historically been upper class hetero sexual Christian male. Anything different from value-laden 'self' has been relegated to the category of the 'other' and by virtue of being 'other' it is 'inferior'. The argument is that science has been partly instrumental in maintaining patriarchal society because of this belief.

One startling revelation is that scientific facts could be appropriated and used by groups with vested interests. For example, Denes (2011) has critiqued the text, entitled, *'The Mystery Method: How to Get Beautiful Women into Bed'* as appropriating research findings of evolutionary and physiological biology to create specific discourses which privilege hetero-sexual men who 'seduce' women, while creating disadvantage for women by teaching men how to use women's bodies against themselves.

3.5 Feminist Theories and Methods

To counteract the above-mentioned shortcomings of science as pointed out by FSS, various theories and approaches have been proposed. Harding (1991) has proposed standpoint theory which emphasises that women have a more objective view of the world than men because women's unique role as mothers and care-givers as gives them a position outside the dominant social order. The emphasis here is on evaluating the value of knowledge of claims based on the context in which it is produced.

Haraway (2020) has expounded the idea of situated knowers to emphasise the fact that people have different points of view from which they see the world. Haraway conceptualises varied research perspectives as different ways of seeing and argues that every view has both blind spots and focal points.

'Feminist Empiricists', as pointed out by Harding (1991), are those feminists scholars who believed that andro-centric bias could be removed from knowledge construction by adhering more strictly to the tenets of scientific positivism and by adding women and excluded groups to research sample. The implicit belief is that andro-centric science is a result of 'bad science', which happens if the guidelines and standards of science have not been stringently followed. Empiricist feminists approve of scientific methodology and positivist objectivity.

Longino (1990) argues for 'contextual empiricism', where she gives due importance to standards of science to measure truth claims against available evidence, but at the same time, she urges scientists to acknowledge the biases they have.

Examples of feminist questions and approaches that look beyond the social and cultural construction of science language are excellent works in the area of the medicalisation of women's lives and bodies (Rapp, 2001; Blizzard, 2007). Studies in this area address the issue of separation between the scientists producing knowledge and those using the science's knowledge and situate scientific knowledge on the bodies and lives of women. This line of thought emphasises the importance of including and integrating the personal lived experience within the theories. Blizzard's (2007) in her ethnography of the sociocultural development of foetoscopy applies a constructivist framework to show how 'patient-mothers', physicians, clergy and others in a social network actively affect the process of development and acceptance of foetoscopy.[5]

On the other hand, Webers (2007) has critiqued the tensions created between nature and constructionism by postmodernist feminist discourses on science. According to Weber, the feminist thought has engaged with the process of 'denaturalisation' to reveal social and political construction of scientific concepts such as 'nature', 'sex', 'woman' and so on. Weber has argued that in contemporary feminist literature of the west, the concept of 'denaturalisation' itself has been naturalised, acting as a blind-spot and is, therefore, problematic.

3.6 Gendered Research and Innovations

A number of research articles deal with the issue of gender bias or gender underrepresentation in science and technological research and innovations.

Gendered Research and Innovation (GRI) is a concept that espouses integrating sex and gender dimension in every step of the research process (Buitendijk & Maes, 2015). Lack of sex and gender analysis in the research process may have serious adverse consequences, especially in the field of health and medicine.

3.7 Feminist Works on Science From India

As we have seen above, most of the works have been conducted western scholars and that too in the western context. Feminist literature available on science from outside western diaspora is scant. In India, where most of the critiques on science come not from mainstream scientists, but from sociologists, the case is not different. Some of the feminist works on science from India are illustrated below:

Post-colonial works on science (Chadha, 1997; Subramaniam, 2009) have refuted the claim of science to universality by elucidating how historical, mythological and colonial moorings have shaped and continue to shape science and how modern science has worked by appropriating indigenous ideas, concepts, practices and philosophies.

Sur, a scientist turned historian of science, through her study of women scientists employed in C.V. Raman's laboratory has examined the confluence of caste, nationalism and gender in science and argued that science in India was organised in the colonial context.

Pointing to how women scientists struggled to integrate passion for their scientific work with their feminity, Chadha (1998) has challenged the 'enlightenment ideology' of modern science. She has thrown light on how so-called 'scientific temper' leads to compartmentalisation of lived experiences by separating 'personal, social and political from the neutral and the scientific'. She has refuted the claim of science to universality by pointing out that modern science was also 'local' in having its roots in a 'particular phase of European history'.

An interesting study was done by Kumar (2001) where using the case study of Indian scientists, she explored whether scientific values were context bound or universal in nature. Findings of her research point towards the universal nature of research values held by the scientists, indicating the fact that notwithstanding their cultural and social context, all the scientists included in the study believed that scientific values were beyond bias.

In her more recent work (2012), Kumar has analysed the relation between gender and science in different cultural contexts. The findings of her study reveal that certain patterns of gendered science have universal nature across varying cultures, such as absence of women at higher levels of academic science, technology, engineering and maths (STEM) fields. Similarly, the nature of subtle biases favouring men was also found to be universal. However, in other aspects such as opportunities in STEM fields, there were considerable differences across culture. For instance, while in countries such as Malaysia and Vietnam, more number of women were present in computer sciences, in Saudi Arabia and India, there was greater participation of women in engineering fields. We can say that very few but important feminist studies have been done by the Indian scholars outside the western context.

3.8 Location of Women in STEM Fields: Factors Behind Underrepresentation

One important and one of the earliest areas of study for FSS was pointing out and challenging the absence of women and other minorities from science. The question of location of women and other minorities in science and their absence from science is important not only to improve the number of minorities in science but also for the quality and output of science. Rossiter's work (1982, 1995) '*Women Scientists in America*' was an early important work that questioned the priorities of science and raised questions on the location of women in science.

Under-representation of women in scientific work force is a major concern of FSS. A wide gender gap has persisted over the years at all levels of science, technology, engineering and medicine disciplines throughout the world. Science fields have been untouched by the developments in feminist studies of science for several reasons. Wyer (2018) has given the following reasons for this:

Firstly, if the subject matter of science discipline in question does not involve people, it may be considered irrelevant to consider if or not women are taken as subjects of the study. Secondly, absence of women in decision-making positions within organisations may fail to bring changes. Thirdly, not necessarily having training in gender aspects, most scientists take for granted the 'objectivity' of scientific perspective assuming that science is beyond the influence of social dynamics. Fourthly, as most feminist scholars belong to the fields of social sciences, they may lack expertise to challenge issues in scientific fields. Lastly, most institutions reinforce disciplinary boundaries. Such restrictive environment does not permit that questions beyond the boundary restrictions be raised. Given below are various theories explaining the location of women in science.

3.9 Lack of Innate Ability

For centuries, science has been a source of theories reeking of sexist ideology that justify gender subordination of women. Producing scientific texts representing women in such a way as to legitimise their societal roles, science has worked to keep women out of intellectual pursuits including science (Sheffield, 2004).

Time and again, science has used biology of women's bodies to perpetuate ideas that work against women. In 18th and 19th centuries, science worked in tandem with societal ideologies to prove that it was beneficial for society if women kept out of educational and intellectual pursuits, as they taxed their bodies and minds and impaired reproductive functions (Sheffield, 2004).

For decades, science has propounded theories of biological and intellectual inferiority of women to profess that women have lesser spatial/mathematical ability (Dusek, 2006). Seymour (2002) has proved that there is no evidence of cognitive factors contributing this high female attrition rate from science fields. For centuries, science has legitimised research exploring the biological differences between men and women. Whatever the difference, scientific theories end up showing as men being 'better' and 'superior' (Dusek, 2006).

However, other studies have provided evidence to refute the above claim. Study conducted by Ceci et al. (2009) on men and women's ability in science and mathematics did not find any significant difference between the two.

3.10 Family Role

Research has shown that strong family encouragement plays a very important role in women's perception of self-capacity and taking up science subjects at university level and her selection of a field of study (Hazari et al., 2007).

Studies have also shown that women who take up sciences also belong to a specific socio-economic as well as social background, have high levels of self-confidence (Doolen & Long, 2007) and often have at least one of the parents in a profession in one of the STEM disciplines.

3.11 Chilly Climate in the Classroom/Gendered Images/Stereotypes/Gender Segregation in Choice of Subject

It appears that women having high self-confidence regarding their mathematics and science abilities enter STEM fields (Tyson's et al., 2007). This self-conception of women as being capable of mathematics and science abilities plays an important role in their choice of subjects and careers. A study conducted by Tyson's et al. (2007) study revealed that liking and preference for science and mathematics courses in secondary schools is one of the significant factors of taking up science subjects at higher levels.

There is gender segregation in the choice of subjects by women in the United States. Studies from the United States reveal that women's presence in health and biological sciences is now equal to or greater than men's, while in physical sciences, engineering and maths-intensive fields women remain a minority (Smyth & Nosek, 2015).

Research suggests that gender gap in science fields at educational level could be because female students do not find science appealing (Tyson et al., 2007). Again, many theories go into explaining this lack of interest in sciences on behalf of girls. Biological science has a theory that girls are left-brained, hence more emotional and intuitive, and less logical with poor reasoning skills. Hence, they are inclined to non-science subjects.

The common perception of STEM fields as nerdy and lonely subjects and eventually a lonely career path tends to discourage girls from choosing these courses at school and later on at college (Sullivan & Guerra, 2007).

One reason given for dropping out of female students from science research fields is a 'chilly climate' in classroom. Several factors add to the 'chilly climate' such as treatment of the girls in the classroom, interaction of girls with male teachers and male students, faculty's teaching style, etc. Evidence for 'chilly climate' for girls in the United States is provided by Brainard and Carlin (1998) who found that highly competent female students often dropped out, while only the males of low ability dropped out of math and science courses. Seymour and Hewitt (1997) found out that students attributed cold and impersonal behaviour of professors for dropping out of science majors.

Research also proves that girls chose their careers to suit social norms, cultural stereotypes and prefer careers that are compatible with family responsibilities, such as education, psychology or medicine (Suter, 2006). According to Xie et al. (2006), women may find it harder to combine family and work in some fields (e.g. those that demand many lab hours) than in other fields (e.g. social sciences). A study conducted in Switzerland (Tacsir et al., 2014) points out that young women make their career choices motivated by social and/or political commitments, whereas men make their choice mostly based on career prospects.

Sadker and Sadker (2010) have explored how the education system in the United States is gendered in many ways. In doing so, their study has exposed gender biases in curriculum and textbooks that emphasise male dominance in the professional world as well as bias in the treatment of boys and girls in the classroom by the teacher.

There is a mismatch between cultural stereotypes of how a girl should be, or what they should do and image of a scientist. There is a dearth of female role models. Such stereotypes are further strengthened by science curricula in schools, language and pictures in text books and general environment of the classroom. All this is a huge discouragement for young girls to aspire for career in science.

3.12 The Leaky Pipeline

The standard model that scholars in the United States use in depicting women's exit from science fields is that of a 'leaky pipeline'. This pipeline depicts women as dropping out of sciences at various points along their education and career – beginning with girl students' losing interest in sciences in school and continues by not pursuing the field at university or at higher levels, and finally, leaving STEM fields after obtaining educational credentials (Doolen & Long, 2007). This phenomenon is progressive (the farther along the pipeline, the fewer the women and persistent (the problem persists in spite of remedial measures taken). Much empirical research has been done to find out what factors stimulate or hinder female students to take up science.

Xie et al. (2003) have shown that women in the United States face far more barriers in becoming scientists or engineers than do men with comparable educational credentials.

In one study, Moss-Racusin et al. (2012) have shown that both male and faculty at a university were biased against female students. Despite earning higher math and science grades than males throughout schooling, females make a choice of not opting for STEM fields. Many explanations are given to explain this choice by females such as expectations about their social roles, anticipated family roles and responsibilities.

On a different note, Ceci et al. (2009) have pointed out that in the Unites States, there is no longer any discrimination in interviewing and hiring, grant and manuscript reviewing, etc. The cause of the gender gap, according to them, is rooted in cultural and stereotypical factors which prevent women from participating in mathematics intensive fields.

Etzkowitz et al. (2000) have pointed out that in the United States, experience of women in academic science is far difficult and arduous than that of the men in the same field. The study revealed that men, irrespective of their performance in graduate school, went on to have a successful career. But it was not so with the women. Those women who entered professional science faced invisibility and were denied professional identity.

3.13 Matilda Effect

It is now well known that women's work in science has been ignored, overlooked and not acknowledged throughout the progress of modern science. When it comes to famous women in science, there are not many names that come to mind. Ada Lovelace is credited with the achievement of developing world's first algorithm more than a century before the arrival of the first general purpose computers. Marie Curie is the only woman who comes to mind as having a notable achievement in science. Other than her, there are hardly any other women in science that are well recognised.

Studies suggest there have been many women throughout the history of science, who have significantly contributed towards the shaping of modern science. However, their efforts have simply been overshadowed by male counterparts in getting recognition (Rossiter, 1997). This systematic bias in science has been termed as 'Matilda effect' by science historian Margaret Rossiter.

For instance, Nettie Stevens was not credited for her groundbreaking discovery of sex linkage to chromosomes. It was Edmund Wilson who was a well-known male scientist who was credited for this discovery (Schindler, 2021).

Similarly, Jocelyn Bell discovered the radio pulsars, but the nobel prize for this discovery was awarded to her thesis supervisor Anthony Hewish (Modgil et al., 2018).

Rosalind Franklin, who led the team that created the famous photograph that led to the discovery of double helical structure of DNA, was mentioned cursorily at the bottom of the paper by Watson and Crick, as having 'stimulated' the authors, but was not included as an author (Benderly, 2018).

4. GENDER IN ORGANISATIONS: FEMINIST ORGANISATIONS THEORY

Feminist organisation studies bring to forefront how organisations exclude women. As in other social spheres, in organisations, gender is a very relevant and important criterion for structuring and differentiation. The question of organisation and gender has long been raised, and many attempts have been made to answer it. While 'mainstream' organisation theories assume organisations to be gender-neutral, feminist studies point out that organisation structures, far from being gender-neutral, are inherently gendered (Wilz, 2001). Most formal processes, supposed to be gender-neutral, are inextricably linked to inner and outer organisational structures, institutions, norms and assumptions (Wilz, 2001).

The liberal feminist agenda promoted gender equality within the work place as an important agenda in the latter half of 20th century. Since the wake of liberal women's movement, place of gender in organisations has been paid more and more attention to. Feminist studies have tried to answer why so many policies fail to address the issue of gender inequality in workplace. Feminist studies have brought new perspectives in trying to answer this question. For instance, feminist studies played an important role in bringing out the artificial dichotomy between home and work. The policies trying to bring balance between the responsibilities of home and work have been revisited. New ways of thinking have emerged to explain the ineffectiveness of gender neutral policies in the facilitation of gender equality.

The feminist organisation theories challenge the traditional notion that organisations are gender-neutral entities and identify the work place as a system of organised male privilege linking gendering within organisations to the artificial dichotomies of 'personal' and 'professional' lives and subsequently 'life' and 'work' (Acker, 1990). Further, the capitalist values embedded within the organisational structure assist in producing and maintaining institutional inequality (Wilz, 2001).

4.1 Gendered Organisations Theory

Joan Acker is credited for theorising and developing gendered organisations theory which posits that rather than being gender-neutral, organisations are inherently gendered structures. Acker's (1990) theory of gendered organisations is a useful perspective for understanding how academic STEM fields are sites in which gender relations are played out.

Acker's theory of gendered organisations is based on the concept of organisational logic (Acker, 1990). The concept of organisational logic draws attention to the existence, rationalisation and legitimitisation of organisational hierarchies. Acker describes organisational logic as the taken-for-granted policies and principles that are used to exercise legitimate control over the workplace. Workers comply because they view these policies and principles as 'natural' or normal business practices.

The organisational logic encompasses the logical systems within organisations such as work protocols, job descriptions, pay scales and job evaluations that are integral to most work organisations and provide guidelines for behaviour and interaction (Acker, 1990). According to Acker, the organisation logic is guided by stereotypical cultural and societal beliefs. Further, cultural gender beliefs are built into practices and assumptions, or workers conduct themselves in a gendered way on the job, and gendered organisational structures and norms shape the criteria used to evaluate workers.

Acker argues that logical principles used by organisations to develop job descriptions and determine salaries or promotion are not neutral but are built upon gender stereotypes, privileging qualities associated with men and masculinity. Acker argues that gender discourses are embedded in organisations, and ultimately result in rampant gender inequality.

Previously, this theory has been used by Husu (2001) for studying gender based discrimination in academia. Kantola (2008) has used this theory to examine gendering processes in political science department of a university.

Williams et al. (2012) have extended this framework by 'identifying the mechanisms that reproduce gender inequality in the twenty-first-century workplace'.

4.2 Components of Gendered Organisation Theory

Gendered organisation theory proposed by Acker (1990) consists of four dimensions that include a set of processes contributing to gendered organisation.

4.2.1 Unofficial Division of Labour

This includes creating unofficial or informal divisions along gender lines (occupational sex segregation). According to the theory, this informal division of labour is the first step at which gender hierarchies are produced. For example, in a university organisation, the women's role might be to act as caregivers, taking up the role of 'mothers of the department' (Kantola, 2008).

4.2.2 Gendered Interaction and Communication

Secondly, theories of gendered organisation also bring into light different ways in which informal interaction and communication in an organisation is gendered. Also included in this organisational culture of gendered interaction are gendered evaluations of scientific success – so that the work of women and men might be evaluated in different ways (Acker, 1990).

4.2.3 Gendered Symbols, Images and Forms of Consciousness

This includes the use of gendered symbolism to reinforce sex segregation and create a gendered organisational logic which influences workers individual gender identities and interactions with co-workers (Acker, 1990). For example, use of titles such as 'masters' and 'fellows' carry a masculine sign (Kantola, 2008).

4.2.4 Different Attitudes

This brings to light the different ways of positioning oneself in the organisation. For example, different attitudes of men and women in similar circumstances (Kantola, 2008).

4.2.5 Science Research Organisation as a Gendered Site

Work organisations in universities and academic STEM fields are gendered in that STEM fields promote professional practices that are portrayed as gender neutral but are often based on the underlying belief that the ideal worker is the one who has minimum obligations outside of work. This image of an ideal worker, in most instances, translates to the ideal worker being a man (Acker, 1990).

The preference for ideal worker and the occupational and organisational practices associated with it leads to direct or indirect exclusion of many women, given the fact that they bear the primary care responsibilities for most families.

The ideal worker belief, embedded in the structure of STEM occupations, shapes evaluations of workers' performances, occupational and organisational practices and ideology and interactions as well as criteria for success, to the extent that they support this ideal worker model, will advantage men as a group over women (Acker, 1990).

This 'ideal worker' model creates conflicts for women when it comes to childbearing and family responsibilities. As a result, women often feel compelled to comply with the 'ideal worker' models to the extent possible, often making modifications in their professional or personal lives in order to accommodate organisational models of an 'ideal worker'. Organisational logics in universities and in STEM fields also promote an image of a scientist that is most often white and male. This gender- and race-based imagery combines with normative standards for professional conduct to influence the types of practices and interactions in which workers engage.

Studies have pointed out that the very mode in which science is done in Indian science organisations could be gendered (Chandra, 2013). The mode of research, time commitment and 'continuity of career' are all based on a male pattern of work and career. The same study also questions the requirement of single mindedness, that is, absorption in science to the exclusion of all else in life and aggressiveness as an essential quality for a successful scientist.

4.2.6 Gender Strategies

The concept of gender strategies emerged out of social constructionist approaches of gender (Bird & Rhoton, 2011). A 'gendered strategy' is a personal plan of action for organising personal practices shaped by personal beliefs about how men and women should act in their social lives. This concept when applied to the experiences of women working in science fields makes women negotiate their position compared to others in the organisation. Most women who are working in male dominated fields, as a result of extensive education, must already believe in a strong sense of themselves as equally capable and qualified as men. Reconciling gaps between their career aspirations and career opportunities require gender strategies. As noted previously, organisations are premised on the belief that the ideal worker is one unencumbered with obligations outside the workplace; historically, this has meant that the ideal worker is a male (Acker, 1990). This belief, embedded in the structure of organisations, shapes evaluations of workers performance as well as criteria for success. Workers construct work personas in accordance with the demands of their occupation, the norms and ideologies of the organisation or workplace and in accordance with gender and race based societal expectations (Dellinger, 2004). The resulting effects of these expectations on workers are patterns of differential work execution by gender as well as differential occupational requirements for men and women (Dellinger, 2004). For women, managing gender is an important aspect of succeeding in occupations emphasising male standards; women who appear too masculine are disparaged as are women seen as too feminine (Britton, 2000). The culture of male-dominated occupations makes gender highly salient for women (Ridgeway

& Correll, 2004), resulting in a 'balancing act' in which women must construct work personas.

Bird and Rhoton (2011) have studied the gender strategy of distancing among women scientists to understand how their gender practices created barriers. Using a social constructionist approach, Bird and Rhoton (2011) have explored the individual and personal strategies deliberately adopted by professional women to negotiate barriers and overcome exclusionary practices associated with their being women in an organisation. They view professional women's gender strategy as a gendered 'plan of action' for 'organising personal practices' that are shaped by personal beliefs about how they as women should act. The gender practices are shaped by the opportunities and resources available to the women. They have identified six gender strategies in which women construct work persona by adopting practices that more or less be categorised into the following groups: how they, as women, should act. These strategies are described below:

4.2.7 Aligning with White, Hegemonic Practices of Masculinity

This includes adoption and support of masculine practices and belief systems built into organisations and institutionalised arrangements by many women professionals who work in male-dominated professional organisations. For instance, women in male-dominated occupations may try to behave like men to get approval.

4.2.8 Aligning With Conventional Practices of Femininity

This includes adoption of practices considered appropriate according to stereotyped notions of 'femininity'. Such practices are socially valued and yield professional opportunities and rewards similar to hegemonic practices of masculinity in male-dominate professional work organisations. For example, women may approve of patronising attitudes by male superiors.

4.2.9 Claiming Gender Neutrality

Women professionals in male-dominated professional organisations adopt gender strategies that involve a variety of 'gender neutrality' claims, such casting oneself or one's actions as gender-neutral, rejecting others' attempts to frame one's actions as 'gendered' and supporting the idea that organisational structures, cultures and practices are gender-neutral. Women use such strategies to demonstrate to their male colleagues that women view men as colleagues and teammates and not as discriminators. For example, women may say that their choice of career was based on their individual preference and not gender.

4.2.10 Framing Gender-Based Policies, Practices and Programmes as 'Political'

Many times to strengthen their claims of 'gender neutrality', women professional use the claims that overtly gender-based policies, programmes and practices are inappropriately 'political'. Many women professionals reject policies such as affirmative action and programmes oriented towards empowering women, for example, labelling them as negatively 'political'. For example, women may be against affirmative actions to help women in organisations (for example, special schemes or quotas) citing reason that all decisions about hiring, salaries and promotions in organisations should be on merit and employees' credentials.

4.2.11 Using Multiple Gender Strategies

Women professionals often experiment with and use multiple strategies throughout their careers. Life circumstances, such as getting married, or becoming pregnant or caring for a parent with a prolonged illness, are key reasons leading to women professionals to switch strategies.

Long work hours, extensive business travel and maintaining a singular focus on work are all expectations that conflict with pregnancy, infant care and raising young children, etc. and force those women who align with hegemonic practices of masculinity to question their adopted gender strategy.

Similarly, those women professionals who initially employ gender strategies that involve aligning with conventional femininity practices may also come to realise the limitations of their strategies. Women who employ such strategies, for example, are often taken less seriously by their colleagues, viewed as followers rather than leaders and find that they have to work much harder than equally qualified men in order to be appropriately recognised and rewarded for their work. Such women may decide that their best option is to embrace a gender strategy that involves lowering personal career aspirations in order to distance themselves from what they view as unjust circumstances or to invest more time in their families.

4.2.12 Challenging Gendered Organisations

Still some women, when faced with limitation or barriers, may adopt gender strategies that involve challenging gendered professional organisations. In organisations, those with the most power to effect change are the least likely to pursue it as they are the ones who benefit most from the existing organisational arrangements. In such a situation, some women may bring critical consciousness about organisational structures and practices and awareness about alternative models for organising equitable work processes and policies into decision-making processes via the organisational roles that they play. These women act as leaders in producing gradual changes in organisational structures and practices, which can result in significant changes over time.

5. CONCLUDING REMARKS

In this chapter, we overviewed major strands of discourses prevailing in the feminist epistemology of science, including a few illustrations from within the feminist studies of science emanating from India.

Also, we looked at the theories explaining the location and position of women in science. As part of these theories, we examined the feminist theories on gendered organisations, and how science fields could be gendered. Finally, we looked in detail at the two theories of gendered organisations and gender strategies. While the theory of gendered organisations posits that organisations are inherently gendered sites, the theory of gender strategies throws light on the practices adopted by both men and women within organisations to create work persona to suit cultural and organisational stereotypes.

NOTES

1. Primotology is the scientific study of primates such as lemurs and chimpanzees.
2. The term androcentrism in science is a concept that denotes the practice of placing male human beings or a masculine point of view at the centre of scientific world view. The implied meaning is that masculinity is normative, and all things outside of masculinity are defined as other.
3. Evolutionary studies investigate the evolutionary processes that produced diverse forms of life on Earth.
4. Endocrinological research is the study of the endocrine system in the human body which secrete hormones.
5. *Foetoscopy* is an endoscopic procedure during pregnancy to allow access to the foetus, the amniotic cavity, the umbilical cord and the foetal side of the placenta.

REFERENCES

Acker, J. (1990). Hierarchies, jobs, bodies: A theory of gendered organizations. *Gender & Society*, *4*(2), 139–158.

Benderly, B. L. (2018, August 1). Just a momenRosalind Franklin and the damage of gender harassmentt... Just a moment.... https://www.science.org/content/article/rosalind-franklin-and-damage-gender-harassment

Biagioli, M. (1999). *The science studies reader*. Routledge.

Bird, S. R., & Rhoton, L. A. (2011). Women professionals gender strategies: Negotiating gendered organisational barriers. In E. L. Jeanes, D. Knights, & P. Yancey Martin (Eds.), *Handbook of gender work and organisation* (pp. 245–262). John Wiley & Sons.

Bleier, R. (1984). *Science and gender: A critique of biology and its theories on women*. Pergammon Press.

Blizzard, D. (2007). *Looking within: A sociocultural examination of fetoscopy*. MIT Press.

Brainard, S. G., & Carlin, L. (1998). A six year longitudinal study of undergraduate women in engineering and science. *Journal of Engineering Education*, *87*(4), 369–375.

Britton, D. M. (2000). The epistemology of the gendered organisation. *Gender & Society*, *14*(3), 418–434.

Buitendijk, S., & Maes, K. (2015). *Gendered research and innovation: Integrating sex and gender analysis into the research process*. League of European Research Universities (LERU).

Ceci, S. J., Williams, W. M., & Barnett, S. M. (2009). Women's underrepresentation in science: Sociocultural and biological considerations. *Psychological Bulletin*, *135*(2), 218–261.

Chadha, G. (1998). Sokal's hoax: A backlash to science criticism. *Economic and Political Weekly*, 2964–2968.

Chandra, N. (2013, November 10). Female scientists underrepresented in Indian research. http://www.dailymail.co.uk/indiahome/indianews/article-2496424/Femalescientists-underrepresented-Indian-research.html. Accessed on November 11, 2015.

Daston, L. (2009). Science studies and the history of science. *Critical Inquiry*, *35*(4), 798–813.

Dellinger, K. (2004). Masculinities in "safe" and "embattled" organizations accounting for pornographic and feminist magazines. *Gender & Society*, *18*(5), 545–566.

Denes, A. (2011, October). Biology as consent: Problematizing the scientific approach to seducing women's bodies. *Women's Studies International Forum*, *34*(5), 411–419.

Doolen, T. L., & Long, M. (2007). Identification of retention levers using a survey of engineering freshman attitudes at Oregon State University. *European Journal of Engineering Education*, *32*(6), 721–734.

Dugdale, A. (1985). Can a feminist critique of the masculinity of scientific knowledge provide a blueprint for a less inhumane science? Evelyn Fox Keller and the feminist dream of a degendered science. *Contributors and Editors*, 53.

Dusek, V. (2006). *Philosophy of technology: An introduction*. Blackwell Publishing.

Etzkowitz, H., Kemelgor, C., & Uzzi, B. (2000). *Athena unbound: The advancement of women in science and technology*. Cambridge University Press.

Gilligan, C. (1982). *In a different voice*. Harvard University Press.

Griffin, S. (2015). *Woman and nature: The roaring inside her*. Open Road Media.

Halpin, Z. T. (1989, December). Scientific objectivity and the concept of "the other". In *Women's studies international forum* (Vol. 12, No. 3, pp. 285–294). Pergamon.

Haraway, D. (1988). Situated knowledges: The science question in feminism and the privilege of partial perspective. *Feminist Studies*, *14*(3), 575–599. https://doi.org/10.2307/3178066

Haraway, D. J. (1989). *Primate visions: Gender, race, and nature in the world of modern science*. Psychology Press.

Haraway, D. (2020). Situated knowledges: The science question in feminism and the privilege of partial perspective. In *Feminist theory reader* (pp. 303–310). Routledge.

Harding, S. G. (1986). *The science question in feminism*. Cornell University Press.

Harding, S. (1991). *Whose science? Whose knowledge? Thinking from women's lives*. Cornell University.

Hazari, Z., Tai, R. H., & Sadler, P. M. (2007). Gender differences in introductory university physics performance: The influence of high school physics preparation and affective factors. *Science Education*, *91*(6), 847–876.

Hesse-Biber, S. N., & Yaiser, M. L. (2004). *Feminist perspectives on social research*. Oxford University Press. https://philpapers.org/rec/HESFPO

Hubbard, R. (1990). *The politics of women's biology*. Rutgers University Press.

Husu, L. (2001). On metaphors on the position of women in academia and science. *NORA - Nordic Journal of Feminist and Gender Research*, *9*(3), 172–181. https://doi.org/10.1080/713801035

Irigaray, L. (2005). In science, is the subject sexed? In Gutting, G. (Ed.), *Continental philosophy of science*. John Wiley & Sons.

Kantola, J. (2008). 'Why do all the women disappear?' Gendering processes in a political science department. *Gender, Work and Organization*, *15*(2), 202–225.

Keller, E. F. (1985). *Reflections on gender and science*. Yale University Press.

Kumar, N. (2001). Gender and stratification in science: An empirical study in the Indian setting. *Indian Journal of Gender Studies*, *8*(1), 51–67.

Longino, H. E. (1990). *Science as social knowledge: Values and objectivity in scientific inquiry*. Princeton University Press.

Longino, H., & Doell, R. (1983). Body, bias, and behavior: A comparative analysis of reasoning in two areas of biological science. *Signs: Journal of Women in Culture and Society*, *9*(2), 206–227.

Martin, E. (1991). The egg and the sperm: How science has constructed a romance based on stereotypical male-female roles. *Signs*, *16*(3), 485–501. http://www.jstor.org/stable/3174586

Merchant, C. (1979). The death of nature. *Organization & Environment*, *11*(2), 198.

Modgil, S., Gill, R., Lakshmi Sharma, V., Velassery, S., & Anand, A. (2018). Nobel nominations in science: Constraints of the fairer sex. *Annals of Neurosciences*, *25*(2), 63–78. https://doi.org/10.1159/000481906

Moss-Racusin, C. A., Dovidio, J. F., Brescoll, V. L., Graham, M. J., & Handelsman, J. (2012). Science faculty's subtle gender biases favor male students. *Proceedings of the National Academy of Sciences*, *109*(41), 16474–16479.

Rapp, R. (2001). Gender, body, biomedicine: How some feminist concerns dragged reproduction to the center of social theory. *Medical Anthropology Quarterly*, *15*(4), 466–477.

Ridgeway, C. L., & Correll, S. J. (2004). Unpacking the gender system a theoretical perspective on gender beliefs and social relations. *Gender & Society*, *18*(4), 510–531.

Rose, H. (1994). *Love and power in a scientific climate*. Indiana University Press.
Rossiter, A. B. (1997). A perspective on critical social work. *Journal of Progressive Human Services*, *7*(2), 23–41.
Sadker, M., & Sadker, D. (2010). *Failing at fairness: How America's schools cheat girls*. Simon & Schuster.
Schiebinger, L. (1991). *The mind has no sex?: Women in the origins of modern science*. Harvard University Press.
Schiebinger, L. (2001). *Has feminism changed science?* Harvard University Press.
Schindler, T. E. (2021, August 19). The Matilda effect: Joshua Lederberg's brilliance obscured his wife's reputation. In *A hidden legacy: The life and work of Esther Zimmer Lederberg* (online edn). Oxford Academic. https://doi.org/10.1093/oso/9780197531679.003.0010. Accessed on February 7, 2024.
Seymour, E. (2002). Tracking the processes of change in US undergraduate education in science, mathematics, engineering, and technology. *Science Education*, *86*(1), 79–105.
Seymour, E., & Hewitt, N. M. (1997). *Talking about leaving* (Vol. 34). Westview Press.
Sheffield, S. L. M. (2004). *Women and science: Social impact and interaction*. ABC-CLIO.
Shiva, V. (1988). *Staying alive: Women, ecology and development*. Zed Books.
Smyth, F. L., & Nosek, B. A. (2015). On the gender–science stereotypes held by scientists: Explicit accord with gender-ratios, implicit accord with scientific identity. *Frontiers in Psychology*, *6*, 415.
Subramaniam, B. (2009). Moored metamorphoses: A retrospective essay on feminist science studies. *Signs: Journal of Women in Culture and Society*, *34*(4), 951–980.
Sullivan, J. R., & Guerra, N. S. (2007). A closer look at college students: Self-efficacy and goal orientation. *Journal of Advanced Academics*, *18*(3), 454–476.
Sur, A. (2011). *Dispersed radiance: Caste, gender, and modern science in India*. Navayana Press.
Suter, C. (2006). Trends in gender segregation by field of work in higher education. In *OECD, women in scientific careers: Unleashing the potential* (pp. 95–104). Organisation for Economic Co-operation and Development.
Tacsir, E., Grazzi, M., & Castillo, R. (2014). *Women in science and technology: What does the literature say?* https://publications.iadb.org/publications/english/document/Women-in-Science-and-Technology-What-Does-the-Literature-Say.pdf
Tuana, N. (1988). The weaker seed. The sexist bias of reproductive theory. *Hypatia*, *3*(1), 35–59.
Tyson, W., Lee, R., Borman, K. M., & Hanson, M. A. (2007). Science, technology, engineering, and mathematics (STEM) pathways: High school science and math coursework and postsecondary degree attainment. *Journal of Education for Students Placed at Risk*, *12*(3), 243–270.
Van den Brink, M., & Benschop, Y. (2012). Gender practices in the construction of academic excellence: Sheep with five legs. *Organization*, *19*(4), 507–524. https://doi.org/10.1177/1350508411414293
Webers, J. (2007). Who's afraid of Nature? The rise and Fall of denaturalization in contemporaary feminist thought. In D. Orr (Ed.), *Feminist politics: Identity, difference, and agency* (p. 274). Rowman and Littlefield Publishers, Inc.
Whelan, E. (2001). Politics by other means: Feminism and mainstream science studies. *Canadian Journal of Sociology/Cahiers canadiens de sociologie*, 535–581.
Williams, C. L., Muller, C., & Kilanski, K. (2012). Gendered organizations in the new economy. *Gender & Society*, *26*(4), 549–573. https://doi.org/10.1177/0891243212445466
Wilz, S. M. (2001, June). Rethinking gender, work and organization–thinking about organization. In *Gender, work & organization conference* (pp. 27–29). Keele University.
Wyer, M. (2018). In the company of feminist science. In *APA handbook of the psychology of women: Perspectives on women's private and public lives* (Vol. 2, pp. 459–474). American Psychological Association.
Xie, Y., Shauman, K. A., & Shauman, K. A. (2003). *Women in science: Career processes and outcomes*. Harvard University Press.

THE INTERPLAY OF ICT AND ENVIRONMENT IN SMALL ISLAND STATES

Verena Tandrayen-Ragoobur, Sheereen Fauzel, Nandikesh Juglal and Bibi Nabeeha Jaunoo

University of Mauritius, Mauritius

ABSTRACT

Small islands are particularly vulnerable to environmental impacts, as multiple environmental as well as socio-economic changes are impacting their local communities and especially the most vulnerable segments of their population. Information and communication technologies (ICTs) are increasingly viewed as an opportunity for small islands to mitigate and adapt to climate change. ICT may help to monitor short-term and long-term climate trends, raise awareness, help protect the environment and reduce carbon emissions. Though the ICT sector has been recognised as crucial in ensuring sustainable development, it is also important to address its potential adverse impacts like energy consumption, electronic waste generation and digital inequality among others. The ICT-environment link is thus rather complex. While there is extensive literature on the ICT-climate change nexus, the evidence remains mixed. The evidence on small island economies is rather scant. The objective of this chapter is to investigate into the ICT and environment linkage for small islands taking on board the specificities of island economies. The Panel Vector Error Correction Model (PVECM) is used on 38 small islands over a period 2000–2020, and the long-run results show that higher use of ICT has resulted in lower carbon emissions.

Keywords: ICT; environment; CO_2 emissions; sustainability; small islands

Social Responsibility, Technology and AI
Developments in Corporate Governance and Responsibility, Volume 23, 203–222
Copyright © 2025 Verena Tandrayen-Ragoobur, Sheereen Fauzel, Nandikesh Juglal and Bibi Nabeeha Jaunoo
Published under exclusive licence by Emerald Publishing Limited
ISSN: 2043-0523/doi:10.1108/S2043-052320240000023011

1. INTRODUCTION

Small island nations are highly influenced by the impacts of climate change, along with other crisis like the health pandemic, cost of living crisis, fuel prices and geopolitical risks, to name a few. However, climate change remains the main battle which they have to confront. Islanders especially those living in the coastal areas and those in poverty are highly impacted by changes in climatic conditions. The vulnerability of communities across different islands is compounded by social economic factors like poverty, inequity and inequality. Climate change exacerbates these existing inequalities and inequities, affecting disproportionately the marginalised groups. Owing to these structural inequalities, the effects on some communities tend to be more pronounced, affecting their livelihoods and their daily life. It is often argued that technology and innovation can help in mitigating the effects of climate change. The role of information and communication technologies (ICT) can emerge as a potential game changer offering the capacity to reduce the adverse impacts of climate change and at the same time enable adaptive mechanisms to build preparedness and resilience. The use of ICT can help in monitoring the short-run and long-run effects of climate trends as well as raising awareness, fostering environmental protection and reducing carbon emissions (Charfeddine & Umlai, 2023). However, the link between ICT and the environment is not straightforward and is rather complex. Despite the potential benefits that can be derived from digitalisation, ICT and innovation, in terms of smart grids for the generation and consumption of energy (Ishida, 2015), the application of big data analytics for intelligent transport systems (Adedoyin et al., 2020; Noussan et al., 2020), the use of Internet of Things (IOT) for green manufacturing and construction (Nidumolu et al., 2009), the ICT sector necessitates important energy resources. ICT may increase energy utilisation and greenhouse gas (GHG) emissions and overall environmental degradation owing to its lifecycle (Lange et al., 2020; Raihan, 2023). Emissions are released during the extraction of the raw materials needed to produce ICT tools, in its production till its transportation to businesses and customers (Charfeddine & Umlai, 2023). In essence, ICT-related emissions are estimated at around 2% of global emissions, which is similar to emissions from the global aviation sector (Salahuddin & Alam, 2015). With recent innovations in the ICT industry through blockchain, cryptocurrencies and digital ledger technology, the negative impact on the environment is likely to be enhanced.

The existing empirical literature shows both the positive and negative effects of ICT on the environment by estimating and quantifying the environmental effects of digitalisation and ICT innovation. Belkhir and Elmeligi (2018) estimate the global carbon footprint of ICT to range between 1.9% and 2.3%, while Malmodin and Lundén (2018) obtain a range of world carbon footprint from ICT between 1.8% and 2.8%. Other studies between 2002 and 2012 obtain a similar range of 1.8%–2.8% for global GHG emissions from the ICT sector. Nonetheless, the empirical evidence remains mixed and diverges across regions and countries. For instance, Asongu and Le Roux (2017) study the ICT–environment nexus for sub-Saharan African countries and find that the increase in ICT through mobile phones and internet connection has a positive net effect on CO_2 emissions per capita. N'dri et al. (2021) assess the importance of ICT on sustainable environment for 58 developing countries. Their results indicate that the use of ICT is environmentally favourable for relatively low-income developing economies, while there is no evident link for relatively high-income developing economies. The bulk of research on the ICT–environment nexus has been focusing on developed, emerging and developing countries; the evidence for small islands remains therefore very scant.

This chapter assesses the intricate link between ICT and the environment in the context of small islands which are highly vulnerable to climate change impacts. The objective of the study is to analyse the dynamics of the relationship taking into account the challenges and opportunities which ICT can bring for small island states. Using a comprehensive dataset covering 38 small islands over two decades from 2000 to 2020, the paper uses as proxy for ICT penetration, mobile cellular subscriptions (per 100 people). The ICT indicator is analysed with respect to its short-term and long-term effects on the environmental index of CO_2 emissions. The study contributes to the global discourse on ICT and sustainable development and in particular the role of ICT in shaping the environmental resilience of small islands.

This chapter is structured as follows. Section 2 reviews the literature on ICT and environment linkage, while section 3 analyses the data on ICT and CO_2 emissions across island economies. Section 4 sets out the data and methodology used and specifies the econometric model to be estimated. Section 5 discusses the findings, and this chapter concludes in section 6 with policy implications.

2. LITERATURE REVIEW

The existing literature on the socio-economic impacts of ICT has been categorised in three segments. First, those studies analysing the economic impacts of ICT (Polák, 2017; Vu et al., 2020) in terms of productivity (Niebel, 2018; Timmer & Van Ark, 2005) or economic growth. The second strand of the literature concentrates on the environment impact of ICT (Bieser & Hilty, 2018; Wang et al., 2021) whether through its negative environmental effects in terms of increased energy consumption (Cheng et al., 2019; Wang et al., 2016) or through energy conservation and reduction in emissions (Han et al., 2016; Li & Du, 2021). The last category investigates as to whether or not ICT promotes sustainability, that is, its effects on environmental performance (Godil et al., 2020; Nguyen et al., 2020).

The literature on the ICT and environment nexus is rather extensive with an attempt to probe into the complex and multidimensional linkage between the two variables (Elliot, 2011; Gholami et al., 2016; Klimova et al., 2016; Melville, 2010; Watson et al., 2012). While the literature on the impact of ICT on economic growth tends to show a positive and significant effect of ICT investment on productivity and output growth across countries in particular developed economies (Dimelis & Papaioannou, 2011; Ollo-López & Aramendía-Muneta, 2012; O'Mahony et al., 2005), there is mixed evidence on the ICT–environment link. The literature also discusses the role of ICT in poverty alleviation, increasing productivity and economic performance in developing countries (Jorgenson et al., 2008). Studies like Dimelis and Papaioannou (2010) and Dedrick et al. (2013) have shown the positive and significant productivity gains of ICT investment across upper income developing countries, and these productivity effects in Dedrick et al. (2013) are moderated by factors like human capital and openness to foreign direct investment (FDI).

The intersection between ICT and the environment remains rather complex. The positive and negative impacts of ICT on the environment have been assessed in terms of three different levels namely the first-order or direct effects, the second-order or indirect effects and the third-order or systemic effects (Berkhout & Hertin, 2001; Mahdavi & Sojoodi, 2021). Similarly, Köhler and Erdmann (2004) and Hilty et al. (2006) have defined the effect as first-order or primary effects in terms of environmental impacts of production, usage, recycling and disposal of ICT equipment. In terms of the first-order effects, ICT production, use and disposal have negative environmental impacts and increase CO_2 emissions. The ICT industry is viewed as a power drainer where intermediate systems or networking devices contribute heavily to ICT footprint. This growth in emissions from the ICT devices and therefore their environmental and climatic impacts come from energy consumption used both in manufacturing and functioning of these devices (Røpke & Christensen, 2012). ICT is initially introduced across industries as part of the growth process, thereby contributing to their expansion but at the same time greater emissions through the scale effect. In addition, mining for earth metals used in manufacturing of ICT devices and waste disposal are additional contributors to the total ICT industry CO_2 footprint (Belkhir & Elmeligi, 2018). ICT infrastructure in particular the data centre industry which serves as the backbone of both the internet as well as the telecom industry amplifies the ICT's contribution to total CO_2 emissions. Further, the relative GHG emission footprint contribution of smartphones has been rising over the years. This is not only the result of the explosive proliferation of mobile phones around the world but more so of the combined effect of the high production footprint and the short lifespan of these products. Many ICT devices and equipment cannot be easily recycled. Improper recycling of such devices represents a significant source of environmental pollution (Williams, 2011). The incineration of ICT devices along with other wastes lead to the release of hazardous compounds that have important socio-economic implications.

The secondary or second-order effects relate to the indirect environmental impacts of ICT through energy use in production and transportation. The second-order effects also include the positive impact of ICT on sustainable development as with the use of ICT, many countries have moved towards more environmentally friendly products and services (Hertin & Berkhout, 2001). ICT has revolutionised the way people communicate and work. For instance, e-commerce, tele-working and video conferencing have reduced the worldwide travelling of both people and goods and hence the consumption of petroleum and the emission of GHGs (Yi & Thomas, 2007). ICT has also helped towards providing intelligent and automated solutions within different sectors, thus improving energy efficiency and reducing GHG emissions (Bekaroo et al., 2016). Furthermore, wireless sensors and monitoring technology has enabled countries to develop the concept of so-called 'smart grids', 'smart homes' and 'smart buildings' to better optimise energy management, operational efficiency, energy supply quality reducing the negative impact on the environment (Chwieduk, 2003; Gharavi & Ghafurian, 2011; Houghton, 2010; Paetz et al., 2012).

Lastly, the third-order or tertiary effects are medium- or long-run adaptation or behavioural change moving towards the greening of ICT both in terms of consumption as well as production patterns. The third order effects, which are known as systemic (rebound) impacts are linked to the outcomes that follow the direct or indirect impacts of ICT on the environment (Mahdavi & Sojoodi, 2021). The 'ICT for green' view contemplates ICT as a possible solution to many environmental problems. ICT can improve carbon productivity as inputs to production systems and by optimising production processes (Dedrick, 2010). The input and output effects are also possible. Watson et al. (2010) discuss the transformative ability of ICT in order to create an environmentally sustainable society. ICT-based solutions have greatly impacted the environment in a positive manner by reducing GHG emissions. Yilmaz et al. (2019) showed that ICT has a positive (reducing) effect on deforestation by making it easier to map and monitor forest hazards and threats.

ICT helps in the production of more goods and services leading to higher economic growth, but at the same time, greater level of economic development leads to a greater demand for ICT goods and services that necessitates more electricity consumption and as such greater CO_2 emissions (Lee & Brahmasrene, 2014). As per the Environmental Kuznets Curve (EKC) hypothesis, pollution per capita initially worsens as countries develop, but in the long run, it improves with high economic growth (Ghosh & Yamarik, 2007; Aslanidis, 2009). This can be explained by several effects namely the scale effect, the output effect, the input effect and the technology effect. The first one related to a situation where emissions rise with a larger scale of economic activities while the output effect is explained by changes in the structure of production from basic manufacturing to more sophisticated value-added activities that may result in a reduction of carbon emissions per unit of output. The third effect is the input effect whereby enterprises adopt increasingly less environmentally damaging inputs and move towards more environmentally friendly production techniques that reduce emissions per output. Lastly, technology effect is the adoption of new technologies that improve production processes with minimal negative impacts on the environment. At the early stages of economic growth, the scale effect outweighs the other effects, while at later stages of growth, the other effects prevail, leading to invested U-shaped link between growth and environment. However, while the literature postulated this inverted U-shaped connection, the empirical evidence supporting the EKC is rather mixed and highly country specific (Van Alstine & Neumayer, 2010).

The EKC has been linked to ICT. For instance, Van Alstine and Neumayer (2010) show that ICT contributes to the firms' growth and expansion via the scale effect through greater emissions. This ICT relates mainly to investment in computers and software which tend to increase emissions, but once the basic ICT capital is in place, the additional ICT investment will focus more on optimising production processes, increasing energy efficient and reducing emission intensity in which case the technology effect prevails over the scale effect (Higón et al., 2017). The input and output effects are also relevant as ICT ensures the use of cleaner inputs and the production of more ICT-based output. Hence, there may exist an inverted U-shaped link between ICT and CO_2 emissions where the latter is expected to increase as ICT development proceeds, but at more advanced stages of ICT expansion, CO_2 emissions may fall (Higón et al., 2017). With further development of the ICT sector and changes in the economic structure, it becomes easier to pursue environmental sustainability. ICT reduces CO_2 emissions through innovative technologies so much that the development of a strong ICT sector with high levels of human capital can potentially reduce CO_2 emissions.

The inverted U-shaped link can also be explained via resource and energy utilisation linked with ICT which has important implications for the environment. ICT has also placed significant pressure on the environment through resource and energy utilisation (Barış-Tüzemen et al., 2020), but ICT penetration may increase sustainability and eco-friendly practices by preventing wastage of resources. The use of automation systems across sectors such as agriculture, manufacturing, construction and services can reduce the need for resources and energy. In the financial services sector, the use of e-banking systems and online transactions has helped in decarbonising the financial system (Kouton, 2019). Further, the use of mobile phones and internet technologies prevent wastage of resources through the use of e-services like e-commerce (Shabani & Shahnazi, 2019). In addition, the use of smart devices and applications like online meeting applications reduce international travels, save costs and mitigate CO_2 emissions (Atsu et al., 2021).

The empirical evidence on the ICT and environment nexus remains mixed. For instance, Mahdavi (2021) find evidence of the positive role of ICT development in reducing environmental pollution in selected countries. Their conclusion is consistent with the results of Chowdhury (2012), Stewart (2015) and Zhang and Liu (2015) but contradicts the findings of Arushanyan et al. (2014), Amri et al. (2019) and Avom et al. (2020). With the advent of ICT, people's lifestyles have changed, and ICT has created many tools and opportunities for efficiency improvement. This can be expected to alleviate environmental degradation. The increasing use of technologies in transportation networks can lead to a decrease in the CO_2 emissions. Increasing level of ICT utilisation in a variety of fields also triggers a substitution trend, which means the reorganisation of production processes to make them more energy-efficient. However, Arushanyan et al. (2014) show that the use of ICT products and services has a notable negative impact on global energy consumption and global warming. The efficiency improvement resulting from the use of ICT can lead to increased energy consumption. This is known as the rebound impact. Furthermore, the high ICT-dependence of production processes causes higher energy consumption in the sector.

Salahuddin et al. (2016) analysed the complex relationship between internet usage, economic growth and CO_2 in the Organization for Economic Cooperation and Development (OECD) countries between 1991 and 2012. They found evidence of a positive, albeit small, long-run relationship between internet usage and CO_2 emissions, but no causal association exists. Their analysis advocates leveraging ICT-enabled emissions abatement potential across different economic sectors in order to allow OECD countries to balance internet growth with environmental stability. The use of modern technologies and implementation of environmentally friendly practices can be adopted to encourage a gradual transition to a green internet environment. There is thus a need for appropriate coordination between ICT and green energy development policies to address the climate change challenges on a global level.

The link between ICT and environment is also analysed for developing countries and in particular for African countries (Avom et al., 2020; Awad, 2022; Mamadou Asngar, 2022). For instance, Avom et al. (2020) show that ICT affects the environment across 21 sub-Saharan African countries through both direct and indirect effects on CO_2 emissions. The direct effect leads to a rise in CO_2 emissions, while the indirect impacts are divided into two parts, first a positive indirect impact via energy consumption and financial development and second a negative indirect effect through trade openness. The total effect is however positive indicating that ICT worsens environmental quality in the region. To mitigate the negative effects of ICT, it is proposed that appropriate policies should be designed to improve energy efficiency and promote the use of renewable energy as well as provide the financial incentives to develop green technologies. Likewise, Mamadou Asngar, (2022) probe into the impact of internet and mobile phone penetration on environmental sustainability measured by CO_2 emissions in 38 sub-Saharan African economies. Their results indicate that investment in ICT infrastructure improves environmental sustainability across all countries, irrespective of their level of income. As such, universal ICT usage is to be promoted in the region. Awad (2022) adopts a larger sample of 47 sub-Saharan African countries to investigate the impact of ICT on environmental quality and employ advanced econometric techniques. There is evidence that ICT services have a favourable but statistically insignificant impact on environmental quality across selected economies. There seems to be no trade-off between increasing ICT infrastructure and sustaining the environmental quality in the region. The only study on small islands relates ICT to economic growth (Qureshi & Najjar, 2017). Their analysis shows the positive multiplier effects of ICT usage on economic growth across 32 very small island states. The evidence on the link between ICT and environment remains mixed for both developed and developing countries, and to the best of our knowledge, there seems to be no evidence for small islands. This chapter bridges the gap by analysing the complex link between ICT and the environment in the context of 38 Small Island Developing States (SIDs) over the last two decades.

3. ICT PENETRATION AND CO_2 EMISSIONS IN SIDS

SIDs contribute less than 1% of global GHG emissions and represents less than 1% of the world's population. However, they are most affected by climate change as they are located in regions prone to extreme weather events, such as hurricanes, cyclones and storm surges, and their geographical position makes them highly susceptible to the impacts of climate change, including sea-level rise. Fig. 1 shows CO_2 emissions per capita across SIDs in 2020, and this confirms the low level of carbon emissions with the exception of Bahrain which seems to be an outlier in the sample.

Next, the ICT index used in this study includes information about mobile cellular subscriptions (per 100 people). The link between ICT usage and CO_2 emissions is analysed as per Fig. 2.

The relationship between these two variables provides an understanding of the extent to which increasing mobile technologies used as a proxy for ICT can affect carbon emissions. The data reveal a positive relationship initially, but this connection seems to decline over time. The positive association may indicate the environmental costs of technology usage. The adverse impacts of ICT on the environment can be explained by different factors. First, the negative effects are shown in terms of increased CO_2 emissions which stem from electronic waste. Rapid technological advancements and shorter product lifecycles contribute to significant rise in e-waste which contains hazardous materials like lead or mercury. These are potential threats to the environment and sustainable development. Resource depletion, environmental degradation and loss of biodiversity are important impacts which result from the extraction of raw materials such as earth metals and minerals for the production of ICT devices. The ICT industry also demands substantial energy mainly from non-renewable sources. This energy is

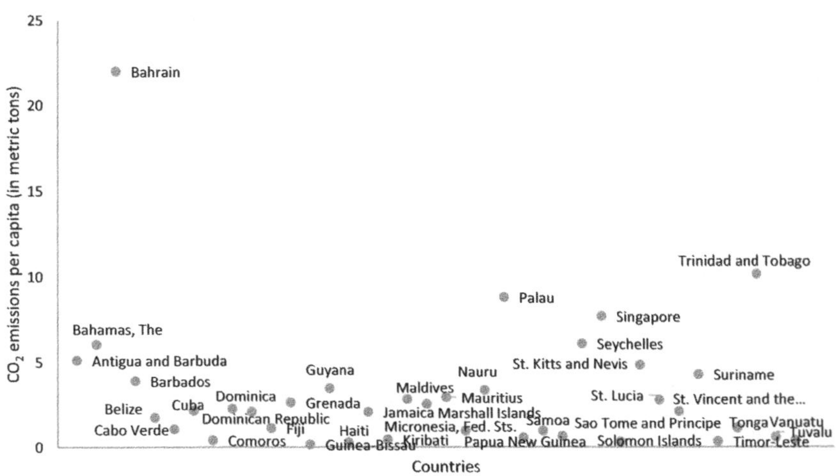

Fig. 1. CO_2 Emissions (Metric Tons per Capita) Across SIDs in 2020.
Source: Compiled from World Bank Indicators, 2023.

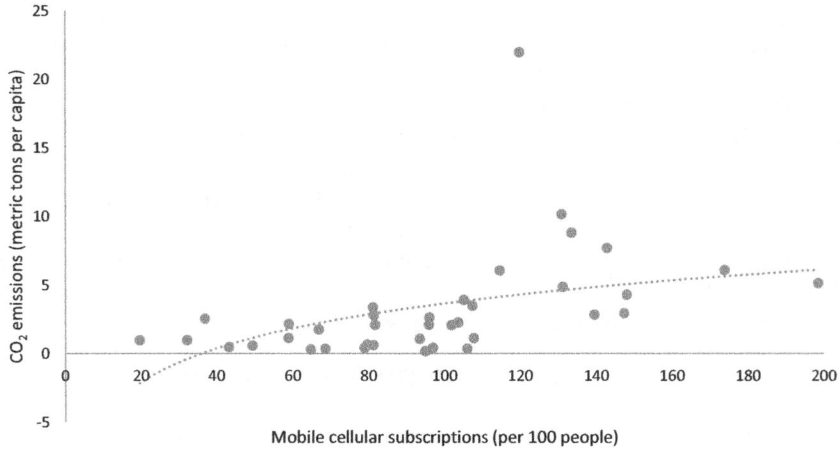

Fig. 2. CO_2 Emissions (Metric Tons per Capita) and Mobile Cellular Subscriptions (per 100 People) Across SIDs. *Source:* Compiled from World Bank Indicators, 2023.

needed to manufacture, operate and transport ICT tools. For instance, data centres which represent an important component of the ICT infrastructure consume significant amount of energy for processing and storage. High carbon emissions and energy consumption increase the overall carbon footprint of the ICT sector. The manufacturing of ICT components further necessitates the use of environmentally harmful substances which increase GHG emissions, hence pollution, resource depletion and adverse effects on the ecosystem. Lastly, in small islands, in particular, the uneven access to ICT can lead to disparities in digital literacy across communities. The marginalised communities may find themselves at a disadvantage affected not only by difficult access to ICT but also more likely to be impacted by the negative consequences of electronic waste disposal. In the long run, advancements in ICT and as such mobile technologies are argued to coincide with more sustainable practices and lower carbon emissions. The positive impacts are likely to be felt over the long run provided e-waste, energy consumption and extraction of raw materials amongst others are properly managed to ensure sustainable development.

4. DATA AND METHODOLOGY

Data was collected from the World Development Indicators 2023; World Bank, 2023) for 38 small islands. The economies included in the study include Antigua and Barbuda, Bahamas, the Bahrain, Barbados, Belize, Cabo Verde, Cuba, Comoros, Dominica, Dominican Republic, Fiji, Grenada, Guinea-Bissau, Guyana, Haiti, Jamaica, Kiribati, Maldives, Marshall Islands, Mauritius, Micronesia Fed. Sts, Nauru, Palau, Papua New Guinea, Samoa, Sao Tome and

Principe, Seychelles, Singapore, Solomon Islands, St. Kitts and Nevis, St. Lucia, St. Vincent and the Grenadines, Suriname, Timor-Leste, Tonga, Trinidad and Tobago, Tuvalu and Vanuatu.

The objective of this study is to investigate the effect of ICT on the environment in the case of small island economies over the period 2000–2020. As per Zhang et al. (2022) where carbon emissions are used as a measure of environment, an econometric model is presented in Eq. (1). Other control variables such as economic growth, local investment, FDI and the usage of renewable energy have been used to investigate the impact of ICT on environmental in small islands (Kayani et al., 2023).

The following model is used in the present study:

$$CO_2 = f(\text{ICT}, \text{RGDP}, \text{GDCF}, \text{FDI}, \text{RENEW}) \tag{1}$$

where carbon dioxide per capita is proxied by CO_2, RGDP is real GDP, while local investment and FDI are proxied by GDCF and FDI, respectively, and renewable energy consumption as a % of total final energy consumption is represented by RENEW.

4.1 Definition of Variables

4.1.1 Dependent Variable

Carbon dioxide (CO_2) accounts for the largest portion of GHG emissions and is a major source of environmental problems. CO_2 emissions, measured in metric tons (Dogan & Seker, 2016; Ozbugday & Erbas, 2015; Piłatowska et al., 2020; Shafiei & Salim, 2014; Waheed et al., 2018), were transformed into a per capita measure to adjust for the population size of the island economies. This is an exogenous variable in the regression widely used by scholars in related studies and represents better environment quality if it is a lower level.

Telecommunications and the mobile industry have experienced significant development all over the world (Edquist & Bergmark, 2023). There is a high use of mobile phone which results in an increase in electronic activities like e-banking, e-commerce, e-trade and so on. Technology has been reported to be a determining factor in mitigating climate change. The economic impact of digitalisation has increased tremendously with the heavy usage of computers, smartphones and tablets, allowing the world to be connected. At the same time, the use of ICT can have important adverse effects on the environment and sustainable development through high carbon footprint resulting from increased energy consumption, e-waste, depletion of raw materials and use of environmentally harmful resources, to name a few. The present study follows Edquist and Bergmark (2023) and includes mobile broadband penetration as measured by mobile cellular subscription in the island economies.

Another control variable is economic growth proxied by the real GDP. The link between environment and aggregate economic activity has been extensively researched. For instance, Mikayilov, Hasanov et al. (2018) used GDP per capita as a measure of economic growth to investigate its impact on carbon emissions in a time series setting and found a positive and statistically significant impact on the emissions in the long run. Similar results were obtained by Hasanov et al. (2019) who investigated the CO_2 emissions–economic growth relationship. Hence, real GDP is integrated in the model to investigate its link with carbon emissions for small island economies.

In addition to economic growth, FDI is as well observed to have an impact on the environment. However, the literature does not really have a consensus on the link between FDI and environment. For instance, developing countries with low environmental standards is prone to have more pollution from economic activities from both local and foreign investment. Since, developed countries have strong environmental standards, firms shift their production in developing countries, thereby turning these economies into 'Pollution haven'. Hence, to further investigate whether this situation holds for the small island economies considered under the present study, we included inward FDI inflow as a percentage of GDP in the model (Dinda & Coondoo, 2006; Fauzel, 2017; Grimes & Jeffrey Kentor, 2003; Halicioglu, 2009). Similarly, we also included local investment as a % of GDP (GDCF) to investigate the impact of local investment on carbon emissions.

Moreover, renewable energy consumption (RENEW) has been considered in environmental pollution studies. By reducing energy consumption, CO_2 emissions can be reduced and thus improves the environmental quality. Hence, policymakers have been interested in examining alternative energy sources such as renewable and nuclear energy as a substitute for fossil fuels (Alper & Onur, 2016). Similarly, Owusu and Asumadu-Sarkodie (2016) argue that the use of cleaner renewable energy sources and technologies produces small amount of secondary waste, thus offers energy security, meets current and future economic and social needs and reduces environmental issues. Hence, renewable energy consumption as a % of total final energy consumption is included to analyse the impact of renewable energy usage on carbon emissions for the small island economies.

The variables are converted in natural logarithm to reduce the problem of heteroscedasticity. The following equation is thus rewritten as:

$$\begin{aligned}\mathrm{lnCO}_{2it} = {} & \beta_0 + \beta_1 \mathrm{lnICT}_{it} + \beta_2 \mathrm{lnRGDP}_{it} + \beta_3 \mathrm{lnGDCF}_{it} + \beta_4 \mathrm{ln3FDI}_{it} \\ & + \beta_5 \mathrm{lnRENEW}_{it} + \epsilon_{it}\end{aligned} \tag{2}$$

where i represents country, t represents time, ϵ is the random error term. The parameter estimates are $\beta_1 \ldots \beta_5$, and the random disturbance term is ε_{it}.

5. FINDINGS AND DISCUSSIONS

Table 1 reports the correlation matrix between the variables. The figures indicate that the variables are not correlated with one another, and there is no evidence of a high degree of multicollinearity.

Table 1. Correlation Matrix.

	CO_2	ICT	RGDP	GDCF	FDI	RENEW
CO_2	1	0.148	0.295	0.207	0.213	−0.523
ICT	0.148	1	0.714	0.026	0.570	−0.096
RGDP	0.295	0.714	1	0.077	0.938	−0.263
GDCF	0.207	0.026	0.077	1	0.061	−0.454
FDI	0.213	0.570	0.9380	0.061	1	−0.210
RENEW	−0.523	−0.096	−0.263	−0.454	−0.210	1

Source: Authors' compilation, 2024.

5.1 Panel Unit Root Tests

It is crucial to investigate the time series properties before estimating the model. As identified by Granger and Newbold (1974) and Phillips (1986), one may get biased results from regressing time series data mainly because of the likelihood that the data might be non-stationary. Hence, the panel unit root tests are performed to analyse the order of integration of the different variables used in the study. Im et al.'s (2003) panel unit root tests have been used, and the findings show that stationarity is achieved after differencing each variable once. This implies that the variables are integrated of order one.

5.2 Panel Cointegration Test

After checking for stationarity of the variables, the existence of cointegration between the variables is assessed, that is, whether there is a long-run link between the variables. The Kao Residual Cointegration test shows the existence of cointegrating association amid the variables. Hence, the study proceeded with the use of a panel vector error correction model.

In the presence of cointegration, a Panel Vector Error Correction Model (PVECM) is adopted as it caters for dynamism in the model. By adopting a PVECM, the study not only analyses the potential effect of ICT on environment in small island economies but also assesses any reverse causality which may prevail between them. An investigation of other feedback and indirect effects in the hypothesised link is also possible. This framework resembles a series of equations where each determinant comes as the explained variable in a system which is then solved simultaneously. A VAR in an error correction model (VECM) is estimated, and the pth order PVECM is specified as follows:

$$\Delta Z_{it} = \prod_i Z_{i,t-1} + \Gamma_{i1}\Delta Z_{i,t-1} + \ldots\ldots + \Gamma_{i,p-1}\Delta Z_{i,t-p+1} + \mu_{it} \quad (3)$$

$$Z_{it} = [CO_{2\,it}, ICT_{it}, RGDP_{it}, GDCF_{it}, FDI_{it}, RENEW_{it}]$$

The VECM linking short-term and long-term causality between ICT and sustainable development is set as follows:

$$\Delta \ln CO_{2\,t} = \alpha_0 + \sum_{j=1}^{n} \alpha_1 \, \Delta \ln ICT_{t-j} + \sum_{j=1}^{n} \alpha_2 \, \Delta \ln RGDP_{t-j} + \sum_{j=1}^{n} \alpha_3 \, \Delta \ln GDCF_{t-j} \sum_{j=1}^{n} \alpha_4 \, \Delta \ln FDI_{t-j} + \sum_{j=1}^{n} \alpha_5 \, \Delta \ln RENEW_{t-j} + \eta ECT_{T-1} + \epsilon_t \tag{4}$$

i denote the different countries in the sample, and t denotes the time dimension. μ is a standard white noise process. The PVECM is estimated by using an optimal lag length of 1, and the results of the model are reported in Table 2.

Analysing the results from Table 2, it is observed from column 2 that the coefficient measuring the impact of ICT on environment is negative and significant. It implies that a 1% increase in ICT use decreases carbon emissions by 1.12%. This result is in line with Bekaroo et al. (2016), Shabani and Shahnazi (2019), Elliot (2011) and Higón et al. (2017). Indeed, the use of technology and green innovation has been a crucial element in reducing carbon footprint of existing activities in small islands. By using ICT, there has been a reduction in emissions (Ismagilova et al., 2019, Legner et al., 2017). Moreover, ICT-supported solutions such as emails instead of paper usage, e-commerce as well as e-banking, all contribute positively to the environment (Bekaroo et al., 2016). ICT-supported products also have an important effect on lowering the ICT carbon footprint (Elliot, 2011). Digitalisation usage improves the environmental quality through the development of smart cities, better transportation system, network system, industrial production operations and energy-efficient products (Higón et al., 2017).

Analysing the impact of an increase in economic activity on environment and CO_2 emissions, a positive and significant result is obtained. A 1% increase in economic activity results in 0.77% increase carbon emissions. Several scholars have found similar results (Danish Hassan et al., 2019; Mikayilov, Galeotti, et al., 2018; Mohsin et al., 2021; Nathaniel et al., 2021; Özbay & Pehlivan, 2021; Pata & Caglar, 2021; Zafar et al., 2021). Economic growth relates to an increase in the amount of goods and services produced in an economy and is found to result in an increase in well-being (Stevenson & Wolfers, 2008). However, an increase in output and consumption also has certain costs associated with it. For instance, the environmental impact of economic growth includes the increased consumption of non-renewable resources, higher levels of pollution, global warming and the potential loss of environmental habitats (Everett et al.,

Table 2. Long Run Results.

Variables	Coefficient	t-statistics
LICT	−1.119***	−13.614
LRGDP	0.774***	7.157
LGDCF	0.111	0.475
LFDI	0.194***	2.382
LRENEW	−0.055	−0.762
Constant	−6.072	0.753

Source: Authors' compilation, 2024.

Note: *** represents significance at 1%.

2010). However, not all forms of economic growth result in environmental degradation. It has been observed that developed countries make use of more environmentally friendly methods of production and devote resources to the protection of the environment and thus register lesser pollution as opposed to developing countries.

Further analysis of the results shows that FDI is another variable influencing carbon footprint (CO2) in the sample of small islands considered under the study. A 1% increase in FDI inflows has resulted in 0.19% increase in carbon emissions proving the pollution Haven theory. It is argued that consistent inflow of FDI results in economic growth, and the same has been reported by various scholars like Blin and Ouattara (2009) and Fauzel et al. (2016). While FDI can benefit the economy by promoting economic growth, it can as well harm the economy by increasing the level of pollution (Fauzel, 2017). For example, the study by Beladi et al. (2016) shows that foreign investment adversely impacts on the environment in the South, and the same was found by Blanco-Gutiérrez et al. (2013). While local investment also has a positive impact on carbon emissions as per the above result, it is statistically insignificant. Similar result has been observed for the use of renewable energy on carbon footprints. The value of RENEW is negative and insignificant for the panel of countries studied. Similar results were obtained by Kayani et al. (2023) and the finding is explained by the relatively small time period considered under the study.

6. CONCLUSION AND RECOMMENDATIONS

This chapter assessed the impact of ICT on environmental across 38 small island economies over the period 2000–2020. Carbon emissions per capita are used as a proxy for environment, while mobile penetration is used to measure ICT. The PVECM method is adopted to investigate the association between environment and ICT. The results show that the higher usage of ICT has led to lower carbon emissions across the island economies under study. Though, there seems to be a positive impact of ICT use on the environment, implying that over time the benefits of the ICT industry has outweighed its adverse effects in terms of carbon emissions, it should be noted that the ICT industry is still an important energy-intensive industry as well as a growing e-waste producer. This poses a persistent and long-term environmental challenge contributing to pollution and representing potential health hazards. Technological dependence and obsolescence is a key challenge as the dependence on specific ICT platforms and systems with constant need for upgrades and updates is related to waste generation, resource use and the difficulties to generate sustainable new technologies. In addition to the environmental impacts of ICT, there are also significant economic and social implications. For instance, automation and digitalisation can cause job displacement with low-skilled workers losing their jobs and being replaced by machines. This is likely to have important employment and social implications on communities. The labour market landscape will change necessitating new approaches to employment and skills development. Across islands, vulnerable communities tend to be more impacted by social inequalities and the digital divide. Unequal access to ICT perpetuates a digital divide which has a negative bearing on the education, social and economic opportunities of this segment of the society. The widespread adoption of ICT can also contribute to the neglect or loss of traditional practices and cultural heritage, and this may result in a decline in cultural diversity with potential consequences for sustainable development.

Addressing these long-term negative impacts requires a holistic and proactive approach that integrates sustainability considerations into the design, production and use of ICT. Strategies should focus on promoting circular economy principles, responsible consumption and the equitable distribution of benefits associated with technological advancements. Appropriate policies are therefore required to further tap on the benefits of ICT and digitalisation. ICT has the potential to deal with climate change issues, and as such, policymakers need to design appropriate policies and set out the relevant mechanisms to promote digitalisation across economies. Moreover, promoting investment in digital infrastructure and green technologies will help in reducing pollution and moving towards a sustainable and green development pathway. Educating the population on the benefits of digitalisation in the context of climate change is as well important. There is a need to extend awareness of the benefits of digitalisation and its positive impact on the environment. Policymakers must come with the right regulations to ensure that the use of ICT reduces rather than increases carbon emissions. Digitalisation of economies helps in minimising waste and pollution (through e-banking, e-commerce, e-trade and e-services, among others). Countries need to ensure that activities involved in upgrading digital technologies do not increase carbon emissions. Appropriate regulations are crucial to outweigh the negative impacts of ICT and allow economies to maximise the benefits of its usage. Addressing these long-term adverse effects necessitates a holistic and sustainable approach, including responsible manufacturing practices, circular economy principles and systems, extended producer responsibility and the promotion of eco-friendly technologies. Sustainable Development Goals must prioritise mitigating environmental effects while promoting digital inclusion and equitable access to technology.

REFERENCES

Adedoyin, F. F., Gumede, M. I., Bekun, F. V., Etokakpan, M. U., & Balsalobre-Lorente, D. (2020). Modelling coal rent, economic growth and CO2 emissions: does regulatory quality matter in BRICS economies? *Science of the Total Environment*, *710*, 136284.

Alper, A., & Onur, G. (2016). Environmental Kuznets curve hypothesis for sub-elements of the carbon emissions in China. *Natural Hazards*, *82*, 1327–1340.

Amri, F., Zaied, Y. B., & Lahouel, B. B. (2019). ICT, total factor productivity, and carbon dioxide emissions in Tunisia. *Technological Forecasting and Social Change*, *146*, 212–217.

Arushanyan, Y., Ekener-Petersen, E., & Finnveden, G. (2014). Lessons learned–review of LCAs for ICT products and services. *Computers in Industry*, *65*(2), 211–234.

Aslanidis, N. (2009). Environmental Kuznets curves for carbon emissions: A critical survey. FEEM Working Paper No. 75.2009. https://ssrn.com/abstract=1498484. http://dx.doi.org/10.2139/ssrn.1498484

Asongu, S. A., & Le Roux, S. (2017). Enhancing ICT for inclusive human development in Sub-Saharan Africa. *Technological Forecasting and Social Change*, *118*, 44–54.

Atsu, F., Adams, S., & Adjei, J. (2021). ICT, energy consumption, financial development, and environmental degradation in South Africa. *Heliyon*, *7*(7).

Avom, D., Nkengfack, H., Fotio, H. K., & Totouom, A. (2020). ICT and environmental quality in Sub-Saharan Africa: Effects and transmission channels. *Technological Forecasting and Social Change*, *155*, 120028.

Awad, A. (2022). Is there a trade-off between ICTs and ecological systems in Africa? Evidence from heterogeneous panel methods robust to cross-sectional dependence. *Environmental Science and Pollution Research*, *29*(38), 58263–58277.

Barış-Tüzemen, Ö., Tüzemen, S., & Çelik, A. K. (2020). Does an N-shaped association exist between pollution and ICT in Turkey? ARDL and quantile regression approaches. *Environmental Science and Pollution Research*, *27*, 20786–20799.

Bekaroo, G., Bokhoree, C., & Pattinson, C. (2016). Impacts of ICT on the natural ecosystem: A grassroot analysis for promoting socio-environmental sustainability. *Renewable and Sustainable Energy Reviews*, *57*, 1580–1595.

Beladi, H., Dutta, M., & Kar, S. (2016). FDI and business internationalization of the unorganized sector: Evidence from Indian manufacturing. *World Development*, *83*, 340–349.

Belkhir, L., & Elmeligi, A. (2018). Assessing ICT global emissions footprint: Trends to 2040 & recommendations. *Journal of Cleaner Production*, *177*, 448–463.

Berkhout, F., & Hertin, J. (2001). Impacts of information and communication technologies on environmental sustainability: Speculations and evidence. *Report to the OECD, Brighton*, *21*, 23.

Bieser, J. C., & Hilty, L. M. (2018). Assessing indirect environmental effects of information and communication technology (ICT): A systematic literature review. *Sustainability*, *10*(8), 2662.

Blanco-Gutiérrez, I., Varela-Ortega, C., & Purkey, D. R. (2013). Integrated assessment of policy interventions for promoting sustainable irrigation in semi-arid environments: A hydro-economic modeling approach. *Journal of Environmental Management*, *128*, 144–160.

Blin, M., & Ouattara, B. (2009). Foreign direct investment and economic growth in Mauritius: Evidence from bounds test cointegration. *Économie Internationale*, (1), 47–61.

Charfeddine, L., & Umlai, M. (2023). ICT sector, digitization and environmental sustainability: A systematic review of the literature from 2000 to 2022. *Renewable and Sustainable Energy Reviews*, *184*, 113482.

Cheng, Z., Li, L., & Liu, J. (2019). The effect of information technology on environmental pollution in China. *Environmental Science and Pollution Research*, *26*(32), 33109–33124.

Chowdhury, G. (2012). Building environmentally sustainable information services: A green is research agenda. *Journal of the American Society for Information Science and Technology*, *63*(4), 633–647.

Chwieduk, D. (2003). Towards sustainable-energy buildings. *Applied Energy*, *76*(1–3), 211–217.

Danish Hassan, S. T., Baloch, M. A., Mahmood, N., & Zhang, J. W. (2019). Linking economic growth and ecological footprint through human capital and biocapacity. *Sustainable Cities and Society*, *47*, 101516.

Dedrick, J. (2010). Green IS: Concepts and issues for information systems research. *Communications of the Association for Information Systems*, *27*(1), 11.

Dedrick, J., Kraemer, K. L., & Shih, E. (2013). Information technology and productivity in developed and developing countries. *Journal of Management Information Systems*, *30*(1), 97–122.

Dimelis, S. P., & Papaioannou, S. K. (2010). FDI and ICT effects on productivity growth: A comparative analysis of developing and developed countries. *The European Journal of Development Research*, *22*, 79–96.

Dimelis, S. P., & Papaioannou, S. K. (2011). ICT growth effects at the industry level: A comparison between the US and the EU. *Information Economics and Policy*, *23*(1), 37–50.

Dinda, S., & Coondoo, D. (2006). Income and emission: A panel data-based cointegration analysis. *Ecological Economics*, *57*(2), 167–181.

Dogan, E., & Seker, F. (2016). Determinants of CO2 emissions in the European Union: The role of renewable and non-renewable energy. *Renewable Energy*, *94*, 429–439.

Edquist, H., & Bergmark, P. (2023). How is mobile broadband intensity affecting CO2 emissions? – A macro analysis. *Telecommunications Policy*, 102668.

Elliot, S. (2011). Transdisciplinary perspectives on environmental sustainability: A resource base and framework for IT-enabled business transformation. *MIS Quarterly*, 197–236.

Everett, T., Ishwaran, M., Ansaloni, G. P., & Rubin, A. (2010). *Economic growth and the environment*. MPRA Paper No. 23585. https://mpra.ub.uni-muenchen.de/23585/

Fauzel, S. (2017). The impact of FDI on CO2 emission in a small island developing state: A cointegration approach. *Economics and Business Letters*, *6*(1), 6–13.

Gharavi, H., & Ghafurian, R. (Eds.). (2011). *Smart grid: The electric energy system of the future* (Vol. 99, pp. 917–921). IEEE.

Gholami, R., Watson, R. T., Hasan, H., Molla, A., & Bjorn-Andersen, N. (2016). Information systems solutions for environmental sustainability: How can we do more? *Journal of the Association for Information Systems*, *17*(8), 2.

Ghosh, S., & Yamarik, S. (2007). International trade, technology, and the wage Gap: Evidence from Granger-causality tests. *Review of International Economics*, *15*(2), 321–346.

Godil, D. I., Sharif, A., Rafique, S., & Jermsittiparsert, K. (2020). The asymmetric effect of tourism, financial development, and globalization on ecological footprint in Turkey. *Environmental Science & Pollution Research*, *27*, 40109–40120.

Granger, C. W., & Newbold, P. (1974). Spurious regressions in econometrics. *Journal of Econometrics*, *2*(2), 111–120.

Grimes, P., & Kentor, J. (2003). Exporting the greenhouse: Foreign capital penetration and CO? Emissions 1980? 1996. *Journal of World-Systems Research*, 261–275.

Halicioglu, F. (2009). An econometric study of CO2 emissions, energy consumption, income and foreign trade in Turkey. *Energy Policy*, *37*(3), 1156–1164.

Han, J. H., Lee, M. J., & Hwang, Y. S. (2016). Tourists' environmentally responsible behavior in response to climate change and tourist experiences in nature-based tourism. *Sustainability*, *8*(7), 644.

Hasanov, F. J., Mikayilov, J. I., Mukhtarov, S., & Suleymanov, E. (2019). Does CO2 emissions–economic growth relationship reveal EKC in developing countries? Evidence from Kazakhstan. *Environmental Science and Pollution Research*, *26*, 30229–30241.

Hertin, J., & Berkhout, F. (2001). *Ecological modernisation and EU environmental policy integration*. University of Sussex.

Higón, D. A., Gholami, R., & Shirazi, F. (2017). ICT and environmental sustainability: A global perspective. *Telematics and Informatics*, *34*(4), 85–95.

Hilty, L. M., Arnfalk, P., Erdmann, L., Goodman, J., Lehmann, M., & Wäger, P. A. (2006). The relevance of information and communication technologies for environmental sustainability–a prospective simulation study. *Environmental Modelling & Software*, *21*(11), 1618–1629.

Houghton, J. W. (2010, September). ICT and the environment in developing countries: A review of opportunities and developments. In *IFIP International Conference on Human Choice and Computers* (pp. 236–247). Springer Berlin Heidelberg. Berlin, Heidelberg.

Im, K. S., Pesaran, M. H., & Shin, Y. (2003). Testing for unit roots in heterogeneous panels. *Journal of Econometrics*, *115*(1), 53–74.

Ishida, H. (2015). The effect of ICT development on economic growth and energy consumption in Japan. *Telematics and Informatics*, *32*(1), 79–88.

Ismagilova, E., Hughes, L., Dwivedi, Y. K., & Raman, K. R. (2019). Smart cities: Advances in research—An information systems perspective. *International Journal of Information Management*, *47*, 88–100.

Jorgenson, D. W., Ho, M. S., & Stiroh, K. J. (2008). A retrospective look at the US productivity growth resurgence. *The Journal of Economic Perspectives*, *22*(1), 3–24.

Kayani, U. N., Sadiq, M., Rabbani, M. R., Aysan, A. F., & Kayani, F. N. (2023). Examining the relationship between economic growth, financial development, and carbon emissions: A review of the literature and scientometric analysis. *International Journal of Energy Economics and Policy*, *13*(2), 489–499.

Klimova, A., Rondeau, E., Andersson, K., Porras, J., Rybin, A., & Zaslavsky, A. (2016). An international Master's program in green ICT as a contribution to sustainable development. *Journal of Cleaner Production*, *135*, 223–239.

Köhler, A., & Erdmann, L. (2004). Expected environmental impacts of pervasive computing. *Human and Ecological Risk Assessment*, *10*(5), 831–852.

Kouton, J. (2019). The asymmetric linkage between energy use and economic growth in selected African countries: Evidence from a nonlinear panel autoregressive distributed lag model. *Energy Economics*, *83*, 475–490.

Lange, S., Pohl, J., & Santarius, T. (2020). Digitalization and energy consumption. Does ICT reduce energy demand? *Ecological Economics*, *176*, 106760.

Lee, J. W., & Brahmasrene, T. (2014). ICT, CO2 emissions and economic growth: Evidence from a panel of ASEAN. *Global Economic Review*, *43*(2), 93–109.

Legner, C., Eymann, T., Hess, T., Matt, C., Böhmann, T., Drews, P., … & Ahlemann, F. (2017). Digitalization: Opportunity and challenge for the business and information systems engineering community. *Business & Information Systems Engineering*, *59*, 301–308.

Li, M., & Du, W. (2021). Can internet development improve the energy efficiency of firms: Empirical evidence from China. *Energy*, *237*, 121590.

Mahdavi, T. (2021). Application of the 'theory of planned behavior to understand farmers' intentions to accept water policy options using structural equation modeling. *Water Supply*, *21*(6), 2720–2734.

Mamadou Asngar, T. (2022). Does financial development improve access to electricity in sub-Saharan Africa? *SN Business & Economics*, *2*(9), 146.

Mahdavi, S., & Sojoodi, S. (2021). *Impact of ICT on Environment*. https://doi.org/10.21203/rs.3.rs-1020622/v1

Malmodin, J., & Lundén, D. (2018). The energy and carbon footprint of the global ICT and E&M sectors 2010–2015. *Sustainability*, *10*(9), 3027.

Melville, N. P. (2010). Information systems innovation for environmental sustainability. *MIS Quarterly*, 1–21.

Mikayilov, J. I., Galeotti, M., & Hasanov, F. J. (2018). The impact of economic growth on CO2 emissions in Azerbaijan. *Journal of Cleaner Production*, *197*, 1558–1572.

Mikayilov, J. I., Hasanov, F. J., & Galeotti, M. (2018). Decoupling of CO2 emissions and GDP: A time-varying cointegration approach. *Ecological Indicators*, *95*, 615–628.

Mohsin, M., Kamran, H. W., Nawaz, M. A., Hussain, M. S., & Dahri, A. S. (2021). Assessing the impact of transition from nonrenewable to renewable energy consumption on economic growth-environmental nexus from developing Asian economies. *Journal of Environmental Management*, *284*, 111999.

Nathaniel, S. P., Yalçiner, K., & Bekun, F. V. (2021). Assessing the environmental sustainability corridor: Linking natural resources, renewable energy, human capital, and ecological footprint in BRICS. *Resources Policy*, *70*, 101924.

N'dri, L. M., Islam, M., & Kakinaka, M. (2021). ICT and environmental sustainability: Any differences in developing countries? *Journal of Cleaner Production*, *297*, 126642.

Nguyen, T. T., Pham, T. A. T., & Tram, H. T. X. (2020). Role of information and communication technologies and innovation in driving carbon emissions and economic growth in selected G-20 countries. *Journal of Environmental Management*, *261*, 110162.

Nidumolu, R., Prahalad, C. K., & Rangaswami, M. R. (2009). Why sustainability is now the key driver of innovation. *Harvard Business Review*, *87*(9), 56–64.

Niebel, T. (2018). ICT and economic growth – Comparing developing, emerging and developed countries. *World Development*, *104*, 197–211.

Noussan, M., Raimondi, P. P., Scita, R., & Hafner, M. (2020). The role of green and blue hydrogen in the energy transition—A technological and geopolitical perspective. *Sustainability*, *13*(1), 298.

Ollo-López, A., & Aramendia-Muneta, M. E. (2012). ICT impact on competitiveness, innovation and environment. *Telematics and Informatics*, *29*(2), 204–210.

O'Mahony, M., Robinson, C., & Vecchi, M. (2005). *The impact of ICT on the demand for skilled labour* (No. 1285). National Institute of Economic and Social Research.

Owusu, P. A., & Asumadu-Sarkodie, S. (2016). A review of renewable energy sources, sustainability issues and climate change mitigation. *Cogent Engineering*, *3*(1), 1167990.

Özbay, F., & Pehlivan, C. (2021). Relationship between the use of renewable energy, carbon dioxide emission, and economic growth. In *Handbook of research on strategic management for current energy investments* (pp. 339–355). IGI Global.

Ozbugday, F. C., & Erbas, B. C. (2015). How effective are energy efficiency and renewable energy in curbing CO2 emissions in the long run? A heterogeneous panel data analysis. *Energy*, *82*, 734–745. https://doi.org/10.1016/j.energy.2015.01.084

Paetz, A. G., Dütschke, E., & Fichtner, W. (2012). Smart homes as a means to sustainable energy consumption: A study of consumer perceptions. *Journal of Consumer Policy*, *35*, 23–41.

Pata, U. K., & Caglar, A. E. (2021). Investigating the EKC hypothesis with renewable energy consumption, human capital, globalization and trade openness for China: Evidence from augmented ARDL approach with a structural break. *Energy*, *216*, 119220.

Phillips, P. C. (1986). Understanding spurious regressions in econometrics. *Journal of Econometrics*, *33*(3), 311–340.

Piłatowska, M., Geise, A., & Włodarczyk, A. (2020). The effect of renewable and nuclear energy consumption on decoupling economic growth from CO2 emissions in Spain. *Energies*, *13*(9), 2124.

Polák, P. (2017). The productivity paradox: A meta-analysis. *Information Economics and Policy*, *38*, 38–54.

Qureshi, S., & Najjar, L. (2017). Information and communications technology use and income growth: Evidence of the multiplier effect in very small Island states. *Information Technology for Development*, *23*(2), 212–234.

Raihan, A. (2023). Sustainable development in Europe: A review of the forestry sector's social, environmental, and economic dynamics. *Global Sustainability Research*, *2*(3), 72–92.

Røpke, I., & Christensen, T. H. (2012). Energy impacts of ICT–Insights from an everyday life perspective. *Telematics and Informatics*, *29*(4), 348–361.

Salahuddin, M., & Alam, K. (2015). Internet usage, electricity consumption and economic growth in Australia: A time series evidence. *Telematics and Informatics*, *32*(4), 862–878.

Salahuddin, M., Alam, K., & Ozturk, I. (2016). The effects of Internet usage and economic growth on CO2 emissions in OECD countries: A panel investigation. *Renewable and Sustainable Energy Reviews*, *62*, 1226–1235.

Shabani, Z. D., & Shahnazi, R. (2019). Energy consumption, carbon dioxide emissions, information and communications technology, and gross domestic product in Iranian economic sectors: A panel causality analysis. *Energy*, *169*, 1064–1078.

Shafiei, S., & Salim, R. A. (2014). Non-renewable and renewable energy consumption and CO2 emissions in OECD countries: A comparative analysis. *Energy Policy*, *66*, 547–556.

Stevenson, B., & Wolfers, J. (2008). *Economic growth and subjective well-being: Reassessing the Easterlin paradox* (No. w14282). National Bureau of Economic Research.

Stewart, K. (2015). Assessing the carbon impact of ICT measures: A case study investigation using Latis model. *International Journal of Transportation Science and Technology*, *4*(3), 277–294.

Timmer, M. P., & Van Ark, B. (2005). Does information and communication technology drive EU-US productivity growth differentials? *Oxford Economic Papers*, *57*(4), 693–716.

Van Alstine, J., & Neumayer, E. (2010). *The environmental Kuznets curve*. Department of Geography and Environment and Center for Environmental Policy and Governance (CEPG), London School of Economics and Political Science.

Vu, K., Hanafizadeh, P., & Bohlin, E. (2020). ICT as a driver of economic growth: A survey of the literature and directions for future research. *Telecommunications Policy*, *44*(2), 101922.

Waheed, R., Chang, D., Sarwar, S., & Chen, W. (2018). Forest, agriculture, renewable energy, and CO_2 emission. *Journal of Cleaner Production*, *172*, 4231–4238.

Wang, Y., Han, R., & Kubota, J. (2016). Is there an environmental Kuznets curve for SO2 emissions? A semi-parametric panel data analysis for China. *Renewable and Sustainable Energy Reviews*, *54*, 1182–1188.

Wang, Q., Xu, X., & Liang, K. (2021). The impact of environmental regulation on firm performance: Evidence from the Chinese cement industry. *Journal of Environmental Management*, *299*, 113596.

Watson, R. T., Boudreau, M. C., & Chen, A. J. (2010). Information systems and environmentally sustainable development: Energy informatics and new directions for the IS community. *MIS Quarterly*, 23–38.

Watson, R. T., Corbett, J., Boudreau, M. C., & Webster, J. (2012). An information strategy for environmental sustainability. *Communications of the ACM*, *55*(7), 28–30.

Williams, B. K. (2011). Adaptive management of natural resources—Framework and issues. *Journal of Environmental Management*, *92*(5), 1346–1353.

World Development Indicators. (2023). World Bank. https://databank.worldbank.org/source/world-development-indicators

Yi, L., & Thomas, H. R. (2007). A review of research on the environmental impact of e-business and ICT. *Environment International*, *33*(6), 841–849.

Yilmaz, G., Peh, S. B., Zhao, D., & Ho, G. W. (2019). Atomic and molecular level design of functional metal–organic frameworks (MOFs) and derivatives for energy and environmental applications. *Advanced Science*, *6*(21), 1901129.

Zafar, M. W., Saeed, A., Zaidi, S. A. H., & Waheed, A. (2021). The linkages among natural resources, renewable energy consumption, and environmental quality: A path toward sustainable development. *Sustainable Development*, *29*(2), 353–362.

Zhang, C., & Liu, C. (2015). The impact of ICT industry on CO2 emissions: A regional analysis in China. *Renewable and Sustainable Energy Reviews*, *44*, 12–19.

Zhang, L., Mu, R., Zhan, Y., Yu, J., Liu, L., Yu, Y., & Zhang, J. (2022). Digital economy, energy efficiency, and carbon emissions: Evidence from provincial panel data in China. *Science of the Total Environment*, *852*, 158403.

TWO FACETS OF AI-DRIVEN APPLICATIONS FOR SUSTAINABLE LEARNING AND DEVELOPMENT: A SYSTEMATIC REVIEW OF TECH-ENTREPRENEURIAL BENEFITS AND THREATS TO CREATIVE LEARNING

Lukman Raimi[a], Nurudeen Babatunde Bamiro[b] and Syamimi Ariff Lim[a]

[a]*Universiti of Brunei Darussalam, Brunei*
[b]*Lagos State University, Nigeria*

ABSTRACT

Artificial Intelligence (AI)-powered technologies are revolutionising the landscape of education, ushering in a myriad of possibilities and challenges. This article delves into the dual nature of AI-driven tools in education, spotlighting pivotal advancements like automated grading, personalised learning algorithms, online monitoring, content filtering, AI-based learning tools, Chat Generative Pre-trained Transformer (ChatGPT) and standardised testing (ST) platforms. Ultimately, the examination reveals a spectrum of advantages, risks and considerations associated with AI-driven educational applications. Employing the PRISMA protocol, this study systematically reviews peer-reviewed literature concerning the implementation and ethical implications of AI in higher education. The analysis incorporates 36 scholarly articles, uncovering the entrepreneurial advantages of AI, such as tailored learning experiences, self-assessment opportunities, heightened efficiency, skill enhancement and reduced educational disparities. Concurrently, the research

Social Responsibility, Technology and AI
Developments in Corporate Governance and Responsibility, Volume 23, 223–248
Copyright © 2025 Lukman Raimi, Nurudeen Babatunde Bamiro and Syamimi Ariff Lim
Published under exclusive licence by Emerald Publishing Limited
ISSN: 2043-0523/doi:10.1108/S2043-052320240000023012

identifies potential hazards, including user profiling, plagiarism, academic integrity breaches and excessive reliance on technology that may hinder creative learning dynamics. Crucial concerns emerge, encompassing the possible devaluation of educators' roles, privacy issues inherent in personalised learning platforms and the intrusive nature of online surveillance. Additionally, the study highlights biases embedded within AI algorithms and apprehensions regarding job displacement within the academic community. To steer AI integration responsibly within higher education, the investigation explores ethical frameworks and models, offering pragmatic suggestions for institutions. Recommendations advocate for a balanced approach, emphasising judicious AI utilisation and the formulation of institutional policies. This chapter's distinctiveness lies in its innovative stance, striving to reconcile the technical and entrepreneurial benefits of AI applications with the preservation of creativity in higher education contexts.

Keywords: AI-Driven applications; creative learning; sustainable learning development; tech-entrepreneurial benefits; threats

1. INTRODUCTION

Artificial intelligence (AI) has significantly influenced various aspects of human life, including education. The use of AI-driven applications for learning and development in higher education institutions (HEIs) has sparked mixed opinions. Technology enthusiasts view this as a positive development, while more conservative stakeholders perceive it as a potential threat. To balance these two opposing perspectives, this chapter examines the tech-entrepreneurial benefits and threats to creativity posed by AI-driven applications, such as Chat Generative Pre-trained Transformer (ChatGPT), chatbots, augmented reality (AR) and intelligent content creation tools in education. The hallmark of AI-driven applications is enhancing positive learning outcomes, particularly students' entrepreneurial knowledge, competencies and problem-solving skills. AI-driven applications in education are simply software and systems that use AI and machine learning (ML) technologies to enhance and improve various aspects of the education process (Cope et al., 2021; Perrotta & Selwyn, 2020). These AI applications leverage data analysis, natural language processing and other AI techniques to provide personalised learning experiences, support educators and streamline administrative tasks in educational institutions (Perrotta & Selwyn, 2020; Soelistiono, 2023).

Some AI-driven applications have been integrated into education to enhance teaching, learning and assessment processes. Each application addresses specific challenges and aims to improve overall educational outcomes through intelligent automation and personalised experiences. Some examples include Automated Grading and Assessment (AGS) which utilises AI to automatically assess and gradeassignments, essays and tests. It employs algorithms to evaluate student responses based on predefined criteria, streamlining the grading process and providing quick feedback. Personalised Learning Algorithms (PLA) on the other hand, leverages

AI to tailor educational content to individual students' needs. By analysing data on students' learning styles, preferences and performance, personalised algorithms generate customised learning experiences, adapting to the unique requirements of each learner. Hence, Predictive Analytics for Student Success (PASS) uses predictive analytics to analyse historical student data, identifying patterns and trends. By forecasting potential challenges or success factors, educators can intervene early to support students at risk, enhancing overall student success. Alternatively, Online Proctoring and Surveillance (OPS) employs AI to monitor students during remote exams. It utilises facial recognition, eye-tracking and other technologies to ensure exam integrity, detecting potential instances of cheating or academic misconduct. Also, Content Filtering and Censorship (CFC) involves the use of AI-driven tools to control access to specific information in educational settings. It filters content based on predefined criteria, restricting or allowing access to ensure compliance with educational guidelines or policies. Interestingly, AI Algorithms Learning Tools (AALT) encompass a variety of AI-driven tools designed to enhance the learning experience. These tools may include intelligent tutoring systems, language processing tools or other applications that leverage AI algorithms to assist students and educators in various learning activities. Whereas, ChatGPT is an AI-driven natural language processing tool. It generates human-like responses in conversations, making it useful for answering questions, assisting with tasks and facilitating interactive learning experiences through text-based communication. Lastly, Standardised Testing (ST) involves the use of AI in the assessment process to determine academic and professional performance or provide a more accurate measure of ability (Raimi et al., 2023).

Research studies and scholarly articles show that integrating AI into education is a complicated topic with both possible advantages and disadvantages. While AI can help with a variety of administrative and academic responsibilities, it also raises concerns about how teachers and students should be developed. According to one study, a lack of time, resources and support is the main reason why teachers are not utilising AI extensively in the classroom (Langreo, 2024). However, according to a Quizlet survey, teachers are more likely than students to employ AI, and they also feel more positively about the usage of AI in the classroom (Quizlet, 2023).

Ahmad et al. (2023) claim that because AI completes monotonous jobs and lessens the need for human decision-making, it makes people lazy. According to their research, AI has a significant influence on Chinese and Pakistani society, accounting for 27.7% of decision-making loss, 68.6% of privacy and security concerns and 8.9% of human laziness. This led to the observation that the area most impacted by AI is human sloth. In a paper by Esther (2023) that explores the possible advantages and hazards of AI in education, the worry that it may encourage indolence in instructors and pupils is also brought up. This chapter emphasises how AI may automate administrative duties, giving teachers more time to attend to the unique needs of each student. However, it also raises worries about the possibility that pupils may become overly dependent on AI-generated content and lose their creative edge.

Based on the above background, the purpose of this study is to analyse the two facets of AI-driven applications in education, focusing on key technologies such as automated grading, personalised learning algorithms, online monitoring, content filtering, AI algorithm learning tools and chat to focus on ChatGPT and standardized tests. Ultimately, AI-driven applications were found to bring a mix of benefits, threats and concerns. Specifically, this study provides answers to the following research questions:

- What technological-entrepreneurial benefits do AI-driven applications bring to learning in HEIs?
- What potential threats do AI-driven applications pose to learning in HEIs?
- What ethical, privacy and equity concerns associated with AI-driven applications in educational settings necessitate robust policy and regulatory frameworks, particularly in higher education?

2. METHODOLOGY

Utilising a Preferred Reporting Items for Systematic Reviews and Meta-Analyses (PRISMA) systematic review methodology, this study sought to address three fundamental research topics. This method is a widely used framework to carry out and document systematic reviews and meta-analyses in research (González et al., 2021; Maphosa & Maphosa, 2023). The search, identification and selection of papers for the study's inclusion were done using this method (Page et al., 2021). An objective synthesis of the data is supported by this systematic review methodology (Hemingway & Brereton, 2009). Extracted data were compiled using the systematic review approach and reported in the study's results section (Bamiro et al., 2023). Finding research articles to include in the study is the first step in the research process. The study parameters, such as the search years, quality and categories of articles to be included, are established based on the research question. Databases and journals are chosen next. These databases and journals are searched using a custom Boolean search. After such searches yield a collection of articles, those papers are screened against a set of inclusion and exclusion criteria to decide which studies will be included in the final analysis. The final list of studies' pertinent data is then extracted and coded to correspond with the research questions. An analytical grid, charts and maps were created as part of the review process to efficiently arrange pertinent data that was taken from a few chosen articles and pinpoint research gaps (Utaminingsih et al., 2023). To promote transparency, each of these methods is fully described in the section dedicated to methods.

2.1 Search Strategy

In this systematic review, only peer-reviewed journal papers were chosen for analysis. This guaranteed a degree of assurance regarding the calibre of the chosen studies (Salisu et al., 2024). The search emphasis was restricted by the parameters to encompass papers published between 2014 and 2024. This period was chosen to guarantee that the research was current, which is crucial given how quickly technology and AI are developing in the field of education.

We performed an extensive search across leading databases, notably Scopus and Google Scholar, to locate scholarly articles of the integration of AI in HEIs. This search yielded numerous pertinent articles, offering valuable insights into the diverse advantages and potential risks associated with AI implementation in HEIs, as well as addressing ethical, privacy and equity concerns related to its usage. Our review focused on leveraging the Scopus database to retrieve relevant articles and high-quality papers. Additionally, Google Scholar was utilised to identify papers relevant to our research inquiries. To enhance the search effectiveness, we broadened our scope of keywords and formulated a comprehensive search query, employing Boolean operators, truncation, wildcard entries and phrase searches within both Scopus and Google Scholar. Scopus's functionality enabled us to conduct both basic and advanced searches, refining results based on various criteria such as document type, date, subject, author and recent publications, all while employing Boolean operators. We improved our research by employing the Boolean operator 'AND' on Google Scholar to fine-tune our search parameters. Moreover, we performed a manual search on Google and examined the initial 20 results to pinpoint pertinent articles and findings aligned with our research inquiries, adhering to the prescribed methodology (Salisu et al., 2024). This approach allowed us to gather pertinent scholarly articles that met the academic standards for our study. The search utilised a combination of keywords such as 'AI', 'Artificial intelligence', 'Higher education institutions', 'HEIs', 'Entrepreneurial benefits', 'AI benefits', 'Artificial intelligence benefits', 'AI threats', 'Ethics', 'Ethical issues of AI', 'Privacy concerns' and 'equity concerns'. The selected keywords were used together with the Boolean operators 'AND' and 'OR' to refine our search results and get articles that will specifically answer our research questions.

2.2 Selection Process

With the assigned keywords, 235 articles in all were found in the first search. In addition to removing duplicate articles, the papers were assessed for relevance to the research topic based on their titles and abstracts. Following this procedure, papers that bore no resemblance to the subject of the investigation were eliminated. There were 121 papers left for additional review, suggesting the first level of exclusion. The complete texts of the 121 chosen papers were then carefully examined. We thoroughly examined the methodology, findings and discussion sections to make sure they were appropriate for answering the research objectives. Thirty six papers were found to be relevant and included in the systematic literature evaluation after the exclusion criteria were applied. The comprehensive PRISMA flow diagram of the literature is displayed in Fig. 1.

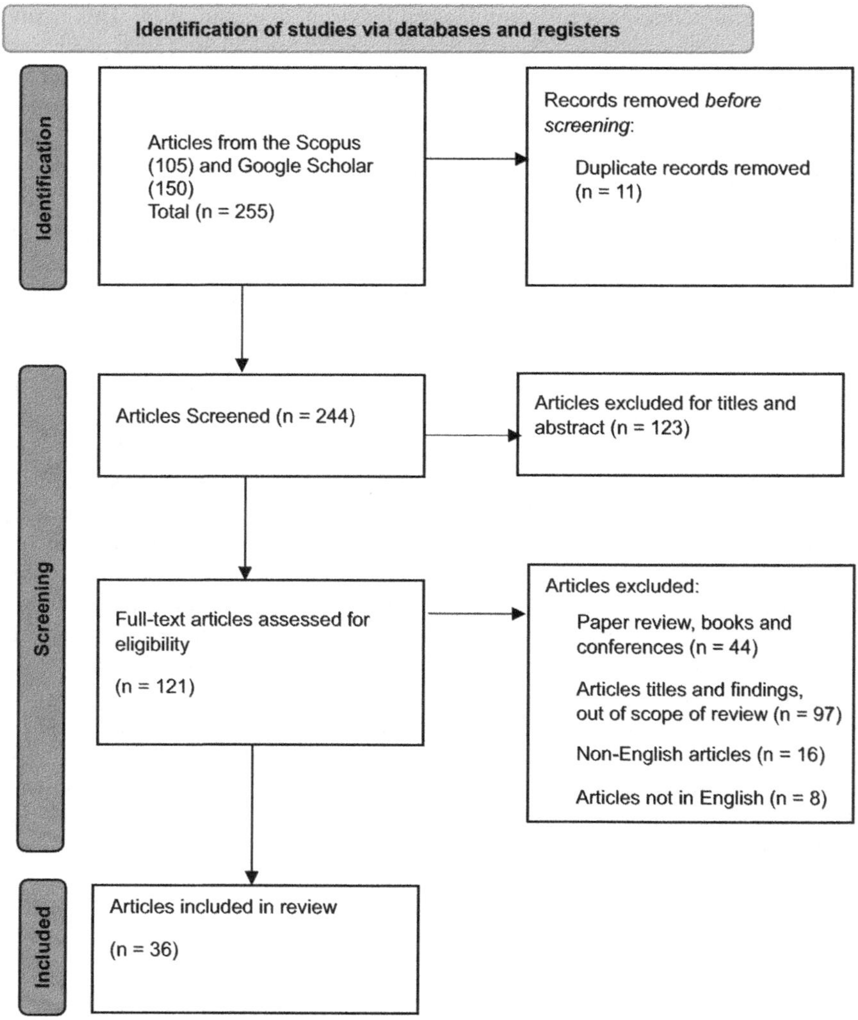

Fig. 1. PRISMA Flow Diagram.

2.3 Eligibility

The final selection did not include conference papers, books, book chapters, non-English articles or duplicate submissions (Table 1). Analyses were conducted on articles that satisfied the inclusion criteria at different phases. In order to ascertain whether the methods, findings and discussion sections were appropriate for answering the study questions, they were also thoroughly examined. This amounts to 36 articles in all. Articles released between 2014 and 2024 were the only ones that were taken into consideration. Peer-reviewed journals select academic publications through a rigorous review process involving subject matter experts.

Table 1. Inclusion and Exclusion Criteria.

Inclusion	Exclusion
Peer-reviewed articles	Books, book chapters, editorials and conference proceedings
Involves HEIs	Not involving HEIs
Involves AI application	Out of scope of AI application
Published between 2014 and 2024	Below 2014
English written articles	Non-English articles

This process ensures that the research methods and findings meet academic standards (Rus et al., 2023).

3. RESULT

3.1 Publication by Year

As illustrated in Fig. 2, a comprehensive analysis of 36 scholarly articles reveals a striking upward trajectory in the utilisation of AI within HEIs over the years under review. This trend is particularly pronounced from 2014 to 2022, demonstrating a consistent rise in the integration of AI technologies within the educational landscape. Notably, the surge in AI applications within HEIs experiences a significant acceleration in 2023, marked by a notable uptick with a total of 21 articles dedicated to this subject. This surge not only underscores the growing significance of AI in educational contexts but also suggests a heightened

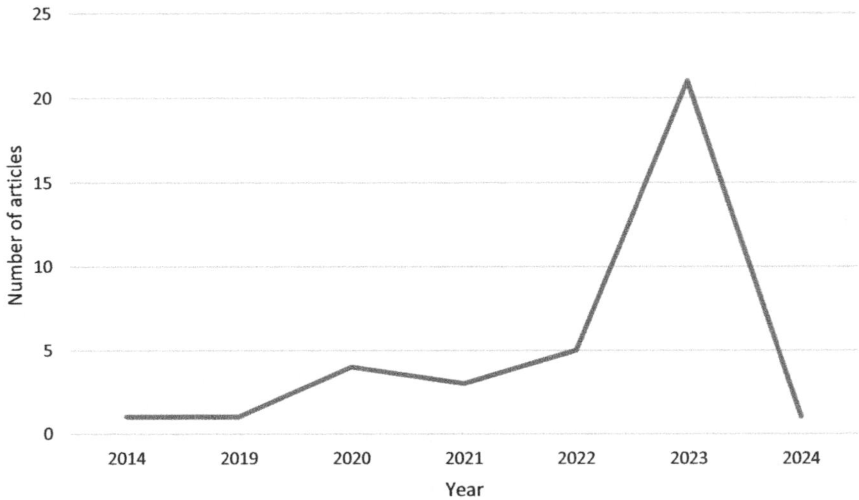

Fig. 2. Distribution of Articles by Year.

scholarly interest and research focus on this burgeoning intersection of technology and academia particularly in the domain of ethical application of AI.

3.2 Research Distribution by Country

The authors' affiliations were utilised to classify the articles within this domain. Among the 36 articles reviewed, the authors hailed from a diverse array of 44 countries. Notably, 28 articles were authored by individuals affiliated with a single country, while eight articles involved authors with affiliations spanning multiple nations. Fig. 3 illustrates the distribution of authors by their country of affiliation.

Interestingly, the data reveals that both the United States and India each contributed authors to five articles, showcasing their significant presence within the research landscape. Furthermore, the figure highlights a predominant affiliation of authors with European countries, indicating a concentration of scholarly activity in this region. However, it's noteworthy that authors from all other geographical regions were equally represented, indicating a global participation in the discourse of this domain.

3.3 Research Distribution by Methodology

In Fig. 4, we present a breakdown of the research distribution based on methodology. It's notable that a significant portion of the articles, totalling 26, opted for the qualitative methodology. This choice reflects a prevailing trend in the literature, where qualitative approaches are often favoured for their ability to delve into the nuances of phenomena and capture diverse perspectives. Among the selected articles, a smaller but still notable contingent of seven articles

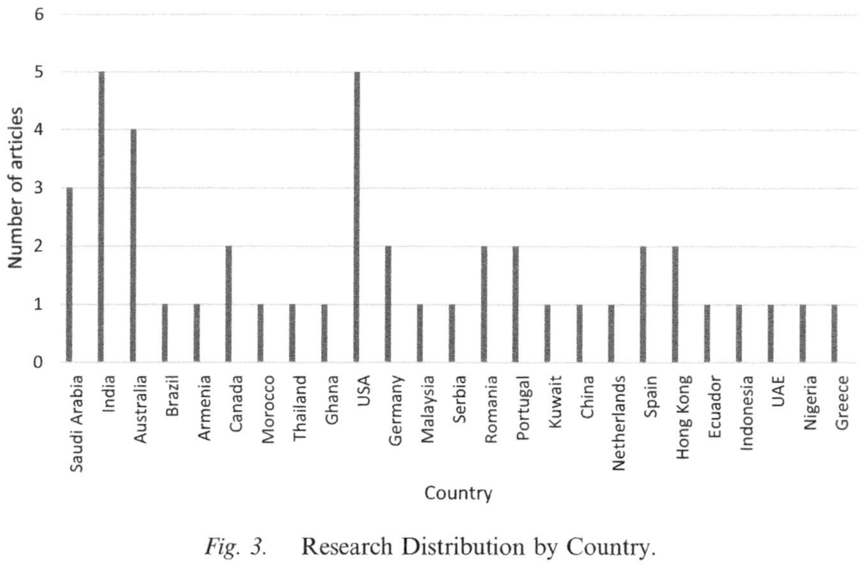

Fig. 3. Research Distribution by Country.

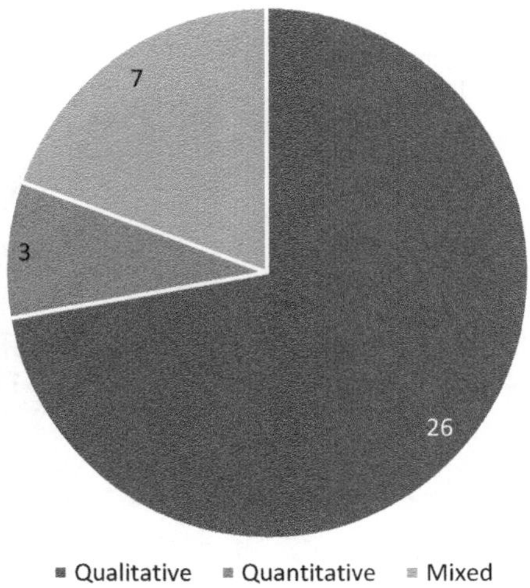

Fig. 4. Research Distribution by Methodology.

employed a mixed methodology, blending qualitative and quantitative techniques to offer a comprehensive understanding of the research subject. Meanwhile, three articles took a purely quantitative approach, a less common but still valuable methodological choice in certain contexts.

The prevalence of qualitative methodology can be attributed to the exploratory nature of many studies included in the analysis (Pisica et al., 2023). Qualitative research, with its emphasis on understanding attitudes, motivations and perceptions, was deemed particularly suited to unravel the complexities surrounding the research objectives. By leveraging qualitative methods, researchers were able to tap into the rich tapestry of opinions and experiences relevant to the research goals, thereby enriching the depth and breadth of the findings.

3.4 Authors Affiliations

The authors' affiliations were classified into four distinct categories, reflecting diverse fields of expertise. Firstly, Science, Technology, Engineering, and Mathematics (STEM) encompassed authors from disciplines such as biology, physics, computer science and medical sciences. It served as an umbrella category, incorporating medical sciences alongside traditional STEM disciplines. The second classification pertained to the realm of business and management, embracing authors involved in fields such as economics, business administration and organisational management. The third category, Arts, encompassed authors affiliated with artistic disciplines, including literature, fine arts and performing arts. Lastly, education and pedagogy comprised the fourth category, housing authors specialising in educational research, curriculum development and pedagogical practices. During the review process, a total of 42 unique affiliations were

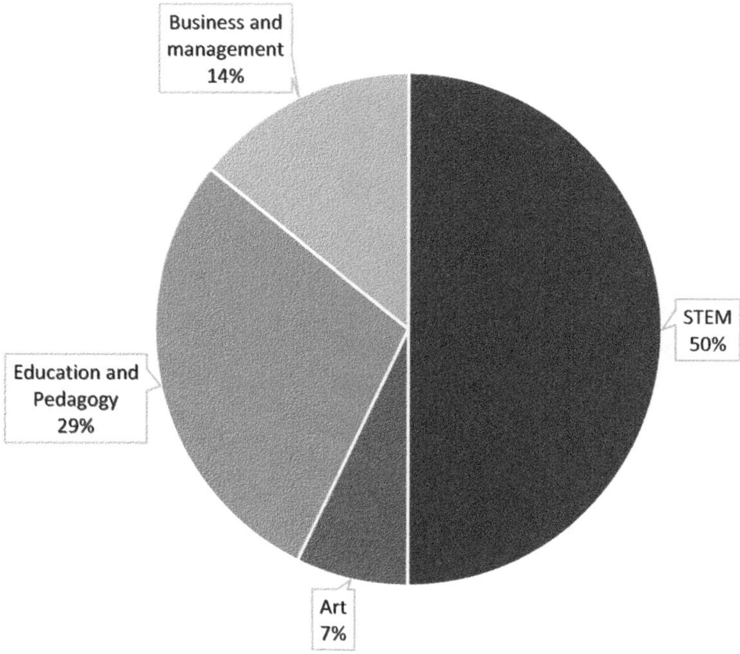

Fig. 5. Authors Affiliation.

identified across the analysed articles. Thirty of these articles were affiliated solely with one category, indicating a clear disciplinary focus. However, six articles (Abgaryan et al., 2023; Dhawan & Batra, 2020; Essel et al., 2022; Hutson et al., 2022; Kuleto et al., 2021; Lund et al., 2020) demonstrated interdisciplinary collaboration by having affiliations across multiple categories.

Notably, the STEM category emerged as the most prevalent, featuring affiliations in 21 of the reviewed articles. This finding underscores the significant contribution of STEM-related disciplines to the body of research on AI application in HEIs. Fig. 5 visually represents the distribution of author affiliations across the defined categories, offering insight into the interdisciplinary landscape of the reviewed articles.

3.5 Thematic Analysis

The analysis of themes within the reviewed articles revealed six main topics extensively discussed and pertinent to our research inquiries. Table 2 presents these identified themes along with their corresponding references.

The thematic analysis reflects some areas of the research. Personalised, adaptive learning and skill development shows to be the most mentioned techno-entrepreneurial benefits of AI in HEIs. ChatGPT appeared to be the most studied AI application from the review articles. Privacy of data and integrity

Table 2. Thematic Analysis.

S/N	Themes	References
1	Personalised learning	Alqahtani et al. (2023), Rasul et al. (2023), Liu (2023), Hutson et al. (2022), Dhawan and Batra (2020), Tanveer et al. (2020), Kuleto et al. (2021), Zouhaier (2023).
2	ChatGPT	Rasul et al. (2023), Sullivan et al. (2023), Borger et al. (2023), Kong et al. (2023), Rane et al. (2023), Kung et al. (2023)
3	Integrity	Rasul et al. (2023), Sullivan et al. (2023)
4	Skill development	Alqahtani et al. (2023), Lainjo and Tsmouche (2023), Liu (2023), Dhawan and Batra (2020), Pisica et al. (2023)
5	Adaptive learning	Alqahtani et al. (2023), Rasul et al. (2023), Dhawan and Batra (2020), Zawacki-Richter et al. (2019)
6	Privacy of data	Borger et al. (2023), Dhawan and Batra (2020), Al Ka'bi (2023).

appeared to be the most ethical concerns of AI application in HEIs as obtained from the reviewed articles.

4. DISCUSSION

4.1 AI-Driven Applications and Concerns of Stakeholders

Conservatives argue that automated grading systems that use AI to score and grade assignments, essays and tests lack the human touch and personalised feedback that traditional grading provides. They believe that the AGS devalues the role of educators and their expertise. Second, conservatives view personalised learning platforms that use AI to tailor educational content to the needs of individual students as invasive or overly data-driven. Critics of this line of thinking worry about the privacy implications of collecting and analysing extensive data about students. When it comes to personalised learning algorithms (PLA), conservatives view personalised learning platforms that use AI to tailor educational content to the needs of individual students as invasive or overly data-oriented driven. Critics of this line of thinking worry about the privacy implications of collecting and analysing extensive data about students. Additionally, the use of AI for online proctoring, where students are monitored during remote exams, has raised concerns about privacy and surveillance. Critics argue that OPS violates student privacy and can be overly intrusive. In some cases, AI-driven content filtering and censorship tools are being used in educational institutions to control access to certain information. Human rights and free expression advocates fear that such tools could stifle open dialogue and limit access to diverse viewpoints. More importantly, people are concerned about bias in AI algorithms used in learning applications. People fear that if these algorithms are trained on biased data, they could perpetuate ideological or political biases in educational content or recommendations. Some conservatives fear that widespread adoption of AI-driven ChatGPT could lead to a decline in the number of human teachers, potentially impacting employment opportunities in the teaching profession. Related to this are the problems of plagiarism, academic dishonesty and abandonment of writing skills or literary creativity. Most conservative people are not positive about the use of AI in ST and college admissions processes. The concern is that holistic assessments of students, including extracurricular activities and character should take precedence over test scores.

4.1.1 Innovation Adoption Behaviour

In the areas of entrepreneurship and technology management, the Diffusion of Innovation Theory (DIT) explains that historically there are five types of innovation adopters based on their adoption behaviour and receptivity to innovation. Attitudes towards AI-driven applications in higher education range from progressive to conservative perspectives and are influenced by the Diffusion of Innovation Theory. Applying the theoretical model of Rogers (2003), this chapter classifies stakeholders in the HEIs into different user categories based on their openness and receptiveness to accepting AI-driven applications and technologies.

Innovators/Technology-Savvy People (2.5%): At the forefront are the innovators, constituting a small percentage. These stakeholders are technology-savvy and often the first to explore and adopt AI-driven applications. Their pioneering spirit contributes to the initial dissemination of AI applications and technologies within the academic realm.

Early Adopters/Progressives (13.5%): Following the innovators are the early adopters or progressives. This group, representing a larger segment of the stakeholders in HEIs, is characterised by their openness to innovation. Early adopters recognise the potential benefits of AI-driven applications and are willing to integrate them into educational practices, fostering early stages of mainstream acceptance.

Early Majority/Pragmatists (34%): The early majority, constituting a significant portion, consists of pragmatists who carefully observe and assess the successes and challenges faced by innovators and early adopters. Once convinced of the practical advantages, they progressively embrace AI-driven applications and technologies, contributing to a broader acceptance within the academic community.

Late Majority/Conservatives (34%): The late majority, comprising a substantial segment of the stakeholders in HEIs, reflects a more conservative stance. These individuals are cautious in their approach, preferring to adopt AI-driven applications only after they have gained widespread acceptance. Resistance may arise from concerns about disruption or uncertainty surrounding these technological advancements.

Laggards/Sceptics (16%): The laggards or sceptics, representing the final category, are the most resistant to change. These individuals are hesitant to adopt AI-driven applications and technologies, often due to deep-rooted scepticism or a preference for traditional methods. Their adoption lags behind the majority, and they may only embrace these technologies when necessary.

Understanding these progressive and conservative attitudes within the Diffusion of Innovation provides insights into the different reactions and acceptance patterns of AI-driven applications in HEIs. This spectrum reflects the dynamic interplay between technological innovation and institutional preparedness within the educational landscape. The DIT logically explains the different reactions to the adoption behaviour of different social classes towards new technologies or innovations (Rogers, 2003).

4.1.2 Case Example: AI-Driven ChatGPT

AI-driven chat Generative Pre-trained Transformer (ChatGPT) is simply an AI tool for generating sentences, phrases, texts and other literary outputs to aid full or partial writing across multidisciplinary boundaries (UNESCO, 2023b). ChatGPT is also a natural language processing tool driven by AI technology that allows users to have human-like conversations with the chatbot to answer questions and assist users with tasks, such as composing emails, essays, poems and computer codes among others.

AI-driven ChatGPT opens doors to a wealth of teaching resources, fostering both knowledge democratisation and decolonisation. Secondly, it streamlines the creation of slides and outlines for educators, offering access to AI tools for editing, proofreading and grammar/spelling checks. Thirdly, it enhances the learning experience, encouraging students to independently search, fact-check and report findings in their own words within the classroom. Moreover, ChatGPT supports case teaching and analysis, providing valuable insights into scientific, historical, management and legal issues. It transforms students' cognitive processes, expanding their thinking beyond traditional boundaries (Grassini, 2023). Finally, it alleviates the challenges of arduous research by serving as an enabler and advisor for both students and lecturers.

In the realm of research, AI-driven ChatGPT serves as a powerful tool, honing researchers' academic writing capabilities and skills through AI generative tools for editing, proofreading and grammar/spelling checks. Additionally, it contributes to the improvement of researchers' written communication skills, offering constructive feedback comments for future enhancements. Moreover, ChatGPT plays a pivotal role in enhancing the critical thinking of researchers, pushing beyond the limitations of their cognitive output during teaching and research endeavours. It acts as a catalyst for innovative thought processes (Haleem et al., 2022). Furthermore, akin to a scholarly consensus, ChatGPT enhances literature searching by leveraging the power of data aggregation, idea integration and synthesis. Notably, it assists in generating contemporary research topics, creating outlines and producing draft versions, thereby contributing to academic enrichment. Finally, ChatGPT transforms the way researchers conceptualise research titles, problem statements and theoretical frameworks. Extending researchers' cognitive powers beyond conventional limits opens new horizons for creativity and imagination in the research domain (Bahroun et al., 2023).

Regarding the techno-entrepreneurial benefits of AI-driven applications in higher education, the study highlights the personalised learning, self-assessment, improved efficiency and reduced inequalities enabled by AI-driven applications. The study acknowledges UNESCO's support and highlights the role of AI in shaping learning policy, accessibility (decolonisation and democratisation of learning) and pedagogy (UNESCO, 2023a). In contrast, the potential threats to creative learning from AI-driven applications in higher education include profiling, plagiarism, intellectual dishonesty and an over-reliance on technology, which hinders positive experiences in creative learning and poses the risk of technological unemployment (Fajrie et al., 2024).

4.2 Technological-Entrepreneurial Benefits AI-driven Applications Bring to Learning in Higher Education Institutions (HEIs)

As depicted in Table 2 of the results, the predominant benefits highlighted in this field include personalised learning, adaptive learning and skills enhancement.

4.2.1 Personalised Learning

Alqahtani et al. (2023) claim that by analysing data on student behaviour and performance, detecting problem areas and offering tailored suggestions for development, AI can provide educators with individualised learning and educational support. Rasul et al. (2023) consider the possibilities of generative AI, such as ChatGPT, in the context of constructivist learning theory in higher education. The study discovered that ChatGPT can scaffold students' past knowledge and experiences to help them construct new information by involving them in conversation and encouraging their participation in the learning process. Furthermore, ChatGPT's customised feedback can aid in this process by expanding on their past understanding and experiences and offering tailored recommendations for more education. By providing teachers and students with the skills to respond more quickly to not only what and how students are learning, but also how they are feeling about the experience, AI has the potential to enable more flexible, inclusive, customised and engaged learning (Hutson et al., 2022).

Tanveer et al. (2020) assert that interactive learning can be facilitated by AI. One of the most innovative aspects of technologically facilitated group education is its application in scenarios where participants are not physically present in the same place. Students can select the time and location of their learning with these vector options. Kuleto et al. (2021) carried out research to look at the advantages of AI and ML at HEIs. The findings demonstrate how AI and ML can improve individualised learning in many ways, including skill development for students, the creation of a collaborative learning environment within the HEI, potential improvements to the security and efficiency of the institution and the provision of a quiet, adaptable and easily accessible computing environment for researchers to allow them to concentrate solely on their research. According to Zouhaier (2023), AI has the power to completely transform education by automating administrative processes, giving quick feedback and tailoring teaching strategies to each student's unique needs. AI can also help with evaluation and grading, freeing up teachers to concentrate on creating curricula and delivering high-quality instruction.

4.2.2 Adaptive Learning

Alqahtani et al. (2023), Rasul et al. (2023), Dhawan and Batra (2020) and Zawacki-Richter et al. (2019) have all contributed to the exploration of the benefits of AI in this domain. Rasul et al. (2023) identified five key benefits of AI, including its potential to facilitate adaptive learning, offer personalised feedback, support research and data analysis, provide automated administrative services and contribute to the development of innovative assessments. Zawacki-Richter et al. (2019) outlined four areas where AI brings benefits to academic support services and institutional administration, encompassing profiling and prediction, assessment and evaluation, adaptive systems and personalisation and intelligent tutoring systems. AI tools are used to support the development of adaptive learning systems, which modify the degree of difficulty of assignments and assessments according to each student's unique needs and abilities. This customised learning experience enables educators to accurately assess each student's learning achievements (Alqahtani et al. 2023).

4.2.3 Skill Development

This study reveals that the development of abilities essential for entrepreneurial success in students is one of the most significant techno-entrepreneurial benefits of AI. To this domain, several studies have contributed. Alqahtani et al. (2023) claim that AI can assist in achieving programme-specific goals while addressing stakeholders' challenges in keeping up with emerging pedagogical approaches and the changing labour market by streamlining course design, creating descriptions, outlining learning objectives and developing assessment methodologies.

The use of AI in HEIs helps students' abilities and competencies, especially in digital fields, to be improved. This improvement includes both new proficiencies resulting from technical breakthroughs and the application of AI, particularly in the area of existing abilities. AI integration in higher education also encourages the creation of novel goods, technologies and business concepts. This encourages academic institutions to host entrepreneurial endeavours, which may result in the development of original businesses, goods and services. These developments in technology and entrepreneurship have the potential to make a major contribution to the advancement of society and all of humanity (Pisica et al., 2023).

AI tools have the potential to provide more focused and efficient career decision-making help for students at HEIs by giving individualised career guidance based on data analysis of their interests, talents and market trends. This link emphasises how AI-driven solutions may enhance the effectiveness and delivery of career services within the framework of higher education (Lainjo & Tsmouche, 2023).

According to Liu's (2023) research, AI improvements enable personalised learning experiences by fostering creative thinking among students and enabling targeted training. This helps students become more innovative while also giving them valuable employability skills like flexibility, problem-solving and critical thinking. AI-driven technologies also enable data-driven decision-making processes, which are essential for educating students for a labour market that is changing quickly. All things considered, these developments act as stimulants to enhance students' employability abilities and career preparedness, closely matching the ever-changing needs of the contemporary labour market.

Apart from the exploration of the emphasised themes, further research has bolstered the understanding of the techno-entrepreneurial advantages of AI applications in the domain of HEIs. Dhawan and Batra (2020) highlighted collaborative learning and the establishment of lifelong alumni connections. Additionally, Singh and Hiran (2022) underscored the accelerated and efficient completion of administrative tasks, such as grading assignments and delivering feedback to students, as key benefits of AI in HEIs.

One notable advantage highlighted in a reviewed article is inclusivity. According to Pisica et al. (2023), their research revealed that nearly a third of respondents noted easier access to education as a benefit for students facing challenges. Through the assistance of AI, individuals with diverse needs and backgrounds will be able to pursue their academic growth thanks to specialised learning approaches tailored to accommodate their requirements.

Abgaryan et al. (2023) assert that the use of AI tools can increase productivity by automating processes like scoring and grading, creating educational content and managing time and effort more effectively. AI-powered chatbots and virtual assistants can be used to increase student engagement by giving them immediate support and guidance, responding to their inquiries, and assisting them in staying motivated and involved while assisting them in overcoming obstacles.

4.3 Potential Threats AI-Driven Applications Pose to Learning in HEIs

In their paper from 2023, Rasul et al. list five possible risks associated with large language models (LLM) like ChatGPT in HEIs. These risks include questions about academic integrity, reliability, the incapacity to assess and validate graduate skill sets, difficulties in determining learning outcomes and the possibility of biases and fabricated data in information processing. They said that there are serious integrity hazards associated with its capacity to incite plagiarism and contract cheating, and that uneven access to learning opportunities is made worse by its restricted accessibility. Moreover, ChatGPT's unreliability in giving accurate information undermines the ideas of constructivist learning theory, undermining critical thinking and problem-solving skills. Furthermore, because the technology lacks the social interactions and real-world experiences necessary for assessing learning outcomes, it is insufficient for assessing and strengthening graduate skill sets.

Sullivan et al. (2023) looks at news stories ($N = 100$) concerning how ChatGPT is changing higher education using content analysis, with a focus on

Australia, New Zealand, the United States and the United Kingdom. Concerns about academic integrity were the main issue discussed in the articles ($n = 88$). The majority of publications discussed academic dishonesty, cheating and abuse in general terms.

Abgaryan et al. (2023) identified prejudice, fairness and data privacy and security as possible risks associated with AI in HEIs. The report went on to say that using AI systems in higher education necessitates gathering and analysing vast volumes of student data, including academic records, personal information and learning preferences. This raises concerns regarding data security and privacy. Furthermore, the quality of AI systems depends on the data they are trained on. An AI system may generate biased findings if the data it was trained on is skewed, which could reinforce already-existing discrimination and inequality in higher education.

Dhawan and Batra (2020) and Borger et al. (2023) also emphasised privacy and security as a major risk to AI applications in HEIs. One of the main worries is the technical challenges and security issues. Since AI systems include a great deal of data synthesis and analysis, they have inherited nearly all data-related problems, including misleading, skewed and discriminatory data as well as worries about data privacy (Dhawan & Batra, 2020).

AI can do more complex educational tasks in the future. In this context, unresolved questions arise, such as whether 'human-like AI' possesses the capability to make sound moral or value-related judgements, whether they will entirely replace teachers, and whether they will endeavour to intentionally comprehend learners. The evolution of AI may challenge the conventional ethics of education as it transforms the role of educators (Bu, 2022).

Pisica et al. (2023) claimed that three possible risks associated with AI – psychosocial consequences, data security and ethical considerations – were identified by researchers. Regarding psychosocial implications, the primary worry raised by respondents was the possibility that students (and not only them) would experience socio-psychological effects because of spending a lot of time in the virtual environment. One of the most sensible elements of using AI in HEIs was addressed about data security and protection. 'Loss of privacy', 'confidentiality' and 'data storage security' were the aspects of the virtual environment that are most vulnerable to hackers and other criminals. However, 'cheating', 'responsibility' and 'inaccurate evaluation' were the most often listed ethical standards.

Rusandi et al. (2023) state that the main worry about AI is that researchers and students could become too dependent on the system and impede their ability to develop critical thinking skills. They go on to say that LLM, like ChatGPT, may discourage critical and creative thinking if it is thought of as a quick fix for coming up with solutions or fixing issues. Furthermore, there is a great deal of worry regarding the possibility that educational disparities will worsen. Inequalities in learning outcomes could result from unequal access to these technologies.

A significant finding highlighted in the reviewed literature pertains to the intersection of copyright and AI. Zhang (2024) discusses the current inadequacy of legal frameworks in granting legal personality to intelligent robots, emphasising the need for precautionary measures and theoretical discussions. Concerning copyright challenges posed by AI and the abundance of content it generates, Zhang advocates for an open and inclusive approach within the copyright system. Rather than excluding AI-generated works due to uncertainties, there's a call for actively seeking a regulatory path that balances reasonable protection while accommodating the unique nature of AI-generated content (Abbott, 2016). Additionally, Bukhari et al. (2023) assert that AI poses fundamental challenges to established principles of copyright law. Traditionally, copyright protects original works stemming from human creativity, whereas AI-generated content blurs the line between derivative and original creation by drawing from existing patterns. Identifying the 'author' of AI-generated content becomes complex, involving considerations of the AI system, its programmer, the user or the entity owning the AI. Moreover, conventional copyright norms require works to be fixed in tangible mediums, but AI produces dynamic content that evolves. Duration of copyright protection also presents challenges with AI-generated content, as determining the timeframe becomes intricate. Lastly, moral rights, safeguarding the personal and reputational aspects of a work for its creator, become ambiguous in the context of AI, which lacks intent or emotion (Bukhari et al., 2023).

4.4 Ethical, Privacy and Equity Concerns Associated With AI-Driven Applications in Educational Settings Necessitate Robust Policy and Regulatory Frameworks, Particularly in Higher Education

Numerous research endeavours delved into the ethical, privacy and equity dimensions of AI implementation in HEIs. A significant revelation from this analysis indicated that most of the examined articles categorised privacy and equity concerns of AI under the umbrella of ethical considerations. In their study, Memarian and Doleck (2023) noted ethics as the least emphasised term among their reviewed literature, suggesting that it is perceived as a broader concept and serves as an overarching framework in the reviewed literature.

This portion of the review examined established frameworks and policies aimed at addressing ethical considerations in AI. Furthermore, it investigated the European Digital Competence Framework for Citizens (DigComp) and UNESCO's AI ethics recommendations to construct a conceptual framework for the ethical use of AI in HEIs. There is a call for the development of regulations concerning ethical and privacy issues associated with the utilisation of ChatGPT in academic and research settings (Guleria et al., 2023). Promoting ethics education and training in this area will lead in the future to the creation of manuals and regulatory standards in higher education (Vera et al., 2024).

Regarding ethical, privacy and equity concerns related to AI-driven applications, a study by Rane et al. (2023) asserted that one of the biggest ethical issues with ChatGPT in the educational setting is the possibility of plagiarism. Because AI-generated content is so easy to use, researchers and students may be enticed to use it without giving credit where credit is due, making it difficult for publishers and institutions to identify and stop academic misconduct. Abbas (2023) asserts that a wide range of concerns, such as data privacy and security, algorithmic bias and fairness, learner autonomy and agency, accountability and transparency and the equitable distribution of AI-enabled opportunities and resources, are ethical considerations in AI-enhanced education. Johnson (2014) and El-Haggar et al. (2023) described privacy was also a major worry.

In a research by Ghotbi et al. (2022), students at HEIs were asked to rank the top one ethical concern related to AI from a list of nine ethical issues put forth by the World Economic Forum, and to provide justification for their selections. The following were chosen as the main ethical concerns of AI applications: unemployment, AI's effect on human behaviour and emotions, growing inequality, AI's power over society, AI discrimination (racist or bias), malevolent and evil AI, AI security and AI errors. Survey research by Holmes et al. (2022) demonstrates several ethics related to AI using student data; these include data ownership and control, privacy expectations, data limits, bias and representation.

Bu (2022) identified three major ethical dangers associated with the application of educational AI: the risk to educational data security; the risk of educational inequality and the breakdown of the teacher–student role structure; and the risk of alienation from the educational objective. This is presented in Fig. 6.

This review explored various models, theories and frameworks concerning the ethical implementation of AI in HEIs. Chatterjee and Bhattacharjee (2020) investigated the potential adoption of AI in HEIs in India by stakeholders,

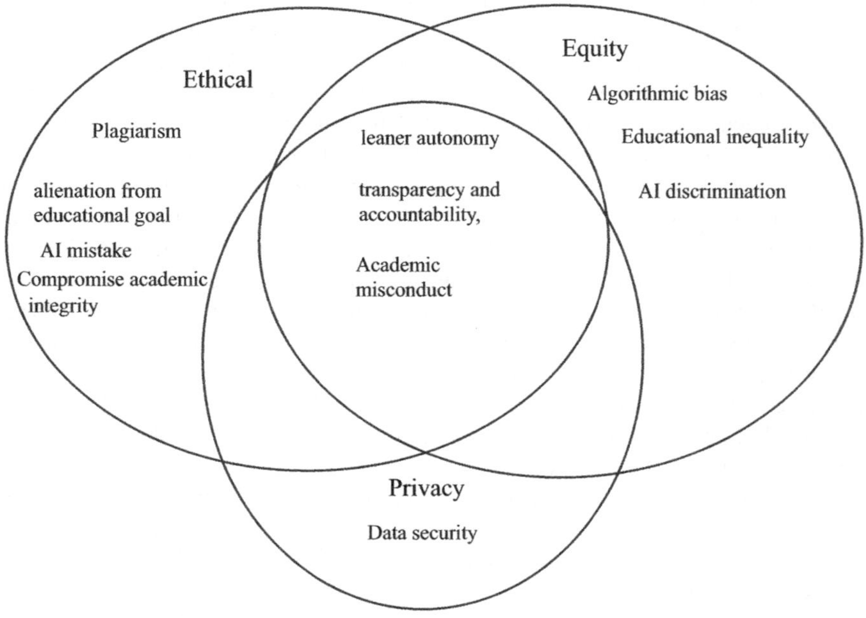

Fig. 6. Ethical, Privacy and Equity Concerns of AI in HEIs Adapted From Reviewed Articles. *Source:* Authors' configuration.

utilising multiple adoption theories and models, including the 'Unified Theory of Acceptance and Use of Technology' (UTAUT). Their findings indicate that the UTAUT model can aid authorities in facilitating AI adoption in higher education. The UTAUT model identifies four exogenous factors: performance expectancy, effort expectancy, facilitating conditions and social influence. The study underscores that Perceived Risk (PR) and Effort Expectancy (EE) significantly influence the attitudes of stakeholders in Indian HEIs towards AI adoption. These attitudes, in turn, drive users' intentions to embrace and integrate AI. Moreover, the research underscores that comprehending the ethical implications of AI applications can significantly impact its prudent adoption.

As envisioned in Roger's Diffusion of Innovations model, Lund et al. (2020) employed the technology adoption model to explore the evolution of public views towards innovation and the relationship this has with the adoption of developing technologies. According to the findings, those who accept new technologies like AI more quickly also seem to think they know more about these technologies and have a more positive attitude towards them.

Fidas et al. (2023) involved stakeholders from three European HEIs in a longitudinal study that lasted for 18 months. Based on intelligent face and voice identification algorithms, the TRUSTID system is robust and effective against impersonation assaults. It also scored highly in usability and user experience, according to a user evaluation with HEI students ($n = 133$).

A policy framework for AI ecological education is proposed by Chan (2023) study to handle the complex ramifications of integrating AI into university teaching and learning. Three dimensions make up this framework: Pedagogical, Governance and Operational. While the Governance component addresses concerns about privacy, security and responsibility, the Pedagogical dimension focuses on employing AI to enhance teaching and learning results. The operational dimension deals with issues related to training and infrastructure. This study also delved into the Digital Competence Framework for Citizens (DigComp) created by the European Union Commission, along with the ethical AI recommendations put forth by UNESCO. A standard definition of digital competence is provided by the European Digital Literacy Framework, also known as The Digital Competence Framework for Citizen (DigComp). The DigComp framework delineates the fundamental constituents of digital competency across five domains (Dimension 1). Information and data literacy, teamwork and communication, producing digital content and safety are among the topics covered. Dimension 2 lists the titles and descriptions of the 21 competencies that are relevant to these fields. Dimensions 1 and 2 combined make up the conceptual reference model.

In order to 'create a framework to make AI systems function for the good of humanity, individuals, society and the environment and ecosystems, and to prevent harm', UNESCO issued the Recommendation on the Ethics of Artificial Intelligence in 2021. (UNESCO, 2021). Along with a list of ideals and principles that all parties involved should uphold, the recommendation places a strong emphasis on gender equality and the preservation of the environment and ecosystems.

The following values and tenets make up the UNESCO Recommendation on the Ethics of AI:

Values: Respect, protection and promotion of human rights and fundamental freedoms, and human dignity, Environment and ecosystem flourishing, ensuring diversity and inclusiveness, Living in peaceful, just and interconnected societies.

Principle: Proportionality and Do No Harm, Safety and security, Fairness and non-discrimination, Sustainability, right to privacy and data protection, Human oversight and determination, Transparency and explainability, Responsibility and accountability, Awareness and literacy, multi-stakeholder and adaptive governance and collaboration.

This study created a conceptual framework for the moral implementation of AI in HEIs by including the European Digital Literacy Framework and the UNESCO Recommendation on the Ethics of AI. This is detailed in Fig. 7.

Several articles that included concepts from the conceptual framework also addressed ethical AI application usage suggestions in HEIs. The Belmont Report's ethical guidelines are as follows: '(1) the use of AI should not violate human autonomy; (2) the benefits of AI should outweigh the risks; and (3) the benefits and risks of AI should be distributed equally (Autonomy, beneficence/ nonmaleficence and fairness)' are reflected in the Kong et al. (2023) study. According to Abbas (2023), professional development opportunities and training in AI ethics, digital literacy and ethical usage of AI technologies should be made

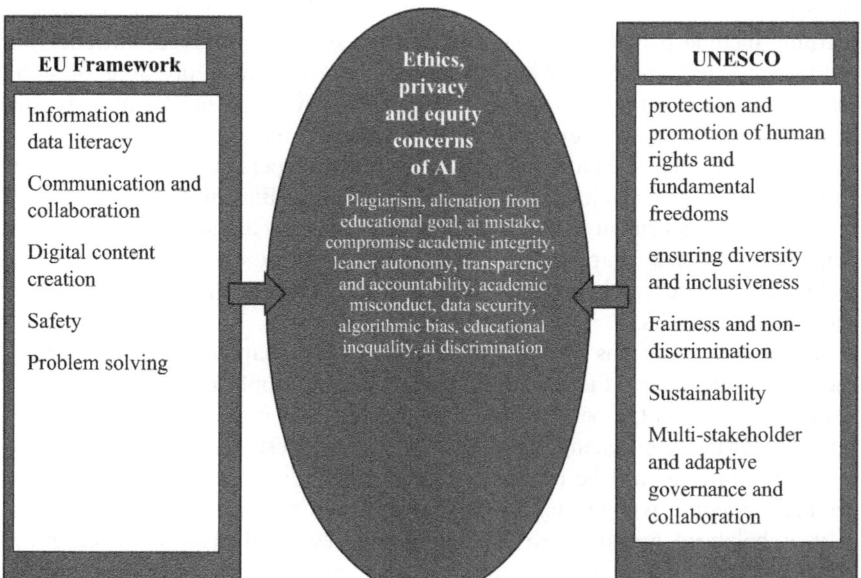

Fig. 7. Ethical Application of AI in HEIs Adapted From the DigComp Conceptual Framework (Vuorikari et al., 2022) and UNESCO Recommendation on the Ethics of Artificial Intelligence (2021).

available to educators. AI in educational settings will be used more ethically if educators are equipped with the knowledge and abilities to handle moral conundrums. All of these suggestions are in line with the DigComp conceptual framework (2022).

According to Köbis and Mehner (2021), the IEEE Global Initiative on Ethics of Autonomous and Intelligent Systems released an updated list of eight guidelines for an AI that is just, transparent and human in 2019. From an AI developer's point of view, these eight factors – human rights, well-being, data agency, efficacy, responsibility, awareness of misuse, transparency and competence – should be taken into mind when developing AI.

According to Mhlanga (2023), responsible and ethical use of ChatGPT in education includes respecting students' privacy, treating everyone equally and without discrimination, acknowledging that ChatGPT cannot replace human teachers, being transparent in ChatGPT use, and providing accurate information.

5. CONCLUSION, IMPLICATIONS AND FURTHER RESEARCH DIRECTION

This chapter analyses the two facets of AI-driven applications in education, focusing on key technologies such as automated grading, personalised learning algorithms, online monitoring, content filtering, AI algorithm learning tools, ChatGPT and ST. Ultimately, AI-driven applications were found to bring a mix of benefits, threats and concerns. The benefits of AI-driven applications in learning include personalised learning, self-assessment, improved efficiency and reduced inequalities. Meanwhile, potential threats include profiling of users, plagiarism, intellectual dishonesty and an over-reliance on technology that impacts creative learning experiences. Key concerns include the potential devaluation of the role of educators, privacy issues with personalised learning platforms and the intrusive nature of online surveillance. Bias in AI algorithms and fears of job displacement within the learning community are also highlighted. The originality of this chapter lies in its creative approach to reconciling the techno-entrepreneurial benefits of AI applications with the threats to creativity in the context of HEIs.

The four implications that have emerged from this chapter are discussed. First, the study underscores the inevitability of AI-driven applications in higher education. To harness the benefits and address concerns, institutions need strategic adoption plans. Embracing these technologies and establishing effective management strategies will be crucial for responsible advancement in teaching and research. Second, recognising the diverse attitudes within the learning community, a balanced approach to AI adoption is essential. This involves understanding and addressing the concerns of conservatives while fostering an environment that encourages progressive engagement. Striking a balance will be instrumental in achieving widespread acceptance. Third, stakeholders must prioritise ethical considerations, privacy and safety when integrating AI-driven applications. Collaborative efforts involving diverse stakeholders are necessary to ensure responsible AI adoption. This includes developing and adhering to institutional policies that safeguard privacy and address ethical concerns. Fourth, this chapter emphasises the transformative role of AI-driven applications, particularly ChatGPT, in enhancing teaching and research. Institutions should invest in empowering educators and researchers to leverage these technologies effectively. This involves providing training and support to ensure optimal utilisation and positive outcomes. This is an exploratory study with useful insights, but future research in these directions will contribute to a more nuanced understanding of the evolving relationship between AI-driven applications and education and guide the development of policies, practices and technologies that promote responsible, equitable and equitable education promote innovative learning experiences.

REFERENCES

Abbas, T. (2023). Ethical implications of AI in modern education: Balancing innovation and responsibility. *Social Sciences Spectrum*, *2*(1), 51–57.

Abbott, R. (2016). I think, therefore I invent: Creative computers and the future of patent law. *Boston College Law Review*, *57*, 1079.

Abgaryan, H., Asatryan, S., & Matevosyan, A. (2023). Revolutionary changes in higher education with artificial intelligence. *Main Issues of Pedagogy and Psychology*, *10*(1), 76–86.

Ahmad, S. F., Han, H., Alam, M. M., Rehmat, M., Irshad, M., Arraño-Muñoz, M., & Ariza-Montes, A. (2023). Impact of artificial intelligence on human loss in decision making, laziness and safety in education. *Humanities and Social Sciences Communications*, *10*(1), 1–14.

Al Ka'bi, A. (2023). Proposed artificial intelligence algorithm and deep learning techniques for development of higher education. *International Journal of Intelligent Networks*, *4*, 68–73.

Alqahtani, T., Badreldin, H. A., Alrashed, M., Alshaya, A. I., Alghamdi, S. S., bin Saleh, K., Alowais, S. A., Alshaya, O. A., Rahman, I., Al Yami, M. S., & Albekairy, A. M. (2023). The emergent role of artificial intelligence, natural learning processing, and large language models in higher education and research. *Research in Social and Administrative Pharmacy*. https://doi.org/10.1016/j.sapharm.2023.05.016

Bahroun, Z., Anane, C., Ahmed, V., & Zacca, A. (2023). Transforming education: A comprehensive review of generative artificial intelligence in educational settings through bibliometric and content analysis. *Sustainability*, *15*(17), 12983.

Bamiro, N. B., Zakariya, Z. B., & Nasiru, B. A. (2023). Development of halal entrepreneurship framework through business incubator service for sustainability using PRISMA. In *Contemporary discourse of halal and Islamic entrepreneurship* (pp. 79–97). Springer.

Borger, J. G., Ng, A. P., Anderton, H., Ashdown, G. W., Auld, M., Blewitt, M. E., Brown, D. V., Call, M. J., Collins, P., Freytag, S., Harrison, L, C., Hesping, E., Hoysted, J., Johnston, J., Mclnneny, A., Tang, P., Whitehead, L., Jex, A. & Naik, S. H. (2023). Artificial intelligence takes center stage: Exploring the capabilities and implications of ChatGPT and other AI-assisted technologies in scientific research and education. *Immunology and Cell Biology*, *101*(10), 923–935.

Bu, Q. (2022). Ethical risks in integrating artificial intelligence into education and potential countermeasures. *Science Insights*, *41*(1), 561–566.

Bukhari, S. W. R., Hassan, S. U., & Aleem, Y. (2023). Impact of artificial intelligence on copyright law: Challenges and prospects. *Journal of the Law Society of Scotland*, *5*(4), 647–656.

Chan, C. K. Y. (2023). A comprehensive AI policy education framework for university teaching and learning. *International journal of educational technology in higher education*, *20*(1), 38.

Chatterjee, S., & Bhattacharjee, K. K. (2020). Adoption of artificial intelligence in higher education: A quantitative analysis using structural equation modelling. *Education and Information Technologies*, *25*, 3443–3463.

Cope, B., Kalantzis, M., & Searsmith, D. (2021). Artificial intelligence for education: Knowledge and its assessment in AI-enabled learning ecologies. *Educational Philosophy and Theory*, *53*(12), 1229–1245.

Dhawan, S., & Batra, G. (2020). Artificial intelligence in higher education: Promises, perils, and perspective. *Expanding Knowledge Horizon. OJAS*, *11*, 11–22.

El-Haggar, N., Amouri, L., Alsumayt, A., Alghamedy, F. H., & Aljameel, S. S. (2023). The effectiveness and privacy preservation of IoT on ubiquitous learning: Modern learning paradigm to enhance higher education. *Applied Sciences*, *13*(15), 9003.

Essel, H. B., Vlachopoulos, D., Tachie-Menson, A., Johnson, E. E., & Baah, P. K. (2022). The impact of a virtual teaching assistant (chatbot) on students' learning in Ghanaian higher education. *International Journal of Educational Technology in Higher Education*, *19*(1), 1–19.

Esther, M. (2023). AI and education: Will AI make our kids dumber? A critical overview of AI and its potential impact on future generation. *Innovation Insider*. https://www.linkedin.com/pulse/ai-education-make-our-kids-dumber-critical-overview-its-esther-musau/. Accessed on February 17, 2024.

Fajrie, N., Purbasari, I., Bamiro, N. B & Evans, D. G. (2024). Does art education matter in inclusiveness for learners with disabilities? A systematic review. *International Journal of Learning, Teaching and Educational Research*, *23*(1), 96–124.

Fidas, C. A., Belk, M., Constantinides, A., Portugal, D., Martins, P., Pietron, A. M., Pitsillides, A., Avouris, N. (2023). Ensuring academic integrity and trust in online learning environments: A longitudinal study of an AI-centered proctoring system in tertiary educational institutions. *Education Sciences*, *13*(6), 566.

Ghotbi, N., Ho, M. T., & Mantello, P. (2022). Attitude of college students towards ethical issues of artificial intelligence in an international university in Japan. *AI & Society*, 1–8.

González, V., Prendes, P., & Roig, R. (2021). Artificial intelligence for student assessment: A systematic review. *Applied Sciences*, *11*(12), 5467. https://doi.org/10.3390/app11125467

Grassini, S. (2023). Shaping the future of education: Exploring the potential and consequences of AI and ChatGPT in educational settings. *Education Sciences*, *13*(7), 692. https://doi.org/10.3390/educsci13070692

Guleria, A., Krishan, K., Sharma, V., & Kanchan, T. (2023). ChatGPT: Ethical concerns and challenges in academics and research. *The Journal of Infection in Developing Countries*, *17*(09), 1292–1299.

Haleem, A., Javaid, M., & Singh, R. P. (2022). An era of ChatGPT as a significant futuristic support tool: A study on features, abilities, and challenges. *BenchCouncil transactions on benchmarks, standards, and evaluations*, *2*(4), 100089.

Hemingway, P., & Brereton, N. (2009). What is a systematic review. *Hayward Medical Communications*, *2*, 1–8.

Holmes, W., Porayska-Pomsta, K., Holstein, K., Sutherland, E., Baker, T., Shum, S. B., Santos, O., Rodrigo, M. T., Cukurova, M., Bittencourt, I. I., & Koedinger, K. R. (2022). Ethics of AI in education: Towards a community-wide framework. *International Journal of Artificial Intelligence in Education*, 1–23.

Hutson, J., Jeevanjee, T., Vander Graaf, V., Lively, J., Weber, J., Weir, G., Arnone, K., Carnes, G., Vosevich, K., Plate, D., Leary, M., & Edele, S. (2022). Artificial intelligence and the disruption of higher education: Strategies for integrations across disciplines. *Creative Education*, *13*(12).

Johnson, J. A. (2014). The ethics of big data in higher education. *International Review of Information Ethics*, *21*, 3–10.

Köbis, L., & Mehner, C. (2021). Ethical questions raised by AI-supported mentoring in higher education. *Frontiers in Artificial Intelligence*, *4*, 624050.

Kong, S. C., Cheung, W. M. Y., & Zhang, G. (2023). Evaluating an artificial intelligence literacy programme for developing university students' conceptual understanding, literacy, empowerment and ethical awareness. *Educational Technology & Society*, *26*(1), 16–30.

Kuleto, V., Ilić, M., Dumangiu, M., Ranković, M., Martins, O. M., Păun, D., & Mihoreanu, L. (2021). Exploring opportunities and challenges of artificial intelligence and machine learning in higher education institutions. *Sustainability*, *13*(18), 10424.

Kung, T. H., Cheatham, M., Medenilla, A., Sillos, C., De Leon, L., Elepaño, C., Madriaga, M., Aggabao, R., Candido, G., Maningo, J., & Tseng, V. (2023). Performance of ChatGPT on USMLE: Potential for AI-assisted medical education using large language models. *PLoS Digital Health*, *2*(2), e0000198.

Lainjo, B., & Tsmouche, H. (2023). The impact of artificial intelligence on higher learning institutions. *International Journal of Education, Teaching, and Social Sciences*, *3*(2), 96–113.

Langreo, L. (2024). Most teachers are not using AI. Here's why. *Education Week*. https://www.edweek.org/technology/most-teachers-are-not-using-ai-heres-why/2024/01. Accessed on February 17, 2024.

Liu, L. (2023). AI and big data-driven decision support for fostering student innovation in music education at private underground colleges. *Journal of Information Systems Engineering and Management*, *8*(2), 23646.

Lund, B. D., Omame, I., Tijani, S., & Agbaji, D. (2020). Perceptions toward artificial intelligence among academic library employees and alignment with the diffusion of innovations' adopter categories. *College & Research Libraries*, *81*(5), 865.

Maphosa, V., & Maphosa, M. (2023). Artificial intelligence in higher education: A bibliometric analysis and topic modelling approach. *Applied Artificial Intelligence*, *37*, 1. https://doi.org/10.1080/08839514.2023.2261730

Memarian, B., & Doleck, T. (2023). Fairness, Accountability, Transparency, and Ethics (FATE) in Artificial Intelligence (AI), and higher education: A systematic review. *Computers and Education: Artificial Intelligence*, 100152.

Mhlanga, D. (2023, February 11). Open AI in education, the responsible and ethical use of ChatGPT towards lifelong learning. *Education, the Responsible and Ethical Use of ChatGPT Towards Lifelong Learning*. https://doi.org/10.2139/ssrn.4354422

Page, M. J., McKenzie, J. E., Bossuyt, P. M., Boutron, I., Hoffmann, T. C., Mulrow, C. D., Shamseer, L., Tetzlaff, J. M., Akl, E. A., Brennan, S. E., Chou, R., Glanville, J., Grimshaw, J. M., Hróbjartsson, A., Lalu, M. M., Li, T., Loder, E. W., Mayo-Wilson, E., … Moher, D. (2021). The PRISMA 2020 statement: An updated guideline for reporting systematic reviews. *PLoS Medicine*, *18*, e1003583.

Perrotta, C., & Selwyn, N. (2020). Deep learning goes to school: Toward a relational understanding of AI in education. *Learning, Media and Technology*, *45*(3), 251–269.

Pisica, A. I., Edu, T., Zaharia, R. M., & Zaharia, R. (2023). Implementing artificial intelligence in higher education: Pros and Cons from the perspectives of academics. *Societies*, *13*(5), 118.

Quizlet. (2023). Quizlet's state of AI in education survey reveals teachers are surprise ai champions. *PR Newswire*. https://www.prnewswire.com/news-releases/quizlets-state-of-ai-in-education-survey-reveals-teachers-are-surprise-ai-champions-301884427.html. Accessed on February 17, 2024.

Raimi, L., Bamiro, N., & Raimi, B. (2023). Two faces of AI-driven applications for sustainable learning and development: Revealing the techno-entrepreneurial benefits and threats to creative learning. In *Presentation at the Learning and Development Africa Conference 2023, held in Ghana on September 15, 2023*.

Rane, N. L., Choudhary, S. P., Tawde, A., & Rane, J. (2023). ChatGPT is not capable of serving as an author: Ethical concerns and challenges of large language models in education. *International Research Journal of Modernization in Engineering Technology and Science*, *5*(10), 851–874.

Rasul, T., Nair, S., Kalendra, D., Robin, M., de Oliveira Santini, F., Ladeira, W. J., Sun, M., Day, I., Rather, R. A., & Heathcote, L. (2023). The role of ChatGPT in higher education: Benefits, challenges, and future research directions. *Journal of Applied Learning and Teaching*, *6*(1), 41–56.

Rogers, E. M. (2003). *Diffusion of innovations*. Free Press.

Rus, R. C., Salisu, M. A., Hussain, M. M., Kamal, M. M., Hanapi, Z., Idris, M. O., Bamiro, N. B., & Kayode, B. K. (2023). Systematic review of Malaysia technical and vocational education (TVET) sustainability framework to increase the marketability of graduates using PRISMA. *Jurnal Kejuruteraan*, *6*(2), 51–63. https://doi.org/10.17576/jkukm-2023-si6(2)-06

Rusandi, M. A., Ahman, Saripah, I., Khairun, D. Y., & Mutmainnah (2023). No worries with ChatGPT: Building bridges between artificial intelligence and education with critical thinking soft skills. *Journal of Public Health*, fdad049.

Salisu, M. A., Ridzwan, C. R., Oyebamiji, Y. O., Usaizan, N., Abioye, A. E., Biola, I. F., Bamiro, N. B., Omowunmi A. K., & Luqman, H. (2024). Disruption of the Covid-19 pandemic on the agri-food sector: A systematic review of its implications in post-pandemic and future of food security. *AIMS Agriculture and Food*, *9*(1), 148–168. https://doi.org/10.3934/agrfood.2024009

Singh, S. V., & Hiran, K. K. (2022). The impact of AI on teaching and learning in higher education technology. *Journal of Higher Education Theory & Practice*, *12*(13).

Soelistiono, S. (2023). Educational technology innovation: AI-integrated learning system design in AILS-based education. *Influence: International Journal of Science Review*, *5*(2), 470–480.

Sullivan, M., Kelly, A., & McLaughlan, P. (2023). ChatGPT in higher education: Considerations for academic integrity and student learning. *Journal of Applied Learning and Teaching*, *6*(1).

Tanveer, M., Hassan, S., & Bhaumik, A. (2020). Academic policy regarding sustainability and artificial intelligence (AI). *Sustainability*, *12*(22), 9435.

UNESCO. (2021). *Recommendation on the ethics of artificial intelligence*. https://unesdoc.unesco.org/ark:/48223/pf0000381137. Accessed on February 10, 2024.

UNESCO. (2023a). *Guidance for generative AI in education and research*. PP-1-44. https://unesdoc.unesco.org/ark:/48223/pf0000386693. Accessed on February 10, 2024.

UNESCO. (2023b). *Chat GPT and Artificial intelligence in higher education*. https://www.iesalc.unesco.org/wp-content/uploads/2023/04/ChatGPT-and-Artificial-Intelligence-in-higher-education-Quick-Start-guide_EN_FINAL.pdf. Accessed on February 26, 2024.

Utaminingsih, S., Fajrie, N., Bamiro, N. B., & Azman, M. N. A. (2023). Teachers and students perception of technology and sustainable adoption framework in the pedagogical process: A systematic review. *International Journal of Learning, Teaching and Educational Research*, *22*(12), 162–186.

Vera, I. A. D., Briones, W. L., & Heredia, M. I. V. (2024). Ethical perspectives on the application of artificial intelligence in higher education. *Sinergias Educativas*, *9*(1).

Vuorikari, R., Kluzer, S., & Punie, Y. (2022). *DigComp 2.2: The Digital Competence Framework for Citizens – With new examples of knowledge, skills and attitudes*. EUR 31006 EN, Publications Office of the European Union. ISBN 978-92-76-48882-8, JRC128415. https://doi.org/10.2760/115376

Zawacki-Richter, O., Marín, V. I., Bond, M., & Gouverneur, F. (2019). Systematic review of research on artificial intelligence applications in higher education–where are the educators? *International Journal of Educational Technology in Higher Education*, *16*(1), 1–27.

Zhang, X. (2024). Analysis of the copyright issues of AI-generated materials. *Science of Law Journal*, *3*(1), 25–29.

Zouhaier, S. (2023). The impact of artificial intelligence on higher education: An empirical study. *European Journal of Educational Sciences*, *10*(1), 17–33.